Beautiful Feelings of Sensitive People

Screen grabs of British Poetry in the 21st century

Selected previous publications by Andrew Duncan

Poetry

In a German Hotel
Cut Memories and False Commands
Sound Surface
Alien Skies
Switching and Main Exchange *
Pauper Estate *
Anxiety Before Entering a Room. New and selected poems
Surveillance and Compliance
Skeleton Looking at Chinese Pictures
The Imaginary in Geometry
Savage Survivals (amid modern suavity) *
Threads of Iron *
In Five Eyes *
On the Margins of Great Empires. Selected Poems *
With Feathers on Glass *

Criticism

The Poetry Scene in the Nineties (internet only)
Centre and Periphery in Modern British Poetry **
The Failure of Conservatism in Modern British Poetry **
Origins of the Underground
The Council of Heresy *
The Long 1950s *
A Poetry Boom 1990-2010 *
Fulfilling the Silent Rules *
Nothing is being suppressed *

As editor

Don't Start Me Talking (with Tim Allen)
Joseph Macleod: *Cyclic Serial Zeniths from the Flux*
Joseph Macleod: *A Drinan Trilogy: The Cove / The Men of the Rocks / Script from Norway* (co-edited with James Fountain)

* original Shearsman titles
** revised 2nd editions from Shearsman

Beautiful Feelings of Sensitive People

Screen grabs of British Poetry in the 21st century

Andrew Duncan

Shearsman Books

First published in the United Kingdom in 2024 by
Shearsman Books Ltd
PO Box 4239
Swindon
SN3 9FN

Shearsman Books Ltd Registered Office
30–31 St. James Place, Mangotsfield, Bristol BS16 9JB
(this address not for correspondence)

ISBN 978-1-84861-941-8

Copyright © 2024 by Andrew Duncan.

ACKNOWLEDGEMENTS

Reviews of Cris Paul and Rhys Trimble
were previously published in *Poetry Wales*.

Reviews of *Portland Triptych*, *Edge of Necessary*, *Winter Journey*,
Elisabeth Bletsoe, Khaled Hakim, Will Harris, Kevin Nolan
and Molly Vogel were previously published in *Tears in the Fence*.

Reviews of Dorothy Lehane and Steve Ely
were previously published in *Litter*.

My thanks to the editors concerned.

Detailed acknowledgements may be found on p.336 *et seq*.

Contents

Introduction	9
Generalisations About the Poetry World	15
Theories of style time	23
Language is made of rules	39
Foundation Texts (*Loving Little Orlick; Ffynhonnau Uchel; Englaland; Incendium Amoris; Cloud. A coffee cantata*	52
Their trajectory was just large (*Flatlands; Terrain Seed Scarcity; Implacable Art; Unsung; Birdhouse; a.m.; The President of Earth; The Itchy Sea; Capital; The Hutton Inquiry; Natural Histories; Vacation of a Lifetime; Andraste's Hair; Galatea; The Missing; The Midlands; The Land of Green Ginger*)	81
Cultural Asset Management	107
Verticegarden (*Octet; Nekorb*)	118
Insignificance; or, Structure Engulfed by Surface	129
Poems on Communal Wellbeing (*Songs for Eurydice; Black Sun; Winstanley; Surge*)	139
Local Knowledge (*Birds of the Sherborne Missal; Portland: A Triptych*)	153
Devolution/Disassembly — Scottish Poets (*Zonda? Khamsin? Sharaav? Camanchaca?; Hand Over Mouth Music; Florilegium; The Sleep Road; makar /unmakar*)	165
Serial (*The School of Forgery; Winter Journey; Exotica Suite*)	183
British South Asian Poets (*Brilliant Corners; Small Hands; The Voice of Sheila Chandra; The Routines*)	201

Splendours and Chagrins (*Rendang; Plague Lands & other poems; Amnion; Katabasis; Writing the Camp*) 215

Anglo-Welsh (*Edge of Necessary; stenia cultus handbook; Keinc; King Driftwood*) 229

Short Strings, Polyrecombinant (*Duetcetera*) 244

West-bloc Dissidents: Alternative Poetry (*Arrays; Lines on the Surface; INSTANT-fLEX 718*) 252

Triumphs and Panics (*Ephemeris; False Flags; Somnia; Makers of Empty Dreams; Forms of Protest; Self Heal; The Cook's Wedding*) 266

The Human Voice (*rabbit; Beautiful Girls'; Venusberg; Rookie; Soft Sift; Kim Kardashian's Marriage*) 283

Pistachio Euphoria Sorbet (*the arboretum towards the beginning; Leave Bambi Alone*) 294

Sociolinguistics (*Tippoo Sultan's Incredible White-Man-Eating Tiger Toy-Machine!!!; Wilia; Knitting drum machines for exiled tongues; Northern Alchemy; The Unquiet*) 299

Privatisation and Religion (*The Palace of Oblivion; Ascension Notes; Monica's Overcoat of Flesh; Stranger in the Mask of a Deer*) 311

By Land and Sea (*Disappearance; Green Noise; Continental Drift; Else*) 318

Afterword 329

Bibliography 330

Permission Acknowledgments 336

Index 342

After I'd invented mountaineering
& the dark ages I decided
I'd try my hand at making up the self
ready for the rise of the bourgeoisie
—Peter Hughes

"The most inadequate catalogue, however, was generally preferable to being shown over the [poem] by an illiterate or ill-informed housekeeper or servant. Most tourists agreed that servants were both ignorant and insolent, and housekeepers proved so full of pretentious and wholly unreliable information that John Dodd could only conclude that it was a 'laudable Custome of England that they should be unacquainted with what they were showing.' J J Hunsecker would vent his feelings at such treatment in the pages of his diary, storming at 'being dragged about by a foolish [bard-tender] of very drunken, dawdling appearance.' 'A katavasia of bazaar connoisseurship ... froufrou of polysyllables... tortuous subtexting in a Yarmouth accent... down long poorly lit galleries debouching wrong explanations of each picture in its turn... coquettishly striking poses in front of mythological tableaux... munching a slippery patter in the mop cupboard... approaching hidden symbolism by way of the wine-cellar[.]' 'No-one shou'd suffer his [symbolic arrangements] to be visited, but with intention to make these visitors happy' he wrote after a particularly unfortunate outing to Grimsthorpe in 1781, 'and shou'd equip his servants with attention and civility.' The final insult, of course, was that these [cultural critics] expected to be tipped handsomely for their trouble."
—Inigo Morguevilliers,
History of the Tourist (unpublished MS)

Introduction: Everybody is peripheral

The Sound of Now

Partway through writing this book I had a discussion with another Nottingham poet where he said that the reference to "21st century" poetry was absolutely fatal because it evoked something I couldn't do, and that it was better to have a restricted subject (poets of Nottingham and the Erewash Valley, maybe?) which had a bounded shape and where the book could match that shape. I didn't buy this, because the main feature of the scene now is the large number of poets and the only route was to unfold a matrix with sites for all of them. The book uncovers part of the matrix.

If you publish a book about contemporary poetry people expect you to identify the style distinctive for a decade or a generation – the Sound of Now. Of course, doing that would instantly define all the other poets as being non-central. My thesis is instead that since the cultural mechanism which authorises central styles broke down in the 1990s there are a dozen valid styles and even conformist poets have a great range to choose from. People may be converging all the time but they are convergent on a dozen different patterns. We can hope to recover the history of localised subsets of the total production. These histories will always seem partial.

I do have a feeling about the Now and it is roughly that the problems which wrecked most English poets thirty years ago, the absurd fantasies and inhibitions, have been resolved and that there is a whole world of poets who have just walked out of that conservative and repressed situation. Roughly 86% of the poets I trawled up began publishing after 2000. Legacy positions do not seem relevant, because so many new poets and readers have been arriving that the old landscape has been simply buried under several new ones. My legacy position was shared boredom with the mainstream and its satraps. At one level, that abolishes my stock in trade – the critique which we, collectively, voiced in the 1990s is now accepted. That mainstream has been effectively swept away. I think it lost power because it produced far too much weak poetry, and because there were many other arts which showed poets what art could do. It wasn't humiliated on the field of combat by an Alternative which was barely visible in the retail outlets and libraries. The Alternative did not win as the mainstream lost. We fought as a single opposition, unified as a conscious anti-principle, but I suppose in retrospect that the relief for cultural critics, in the Eighties or Nineties, was moments of realising that the avant-garde exit was surrounded by dozens of other routes, more travelled and certainly less theorised. The future was actually not going to be a re-run of the modernist revolution of the 1920s or of the flourishing of the American avant-garde in the 1950s. Those narratives of longing wove an overall pattern which apparently stabilised everything but in doing that was impervious to new facts. I don't think the Alternative was defeated on the field of combat, either, but I don't think it is set to inherit the earth.

There is actually a frequent genre, and this is the Nature Poem with Politics. If I pick up five new books, three seem to be about Landscape (am I exaggerating?). There is a profusion of Place poems. Since the Place thing has never slowed down since 1966 (the start of the *English Intelligencer* project, myth geography landscape) it can't be the new thing. It is too ordinary to be the forefront. In fact there seems to be a lot of interest in deleting the history of the genre. But, everyone is reading these poems all the time – one has to acknowledge that.

The jacket of the 2011 anthology *The Salt Book of Younger Poets* announces that these are the "poets who will dominate UK poetry in years to come". That hasn't proved to be so – the number of poets on the market is just too large. The fifty poets in that volume, incredibly gifted as a collective entity, are only a fraction of the poets achieving success in the world of 2022. There is no "generational sound" to define a generation. Is there a pattern whereby people peak with their first book, after years of endeavour, and then drop out rather than write a second book? Another question would be if the dropping-out is actually what their *audience* do; so that poets have readers of exactly their age, and after a few years their market share freezes. Maybe, in the rush of ever more rapid cultural change, the market is divided into chronological segments, mini-generations who feel very distinct from older people, and in turn seem tired to people younger than them. This is a bit speculative – the pattern may simply be a very brief phase of attention for each poet.

Notes on volumes of publication

The Poetry Book Society has a quarterly page of Suggested New Books, maybe 80 titles a quarter. That *is* a lot of books, isn't it? I indulged myself and copied down a five-year series of titles from the fabulous PBS web page. I gathered 1,140 titles from 972 British poets. This is certainly a luxury experience, things being offered for your pleasure in senseless profusion. It is more than anyone can take in. The luxury aspect is also that I am not obliged to buy any of them – I am free of responsibility and that is a wonderful feeling. I can't read all these texts.

About 55% of those names were women. I checked and, out of 74 names in the classic 2013 anthology *Dear World and Everyone in It*, 52 do not appear in this PBS series. Why do this check? Because poets have a fear of being left out; it is like children being afraid of the dark. So as we gaze in fascination at the 1,140 titles displayed on the PBS pages, we have to ask whether we are leaving space for the ones who are, at certain hours of the day, in shadow. *Dear World* included poets under 35 – who, by 2020, would be at the prime of their careers. It is likely that all of them published a book between 2017 and 2022. I don't know how the PBS filter the raw industrial output, but *all kinds of stuff* must have been omitted. So for the five years in question it is plausible that we would want to read 2,280 titles rather than 1,140. And, obviously, those 52 names from *Dear World* can only be a visible marker for a much larger group of poets we are *not seeing*. The PBS site is exactly a shop window and not a magical truth engine which would find for us everything significant, creative, exciting, unheard-of, for that period.

How did the stories turn out

Beautiful feelings of sensitive people is just a five-word way of explaining to someone who never reads poetry what we are hoping to find in a book of poems. It is the most unifying (and featureless?) description I could find. It is not there to exclude political poetry – to have beautiful feelings and not wish for a beautiful world would be like lying on a beach for eight hours and not noticing that there is an ocean just in front of you. In fact, wanting to be Greta Thunberg is a beautiful feeling in itself. It describes a wide range of 21st century poetry but perhaps not the majority. The figures suggest that there is a public verdict on the poetry of the past, so of the period say 1970 to 2000, which is utterly favourable – people have an image of Being a Poet and they want to go and inhabit that image. It is a Yes vote. Maybe all those struggles were not in vain. But, that wish to be a poet does not necessarily mean you have much interest in the work of other poets.

Dates

I have noticed that over many publications women poets have avoided printing their date of birth. The contextual reasons for this are apparent and this is not just an individual thing. In order to be polite, I have avoided giving dates of birth for anybody, although not completely. There really are patterns of change which are revealed by scrutinising people linked by age, or separated by (even) five years; but we can bypass these.

Because I do not want to write about sensations I haven't had, the book is confined to sensations I have had. This raises a question whether someone born in the 1950s, as I was, can still battle it out with new and advanced poetry. The idea of a country of the incomprehensible, too subtle to show up in photographs, and extending its borders stealthily as the old country dissolves in the warming waves, will always remain attractive. Who will tell the story of those whose talent was invisible?

Unmeasured

I am uneasy about operating with these figures, because obviously that is reducing poets to parts of a featureless quantity and they all want to be unique, and to stress their uniqueness. A lot of the discourse around poetry at the moment relates to exclusion and diversity. But, if you have a list of 237 recommended books during a year, you are going to miss out on most of them, even 90% of them. Being left out is basic because it is anchored in the volume of publications. I am doubtful of its force as a theme of debate. It seems to me that if fifty poets swim within view of the camera then fifty more are drifting off camera and into invisibility. It is hard to process this in terms of guilt and neglect. I wonder how on earth I can assimilate this bulk of product. Can it really be 240 significant books a year for 20 years? OMG. All the same that is a plausible figure if you wanted to describe the era. The length of the count makes me want to speed up but the key is to *slow down*, to freeze on a much smaller number of texts, and to make them linger, as if we could make sounds stand still. This is my excuse for writing something which deals with a few dozen while leaving the whole list of 972 somewhere in the warehouse. I would suggest that the annual anthologies (*Best British Poetry 2011*, and so forth) which Salt used to do, and in fact the PBS lists, are vital resources, even if not ideal as surveys. And the PBS website is a very convenient place to buy books.

Introduction 13

Exclusion

As I previously wrote a work in seven volumes on poetry from 1960 up to 1997, I have left the poets who were in that Blair-era grand project, or BGP, out of consideration. I am now only dealing with poets who made a debut (generously defined) after 1997. This clears the decks. Obviously I have not been completely consistent about this. I wrote a previous book, *A Poetry Boom*, about the period 1990 to 2010, which took the line of writing about ideas, relevant to many poets, but discussing only 20 individuals. This time I have taken the opposite line, of exhibiting as many poets as possible. (The poets in *Poetry Boom* do not re-appear, sadly.) If you advance one cell at a time, you are advancing. I think.

Generalisations about the poetry world

The starting point is an unknown number of poetry fans wanting to consume poetry, probably looking for beautiful feelings of sensitive people. The bookshops try to stack up books that people want to buy. (This includes postal retailers.) The fit of the supply to the demand is not exactly tight but a bit better than random. Everyone has a frame limiting what they see. That applies to consumers of poetry as well. Editors push out commodities which readers want to consume. The frame is everywhere and poets are quite well aware of this. There is no management of the production side. It is effectively random. Almost all of it is unnecessary. It fulfils a thousand needs that don't exist. Editors may have goals, but they don't control either production or consumption.

If we have 50+ British Asian poets in our baffling list of 972 it is apparent that they are seeking approval and that they like the institutions which offer them validation, recognition, praise, affection, position. Their endeavours are directed at this. If someone judges them to have won, over some other cluster of poets, that is meaningless if the judges and the other poets are not themselves recognised as excellent. So if you subvert those institutions you nullify the victory of those poets. I think the traditional role of a cultural critic who invalidates everything from an external standpoint (my personal experience of this is via the Punk world but a more typical model is Marxism) is obsolete. The cultural frame is there to offer warmth, validation, an audience for vital symbolic acts. Disrupting it threatens everyone with pointlessness and a cold feeling. I am doubting that there is an external vantage point raised above poetry, and saying rather that the poetry world makes its own laws and its own legitimation. This right is based partly on the number of people involved. I trawled poetry titles from the British Library catalogue to get a count of books published by an individual author in a given year. I did this for three sample years: 2000, 2010, and 2019. The result was a list of 3,710 poets who published a book in one of those three years. It sounds as if the obstacles, if they exist, are ineffective. The count of titles in each year has risen steeply since 1990. This number does not allow us to measure the frustration of people who were stuck outside the door.

There are systems, where the parts are directed towards a shared goal and activity unnecessary to that end is suppressed. Poetry is not one of these. I don't think the set-up gives people exactly what they want.

But it isn't a system at all. You can't optimise it. Measuring inputs and outputs is a bit phony. I am unable to say if the poetry scene is successful or unsuccessful. There is just a lack of external criteria. I am unsure how a good outcome pattern would exist outside the actual outcome pattern. Where is control situated? Everyone does what they want. There is no infrastructure and no switches to control it. I don't want to be blamed for the defects in the industry, and I don't think you can separate the defects from the people. So, the people who are in the poetry world… they are genuinely diverse and want different things. It's like a crowd at a fair; they are all moving around but not actually moving north or south as a group. To generalise, they are empathetic and they don't like being told what to do. There is no control and command system. There is nothing… just rules in the heads of a few thousand people. Not felt as rules but as wishes. Things thinner than air. And people drift into this world because they like the lack of control. They actually fear commands and norms. They are the people you don't want to manage!

The Apex Falls

We are searching for consistent features of the era. We find one at the sociological level in the widening of the cultural apex. This hypothesis states a, that modern poetry is dominated by graduates; b, that its population has grown as the count of graduates in the population has gone up, that its composition is changing as the composition of graduates changes – in particular as regards women and people whose families were fairly recent immigrants. The composition includes very numerous people of working-class origin even though a sociologist might, quite likely, define anyone with a degree as being part of the middle class. So there are two questions. First, about the widening of the apex. Evidently the number of poets publishing in 2020 is a multiple of the poets publishing in 1952. The increase may be a factor of five or seven. But the second question is whether there is also a homogenisation, brought about by the deeply influencing shared experiences of studying for exams, being examined, or of reading poetry and of asking yourself as you write poetry what a willing readership would think and what they would like. So the mind of a poet may be, *prima facie*, a product of reading and writing poetry. Key issues would then be the relationship of poets to communities, in principle not educated, among whom they originated; and the effect of diverse social origins on the poetry world, even as the participants assimilated to the internal rules of the poetry world itself. Any anthology collected later than 1962 will show results radically different from the ones found in Allott's Penguin anthology, with its 39.5% block of Oxford graduates.

If the apex was going to include so many more people it was possible to think that the existing apex would disappear and that there would be a moment of discontinuity, overthrow, of burning the rules and rebuilding. This never happened, but it is only fair to say that many people thought, at various times, that it was going to happen and that they were part of it. Instead you have had constant change and a flow of new talent entering the system and effectively strengthening it, beyond the point where it was able to collapse. I don't think people have any memories of a night of burning the manor house that didn't happen; instead they have memories of themselves breaking through the inhibitions and technical problems of adolescence. The movement that came closest was the alternative sector of the 1970s. However, if you look at the 36 names in Mottram's standard list of the "British Poetry Revival", June 1974, 19 of them were already in Lucie-Smith's Penguin anthology of four years earlier. This was a mainstream anthology and available in most bookshops. Penguin weren't exactly run by Marxist cadres with berets and Kalashnikovs.

Talk of flocks of new names arriving at the apex raises the question of sheaves of old names being thrown out to make way for them. Again, I see this as a gradual and undramatic process, something like dead leaves being swept up and thrown away every autumn. Of course most poets of the 1970s have been forgotten. And of course most poets active in the 1940s had been forgotten by 1974. One high moment was Lucie-Smith's anthology which ejected both Auden and Spender. This was exciting, because they were both Top People and had actually written some significant poems after 1945; but Lucie-Smith was signalling a change of the music, a new era. These events are too numerous to track: finally 500 poets are whittled down to 50. Someone arriving on the scene in 2010 acquires an abbreviated version of the 20th C: a metabolic process has taken place. This does not exhibit the apex dissolving and falling down to ground level. The British scene knows fashions, and fashions that come to an end, but not revolutions. This is a country of stable property values.

Music

There are technical problems in defining the lyrics of songs as not being poetry, so there are advantages in accepting that they are poetry.

So, printed poetry is very much the rarest way of consuming poems. Listening to them as part of music is the norm. The group which likes this choice correlates not just with high verbal intelligence but also with training, in the classroom and in private study.

Printed poetry is not going to debouch into mass popularity because song lyrics are already there occupying that territory. Conversely, poetry needs to satisfy the wishes of the dedicated audience in order to be anything significant. It is reasonable to find these qualities in exaggerating the qualities of abstraction and speculation, of intuition and group feeling, which language possesses and which are restrained by everyday speech.

The shape of poetry is found, we may think, by identifying its edges. Poetry is a minority art and it is easy to find where it stops. It is likely that poetry becomes most successful by taking qualities which other arts do not have and pursuing them in the direction which they naturally possess and where they are capable of extension. If you hear a poem read out in a chat show, for example, it is rational to ask the poem to have qualities which the rest of the chat show does not possess.

Poetry is classically consumed in private and the result of getting rid of the throng of other people is to give the artwork much more capacity to extend and innovate. Simultaneously, the act of reading teaches the reader and extends them in the direction which the poem is pursuing. Artistic speculation accompanies, we may say, intellectual speculation. Poetry as we have it is individualistic. Strands of poetry naturally develop away from other strands and create islands of sensibility. Poetry which is undeveloped in this way is likely to be very unsuccessful. It does not satisfy the demands which it encourages. Innovation is central to poetry (even as cultural managers try to ban its results).

Somatic

Alec Newman (of Knives Forks and Spoons) has remarked that he got into poetry when, many years ago, Martin Stannard came into his class at a school (somewhere near East Bergholt, I don't know the name) and talked about modern poetry. The face-to-face contact was very important. When I mention this I am not commenting on unfairness – private schools are much more into enrichment (to use the trade term). Generally people get into modern poetry after face to face contact with someone who is already into it. My guess is that there is some kind of somatic projection taking place; the poems are abstract but the presence of another person allows you to project into them. After that, they are not abstract because your body is present inside them, with its organs and neural networks. The other person is the gateway. "I saw not with my eyes but with my whole body." This explains the prominence of poetic groups of friends. I don't think I need to discuss these to explain particular poems – but they litter the landscape and people often talk about them. We are talking about a continuous network here – discontinuity is just an accident. Between any two groups there are dozens of intermediate points.

The sound of a decade

In retrospect, it seems that when the number of young Oxford graduates was very small there was only one style which they found exciting, it was easy to find out what it was, and it was highly differentiated from the previously fashionable style, because differentiation was how the new poets won a competition with the old ones. However, the widening of the apex has swept that situation away. Poets now compete with each other essentially by designing variant models. So there is no period style. Looking back, you can see that when the number of central models grew to, say, half a dozen, then even being conformist led to divergent results.

The model requires some more detail, in the sense that in the 1950s, say, there was more than one style. Even if we only remember one blanket Fifties style, John Press's highly detailed contemporary account divides the scene into two factions ("rule and energy" are the groups and the name of his book). Closer examination would probably find that "within the nucleus of highly legitimated youth, there were generally several tendencies of which only one broke through and is remembered". My impression is that the competing cliques were very similar, sociologically; the desire to compete is not based on being social outsiders but on the desire to *win*. (The poetry we like to remember from the 1950s is from losers/outsiders like E.P. Thompson and W.S. Graham.)

Bourdieu

The great modern work on the sociology of art is by Pierre Bourdieu. It is tempting to transfer his findings, but his research is all about French audiences. There is nothing you can say that is true both of France and of

Britain, unless it is terribly vague. So a transfer of French results to Britain would lose all explanatory value. This is especially true for poetry, where there is no interest in France for modern British poetry and the converse is almost equally true. So we don't have a sociology of art in Britain. If we analyse Bourdieu (and this is not something he makes explicit) he sees social memory as involving thousands of acts and scenes. The brain stores these in sets by analogy and extracts patterns, forming a *cultural field*. Social knowledge works in a way like acquiring grammar. An infant starts without language and hears thousands of utterances and extracts from these rules of grammar and uses these to create new utterances, initially with errors, but converging on the shared grammar. The scenes are repeated, it is like going round a housing estate, like the one I live on, looking at all the houses one by one. The house we imagine looks like all the others. In art, the deep patterns take over and repeat. The imagination is malleable but it tends to rebuild reality. Art acquires force by representing what we know and loses force when it ignores the common patterns. It presents wish-fulfilment but what we wish for is dependent on what we have seen but not had, and on what other people wish for. It is possible to depict wishes which people do not have and so to fail to interest them.

Field theory says not only that we experience thousands of scenes as the content of our social lives, but also that these are structured by rigid rules and that our brains are effective at isolating these rules. So, if we accept this, it is likely that British poetry repeats basic patterns which overflow from social experience, and succeeds by capturing these. A proposed result would be this. "The basic thing is organisation of space because there are too many people and land cannot be manufactured. A corollary is the wish to control other people as a fallback from having real control of the space. Fantasy restriction of other people is an outlet for spatial frustration. Other people are made to live through fantasy narratives in which restraints on their actions go partway to clearing them from ground we cover. Abstract knowledge is infected by the wish to control." There is no research basis for this so we can't depend on it and above all we can't enjoy the details which research evidence (questionnaires, in the model) would offer. A project which collects 4,000 questionnaires and reports the common features will find common features. The divergent reactions of any individual will not progress into the report.

Gatekeepers

With the abandonment of further nationalisation the project of socialising the entire economy has disappeared from view. It has given way to accepting capitalism, but there is a new Left project of social mobility in which the State smooths the transition from school to university to workplace. Everyone can see this working, on a mass basis, so it is a valid project.

Focus has shifted onto how people are selected for jobs. The appointments panel is the gate through which the big river flows. The CV and the job interview, in millions, are the gates where the Left project fails or succeeds. This river passes through a thousand sluices and some of these are full of wrecks. We see a rusty sluice. A wreck haven. A gate that masters water. An underwater grille separating fish from wrack. If a poem is a cell of idealised space, the idealisation now takes the form of everyone passing the tests and getting a job. There is a fantasy of being on the job panel and making them make the wrong choice. Poetry loves the version of Self which is self-defined as opposed to the version which other people see. This is a collective act of self-deception.

There is a background to this welcoming project. In the early Sixties, two sociologists researched grammar schools and in particular why working-class children who had scored many marks in the 11-plus and got a place at grammar school dropped out thereafter. The conclusion was that grammar schools were ineffective at bringing class mobility. The reasons for dropping out had to do with congruity. The atmosphere at the schools was hostile to the working-class pupils. The idea of permanently moving into a middle-class environment became unattractive. Meanwhile, it was hard for them to study at home – middle class homes had more space, more quiet, and more acceptance that the children had to do several hours of homework every night. The project of upward mobility relied on designing social space so that it was welcoming to the target group – they were not ridiculed or marginalised. People weren't imitating their accents for a laugh. The in-group wasn't busy crushing the out-groups.

Beside offering education, there is great interest in how work culture accepts people. The idea is of influencing the workplace, not by a shift to collective ownership, but by changing the micro-language, the welcoming and induction functions, so as to open gates for ethnic minorities, for income groups D and E, and for women. The whole project of displacing traditional views of literature is connected to this idea of facilitating social mobility. A shift in the way you read a novel is a proxy for how you read someone's character and decide whether they are fit for promotion or appointment. There is an invariant: it is "judgment of humans", what is common to job panels and essays on literature.

The mobility project has to unfold in parallel with research into the crimes of capitalism, getting the State-capitalism relationship into the right frame. The work of regulators enforces the law. Identifying criminality so that democracy can assert itself over lawless oligarchs. You can't simply hand the economy over to capitalism.

What does this have to offer to someone who is working class and over 25? You can't expect people who failed all their exams to be emotionally in favour of meritocracy. Meritocracy is not simply the *right* way of doing things but has inherent problems. UKIP reached a score of 25% of the vote, at their peak, by abandoning meritocracy.

Class mobility is the central drama: if we were in a major war everyone would be writing about the war, similarly today poetry is about new jobs and a new society. It is inevitable that poetry should re-enact this drama but there are problems in translating this into effective literary form. To be against social mobility would be like wanting Mussolini to win the war, it is an empty site; but potentially one can be bored by a theme that repeats. There is no obvious mechanism by which theorising about diversity affects the workplace. I can't see literature as an amateur form of diversity training.

If we try to define a style we might say that verbal space exists already and all the time but that a sensitive writer can create a locally divergent space which has new characteristics and which changes your state of mind when you are in it. This often has to do with the removal of aggression and the introduction of fine distinctions. This redesign of shared space has an obvious affinity with the attempt to design spaces in schools and in workplaces so that they are non-specific and so welcoming to people who initially feel uncertain and alien in them. I emphasise that these are small-scale effects. However, if you look at the appeal of poetry as a social world you will probably conclude that this low pressure and high receptivity are its biggest assets and that their small scale does not put a block on this.

Theories of style time

As we start we may as well ask what was happening in 2000. The figure I have is 1,113 books by individual authors. The 2000 figure already sounds infeasibly large, but the poetry world was attractive to an increasingly large number of people and printing/setting technology was getting cheaper and better.

I counted twelve books by British Asian writers (based on name). This does not sound like a lot. The count for 2019 is 82. Clearly this was a growth area. The overall count of titles being published was set to grow by 47% by 2019. If you had a growth of titles by women or by British Asians within a static total you would be seeing white male writers being squeezed out. Evidently this didn't happen, and the expansion of overall output accommodated the arrival of poets in the field. Poetry succeeded by developing new space, social, linguistic, or psychological.

We see a late pamphlet (*At St Pancras Station: a poem*) by John Heath-Stubbs, born 1918, who in the Forties had tried to express the incompatibility of being gay with being Christian, in tortuous and highly-wrought poems telling a personal myth. Sometime in the 1950s he decided that this was just too difficult, and became a sociable and undemanding poet. To the best of my knowledge he had not written a decent poem since the 1950s. James Kirkup, also born 1918 (although his claimed date of birth was 1923) had announced in 1963 that he was giving up poetry, disappointed. He wrote voluminously after that, but without ambition and apparently without effort. We see in 2000 a volume *A tiger in your tanka: poems songs sequences narratives*. His four-volume retrospective avoids date order, presumably to disguise the fact that he had given up trying. His attempt to write gay poetry in the 1940s remains compelling. The stratification shows these poets born (just) before 1920 and poets born in the 1970s, so a set of curves with poets distributed at various points along them. At some level the 1940s were still happening. The piling of strata, to remind ourselves, also applies to the audience: some people who had been reading Heath-Stubbs and Kirkup around 1945 were still buying books. If we question whether everyone inside the poetry world in 2000 was actually living in 2000 we also ask whether a consensus could exist across a world so utterly broken up into separate aesthetic fragments. This raises a further question, whether what I record can be right, actually, and whether standing and reputation can exist in the absence of consensus.

Some of the new poets were also starting six-decade careers. We can consider time in terms of the *axis* and the *niche*. The axis is the series of time which leads up to the now moment and provides us with an impetus to develop. The niche is the result of time but is small enough to belong to a particular poet and be the ground of their poetry. This gives us a framework to think about collective time as it affects poets whose imperative is to separate themselves from others enough to acquire distinctiveness – but not enough to lose the public. Poets think intensively about the recent past of poetry and about their own estates. Quite a few poets don't accept that they live in the same time as everyone else. We would also have to include the *vintage*. Heath-Stubbs would be vintage 1942, and that would imply a first wave of rejecting Auden, the interest in personal myth, the distrust of documentary. The value of cultural assets can go down as well as up.

Genre A

Everything was simpler in the 1950s and at the cost of pangs of nostalgia I am going to return to the Cold War era to get some perspective on a confusing landscape. The NATO camp was keen on individual choice and the Moscow alliances consequently claimed that personal choice was fictitious and in fact the individual was an illusion. For them, culture was controlled by vast social forces which could not directly be observed but which structuralism set out to find and listen to. Without having ever seen these invisible great powers, I can still say that there is a match here – the line of personal choice and individualism definitely matches a market driven, consumer society. But it does not follow that either poets or poetry readers are pro-capitalist or pro-Cold War – they often found the political and industrial complex in the West to be a source of constraints and oppression. That match is not there to be found.

There are two ways of looking at the mainstream of poetry today. One is to say that privatisation means diversity and the poems are about being special, so what everyone *doesn't* have in common. The other is to say that there is a Genre A and it is a genre even if 5000 people write inside it. This means that it has an outside and that you can flip it over to reveal a history, a set of assumptions, a set of alliances. There is the usual puzzle of reversibility where we ask if the pressure of the market created the genre or the genre created and taught the market.

What is the accepted poetry? The simplest way to exhibit it is to point to *Poetry Review*, the most read magazine. Roughly 80 issues from the current century will exhibit the central area of British poetry, and so offer a window on what we remember. If we inquire after poets not in those issues, we are already venturing into memories which are not collective. It is also worth considering standard anthologies such as *Dear World, Identity Parade*, and the *Best British Poetry* series (of which 5 volumes came out).

PR published roughly 2700 poems between 2000 and 2020, and generalisations about that data field cannot be very accurate. They actually were diverse. However, without stretching the facts too much, we can establish that the typical poem filled about a page of *PR*, was privatised and spoken through or by a central "I", and asked us to identify with that I; that much of the information released related to that I rather than to more impersonal frameworks; that the I was sensitive and humane and attentive to fine details; and that the feelings described were generally beautiful. To this end the poet was not using arbitrary or preset procedures; they rarely used a distinctive or innovative style (as opposed to a *voice*); they generally avoided abstractions; they rarely used a style that was startling or an end in itself (what you could call Mannerist). The voice was designed to be attractive, so that liking one poem would sell you on other poems by that poet, which of course had to prolong the initial feeling. The tone is not exactly lyric: it reflects states of mind rather more complex than that (and less upbeat than pop song lyrics). It is hardly plausible that the large *PR* readership disliked these poems, so in fact they give information about the preferences of that readership. The self is caught in the present moment – not in long durations where rules assert themselves and statistics take over. Surprise and freedom are located in the instant, in brief moments. As the (speaking) individual is a point inside a large field of social events, so the poem draws on a moment which is a point in a large field of points in time.

We can draw an imaginary circle which all of those poems fit inside. Once we have done so it is apparent that there is a realm outside the circle. I am arguing that this represents a hegemony rather than a style. It is permissive. But evidently if your poems fit inside that hegemony then they cannot also claim to be original, challenging, outside the existing rules, or extreme. There are a million ways of irritating people and if someone writes poems which are genuinely appealing then we are right to use terms like *suave* and *smooth* and to admire the effort and skill. This is an unselfish endeavour. But there is a dark side to all this.

We look at [the exit of Christianity Marxism and imperialism] [the prevalence of monologue] [the exit of a sublime register of language] [the demise of verse drama and narrative] [the reliance on domestic themes] [the reliance on intimacy] [the use of small intimate reading spaces] [the lack of distance from the audience] [the tugging of the personality into the centre of artistic appeal] [the distaste for heroism] [the interest in fine stylistic gestures] [the lack of grand themes] [the distaste for abstract ideas] [the reduction of politics to the personal and interpersonal domain] and find that they are all linked. The sound of the era is privatised, personalised, individualistic, small-scale. It dislikes authority. However fascinated we are by poets who break these rules, we need to think about this central area. Evidently it is just one genre but it is rather widespread. I am tempted to say that the poems are like one side of an argument with all the points made by the other side left out. But I don't think that is fair. Even if the poems are usually monologues. It could be more interesting if you altered football so that you only had one team in the game – there would be many more goals. Every manœuvre would work. There would be more climaxes. But is it better with two teams? do we like monologues so much?

If I look at 80 poems by a single poet, it may be that sixty of them fit into the same area, the target area which the poet has defined as their self. We could draw a boundary which contains the sixty and look, we have another circle.

It may not be helpful to describe texts that don't actually exist. However, the idea of unconscious limits presupposes an area which is not at all, or thinly, populated with texts. I think we can give this area substance by looking at other periods when these limits did not hold good. If you go to the opera you are bound to admit that the words are poetry and it is of a kind which people no longer write. We cannot go inside this space.

Poetry was formerly public, in courts or congregations, and dealt with public affairs in an elevated language; it has become privatised, recounting personal issues in venues that deliver intimacy, and couched in personalised language. It formerly dealt with saints and heroes, and now deals with poets. This is really a shift in the distribution of genres: lyric poetry thrived in historic times, and has simply eaten up the other genres. Meanwhile it has lost the lyric quality, it is more banal than traditional lyric poetry. Our time is a disability as well as a community.

It seems that if we have one basic book – the *Popol Vuh*, or the Bible – then there is no clear terrain for each of 972 poets to set up shop on. So the implication of allowing mass creativity is that your utterance is going to be non-collective and sited at the edge of attention. Modern poets claim title to their home ground at the cost of accepting that their work is marginal to the agora, the public space.

We spoke of a circle to divide the centre from everything else. But if we asked ten experts about the site of the circle, would they put it in ten different places? And, if we looked at a number (any number!) of actual texts, would it be ambiguous whether they fit inside the circle or not?

I thought to use the word hegemony, or "leadership", a term coined to express the exclusion of other political possibilities in an Italy which was consensually Fascist. It is customary for British cultural historians to determine what people like and tell them they mustn't like it. It would be attractive at this point to identify a curved edge of repression which implements the wishes of some nefarious interest group and excludes themes of momentous value. But that hardly seems to be the case. Fashions in culture are always based on pleasure, and it is very easy for people to walk out if they aren't having a good time. What I am describing is what people feel comfortable in, what makes them drop their defences and get carried away. What belongs to them as well as the poet. Maybe there is another radio station on the air, if we turn the dial further round.

[1] intimacy, empathy

For some reason intimacy is the key and if we understand it we will understand successful modern poetry – successfully. Poets being told they lack sensitivity will go cold and rigid. It is the asset everyone wants to possess. One version of time is that the era is seeing a constant increase of intimacy. The privatised style lives in short distances and offers a fabulous scope to small scale events. Poets who thrive in this world practice autobiography, introspection, subjective and experimental styles of language. This is parallel to natural history, where close observation yields ever better information and the audience develops even more curiosity. There must be a domain of activity where things are visible and are made clear by actions, and subtlety doesn't find anything to play with. But poets would move quickly away from anything like this. What you get is limited by that original selectivity.

The self knowledge (including knowledge of other selves) is not caused by the availability of better cameras, data storage, scientific psychology, novels, etc., but it uses them as supports. Of course this wealth of self-reflections didn't exist before the 20th C.

The issue of egocentricity is irritating but repays discussion. A fair fraction of the people who never read modern poetry associate it with self-regard, belief that knowledge of the self is better than other knowledge, going on for too long, seeing significance where there is only association with a given person. It is an area that needs to have light shed on it. Probably people who like poetry accept this focus, and others are simply not in the room with us.

I am not trying to exorcise the Marxist interpretation in which the regression to the small-scale is an expression of alienation from other people and records something being taken away. But we must also take into account the aesthetic impact of the intimate. Surely tiny processes in the space connecting two people, corresponding to the tiny signs of a poem, and to tiny processes in the chemistry of the brain and other organs, matter to us because we are human and contained within such processes. They are objectively complex and our experiences of them are objectively intense. Intimacy, empathy, sensibility – these too cannot be exorcised.

Developing economic power for the individual is the equivalent of poetry about the feelings of an individual. *Amour-propre* is like personal property. A theory connects individualism with the rise of the West since 1500 AD (or even since 500 BC). Self regard may find self regard as the explanation for everything – historical investigation tends to dissolve the evidence base for that. Arguably, there was no autobiographical poetry before the 16th C. If so many poets now start with the rule that everything has to be first hand experience, we need to ask why that is and who the legislator was who set it in place.

Attention to details, the fine lens, is integral to modern poetry. It gives us an alternative to the rather sweet ideal of "beautiful feelings of sensitive people" by shifting the motive force to richness of detail and closeness of attention. These create information, and poems are made of information.

Sensitivity involves very small quantities and spaces. Conversely, the revolutionary thing deals with Big Objects – ones it takes no sensitivity at all to detect. Demolishing bourgeois society. Rolling back the last 500 years of history. Proving the Government wrong. Locating design flaws in the world economy. Composing the history of art and 'world historical' innovations. In representations of this grandeur, small feelings are not going to register. They are too small.

[2] Dumbing down

I heard a performance poet say on the radio, in 2022, that the poetry slam was the most important cultural development of the past 50 years. This does not seem very likely. The slam is a game-show format. It is more credible if you never read books. There is a view which holds that in the 1950s, poetry was written by cultured people and was full of culture, and in the 1960s a new minimal poetry came along which was quite like the lyrics of pop songs, never referred to abstract ideas, and contained almost no information. This had barely existed before (it was obviously stupid and not worth writing). It could be delivered live and was aimed at young people. It has flourished ever since 1965 or so. Therefore, banality is modernity. Advertisements can get more elaborate and high-tech, poetry gets more and more simplistic and manipulative. This view bypasses everything that verbal intelligence thrives on – the British Poetry Revival never happened, literary theory never influenced poetry, the influence of conceptual art never happened, poets never tried to do philosophy in poetry, introspection never happened. And if you propose anything else, you are anti-modern and out of date, because the timetable says to get ever more simplistic and ever louder. You don't need to deal with the entanglement between culture and high-quality schools if you promote poetry that visibly isn't cultured and doesn't promote patience and learning.

The argument for dumbing down is that if you have a tiny audience, the poetry which alienates no sections at all will have the widest circulation. This encourages you to remove all content from the poetry – on the basis that it is the content which annoys people. Similarly, you remove all traces of style. Strangely, this process alienates a lot of people. Yet most poetry coming out can be accurately described as dumbed down. I find it hard to think about, because reading it mysteriously drives all thoughts out of my mind and leaves me numb and barely conscious. It is only of interest to notice that the managers doing it most deny that it even exists. To account for it as the main phenomenon of contemporary poetry, you have to notice that it exists.

Dumbing down tends to be solipsistic. Why? Adding information tends to moderate the primary flow of simple and egoistic sensations. This leads us to the next conclusion, that reality is alienation. Information is oppressive. Master these ideas and you will start writing dumbed-down poetry.

The origin of the phrase "dumbing down" was a policy solution in the US school system, where politicians dealt with low pass-rates in standard tests by making the tests simpler. In a meritocratic society, dumbing down is a radical move towards equality. Radically wrong, maybe.

Half a century ago, during the education revolution which brought secondary and higher education to millions of people from the working classes, the perceptions of these outsiders becoming insiders were articulated very frequently and offer a description of the English middle class and its mechanisms of defence. The cultural politics of the last 35 years (I mean roughly 1979 to 2015) have involved a consistent switching of this kind of discourse to a branch line. It is not listened to and is frequently described as boring. However, it is likely to explain the relationship between those other outsiders, the first or second generation immigrants, and the culture around poetry. Giving right explanations is not necessarily the way to gain prestige and popularity among the people whose conduct you are explaining.

Writing poems which are as simple as pop lyrics is not likely to impress connoisseurs of poetry. The literary code, most probably, was developed to make ambitious poetry possible. The language of pop lyrics may have a close relationship to this simplified poetry; and the strata of language which it shears off work more with the rational faculties than with the affective ones. Songs are a simple form of music and we are allowed to enjoy music which is more complex.

[3] innovation; myths and counter-myths of the avant-garde

There was a long tradition of the *modernist* in Britain, something which went along with being an intellectual and being ignored by the public. It was a package deal, and was a recognised Character, like the 'village atheist' a century or so before. At some point, perhaps around 1967, the Modernist role is modified, being replaced in some markets by 'Theory', another package deal associated with Paris, with the student revolts of 1968, and with post-structuralism. Within poetry, the replacing component was the 'underground', which was based on the US avant-garde of the 1950s.

One view is that modernism has been continuous for the last 100 years, that all the really significant artists of the 20th C were modernists, that it is the most legitimate way of doing art, and that everyone not doing it needs an explanation of why they are doing something less interesting. Syllabuses, State museums, and auction houses all confirm this view. To write in a modernist way is to put yourself on the side of people who give out the degrees. As for literary history, the rule is that it is about what changed and so only modernism is historic.

Unsurprisingly, not everyone tells this story in quite the same way. A significant variant is that represented by Hilton Kramer. A society which legitimates its powerful people by saying that they bring innovation about and direct investment towards new ideas is logically going to put its faith in innovative art and use it as an investment vehicle. Modernism was revived in the 1960s but distorted by a fashion cycle and by infantilism which imposed trivial biographical therapy-oriented material on the work and ended any forward motion. There is however a legitimate non-infantile modernism and this is the area which counts. Another variant starts from Harold Rosenberg's 1963 essay on "academic modernism" to say that modernism has forfeited all status as a revolt. Because only rich people can own it, it acts to legitimate the rich and also the rich bestow legitimacy on it.

With the avant-garde and its allies, we can speak of a court of the Crown Prince. Literally, this court has no power. All the same its members are constantly shaping projects for legislation. They are the succession plan of domination – they resemble those who actually hold power and imitate their bearing. They come together because of a theory of Time – the old King will die and they will succeed. The administration will be filled from the ranks of the former exiled court. It is difficult to extract the milieu of the radical, artistic and political, from the habit of forming legislative projects. The more idealistic line of this is even less democratic, as it builds something without any restraints. Imagining a political arrangement in which everyone else has to conform to the laws which you devise is not a forum in which egocentricity has been shed. It is impersonal but in a self-centred manner.

Cultural dynamism may come from a particular kind of person who thrives on high conflict levels and who manipulates situations to make conflicts worse. One way they do this is to degrade things precious to the other side. If any artist conforms to their audience, then an audience which cracks into mutually ignoring fractions forces art to evolve –

10, 100, 1000 times faster. Modernists believe that anyone not at the "cutting edge" is producing sentimental, worthless art. Marxists believe that no-one who isn't a Marxist has any moral worth. If you are both at once you are going to have a limited social life. The Alternative has a two-part theory of time. First, that only the very edge of innovation is artistically valid. Some quite mysterious force invalidates any older style once the new style has been formulated. Secondly, this timetable involves also a transmission of validity: something vital is passed on from the forefront at any time to the successors. This is the shining exception to the universal wearing-out of validity. Describing this "double timetable" is quite demanding. One has to have a model for *how* something in 2010 is connected to the culture heroes and founders of around 1912.

Critics in the anti-modernist line became preoccupied with Englishness, seen as an alternative source of legitimacy. Modernism was seen as foreign. Thus the path of stylistic development is simply closed down, like a railway line being decommissioned. The poet will succeed, supposedly, by finding the typical sound of the times, even if this brings mediocrity in most cases. This line was driven by cultural fear of the USA and by a crisis of national prestige. This theory of Englishness was largely a special plea in favour of mediocrity.

The passage of time made new things old, and so brought a crisis of obsolescence to the sector which consciously defined itself as innovative. Did new things actually crop up or had the storm front of the 1970s really reached the limits of the poem, by uninhibited innovation which stopped only at the edge of incomprehensibility and breakdown of the code? What is distinctively new since 1977? Did reaching an edge transform the 'Alternative' into a poetic school dominated by the past, and by the older members of the group? Being inside classic works that actually exist (*The White Stones, Place, Eternal Sections, A Various Art*, etc.) competed with a purer relationship to the future and the unknown. This thesis has rarely been voiced but has aroused furious disagreement when it has been.

Everyone has a version of what being out of date means. The avant-garde simply has a rigid version of it. If your big thing is innovation, you can't also indulge in genealogy. Two equally important threads were 'the new poetry as the expression of a new generation which finds nothing to admire in English politics and society' and 'conscious experimentation by means of linguistic games whose offspring proliferate and generate new combinations as years go by'.

[4] Another version of time is that this is the era of **cheap information**. Poetry is made of information and changes in the economics of information affect the economics of poetry. I discussed this at length in *The Failure of Conservatism in Modern British Poetry*.

[5] Another version of time is that the modern era sees poetry getting involved with **spatial planning** so that the clashes over use of territory and the various cognitive frameworks in which terrain is perceived and remembered are a major subject. Politics is understood as a routine for regulating disputes about land use.

Poets record limits without knowing why; but they are part of a larger map. Social organisation has a lot to do with the fitting together of various uses of land in a single overall space with multiple internal boundaries. Space is where claims are raised and conflicting wishes are eventually fitted together in a higher-level unity. Conflict ends where boundaries are accepted by all sides.

A theme is mental maps where the version of geography which people can carry around in their heads is taken as a primary reality, a sort of naive art which people rely on to navigate. Poetry is used to record memories of space and even to define it, as a sort of map in narrative form. A primary motive for this would be a distrust of central space as something unreal and giving a home to myths. The ideal is to define and promote a set of distributed spaces which have more real qualities. However, the intent is to set up new myths in these radiating centres, which are smaller and more real. Describing a place is an equivalent for describing a self, bounded in its movement by other selves, as the core of a body of poems. Language tied to a place is a surrogate for dialect.

The lattice of spatial boundaries is the substrate for the knowledge recorded in language. The poems are virtual property with limits implied by contract and defended by convention. The substrate can be represented in various projective grids.

Highly differentiated urban space is concomitant with a highly differentiated division of labour and highly specialised skills as the substrate of advanced processes and products. This was an incitement to elaborated language within a poem. Poets make cultural space more elaborate by partitioning it with stylistic refinements.

We are not seeing poems about farming and woodlands as in the Middle Ages nor yet are we seeing any poems about manufacturing. But this leaves property development and partitioning, severalty, as the residual economic activity which every poet records, even if unconsciously. Recording the boundaries, the transitions. This is also the breach by which perfect and shared space left. The thing which every poet wants to evoke. The poem is suspended in a space which is empty, invisible, total. This idea is set out at length in Richard Sennett's *The Decline of Public Man*.

Verbal space is a mechanism by which we diffuse our anxiety about space.

Being up to date

I am returning to the progress thesis, which logically means that an advance in technique in a particular town causes the validity of poems in every other town to change. It is as if the information stored in black and white on paper in *different* physical locations became corrupted by an event at *one* discrete point. This is not possible. If the texts in question do not physically change then their validity cannot change. We must be talking, therefore, about shifts in the feelings of the market – something by its nature plural and decentralised. The market probably goes off in several different directions. The claim to centralisation bypasses the fact that there is no central point and no mechanism for enforcing central edicts.

I have never really understood the theory of stylistic progress (and devastation) as expounded, for example, by Clement Greenberg. I don't follow his dictum "everything which is not avant-garde is kitsch". But I do have a view on where it came from. Central is a theory of collapse – *everything* has collapsed except the millimetre-thin forefront. This sounds like Spengler's decline of the West – it is an explanation of decline, which is seen as inevitable. The elevation of artistic progress to the status of "world history" also sounds like Spengler. The idea that the way it imagines and represents space is the most significant feature of a civilisation is Spenglerian. This is the supposed link between visual art and the state of civilisation. Finally, Spengler defined the West as the "Faustian" civilisation, which always moved towards its frontiers and tried to extend them. This is the justification for believing that the forefront is the most significant zone for art (and that everywhere else is ruined). I mention this because I don't find that Hegel fits the bill as the source of this progress theory.

The point is less Spengler's low standards of proof for anything than the sense of power of an in-group which believes that it is writing history. If a dozen styles are valid simultaneously, a succession theory which explains why only one is valid is a wrong explanation. It supports something which is not true. What we are seeing is actually a warrant for invalidating rivals.

However conservative the market is, things do become out of date. My feeling is that people writing in a style which was around fifty years ago write boringly because they lack energy – the problem is not in the style, so much, but in the fact that their choice of a tired style was a symptom of them being without energy or direction.

The decline of the mainstream

If we think about the sources of information in poetry, we can quickly identify the sense record. This is what comes in through the five senses and is at least in principle shared by other people, if they are present. Objects are only known by the senses but have a permanence which also means that they are shared by other people. Then there is the record of feelings, inner-body sensations which are felt as heat, cold, pressure, also as pleasure, pain, etc. Then there is the record of thinking, so dealing with patterns and ideas which are not simply sensations, and which in practice are tangled up with feelings. Then there is the intuition record, where we perceive other people's feelings; this is also linked to identification, something crucial in poetry and which some intuitions fall under. This can extend to *group feeling*, so no longer two people in an intimate bond but a larger number with more energy circulating between them. We can describe these channels quickly because they are organic to a human group, any human group, and our nature makes us fluent in all of them. We did not mention an integrator which combines all these sources into a better image, and which has a special relationship to language. It is cross-modal, that is it combines perceptions of different modalities.

Another level is purpose. Human organisms do not passively perceive their environment but organise perception in order to fulfil organic needs. In order to be employed by someone, to be their servant, you have to abandon your own purposes; this is greatly emphasised in education, which evidently wants to turn out employable minds. Education wants minds which can argue for both sides and so argue for whoever pays them. Writing essays that reflect political beliefs, or any attitudes in fact, is stigmatised in higher education.

This basis is necessary to explain how the older poetic ideology known as empiricism worked. The ideology wanted the poet to be distrustful, to be uncommitted, to separate wishes from the sense record, and to describe objects (or anything like an object) accurately and with details. The unstated subtext of this was that channels like feeling, intuition, and especially speculation, were to be repressed as much as possible. The situation of the past 20 years is that poets have shed this limiting ideology. If we talk about a "mainstream" now it is quite different from the mainstream visible in 1975.

The imperative to describe physical objects accurately can hardly be separated from commerce, from the description of objects of exchange which is exact as one condition of a valid contract of sale. Poetry is more ancient than the retail nexus and has to fulfil other imperatives.

The group of ideas we are describing was rather hostile to poems which developed enthusiasm and involvement and ran away with the reader. This sort of excitement and development of new associations and intuitions was labelled as a loss of reason. During the Cold War, teachers and critics who had invested in the war effort were afraid of pupils and students developing socialistic attitudes and asking for greater social equality, for better working conditions, for the sharing of profits. Most social reforms were seen as crypto-communism. Young people were likely to have this reaction to the social order as they became conscious, and poetry was likely to record such feelings. Meanwhile, exact observation, however dull, was to make these people employable. Having never developed political commitment, they were psychologically disposable to develop loyalty to the corporation which was going to hire them, and to think only of their job. In Accounts or elsewhere. The Cold War poem was designed to freeze enthusiasm, although this often raised the question of how one could then become enthusiastic about the poem.

It is possible, as it turned out, to describe trees, sounds, towns, in sensory terms and without using emotive words and still evoke feelings in the reader. However, it was never clear why the poet should avoid expressing their feelings and so arousing intuition and sympathy in the reader, channels capable of greatly amplifying direct sense reactions. Symbolism is where the channels of sensory perception and emotion come together on the same surface and pursue a joint course. There was a phase in the later 20th C when personal symbolism was shouted down, critics instantly separating the two channels and denouncing the rash decision to bind them together. In the end the expression of feeling was exiled because all its means had been re-defined as illogical.

Not a few people perceived that the Cold War conservative style was successful because it was associated with a prestigious and educated group and that there was a wide zone in which poetry of limited aesthetic value was praised because it sounded educated. Actually, this perception gave quite a few people a free lesson in the links between artistic style and social power. A wider knowledge of languages and culture does not naturally make people *more* repressed and conventional, and a key development saw poets exploit education and access to diverse poetry to find alternatives to the Empirical and Conservative style and so (eventually) to make it obsolete.

There was a shorthand term, a while ago (certainly between 1950 and 1980) whereby *empirical* was a loaded word for distinguishing between Marxist and conservative scholars. The Marxists used it to denounce someone, not one of theirs, for being short-sighted and unable to see the wider pattern. Elsewhere, the word was used to criticise any kind of large-scale reform. The existing order based on property and inequality was tried and tested; anything better had not been tried out and was not *empirically proven*. So change was banned altogether and this poetry aligned with neo-liberalism. The distinction between theory and empiricism persisted but the word *theory* gradually became less Marxist and less political. These oppositions were not necessarily helpful to debate and reflection.

Explaining why people disliked the mainstream in the period up to, say, 1990, should also explain why the central current of British poetry has changed so much since then; in fact its success has turned on a rejection of recently powerful traditions and the opening up of new territory. It used to be that I would read magazines and be amazed that people with so much education could take so much effort to write such bad poetry. There were obviously conventions which paralysed their creativity. That is no longer true, and the amazement is obsolete. It is obvious now that the old ideology was having major problems keeping control in the later 1980s.

There is now no orthodoxy. While the new poetry is wonderfully diverse, we can offer the generalisation that it lacks inhibitions about using disparate parts of experience, and to be specific that it uses emotional language, symbolism, complex figures of speech, metaphors, fantasies, exact descriptions of objects or organisms, intuitions about other people's feelings, scientific knowledge, documents, abstractions, and so forth.

Since human beings have a cross-modal faculty, called consciousness, it is natural for poetry also to be cross-modal. This is a stable site for it to occupy. The new pattern is simply an organic one where the naturally available elements of human consciousnesss are freely available for verbal patterning. This has allowed a very impressive diversity which is much less easy to describe than the former monoculture.

Language is made of rules

This chapter is about the operation of rules in poetry, and how they are set and, occasionally, changed. Everybody thinks they are a free agent, so we do not need to spend time on the rule-free aspect of the scene. Instead, we need to ask where the rules are set, how they are debated, how old they are.

The relationship between the educated and the rest, between status and culture, is unstable and accurate statements about it are not available. UKIP stated their conclusion in the form of, *educated people are wrong*. I was taken aback to discover that the lack of patriotic poetry (the drum and trumpet style, indeed) goes back to the 1920s. This raised the spectre of a continuing self-imitation, where young people in any year acquire the rules of poetry from the existing poetry, and learn reactions through deep identification. That would give us a pattern of serenity and stability, broken by rare crises in which the rules are re-set. The stability would be held up both by new people joining and reinforcing the set-up, and by people who disliked the set-up not participating to any extent, departing for other scenes. And not exercising a vote at any decision point. The pattern allows for the arrival of new people who are similar to the ones already there, and for the retention of past decisions and symbolic structures.

A poem is couched in language, which is a public set of rules and virtual objects. So, not only the sounds represented by letters, but also the meaning of words in the lexicon, the behaviour of objects and materials, and the relation of signs of emotion to invisible inner states, are fixed and public. There is also a layer of literary convention, much argued over, which readers are familiar with. All this reduces the ambiguity of poetic statements and symbols to the point where it is possible to read poetry. Its stable and public nature allows us to define misreadings. Poets often deny the existence of rules, but the moment when poets start believing in them is when they accuse someone of misreading their poem – at that point they believe that a form of words invokes all kinds of rules and so constrains the way in which the poem is allowed to be read. Writers think there is a legitimate way of reading a line – and the *lex* root means 'law' and is buried in the word *legitimate*. The line does not have the value which the poet attributes to it but the value which the readers attribute to it.

Rules do not apply in a vacuum but they do apply to poems. By the time you have written half a poem, the rest of it is governed by all kinds of rules. This means you don't have autonomy (and *nomos* is that *law* word, again). But the rules mean other people can read your poems. The poetic order is held in place by the whole set of people who read poetry. Its processes cannot genuinely be accountable, because they are implicit and evanescent. It works on the basis that the actual readers have the right to set the values of verbal structures, on various scales.

A game has shared rules and the rules in a sense are the game. Two games with the same rules are the same game. In culture, the rules are not written down, but implicit and acquired by intuition. The rules may be more obvious in the steps transforming a half-finished poem into a finished one, or in failed poems, than elsewhere.

The Shadow Side

A trawl through the entries for British poets in *The Oxford Companion to Twentieth Century Poetry in English*, edited by Ian Hamilton (1994), hauls up 370 names of whom 111 studied at Oxford University. That is, about 30% of the poets felt to matter for the 20th century. I looked, while writing, at an anthology by Kenneth Allott called *Contemporary Poetry* (in re-issue *Contemporary Poetry 1918–60,* also *The Penguin Book of Contemporary Verse*). Allott included 86 poets of whom 6 were female (7%) and 34 studied at Oxford University (39.5%). These sample "standard repositories" show the power of in-groups. They record the apex, but the next question is how the apex relates to the base. (The total in Allott for Oxford *plus* Cambridge is 60%.)

These two books are a convenient reference site for elitism. Do they show the absence of ethnic minorities? Actually, Allott leaves out the Scots and Welsh but Hamilton includes them. Evidently, if the publication system were different, it would reach a different market, including people who were alienated by people like Hamilton and Allott. Or, that market may remain in the imaginary. It's an agreed generalisation that the most prestigious poetry tends to be written by the people with the most formal education, and within that group, even, by people closest to a socio-cultural pattern present in families with a long tradition of speaking English. The acquisition of poetry-fertile qualities, that is, seems to start in early childhood rather than, say, at age eighteen. There is a geographical factor: if we divide Western Europe into cold and warm zones then it is obvious that peripheral areas are relatively "cold" and that Wales and Scotland are less attractive as areas to set poems in; but as American poets do not suffer from this it seems likely that language use is also very important. Successful poets began, probably, with high verbal intelligence and spent key years on training courses to improve it. Hardly less obviously, the people who judge this success (i.e., in contrast to many factions unsuccessfully ascribing it) themselves conform to this pattern.

There is a competition between makers of taste, which evidently some of them lose. While poetry is a commodity, and people can buy as much or as little as they choose, there are also points where authority does exist: for example, in compiling anthologies, in setting up the school syllabus, and in teaching. Schoolchildren are surely influenceable and good teachers influence them. Pupils write essays about poems and deftly learn what will get high marks. This is not a relationship of equals. One version of literary taste comes out on top, and this wasn't really a free market.

Anyone who looks at these figures will get to the next step, i.e. the possibility that the most cultured people are also the most likely to write effective poetry. It would follow that, in 1960, 40% of the best poets actually were Oxford graduates, so that Allott wasn't biased. The next step would be to overthrow the way things have been done in the past, and enact rules that all anthologies, magazines, etc. have to include poets in numerical ratio to sociological sub-groups within the entire population, rather than choosing them on the basis of artistic merit. Of course, this would produce anthologies, magazines, etc., which were unpleasant to read, because they weren't full of good poems.

The transmission of the implicit as a shared grammar takes place within the poems – the more you read, the more you understand. So if there is an out-group perhaps it doesn't understand what the in-group is saying.

The 1962 anthology gives us the useful image of a duality: the *face* is composed and adorned and dressed in the mirror but the *silhouette* shows more basic physical truths and is not composed – it tells a different story. Thus Allott shows fairness and generosity as the face, and elitism and minority status (unpopularity?) as the three-dimensional shape. What if someone takes the shadow side as the real picture?

Market choice

We keep mentioning rules but modern poetry is notoriously free in at least three ways. First, poets do not have managers. They are not being supervised and do not have to submit individual creativity to a collective scheme, as in a film crew. Editors do not actually tell poets what to do – they may make suggestions. Next, we are free inside the poem. The way we react to a line is largely personal and we can sail off into personal fantasies as part of absorbing the line. This is less possible in a performance but private reading is the key process. The poems not only ask for but use free association. Images follow each other according to the logic of fantasy. Thirdly, we are free to choose what to buy and the business is focused on making that choice as wide and attractive as possible. However many times I have been in a bookshop, I have yet to hear someone say, you have to buy that book, or you can't buy that one. The degree of freedom in poetry is high and obvious. It is a descriptive challenge to explain how this liberty is compatible with a pervasive field that subtends rules of taste which change and which are promoted or challenged by strong personalities. Outside formal education, I think it is all happening in the bookshops, and that each book has a separate biography as a commodity. I concede that individuals consume using rules, so they may either decide "I will buy a book by someone I have never heard of" or "I will buy a book because I have heard of the author", and those are rules. I am just saying that I don't see how those rules are *centralised*.

If we look at the scene in 2000 or 2010, the striking feature is that there are a dozen different stylistic models and none could have the force of law unless the others were somehow shut down and rendered null. We noticeably have dissident poets who must, previously, have been dissident readers. The interaction of the elite and the market is that someone can float a literary idea and it reaches the public through magazines and the bookshops (and the Net) and then it can succeed or fail according to their response. So a key phenomenon is failed projects for renewing taste, and we can locate these with a little effort. Eric Mottram's stint as editor of *Poetry Review* may have been one of these, although the extent of its success is also noticeable and worth arguing over. Perhaps no project fails altogether.

We can reconcile the demands of retail freedom and impressive influencers by talking about temporary consumer identities. You need to offer these identities in order to sell either clothes or books. This acknowledges that Michael Roberts did not have any institutional power by saying that his idea of the Modernist was a package which many people could adopt as a temporary identity. Roberts' three anthologies of the 1930s wrapped up the temporary identity we are talking about. So Roberts was not the boss but like someone whose style of dress is arrestingly new and able to be imitated by anybody else. After the imitation, you feel that the style is yours and says something about you. So the 1930s saw many poets, almost all of them under 30, being influenced by his anthologies, but far more people publishing without being influenced by him. A conservative identity is also a package which you can adopt. Few conservatives are uniformly so, more probably they decide how to react afresh with every new poem – which is what the subjects report about their own experience of it.

Anti-meritocratic feelings

The rise of UKIP was the most striking feature of politics in the period after the 2008 crash. Actually, the line of right-wing populism was broader; first, the BNP got 943,000 votes in the 2010 general election, then UKIP gobbled up all those voters and a lot more, then a populist faction destroyed the May administration and seized the Conservative party leadership.

    I spent a lot of time reflecting on this. To start with, where the UKIP bloc took the law made by Brussels and Westminster and rejected all of it because they regarded the elite as corrupt, I could see that poetic taste as we have it was also the result of legislative acts carried out by an elite. If Allott's standard anthology had names of whom 60% had studied either at Oxford or at Cambridge, that pretty well defined the elite. Changes since his halt point, in 1960 (the book reached publication slightly later, in 1962) have much diluted the Oxbridge hegemony but the new regime was much more dominated by graduates – an elite which is so large that it is almost not an elite. Until Brexit polarised the graduates against the rest and UKIP defined the universities as bad places which manufactured people who voted against Brexit.

    Poets expect people to find them appealing but their line did not go over well with UKIP supporters.

I am sensitive. *You want special treatment. You want to jump to the head of the queue.*
I am intelligent. *That is so wrong*
I am fluent in abstract ideas. *Abstraction is inherently wrong and controlled by foreigners. We only believe in things and hatred.*
I have a wide knowledge of culture. *This means that you like foreigners. You aren't loyal. And you have swallowed all their disloyal ideas.*
I have a wide vocabulary. *This just means that you can cheat people. You are not trustworthy.*
I have a knowledge of cultural heights and food sensations that you are not yet familiar with. *That is repulsive. We don't want your sort around here. You have been putting us down all our lives. We will be liberated by overthrowing you.*
I have a wide knowledge of foreign countries where I wandered around having unexpected and carefree and exciting sensations. *You like foreigners.*

So UKIP was not giving out sounds that poets wanted to hear. The scene is left-liberal and internationally oriented. How bad is this anyway? Some people may dislike all this but they aren't the people who pursue poetry. The poem as grand act of xenophobia was quite prevalent during the period of Great Power naval rivalry and then the Great War.

"'Lie down men', he said, although he sat on horseback, exposed to the fire as calm as possible. 'This shall be a glorious day for Old England, if these bragadocian rascals dare but stand their ground, we will display the point of the British bayonet, and where it is properly displayed no power is able to withstand it. All I request of you is to be steady and obey your officers.'"

This is strong language and poetry exploited it for a long time. The abandonment of poetry about naval battles, of poetry about killing foreigners in general, was a shift about 100 years ago which has never been reversed. But the "emotional identity" of aggressive nationalism persisted, even if it was increasingly a minority attitude, in other strata. People with this attitude are generally not in the government. Poets writing sensitively about beautiful feelings are not what UKIP supporters want. They are on a war footing and do not want to be distracted by beautiful and intricate things. So they have a case – the literary world is not now producing patriotic propaganda poems and so is not acting according to their wishes.

My research may have been a waste of time. After all, I didn't find either UKIP poets or even right-wing poets in the period after 1960. Why explain what didn't happen? Poetry does not write patriotically about wars and conquests. The joke version is that UKIP members have a special anthology just for them called "100 poems about killing foreigners". But, the UKIP platform was that the legislators both at Brussels and in Westminster had passed bad laws and there was a happy life to be recovered by scrapping all that legislation. This maps onto cultural life if you decide that the set-up *is* the product of legislation and that this was the self-enactment of a *minority*. It is clear that poetry had been involved with naval and military affairs (from about 1897 on) and that this stopped abruptly around 1920. The rules changed. Even the celebrated Battleship Poets, still in their prime, stopped writing that kind of poetry. There are a dozen or so collective changes of the 20th century and I have chosen this one because it was never reversed, its consequences were still visible in the 1980s and still in 2020. There was no legislation to annul it. Every generation of young people arriving saw the set-up and accepted the findings. The scene reproduced itself.

If there are laws of taste and they change, then we are entitled to ask how they changed, who led the change, how many proposals for change failed in the market. I identified a dozen changes to the rules, during the 20th C, and tried to reconstruct their biographies. I looked at the purge of rhetoric, a striking feature of the inter-war period, and found that very similar changes had happened in other areas of public emotional speaking, namely the theatre, politics, and the law courts. One of the key figures, identified by some very interesting legal history, was Patrick Hastings, a barrister who was also a playwright and also a politician with Cabinet rank.

(There is a very long series of posts on this on my website.) The shift of sensibility could not possibly have taken place inside poetry, which in this case was not autonomous. Literary critics may have organised the response but the change flowed in from a wider world.

The reasons why militarism became suspect are super obvious and they don't attach to a few supercilious supervisors forcing a policy through that nobody wanted. I believe that the same limit applies to all the other legislation on poetic taste in the 20th C. The patterns of culture are there because they give pleasure and not because of external, schematic, frames of compulsion.

Wastewater to underground water

Maybe we can revisit the legislation metaphor. The outcome is that if you give a reading some people will like it, some will dislike it, and some won't really react. So taste is unlike law and it is always up to the individual. However, access to publication is restricted by editors. Your poem gets returned to you because it fails by the rules and poetry is, like football, played by the rules. The verdict, here, is that the editor didn't enjoy it. You are unhappy. You try to analyse what the editor enjoys (as the line bounding what they don't enjoy). Rejected poets rarely want editors to have the freedom to reject them. Next year there will be another editor with a different set of feelings. The border where feelings turn into rules or vice versa is of great interest. Feelings show patterns and even have history.

As if we were considering an industrial process, we should consider the biography of the waste as much as that of the commodity. It is key to Allott's staging of things if we identify a process that prevented people not in his anthology from writing ambitious poetry, instead of or as well as Allott turning down poetry that had actually been composed. If I use the words *grey material* to refer to these poems it is an allusion to grey water (you wouldn't want to drink it) and also to the lack of light falling on it at every stage. This is in contrast to the light falling on, and bouncing back off as aura, Geoffrey Hill or Charles Tomlinson. Information on the waste channel is limited at every stage. We can say that the exclusion of Kathleen Raine from Lucie-Smith's anthology was a drama, not least because it is part of a whole process by which she was moved out of the elite centre. But that is one person out of a mass. If you collate *Identity Parade* (2010) with *Dear World* (2013), you find that only 5 out of 85 names in *IP* made it into the later anthology. I don't want to suggest that the others had stopped being successful. I just want to say how little information we have on the decision to omit, or on the armies of poets omitted from various scenes. The more they were affected, the less we know about their poetry.

It is no secret that different judges would select different poets, and retrieve segments of the Rejected. Or, that the rejected themselves would like to have different judges. Or that the Fifties had rather little to show in the way of upscale suppressed writers. The idea that the editors could be wrong in rejecting you didn't really catch on until the later Sixties. Prior to that people, after rejection, stopped writing poetry, or largely gave up trying at it.

The poetic process involves an aestheticisation which is selective in several ways and so leaves a residue in silence, which logic tells us must exist, and which contains everything which is not aesthetic. We have found a way of defining the aesthetic activity: *socially* to locate the good poems and *internally* to discard dull material and to intensify the chosen moments of language.

In the end you get the return of the repressed. If you have someone who recovers information about the invisible, about the 99% of poets who are marginally visible (and that percentage may be *higher*), the result must shed light not only on the literary process but also on social reshaping of memory. It may also be hard to read and make sense of.

Micro-rules

The civilisational rules also concern conduct. If you look at a group of people who show unusual inhibitions, it is credible that this present state reflects past aggression. Inhibition is part of a social function and the civilisational process (as Norbert Elias describes it) involves the renouncing of this aggression. Bullying and machismo are big parts of the collective story and the discussion now has to do with public space, in which they have played a formative role. If a lot of attention has been given to changing the micro-rules of public space, this is because they had to change a lot, notably to do with work spaces which had been all male expanding to include young women, notably young professional women. The rule that a lawyer had to be a man, for example, had to dissolve as women qualified and became lawyers.

Probably too much fuss has been made about the rather inevitable process of changing these micro-rules, as people do not like being rebuked and are quick to notice that these rules are not made in exactly a democratic way and that the process tends to be led by articulate people – who can be attacked because they are vocal. I have to recall that literature has always supplied models of manners and conduct, and that people have always picked up, from poetry, rules of conduct which they did not already observe. Public space is a tissue of micro-rules. A key issue is safe space and this can involve excluding individuals to make it safe. Evidently domination and space are intertwined.

One has to ask what is the difference between poems and undifferentiated social space, and the answer lies in a complex but vital shift of rules, involving idealisation, harmony, self-restraint, and also freedom.

The absence of aggression is surely part of its charter clauses. If poems are written as model spaces, among other things, I have to review them *as* model spaces to pursue the intent.

If you go back to the school milieu, teachers quite often have the opinion that children are self-determining at a certain age and that their expectations of what they will become as adults are a critical limit on their attitude to school work. Changing the public image of selective workplaces, the ones where you get to have high earnings, is also part of how teachers think. 14-year-olds, acting on incomplete information, maintain, repair, and even invent the class system (and its geographical implantation). I don't think the checks on social mobility are quite so simple, but this issue of "defining what space it is appropriate for you to enter and take part in" is part of social management. It is important to detect this double push, to alter the perceptions of children and to make the labour market open. The passage involves a single individual but crosses an interval of 10 years or even more. I just wonder if I have any readers who are *against* class mobility.

There is some affinity between the poem co-opting you into its inner space and society co-opting you into a situation where you are able to carry out a role (or a job?). But how does this happen exactly? And what are the differences?

Who owns the rules

There is a new feeling about the possibility of changing unconscious rules of conduct. Part of this is an awareness that the rules of the scene are the product of human action and collusion rather than of something impersonal (like the rules of stress in the English language, let's say). And part of it is the impact of social media on discussion around poetry. The level of communication of reactions and opinions has gone up greatly, so that there is much more visibility of the ethical content of a poem (or a reaction). So it has become much more credible that social pressure would change the collective rules.

There is widespread agreement that the effect of social media, of websites showing discussion, etc. on poetry has been to create, not a community, but an archipelago of islands on which multiple communities evolve in different directions. It is like the magazines scene. We can theorise that a central space might emerge, which would be so popular that you would have to follow it, as it would be the web chronicle of record; but as things stand the Internet has no centre and has demolished central place yet again.

Primal panic

Light can be shed on the word *sensitive* and its implications, by looking at the *Jeremy Kyle Show* (the "voice of the people" according to its own advertising). The standard content of the show includes grievance and projection of guilt. The show, notoriously, foregrounded people in a kind of infantile panic of unappeased dependency. There is in humans something original and locked-in which is broken down by language and perceptions, to form a later world whose parts are *different* from each other. In the show, this development is seen as a kind of weakness and is blocked. The basic assertion is defeatured to the point of becoming a bludgeon. It does not allow the onlooker a choice about what emotional stance to take up – the guilt is laid on thick so that the onlooker has no choice. Their world-view is 90% grievance and 80% grudge and is protected from any verbal process of testing and debate. This offers us a definition of the word *sensitive* – it is any autobiographical discourse which is not crippled by resentment, which offers the onlooker the chance to be attracted and make their minds up, and in which states of mind fluctuate from minute to minute. This shift will be seen by the Kyle faction as a weakening of the signal. The wish for sensitivity is a demand that art give up the infantile position, in which needs are unqualified and other people are there only to do exactly what the ego wants. Of course some poetry is written from this position, and this is the force of the word *sensitivity*. I am not attacking the Kyle show and its watchers, just observing an opposition in the cultural field. This separates literary from non-literary. The separation is the site of rules. A rule is that literature is found in the literary realm.

Feelings

I am clear how knowledge of other countries and of abstract ideas allows a minority to emerge as victors. But if poetry is about feelings then it is less clear how a minority can win persistently. Doesn't everyone have feelings the same size? I am not going to answer this question because I want to leave it as a crux. It is a source of insight at every point. Of course Oxford graduates don't have feelings bigger than other people's. That is a heresy. And there may be different histories of the same period of poetry – different directions emerging and seizing attention.

The skittery style

This is to bring on stage a verbal manner which has some claim to distinctiveness and which, it is credible, was not present in 1999. It is easier to show in prose than in verse. "[T]here's only one method: throw yourself into the darkness which is (at least) the darkness of ink and death. Lose yourself in strange demotics, flarf-like overspills, sleuthy overhearings, scatological flingings of language, self-reflexive poetics questions: these proverbs of death. If sable smoke is an embarrassed reference to death then these are death grunts after the event, the transcriptions of voices, vampires, the graphology of emphasis for the ear – nothing random. A little openness to punning, infantile abandonment, language-ploy, goes a long way. You'll hear the death rattle laughing." (Blurb by Robert Sheppard for *sable smoke*, Burner Veer series no. 34)

Not everything which is unusual is attractive. The line skitters because it slides off every idea very quickly and whitters because it does not present coherent information. But it is a signal to a specific fraction of the market, which knows its own wishes.

> "To fall out of propriety – ultimately, out of property – what does it mean? The proper order is gone. 'All kinds of sputter suddenly relate to each other.' The way you hear it is going to change – the language: out of control and failing – to measure what it's supposed to. So this is not the master's voice… and the result is a different world, close by but unremarked. And bark leather makes this happen by calling to us with the most un-judging expressions, the ones that speak from intimate and unguarded feeling and from perception of things in whatever place they happen to be, not where they should be. The truth is things are not in their place."
> (blurb by William Rowe for 'bark leather',
> Burner Veer series no. 16)

The phrase *the ones that speak from intimate and unguarded feeling* is revealing because it is so out of place in a stack of Veer blurbs: it refers to poetry reproducing prior feelings rather than being an improvisation in a realm emptied of memories.

The proposal is that randomness actually is the lyric sound, has replaced the former versions of lyric; that rapid responses unconnected from stimuli liberate you from ever reacting to unpleasant stimuli. This is a fundamental gesture. It is a modern pastoral. We have been talking about repetition and reinforcement and it is critical to reflect on a cell which rejects those processes. It is neither expressive nor documentary. The project of deprogramming is connected, almost inevitably, to an idea that society spends tremendous energies in conditioning us to repeat behaviour patterns which we have no opportunity to assess in rational terms. If I am right, the disconnected quality is a protest against authority; because voices of authority tell people that dropping out brings a lack of direction and of purpose, the counter-claim is to possess free and groundless chains of association. So, attention to any matter is felt as a loss of autonomy. The end result is quite like the condition attributed to consumers, where the attention span is very very short. The idea of breaking out of that sick glitter flow, of no longer reacting to it at all, is attractive, even a kind of sublime.

*

I thought to find out how many poets in the 2010 Bloodaxe anthology *Identity Parade* had studied at either Oxford or Cambridge. I reached a figure of 23, or 27%. That includes two poets teaching at those places, and because poets now go to great lengths to disguise any Oxbridge link the data-gathering exercise was irritating and the count may be too low. I think the key may be that people don't want a friend who is more intelligent than they are and poets want to be popular. (If you are this scared of academic success, how scared are you of artistic success?) Anyway, this is a significant drop on the 60% racked up by Allott's anthology. The apex is getting broader, as I suggested. Because collusion implies a game it also implies rules. The rules are only a way of describing a process of collusion and identification which we profoundly enjoy. I can see that identification is where we are captured by the social system. My profound dislike of Brexit leads me to support the liberal legacy of cultural legislation. The poetry scene can only make its rewards available to you by reproducing itself. With all that implies of collusion, consensus, and conservatism.

Foundation Texts

Put your bat clothes on: Kevin Nolan, *Loving Little Orlick* (2006, 81pp)

The starting line is that I think this may be the most important new volume of the 21st century. I find it endlessly fascinating and yet indefinable – it remains mysterious. From scattered conversations I recall that Orlick is a Dickens character – but may also be connected with orlach (variant *ordlach*, Irish for *inch, finger's breadth ... a moment in time*). The author was unhappy that the milieu had failed to produce any 'serious' reviews which traced the thematics of the work. He certainly regarded it as a themed book. I kept quiet because I found the book unreviewable. (Orlick may be a substandard variant of a more familiar surname, Horlick: "meanwhile/ the Lord post-caring rules outright murder and has his medics/ skin and pickle Orlick for the Mad Theory seminar".)

Two immediate points. The text moves very quickly from one idea to another. Secondly, it is full of people's names. This is compatible with a concrete situation with a plot, a drama in fact. The names belong to characters and the poet is, whatever else may be going on, moving the characters around. If you can't explain this you can't explain anything.

The scene recognised in *Orlick* a resemblance to Prynne, specifically the Prynne of *The White Stones*. This is not easy to define precisely, maybe only that quicksilver rapidity of movement, the irrational complexity of human organised action opened up by a few words (that never pause to spell it all out). I don't think it is, really, similar to *White Stones* – but its bebop-like rapidity is enough to make it an envy-object. After all, everyone has tried to write like *The White Stones* – at least in Cambridge.

This poetry is supremely difficult to describe and master at the same time that its individual parts are perfectly clear and fluent. Let me propose that the surface we see in *Orlick* is like one where someone is watching a film and simultaneously talking about it, visualising scenes from other films (with the same actors, scenery, or plot modules) and imagining what is going to happen next. This is based on the knowledge that he has spent many years teaching film studies and has memories of thousands of films.

So the instant visibility of the characters could be because they have walked on screen from another film we have seen. They are familiar, fully fashioned. A chapter of introduction would be superfluous. By examination, I can see that the scenarios are not from actual films: they are therefore invented films – but may for all that live inside the syntax of film plotting and draw on a library of films which the poet has in his memory. All this is compatible with the immediate accessibility of the poetic text.

Orlick is a demonic figure in *Great Expectations*, so the idea of loving little Orlick is an inversion of the possible, a trip into another state which is purely a possibility opened by the text and yet is forbidden by its record. It is dissident, perverse, fantastic. Suppose Orlick were the object of patronage and gifts and not Pip? One passage from the poem 'WRZBRNO' lays out what may be the rules of composition:

> You start as a raw recruit tasked with taking down Paxton Quigley, a serial monster trapped on floor 6 with a plasma cannon and 3 hostages. Already he has grown punitive organelles to irradiate the white goods on level 8. Police liaison is a Canadian female who quickly shoots down all the photographers. Down in the basement is Lech Furiskey, the 64 year old janitor in secret telepathic communication with Quigley. In a late game you get to play him as a beefy, lock-eyed transvestite who sings at the café Nezval most nights. *Didn't youse use to use a used-car dealer in Youghall?* is his first line. **Ex-Dream** is always personal; it's whatever gets you to the position of office-manager fastest. The janitor is a wedding-guest too: you don't have to sound like him till you're ready. No need for implants, the café floor already smells of oil.

'WRZ BRNO' could be a radio station in Brno (in the Czech Republic) or a made-up Slavonic word –'wrz' is a possible letter sequence in Polish. Carroll Quigley is the author of a book uncovering the secret history of British and American foreign policy, a classic of conspiracy theory. 'Quigley' is an Irish name, the same as O'Coiglidh. Furiskey appears in one other poem ('Bacon Dust'), the ambiguous Irish/Polish sounds of the name may have appealed. This is like what a scriptwriter would get as a brief, setting you up to write episode 28 after not being involved in episodes 1-27. More simply, it could be like the TV listings a consumer scans to figure out what scene to spend the evening in. Nezval was a great Czech poet who was minister of cinema after the Communist takeover. He wrote a long poem for Stalin's birthday (1949) which is now hard to obtain. But the reference to 'game' might point us towards a role-playing game.

Kevin at various times has described themes of the book as Irishness, the arms trade, the Qu'ran, and global warming. I have not been able to trace most of these. Evidently the book is bound by themes, a set where different passages reflect or continue each other. K was disappointed that I didn't recognise references to the Qu'ran at first glance. He said that the Orlick book had two opposite meanings of the word *oirlich* which start and end the volume. One is the 'battle-fury' of *The Tain* and the other is a sense 'little one' which means 'dearest', a term of affection for a child. This is the 'little Orlick'. *Great Expectations* is a theme running through the book. He described a reference to a song about the woods of Killarney being destroyed which is picked up in forest themes and connects to the devastation of Nature (probably).

The Tudor arrival of a new regime of intense rule (and misrule) (An Concas) may have been linked to a shortage of old-stand timber in England which meant that naval supplies for masts and long beams were sought in Ireland. This brought English gentleman colonists, and this incited rebellion by the Irish, so that the price of the timber was warfare and eventually the destruction of the native political structure of landholding and great families, in the affected areas. The ships that went out to colonise America were partly built of Irish timber, and the destruction of a social order (in some parts of Ireland) was a side-effect of early imperialism. The Tudor and Stuart Crown responded to rebellion by declaring lands (held under feudal law at the pleasure of the Crown) forfeit, a high-risk policy which created new reasons to revolt. Land-grants to English gentry and their retainers brought into existence a class of landless and disaffected 'mere Irish', a group with a long life as English colonisation subverted different districts, piecemeal over generations. So there is a link (rebels and outlaws: tree cutting) and folk-lore is not wholly wrong. An undated (but printed in 1904) text on the Internet says: "During the wars of Elizabeth it was still a proverb that 'The Irish will never be tamed while the leaves are on the trees', meaning that the winter was the only time in which the woods could be entered by an army with any hope of success; [.]" (http://www.ucc.ie/celt/online/E900000-001/text001.html) (by Caesar Litton Falkiner) – this also shows the woods as the protection of Gaelic-Irish rebels. In 'Kill Michael' Nolan uses the words *Silvatici* and *carceleri*. Carceleri should mean prisoners, the spelling might make it Rumanian. Silvaticus is someone who lives in a wood (silva) and gives us our word

Foundation Texts 55

savage. This matches the Irish phrase, *ceithearnach choille*, the wood-kern, a familiar term for an outlaw, most likely an inhabitant of Ulster after the Settlement and in insurrection against the settlers (and used on p.32). The forest is so the home of resistance, of pristine and egalitarian values. In 'The File on Agrippina' we hear 'Then soldiers of the forest, be effective!/ There never was such shade! Lob clarity/ to the net, there never was such clarity!' These are presumably wood-kerns. The poem concludes 'As corruption immemorial we shall/ graft them. As daybreak splicing/ wavelengths we will separate. As/ sensors theoretical we'll grow rings and bow directly – / meanwhile the trees cut down/ whole swathes of the lucid inevitable…' This is difficult but there seems to be a connection between trees processing light in photosynthesis as the primary energy source of the organic world, and "light" being shed on shady practices (to include the destruction of forests). The "grow rings" bit must suggest "growth rings" – the *speakers* are trees, their growth rings are a record of a primary kind, and they are "sensors" for atmospheric pollution and global warming. The "lucid inevitable" could perhaps be the disaster of economic rationality, an inevitable decline which a forest could replace with cyclical lastingness and leafy darkness. Uncovering a forest theme may be a distraction from the overall shape of the book: mostly it isn't about forests, in fact it shifts themes with a kind of voluptuous subtlety of touch and that velocity is a key tonal value.

The poem 'Eirleach' starts with a lengthy and untranslated quote in Old Gaelic. I should confess that I did Old Irish at university, 45 years ago, and that the quote is from one of the set texts we studied for that paper – it is the *Táin*, 8th century text, 10th century manuscript. I admit that it was only the last sentence which I was able to translate. Anyway I searched the Internet and found out that the story it tells is of Orlab (variant *Orlam*, and perhaps another quasi-Orlick figure), son of Ailill and Medb, who are the king and queen of Ulster. He goes with his chariot-boy to cut wood for chariot-poles in a wood belonging to another kingdom. Cu Chulainn (hero-name for Setanta) comes across the party. He tricks the lad into showing him who Orlam is, outruns the boy, cuts Orlam's head off. And shows it to the men of Ireland (this is the part I could translate). This is the 'eirleach', the slaughter. The story about the cutting of young trees (to turn into chariot-poles) presumably connects to other passages about the cutting of timber. When we come to the poem –

Salacea claimant, blue guest, harbinger berserker: waldteufel. Callsign: eternity. Process: distillation. Element: deuterium. Vector: a kind of bulky demission, hope from antihope outside landline wavebands. Blowback: a kind of allegiance masquerading as opposition, gracenotes for the seizure masked with killer attorneys

It holds six brief prose sections of which this is one. The whole reads like objective description but evidently deals with fictional knowledge. It reads like a handbook where we would look up the callsign of a something. I am unable to find the 'slaughter' in this, or indeed the connection with Cu Chulainn and the lamented Orlam. The handbook could be rules of a game in which 'vector' describes the way a piece is permitted to move on the board. This could connect with the partly ritualised heroics of *The Táin* – Cu Chulainn showed the gory head to the men of Ireland because they were there, obviously, to look on, like a crowd at a football match. The killer quality of the attorney matches the word *eirleach*. Waldteufel means literally 'wood devil', but because hunters were supposed to carry very strong spirits with them in flasks, to mitigate the hardship, it is the brand name of a herbal liqueur. Working back, Salacea could be the name of a character. 'Harbinger' could be the tell-tale sign that she is about to manifest: in this case, a berserker (classified as a wood-devil). *Claimant* connects to *seizure* and gives us a hint of what stories we would expect Salacea to live through. Thus the poem would actually be giving us fragments of plot that are ready for combining; the rules of a narrative game without any instances of the game. The poem is replayable. The game concept is clearer in the next two sections:

> Level seven: passerine error-code, men with teeth missing & pets dyed strange colours, plus the latest updates that find DSO battle ideograms, changing value of 1004 DWORDS to convergence/ bilateral symmetry, (romanticalities = recitationalisme)

Perhaps the game is called *eirleach*. Although property is supposed to have been a weakly developed concept in early Ireland, Cu Chulainn certainly has the concept of rights, as tied to particular pieces of land: Orlam is cutting chariot poles in a wood where he has no title to do this, and his death is a requital for trespassing. DRAM is dynamic RAM so DWORDS should mean dynamic WORDS.

Perhaps we should take a breather there and consider why this poetry is appealing. I find it appealing. The quicksilver quality is key – the separate phrases seem interpretable even if the overall design is puzzling. The speed of transition is seductive. We seem to know that we don't need to retain the details about Salacea – it is not going to come back – so the effect is of speed. It is like listening to Charlie Parker playing saxophone, that ripple of very short staccato notes, higher and purer in tone than the tenor saxophones, usually played legato, which were the pop norm when he started. That move into shorter time values moves the listener's state of awareness, with its suggestion of unnatural, bird-like, lightness and swiftness. The local flow of sense is highly unpredictable – this gives the allegro effect, endless very rapid notes skittering across the page. The landscape is modern for 2006 – it is eye-poppingly unfamiliar and this is enticing. It is chic. 'Life as a Bracket' starts with a simple question to which some of the poem is an answer:

> What is it like to be a bat? To think
> bat by consensus, hard-wired to multiple alliances,
> saw-toothed phrase boundaries
> and shattered guitar-picks? Blue sparks each bone
> in the non-neon air, a beast and
> ten fingers is making the bottleneck
> slide, from his hotel
> microphone, sees the railyard
> smokestack, some strange walking man
> with a leg to stand on, heart of swill,
> and a good long pause after the shot.
>
> But we bats want the art-time immemorial,
> crating it up like millionaires of summer as
> summer fades, north of verbatim, our khaki
> alphabet to whistle near and far, no second take.
> Everything is in the way you hit:
> just a shine hanging in the air,
> held to successive shapes by a
> mucous envelope,
> yet here voice is credit, harp and wood by
> sheet-steel carbon, superstrung on lo-fi scratching acetate.

The label, now we're going to be bats, makes the theme obvious. But rapidly the poem turns into a reflection on music in general and what may be a symbol for the lyric impulse. Perhaps the theme is hearing and the bat is just a symbol. Let's just imagine this as an advertisement for a CD player. Its product is fine sound. The ad starts with a bat with its miracle ears and then cuts to scenes of a blues musician with guitar on back walking the line. Both bat and bluesnik have delicate fingers. The use of folk music is made to suggest intimacy and solidarity, as against high technology (which is actually mediating the folk music to us). Then the ad evokes fame and the unity of people listening to the same song. This is a possible ad. Ads about indulgent purchases use free association to encourage subjectivity. I am suggesting that the flow of images in Nolan's poem is not alien, and that the subjectivity which may shake us off is the key to the pleasure. I don't know about 'blue sparks each bone', this sounds like cyclotron radiation (for seeing inside solid objects). The 'smokestack' recalls 'Smokestack Lightning', one of the most famous of all blues songs, 'smoke stack lightning shines just like gold', cinders flying up the stack of a steam train, maybe the blue light shines in the same way. Walking man could be an itinerant musician, too poor to travel by bus. Heart of swill, he's a drunk, the 'shot' is a glass of spirits. We hear a description of the craving for fame. On a graph, up can be read as 'north'. 'North of' means 'higher than'. 'North of verbatim' could mean 'a legend that surpasses what actually happened'. Fame is still part of our theme of 'hearing'. The 'steel' in conjunction with 'wood' is a guitar string, the carbon in the lattice is what makes iron into steel. Up until the 1970s the master pressings of records were made on a disk made of acetate. The acetate was destroyed by being played back. The scratchy transcriptions were actually the ones made from old vinyl, not acetates. Acetates exist of tracks that were never pressed and put on sale. I don't know what the bracket is. 'Superstrings' are a part of physics and have more dimensions than plain old strings. Links to guitars are dubious. Here the arrival of freedom, the dissipation of the elementary negativity, can give us insight into the less labelled poems in the book. The patter of very high very rapid notes fits Nolan's own style. The poem moves on to convicts in prison and to a musician with a tattooed arm. How do they feel about bats? Maybe they are characters from a blues song or two.

At p.78 is another bit of Gaelic which it might be helpful if I translate: *agus éisteann leis an bhfuaim* … is "and listen to the sound going down and falling back into silence". I believe the unrounding of *titim* indicates that this is 20th century Irish Gaelic, it is *tuitim* in other varieties of Gaelic. Nolan, like most Irish people who grew up in England, is interested in the idea of Irishness. Quoting the *Tain*, a core work of classical Irish culture, is a way of declaring allegiance. Further loyalties might be demanded – and rejected. That sentence about falling into silence might just refer to the Irish language itself.

Maybe I can stop there. The label 'postmodern' fits this work because of its detachment from realist logic, its carefree plunging into the endless serials and vivid characters of popular culture, its disturbingly jazzed and tonally shifting surface. It has a dreamlike fluency and delicacy, the flow of new and surprising images never slows down. Conclusions? The writing is seductive, shimmering, unseizable, ravishing in the way that being able to hear bats' squeaks and feel yourself swooping over a twilight meadow catching hovering insects might be. I will just quote one passage without distracting commentary:

> And the migraine's terrible lifting,
> porch and star. Or someone stands: let him,
> make him with a rhotic R, expletive square,
>   for saints have numbered ears,
>   anti-particles stain each city wall.
> Implacably lidded, what's his lark?
>   What's his *what*?
>   Carving an eye now, this is milk,
>   paperwork from gout and gutter.
>   Faces from the curtain
>   speak of Eve and while
>   night posts its owl,
>   poison tags its cell. Verse, window
>   oubliette, seep to forget,
>   in the White House, the Dark House:
>   transitive, the use of seed.....

* *

Dewi Stephen Jones

This is a partial translation of a review by Bobi Jones (1929–2017) of a book in free verse (*Ffynhonnau Uchel*, Gwasg Gomer, 2012 – the title means "high springs"). I must say I find Bobi deeply unsympathetic, as a nationalist who rejected modernity so far as to become a neo-con, but this is a compelling review. The title is 'Adolygiad unig', or "a solitary review" (possibly, "a review of an isolated man"). The book is by Dewi Stephen Jones, [1940–2019], and the source is Bobi Jones' website.

> This is a remarkable volume which should never have been written. From one point of view the whole publishing system of contemporary Wales was constructed to prevent things like this from happening. This is noticeable right away in a historical context. It is the second volume by Dewi Stephen Jones, after *Hen Ddawns*, 1993. Things like this don't happen every day. In the last century, there is a series of poems by Waldo – 'Cwmwl haf', 'O bridd', 'Mewn dau Gae', and a handful of others – which set a bit of an inexhaustible challenge to careful readers down the years. There are a dozen unusual poems by Saunders Lewis. I don't detect other poems of such a quality before this volume.
>
> Some of Dewi Stephen Jones's amazing work belongs to this band. His powers of suggestion are just as rich as those of his predecessors, and his language as enchanting. In a remote part of the world Dewi Stephen Jones is the most ambitious Welsh poet today. It is hard to believe that anyone is slower in shaping his poems than he is. But in a country which is inclining towards a 'popular' standard as its only measuring line, and also towards poems for children or performance,(with the consequence that so much of its poetry is more elementary and more superficial than any other country I know about), a poet is under suspicion who weighs and measures each word for weeks. Poetry of this kind is as if we were being pulled out of the pit of colonialism. Things like this volume are not, in any century, found on every street corner. People are not expecting it. But I can seriously promise a careful reader many years of excitement in these thirty-six pages. His life was one heavy with being inconspicuous. No poet in Wales was more out of sight than he. He is the Emily Dickinson of our land. But in this hidden state he shaped his secret treasures.
>
> The wisest way, perhaps, of introducing the book would be to gloss two poems in particular. First, let's look at 'The Pigeons'. [*The same word means 'doves' and 'pigeons' in Welsh*, AD] And

let's concentrate for a moment on one chief theme, that is the relationship important in this post-modern age between dividing and unifying. This union of course is the essence of thought and the essence of language, always. And the chief flaw of the whole crazy and worthless post-modernism, in a metanarrative so full of flaws, was trying to separate those two. I will quote the poem complete:

They ignore the dizziness of the slope
and the unstable ground of the observer
as he turns to try and hold the course
of his flock and get an arc of round disappearances
they are not like a shoal of fish, although they are in the blue depth.
Lost wild tenants, turn in my salt skull.

They turn within bounds without following a path.
Last night were the rings of the raindrops, the geometry of glass,
spreading their perfect vibration across the surface of the water of
    a lake
until they died out at the bank. The doves are in the rhythm and
    metre
of their flight, true to the shadow of a place, a wall of nothing
which keeps them from turning into the maps yonder. They
    rebound.

Low, they attack three times, many more,
before drawing a figure of eight, regaining the position
and turning back and forth setting up a pattern
of turning and returning like a circle and its echo
over in the mirror which is nothing but the air of their flight.
When they are high in the softness of breath of the principal wind,
their circuit is wider like the circuits of sadness.

Sometimes without raising my head I hear the strength of wings
and my pigeons come into view suddenly yards away
and turn at such a steep angle until they rise up ahead of me
and appear like a disappearance – an emerald
feather piercing a blind eye – though the power
of their flight is like an earthquake above the loft of the day.

Close to the shed they fly lower than the kite
diving smoothly and rising to scrape the roof
before them. This is a ceremony going round
and round without their great path slowing
and like a fairground ride you are bound to feel resistance.
But the walls do not exist.

Notice how the bard is groping constantly and imaginatively for the unity he feels in this flock of pigeons: *keeping compass … and get an arc … round… turn in my skull… they turn round within bounds without going… circuits… the geometry… perfect vibration…* and so on. Then, let's note the tension of opposition: *dizziness… unstable… disappearances… they are not… loss… parting… until they died out… rebound…* and so on. But the unity of pattern is winning. There is a neat form in the circular movements. In one view, what results is a series of images or separate portraits following each other without a real developing narrative. As in each of Dewi Stephen Jones's poems, we get wonderful depths. Poem after poem, is opened an experience which is thrilling to those who read slowly. No doubt that the pigeon racing is happening in an industrial social background of: *'above the loft of the day'* … *'close to the shed'*… like the life beneath. But in this context society itself is experiencing the same division and union. It is true we are being led to a freedom where 'the walls don't exist'. But this narrative emerges from the thematic harmony, the 'narrow walls'. Striking is the splendid comparison between the pigeons above the shed going 'round and round without their great path slowing/ and like a ride in the fair you are bound to feel resistance'. But the walls do not exist. All of life is in this passage.

What 'lens' was in the first volume, the 'map' is in this volume. Of course mapping is found in the subconscious of the 'Pigeons' themselves. (*translation AD*)

It 'should never have happened' means that the performance poets should have prevented it from happening. I think attributing so much to Saunders Lewis is an exaggeration. But I am very glad that Bobi has gone so far for Dewi Stephen Jones. I am not going to go into the pattern of modern Welsh poetry, either conservative nationalist/Christian poetry or poetry in the modern style, because the problem is abidingly one of translation. I have only translated about 20% of Bobi's review. I think Dewi Stephen might resemble some of Bobi's poems, in his second book, of 1960, for example. Actually, Bobi was one of the pioneers of free verse, back in the Fifties. Bobi was so nationalistic that he went back over the history of Welsh poetry in the past 200 years, identified poets using themes which weren't ancestrally Welsh, and proclaimed that this couldn't be good poetry because it wasn't Welsh enough. Suspected of English influence (supping from the pit of colonialism), etc. This really irritated me. Actually, fanaticism itself is profoundly un-Welsh.

Dewi Stephen only published two books of poetry. *Hen ddawns* came out in 1993. It has a poem about the Gwrygon, a hill-fort which faces his house. W became gw before Welsh was written down, so there is a root *wrok* which gives Viriconium, Wroxeter, and the Wrekin, as well as gwrygon. There is another poem about it in Tony Bianchi's anthology:

> It climbed like a snail
> >overnight into the corner of my window
> changing its shape
> >unchangingly
> not a turret is its flight,
> >its neck towards the south-east
> and the quarrel of the horns out of sight,
> >tumulus, rockpile.
> And on the slant
> >the shape of the shell –
> its softness
> >is at the thickness of the green glass.
> I will inquire
> >how it holds on.
> Isn't the valve beneath it
> >as tense as the shackle
>
> before being loosed?
>
> >…and it turns between the trails of its track
> back into its hole
> >and its delicate darkness.
> >(from 'Y Mynydd: Dinlle Gwrygon')

This elaborate and visually teasing poem about a hill-fort with multiple ramparts breaks Welsh conventions. The valve is called a pseudopod. Dewi prolongs the appearance of the curved hill-fort climbing his window as daylight arrives into a meditation on the passage of time and the relationship between a pre-Roman earthwork and his own life in the same daylight.

Feast and Riot: Steve Ely, *Englaland* (2015, 199pp);
Incendium Amoris (2017, 116pp) (Smokestack Books)
To start with, two differing quotations from *Englaland*. The first evokes Scargill putting Cecil Parkinson MP right:

> the real Yorkshire,
> red or dead in tooth and claw,
> in Docs and denims and donkey jackets,
> the Yorkshire that flew into lines of coppers,
> the Yorkshire that took down a Government;
> there before us on TV, taking them down once more.
> *'There are five points I'd like to make in response*
> *to that, frankly, preposterous assertion...'*
> and in our flat South Riding vowels
> he reeled them off, one after the other,
> fluent as the Dearne, consonants blunt
> as cobbles, arguments sharp as a diamond-bit,
> each word a slap in the face, a punch
> to the stomach, flustering Parkinson's
> brilliantined cool, stammering
> his learned RP.
>   ('One of us')

The King's endowment: lauds in the forest chantry. Plainsong of blackbird and contrapuntal thrush; earthworm and landsnail, the cantarists' perpetual stipends.

I rose with the song and arranged my relics: the osteoporosis femur from the graveyard of St. Lawrence; the blue stone for the roman road; skulls of hare and roadkill badger, bastard-wings of jays; magpie piety, tongue-tied cult of saints.

> Bryony's scarlet beads, Our Father, Hail Mary. Rood of corky elder, apocryphal scoring in the beech bole's elephant folio. Pray for the dead, for God's anointed, Ælfric and Æthelwin, earls and sons of kings.
> ('The Battle of Brunanburh', VII)

The title is Old English and is just the older form of England– *engla-land*, land of the Angles (genitive plural). *Englaland* is vast, reckless, rowdy, colourful, soaked in history and almost everything else, yorkshirophilous, and visibly a modern classic. Steve Ely's first book, *Oswald's Book of Hours*, instantly established him, for those who came across it, in the field. It had a rapid acceptability, partly because the underpinning emotional structures were familiar – from the work of Geoffrey Hill and Ted Hughes, writers evidently admired by Ely and who set up a verbal world in which he could feel confident, relax, and be amazingly productive. He also sounded as if he had absorbed dysmorphic doses of Mark E. Smith and Johnny Rotten at a susceptible stage. The *Book of Hours* has some relationship to King Oswald of Northumbria (not to *Mercian Hymns* and its King Offa) and was mostly about hunting, with the key motif of troubles in the North Country and of resistance to Thatcher, and the woes caused by Thatcher. It was much more political than Hughes and Hill – Ely offered the acts of killing and seizing as marks of our nature and so of what is alienated in an industrial society, but unlike Hughes saw a possible resolution of alienation through better political arrangements and through other people. Widening the view for a moment, all three of these books come from Smokestack Books (Ripon), and their editorial policy involves a strong left-wing connection, a matter of signalling to and gathering an audience which is now justified by this incredibly strong left-wing poetry. Smokestack have created a virtual place where you know you will find a certain signal and where you can play out a certain role. They have enriched the cultural offer. (The Brunanburh poem, in 30 parts, is described in the notes as a "tribute to [...] *Mercian Hymns*", which is acknowledged.)

I was wondering why, in a book written in English, you would keep the Latin title and not use the English version, the fire of love. The problem could be that this has links to a great record by rockabilly god Jody Reynolds, covered with less crispness in the 80s by The Gun Club (also an album title). So, if I used the string *the fire of love* in conversation, people could well start into themes about Jeffrey Lee Pierce and Tav Falco.

Hence the Latin title is retained. The source is a 14th century work in Middle English by Richard Rolle of Hampole, a Yorkshire hermit writing mystic treatises (about love). The last time I saw a reference to Rolle was a few weeks ago when I was analysing Eric Mottram's 1973 poem *Local Movement*. The section about Rolle comes as part of an "associational argument" about stimuli as triggers of behaviour, love in this instance.

With *Incendium*, Ely has published some 420 pages of poetry in a period of five years. There is something overwhelming about this, and the question is more what do we do with this overwhelmed feeling? One step is to say, this is better than what anyone else can do and the territory now gets reorganised around Ely's condition as superior and by virtue of that central. A review has to deliver that as its freight. But other things follow too, which are less clear-cut. For example, Ely can write so fluently because he is in the middle of his home range. It follows that he is down to earth and not lost in theory. This is a distinction from writers (of the Left, normally) whose verbal position comes out of theory, itself vaguely related to facts which took place in countries other than Britain, and is precious because it is unheard-of (and original and so wholly owned). Writing out of your own centre disables the standard right-wing counter-punch about being "up in the air". Being a political writer – that is, as opposed to someone narcissistic writing out of fantasies which claim to be related to society and law – involves an imaginary which other people can share, and which is cellularly bonded to a shared reality, although never wavering from a transformatory optimism. This also involves, to some extent, shared symbolism and an accepted language. We need to set this in the context of an older English poetry because Ely wants to write about the North, about history, and about conflict in history, he uses meaning-bearing structures which poetry readers are already familiar with, which draw up core memories about the communal life as lived and imagined, and which acquired their spatial extension through use in cultural creations – such as *Remains of Elmet*, such as *Mercian Hymns*, such as *The Anathémata*. These are poems about other people and for other people and they are not expounding linguistic privatisation.

Ely's note says that Richard Rolle resided "In the heart of Robin Hood's Barnsdale Forest". In symbolic geography, outlaws and hermits carry out partly analogous functions and dwell in the same uncoded and unowned space. A.J. Pollard's book *Imagining Robin Hood* (2004) describes how Robin was part of the myth of the North (for a 15th century audience) but warns that this carried the autonomous or fantasy elements of myth, not

Foundation Texts

amounting to folk sociology: "The north generally was perceived as wild, uncivilised and lawless. It was a deep-rooted image owing something to literary exegesis. William of Newburgh, writing in the mid-twelfth century, described the site of Fountains Abbey at its foundation as 'a dreadful spot in the deserted wild'. [...] The uncouthness of northerners was reflected also in their language. From William of Malmesbury in the early twelfth century sophisticated southerners commented on their virtual inability to understand what on earth northerners were talking about. [...] It is because the north [...] could be imagined as different and distant [...] that its reputed wildness and lawlessness could be called to mind as the setting for the violent but cleansing lives of bandits, outlaws, poachers and highwaymen. [...] The north, like the greenwood, was strictly a literary locale." Ely is clearly writing a new myth of the North, and the incidents he favours fulfil folk themes of the outdoor life, hunting, poaching, collective violence, Viking invasions, the forest, defiance, heroic contests. *Englaland* is divided into long sections which deal successively with the Battle of Brunanburh in AD 937, a civil war in which the rival generals are the Duke of Wellington and Peter Mandelson, topographical poems, a boxing match, the miners' strike of 1984–5 (described as "The Harrowing of the North"), the Empire and the origins of the peoples now in England, and a poem about the yellowhammer which is about various Northern terrains and events. Ely is wholly connected to this myth ore bed, but it is so old that it can't collapse, it is recognised as the "melody" of the North just as the banjo and fiddle are for the Appalachians. As follows, the power of the poetry is not subject to attenuation by sociology. Broad acres, broad Yorkshire, broad characters.

Ely's poetry constantly, on most pages, deals with contests of strength. Lenin said, famously, *Kto kogo?* Who did it to whom, an idiom which actually means "who won". The idea that one side wins in any situation is part of Leninism. The idea that you can set aside this consideration may be part of an adaptation to being defeated – a policy of weakness which denies the prevalence of competition. The theme links Ely back to Hughes, who again had *contest*, the finding of limits to strength as a primary source of knowledge, and *prevailing* on almost every page. This is also part of a mythical idea of being Yorkshire, that life is about obstinate and powerful men competing and finally winning by dint of might and skill. The outcome of the wins is a cluster of stories. Bourdieu remarks somewhere that the working class have a preference for sport which involves simple strength and endurance (as opposed to esoteric and refined gestures) and this reflected admiration for the virtues which the manual working class needed to win a living – coal miners ahead of anyone else. It is plausible that Ely's sheer productivity is an expression of solidarity with the ordinary people of his home region. His impressive re-creations of archaic texts, as the lost past of the same region, deal often with warrior virtues – precisely, of strength, endurance, courage, manual skill – which fit into the same story. The vigour which foams up in riots is connected to working power, physical size, great appetite, abundance, fertility. Ely has a preference for stories which involve an upsurge of indiscreet energy which makes two parties pour out onto the streets, line out, batter each other, observe vigour triumph without tricks or cavils, and sink down tired but satisfied. This is also an image of an election, where political authority is the prize handed to the faction which is more energetic and more able to reproduce itself. Elections, riots, football matches, rock gigs and mass pickets are here the sites where the collective knows itself and shakes off its bonds, the human deluges which call most to us, as humans, and are the best subjects for poetry.

References (in 'One of us') to biographical events suggest that Ely was around 18 or 20 in 1982. This means he is roughly the same age as I am and raises a puzzle about his poetic career up to 2013. It also sheds light on his poetics, which, historically, do not take on techniques which were not available in around 1974. This may stimulate reflection. To start with, with Corbyn at the helm we are looking forward to policies sketched in the early 1970s as the way out of the bad situation. At the moment, millions of people are, it seems, recognising that what happened after that (the Labour Party adopting neoliberalism in mirror-adulation of the Conservative and Republican parties, to put it simply) was malign and is now not the road to follow for the next 40 years. This makes the burning question of poetics this: given that the "alternative" poetry sector was rooted in the left milieu in which Corbyn was a participating but quite a moderate figure, does this "alternative" now represent the party of progress and legitimacy (simultaneously!), or did its modifications subsequent to 1974 represent such an internalisation of loss, isolation, weakness, that they hold an internalised failure mentality and have no role to play in a dynamic left-wing movement? There are, indeed, significant problems in declaring Ely to be out of date or in believing that he would write better poetry if he did a few seminars on how to read Mottram and Prynne.

I think Ely is better than Hill at history, though not necessarily at verse. Take this passage from 'Yellowhammer':

> Whence the sturgeon?
> Its English redds lie occluded,
> occult. A seven-foot 'vagrant',
> forked bankside at Towton,
> armoured flanks
> packed with hard caviar.
> Others, exhaust kelts perhaps,
> found floating bankside at Barnby Dun
> and Bolham-on-Idle: stoned by frightened farmboys.
>
> Mercian Sabrina,
> Offa's moated failsafe,
> silts glutted with styria
> from Purton to Tewkesbury,
> to stone-bottomed Vyrnwy and Tanat beyond.
> At Oswestry's guffawing table
> the simultaneous interpretation
> of Cadwallon and Penda,
> stripping the plate, unbuckling the bones, cleaving the
>   noble jowl.

Sabrina is the Severn, redds are spawning-grounds of river fish. I associated Styria with styrian hops and was considering that making beer by damming a river and pouring fothers of hops into it is a bit large even for archaeo-Mercians, but *styria* is just Anglo-Saxon for 'sturgeon'. At Oswestry, two pagan kings met their end, sadly, and the carving of a sturgeon (with its archaic armour) is used as a metaphor for the stripping of the panoply and despatching of the two kings. The sturgeon was a royal fish. The heroic feast and the splendid growth and might of the sturgeon are typical Ely themes, along with "the threat to its way of life" which inevitably recalls the South Yorkshire industrial district. The whole passage must be based on learned works on lost species, learning worn lightly and absorbed into a rich textile of symbolic and poetic associations. 'Wealhhnutu' is another example of a text which carries quite complex, and painstakingly won, historical processes into clear and ringing poetry.

The disinherited 70s Left consisted largely of arts graduates. They were highly trained in analysing texts and symbolic codes. This ability was, as it were, their high-speed cars – a status symbol. They thought analysing texts was more important than most people do. Thoughts about production, commodities, industrial tasks, technology, supplying abundance, rarely troubled them, and they disliked people who had any such thoughts. An interest in manipulating information, as opposed to objects, associated them deeply with people in advertising or in manipulating financial instruments. If they wrote poetry, it was poetry which rewarded post-graduate skills in analysing texts and codes. It eschewed character, narrative, or drama, and rarely portrayed conflict. It cut the self out of the poem, dematerialising it. The qualities which win conflicts were sidelined, and the verbal function of winning arguments was deprecated because the function of exhibiting elite knowledge was so central. Distantiation was favoured, as a sign of high educational status. This poetry could generate insecurity but not address political issues. So, I have doubts about its relevance to left-wing politics in 2017, and in particular to Steve Ely's artistic needs.

I don't think *Englaland* is artistically all on the same level. The poems about fights, riots, picket lines, etc. are cheerful and robust but do occasionally end up like sports commentaries. 'Yellowhammer' is an artistic peak, sustaining the thrust and weight of the materials of its 250 lines with lucidity and cohesion. In 'Scum of the Earth', the Mandelson-Wellington verbal battle reads as if written for the voices of Noddy Holder and John Inman. The poem "Little Saint Hugh", in *Incendium Amoris*, is much less narrative (around a pogrom in York) and more about a historical process, the anti-Semitism of high mediaeval England, which led to what Antony Julius credits (in his history of English anti-Semitism) as the first legal interdict of residence of the Jews. The pictorial aspects of the poem illustrate something abstract but for all that potent. 'Scum of the Earth' is rollicking and robust but it fills in all the cracks, like a good pie, and does not allow abstract thought. Thinking about history is possible because of gaps. Ely is here exploring the history of the tabloid mentality and of ethnic aggression, and his attitude qualifies his populism, which is not uncritical or recuperable by a right-wing narrative. The heroic poetry of north-west Europe is all about who did it to whom, about feasts, combats, feats of strength, winning, so textual recuperation produces something so like the central Ely project that you can't tell which is which:

> Silvaticus, phantom of the woods:
> eluder of man-traps, evader of trip-wires,
> master of shadows, crepuscular and fleet.

> Gaitered in dew, belted with coneys,
> dappled like the forest
> in Jack Pyke Lincoln Green,
> the pockets of his long coat
> squirming with polecats:
> lock-knife, hip-flask,
> a crushed pack of Park Drive;
> Wulfric, the one they call wild.
>
> Hard voices in the forest
> calling along the line.
> Bootsnag treeroot, drystick breaking,
> a cordon creeping forward.
> Quarterpatch spaniels working the brambles,
> whimpering and yelping, docked-tails whirring
>   ('Seditiones, caedem et rapinam')

A modern poacher is merged with a 12th century woodland outlaw with a train of *Beowulf*-like adorning epithets. We heard about Silvaticus in Kevin Nolan's book. This sounds (also) like MacSweeney's *Ranter*, but to be honest the verbal forms are so much part of the twirling constellation of the Left/Underground/ outlaw lore that I think they are just catching birds in the same sky.

The radicalising reaction of the 2007 banking crash on poetry has taken some time to build up, but is now obviously central to the whole scene. Many people are hearing this music, but Steve Ely has slashed and burned a central place in it. We hail Eric Mottram. Jody Reynolds. Steve Ely. For lo, their grandeur is legion and their name is legend.

Martin Thom, *Cloud. A Coffee Cantata* (Equipage, 2020, 38pp)
The title of the first section is 'London, 6 September 2019. At the DSEI Arms Fair. Climate Justice Day', but we have already had the initial quotations, which deal respectively with a creation myth from the 16th C Mayan text *Popol Vuh*, from a biography about Swedenborg's coffee-drinking habits, and a Guatemalan saying (expressing fatalism). There follows an illustration from one of Swedenborg's books. The latter, a wood-cut, shows a Machina Sclopetaria, which we can translate (from the Latin caption) as a machine-gun: multiple barrels fired alternately by the rotation of a cog-wheel, in a carriage on wheels. (It has a set of

blades like a windmill and was supposed to work *ope aeris*, by the energy of the air.) By this time we know we have a story about interconnection: different planes of reality are being lit up to show how they are interrelated. The title gives us coffee as the theme. Perhaps the proposal is that Guatemala (inhabited by speakers of Mayan languages) has coffee as its main export, and its politics derive from that; whereas Britain's main export is arms, and its politics, equally, derive from that–and the absence of other exports. Swedenborg's predilection for coffee, and arms design, during his life in England, is the link, and he is the character we are following for much of the poem. (The Swedenborg book is *Daedalus hyperboreus*, or "The Nordic Inventor", 1716.)

The text consists of 140 9-line stanzas, rhyming ABABBCBCC. This exit from free verse into regular metre is a sign of coming out of a private poetic world into a public language, where the statements apply to the world we live in, so that the poet is accountable in the same way as an enterprise. The poem contains a narrative: and this is partly surreal, because this is the nature of an allegory, to animate abstract and hidden relations. The metrical pattern is always incomplete and (from its visibility) always suggesting an arriving completion; this leads us to detect a pattern at the level of argument. But, let's hear some of it:

>   I saw
> Behind his back affinity groups gathering for their action, raw
> And pale at the thought of dreadful war outstared.
>   My comrades they had stepped trepidant across
>   The ribbon of their risk, and on that footing feared
>   The dire distress attends all leaping into loss
>   Yet leap they did to disrupt *la machine atroce*
> As through the lines and dreaming there came the three locked-on.
> Three sleepers lay down on the road, glistening still with frost,
>   The good thief to the bad thief chained, the bad thief to the son,
> A threefold cord withstanding artic or pantechnicon.

This passage about a protest, about DSEI, has solidarity as one of its main subjects, and this persists, as for instance several stanzas deal with the staff brewing and serving at a cafe, where they are sharing labour and help. The design of the poem is one of continuous action, characters going through rapid physical movement. If I had to sum up *Cloud* I would point to its ceaseless discovery of new elements of the real world, its finding of unfamiliarity and dazzling precision in the shifting banks of economy and technology, the things which we share and can examine. It is unusually rich in objects, institutions, and economic relations.

There was a fact circulated, a few years ago, telling us that if you paid £2.50 for your oversize coffee at a brand cafe only 1p of that actually went to the primary producer, the farmer tending the bush and picking the bean. This was a brilliant piece of education: you could get it in a second, and yet it opened up a real complexity, the story of where the money goes –a transcontinental tangle of culverts. It was also a unifier – even people who read the *Daily Telegraph* did not at all think that that penny to the Third World peasants actually doing the work was the right sum, or that we, self-regarding English consumers, were not benefiting from the whole ripple of rip-off. It wasn't all that hard to go on to think that the merchant, commodity trading, interest needed local governments to repress attempts at self-assertion by the peasants, rapaciously claiming three pennies from the global two pounds fifty pence, and that arms deals might be a way of supporting that sort of top-down death grip. Or, that debt might be a way of exacting compliance – and was a tally of luxuries (as well as arms) for local elites, rather than past benefits to the peasants. I want to cite another passage, which I think is mainly decorative, and not part of the political argument:

> I was much impressed by the Sami coat he wore
>   In honour of Linnaeus, Lapland and the trance,
> But also by the Carl-staf of polished bronze he bore
>   A measuring device to make the volumes dance.
> With embroidered chanticleer he'd wave that gleaming lance
> At market, in the warehouse or in a Stockholm hold
> To gauge the perfect packing a sack or barrel wants
> When saving peas or cabbages, salted for the cold,
> Or stacking cannonball and shot, against the shipboard pitch
>   and roll.

Thom also names Swedenborg as a figure of the Enlightenment, so that this metrical staff is also a yardstick, representing the idea of justice which we all have and which is offended by the rich battening on the poor. But I think the link to the Lapps is there because they are the only European example of shamanism, and that is something which anthropologists like to talk about; Swedenborg's habitual intercourse with speaking spirits is *like* what shamans do, even if he was a baron and an engineer. (Some folklorists find *other* traces of shamanism, in Hungary I believe.)

Thom was a Seventies poet, publishing the absolutely extraordinary *The Bloodshed the Shaking House* with X-Press in 1977, and he had studied archaeology and anthropology – a project of which the headline is, virtually, that you are going to have to forget everything about being from the 20th C West in order to write a good essay. This helps us to get his interest in the Mayan culture, which bequeathed its language and genes to the upland farmers of Guatemala, the ones who actually cultivate the coffee.

> 'Your cart it cannot catch', I said, 'the chill rain sheeting down,
>   Nor your eyes retain, by canny cones and rods,
>   That manifold descending in drop and dreep to town
>   Of the fleeting hailstones, the maize seed of the gods,
>   That presage by their rattle the coronated clods.'
> 'There are braided words', the risen man replied,
>   'Combed out by the wind and despite the odds
>   Entered into wisdom books upon the mountainside,
> Memorials to the Mayan Ixil innocents who died.
> From giddy heights a thread leads me out and through
>   Blocks inert and Sartrean in their certain places,
>   Yet with my cart, with scripture and with the *Popol Vuh*
>   I walk a gull-swept line where Mayan Ixil faces
>   Are shaped from banks of sand and silted river traces.'

Quoting the *Popol Vuh* is a provocation – you can put it into English words but you can't really think that you understand it, that you can explain why the parts are there and how they connect. This is a window through which we can see our own inability to understand the global world – a moment of wonder, I hope. If you think about the *Popol Vuh* in relation to the modern Maya-speaking communities, the ones you can visit and talk to about folklore, you come slap up against the impact of imperialism. The Maya who are left are submerged by Hispanic culture. The continuity between primary imperialism and global capitalism is blatant in Latin America, where the withdrawal of Spain still left creole-dominated, racially unequal, regimes in power, but this just leads us towards recognising the regime of globalisation as the legacy of imperialism, a re-branding rather than a reform.

If I am not mistaken, the passage about pots and pans acting on their own (in the *Popol Vuh* quotation) is echoed at stanzas 136-9, the poem literally incorporating the mysterious and non-European. I understand from a glance at the source that the pots rose up because they were tired of being burnt in the fire, and the grindstones rose and ground up their masters because they were tired of being ground down themselves. References to maize people and people formed from mud are also part of the serial creation myth (good, better, best) in the Vuh (also transliterated wuj). Popol Vuh was a psychedelic-era rock band from Munich, which leads Thom to the even better CAN, from Darmstadt, with their astonishing percussionist Jaki Liebezeit (he cites 'Mother Sky', it's on You-Tube) before moving swiftly on to the anthropologist Rodney Needham and his book on the use of drumming. Thom returned to the poetry stage with *Fair*, in 2018 – which was also about an arms fair. This is, I suppose, where he sees poetry blossoming. I react to Nigel Wheale and Ewan Smith publishing *Fair* (with infernal methods), and Rod Mengham publishing *Cloud* (with Equipage). They are trace indicators of a sort of group, of Corbyn's generation, whom I became aware of, at latest, in 1981, with *Equofinality*, and who have persisted and who show no sign of cease and desisting.

As for the title – the cover photograph shows an 1875 photograph of people working at a coffee plantation in Guatemala. The credit says the estate was "Las Nubes" – the clouds. Coffee grows high on hills. *Popol* is usually translated as *mat*, but I understand the root means weaving, so this is why Thom says *braided words*.

Identification

The concept of identification asks for further discussion. If a poem is unsuccessful then the reason is likely to be that the reader fails to identify with the characters, or maybe with the narrator. This suggests that the question of success and failure could be resolved by a better examination of the process of identification. Failed identifications could be the most revealing moments, the telltales.

A simple description of the process treats it as a mirror. The reader mirrors what the voices in the poem tell, not by actions but by movements of the image of their body, the virtual shape by which they plan body movements. Naturally the mirroring involves the emotional and intellectual parts of the self as well.

Considering the identification idea quickly brings up proposals about the failure of poems. For example, at some level the proposed experience has to be desirable. It must favour selves which are harmonious, or rapidly moving, or athletic in the virtual actions they carry out. The mirror process can only mirror what is visible, so identification is going to work with unusually clear and persistent sources of information. A special role attaches to physical action, because humans are built to deal with the physical world and their minds can only function fully with such a substrate. This is called "entanglement". We find our selves through objects and places. Poems need the sense record as part of the music.

Mimesis could almost replace the idea of identification. It means imitation, mimicry, but more specifically the process where a human imitates someone else's state of mind. When the actor on screen seems warm, I feel warm. The idea is that we normally live surrounded by other people and that what fills our normal consciousness is a serial and constant imitation of what they are feeling.

Poetry is reliant on identification and people who read poetry a lot presumably enhance and develop their skills at doing it. This could even be the feature which we find connecting that class of people. You become an insider by having the wish to go inside. But this also raises the possibility of people who are bad at identification. Poetry evidently does not have a force like the big acoustic energy of an orchestra. The force it does have is invisible to a non-participant and is merely part of a self, a sort of virtual image of that self. These metaphors may be unsatisfactory. But we have to find some way of talking about identification and mimesis.

The tale of the human figure in art gives us an analogy for poetry about humans. This is an archaic feature but it is exactly on the scale of the human perceiving it. We could collect a thousand examples of art based on the human figure. It offers a range of possibilities that satisfy the most basic visual needs of humans. Art is the projection of a body image in several ways. I was impressed by an exhibition of the artist Helen Chadwick where a series of three-dimensional objects, looking like furniture, were the size of the artist herself at various stages of life. This was conscious but also exposed a set of unconscious preferences pervading poetry, as well as art. When I compiled a list of long poems of the 1970s, I collected a hundred, of which two were by women. At the time, women generally wanted to be smaller and the men wanted to be larger. A poem is also a projection of the body image. Large scale in art can be grandiose but it is also the source of exhilaration, when we feel our own body-image expand. Of course a body of poetry can fail to inspire any acts of projection. That is when it lacks good gestalt, I imagine.

Do we understand ancient art? The suggestion that we can implies that there are rules which we can apply to interpreting art because human nature is constant and we can understand ancient figure art through the body image. We are trying to recover the meaning of a visual work that is essentially silent. There is no dealer to produce a patter around it. Where there is deduction there are also rules to follow. The recovery of information is a deductive process, not merely visual. It follows also that we recover the meaning of poems through rules. The poems cannot subtract themselves from the reach of these rules. That might be a goal for some writers.

Of course it is possible to argue that we don't understand ancient art. This just raises the question of why we respond so intensively, to, say, the human figures of the Cyclades around 5000 BC. They speak to us through a human figure which has not changed in the interim; while the symbolism is now silent and mysterious.

The idea of body image answers the question of how a fish with eyes at the front knows what the rear half of its body is doing. A body image is a virtual neural pattern which allows the planning of movement and avoiding obstacles. Actually, it probably existed before the arrival of vertebrates. It is genuinely archaic. (It is worth asking why vertebrates don't have light sensors all over them, being all eye.)

Gestalt is no longer used as a conceptual pattern by research psychologists but it has left behind terminology which can be useful to a critic. It is one more way of thinking about it all. The Gestalt school of psychology was interested in the way the mind organises fragments to construct wholes. The construction relies on the constancy of body shapes, so that a part of a predator reliably indicates that a whole predator is there. Detecting entire shapes from fragments of a shape. This faculty worked in early visual landscapes where creatures might be hidden behind bushes so that you only see part of a shape and only for a short time. The software turns this stimulus into a perception of a whole. This relates to the implicit content of a poem. This is not in the words anywhere but is supplied by our processing software. The whole is called a gestalt, and the school is named after this part of the theory.

The implicit is not accessible to innovation. It is conservative. The efficiency of gestalt perception depends on the constancy of shapes. Is the implicit derived from other texts? only partly. Because our minds really do use gestalt principles, it is enough to show a fragment and the mind will construct the rest. Poetry is all reliant on implicit information. What information is that – it is somatic information about the body image and the internal state of the other person. Intuition and gestalt give it to you. You don't have to read Merleau-Ponty. Or spend 30 years on the reading list before starting on the poetry. That is not the way to go. It is the poet's brain which is complicated and not the books they have read in the past 10 years. The stretches of information which bad readers fail to take in are not quotes, and the way in is to relax and empathise and not reject what is being said.

The poem that gets printed does not contain feelings. To be exact, it is just a string of letters and blank spaces. If presented with such a string, the reader who knows the English language will be able to allocate the stresses to syllables with almost no errors, based on recognising the words as part of a public and agreed lexical set. Stress is fundamental to poetry but it is also set by a set of prestructured rules, of which everyone owns a copy. I mention this to underline how people find emotions in a poem. The poem consists of sounds and we project feeling into it by applying preset rules about how human feelings work. The less the feelings are indicated, the more reliant the process is on stored rules – the social knowledge. The words direct us to project feelings.

Imagine yourself in a pit which is covered over. The only light source is a signal from outside. The signal is part of a poem and when it speaks of a toe you can feel your toe and when it speaks of a mouth you can feel your mouth. You can have the most refined sensations as long as they are there in the poem. But you are shut inside the poem. It is intensely frustrating to be so dependent on someone else's decisions. But in exchange you can have memories of experiences you never had, live through roles you never occupied, recall countries you have never visited. The frustration awakes desires you never had and the sensory deprivation gives them a vividness and an accumulation of detail which touch does not vouchsafe. This is empathy. I am in darkness and each square inch of light in the poem lights up a square inch of my being. This is another way of looking at the poem. It allows us to become aware of our own feelings but this is restricted by the boundaries of the poem. Each extension of the poem adds another part to the virtual body which we are experiencing within the poem.

'How can an individual understand another's expressions objectively and validly? It is possible only on the condition that the other person's expression contains nothing which is not also part of the observer.' — Dilthey. This implies that a man can never fully understand a woman and a woman can never fully understand a man. That is, poetry is fundamentally reliant on empathy and empathy is fundamentally flawed. But perhaps we can twist this around. And say language is a median realm where one person can externalise what they feel inside and another person can learn to recognise what they have never felt.

Popularity is often a result partly of predictability. A poet acquires a brand identity by being predictable. The consumer can remember the style and returns for more. It is easier for them to retrieve a feeling if the feeling is familiar and steady. But this predictability is a feature of procedures that do not change.

This is the result of gestalt psychology, that we are incredibly good at predicting emotions from small signs, and that swiftness of response is based on the archaic and repetitive nature of emotions. The environment of other humans is predictable in the same way that an early environment, of savannah or grassy plains, was predictable. Risk is sudden but patterned, and it was safe only if you exploited the regularity of the unseen and reacted swiftly to signals.

It is credible that the area which evokes conscious thought is the one where we experience freedom – because it is the most unpredictable and the most confusing. Because we are aware of divergent close possibilities, we rightly feel ourselves free to choose. There is also the unconscious, and the content of poetry is frequently fantasy and distortion, from what Freud called the primary process. This material is irrational – he has fascinating things to say about it lacking any concept of Time. However, that is not the same as being impossible to follow. This is a stratum, or process, which we all share. We recognise everything which is already inside us. Folklore is full of magic and monsters and this does not cause problems.

One definition of the success of a work of art is to have two unconscious minds hearing the same music. This is hardly possible if the poem is not presenting an unconscious level at all. It is normal for deep identification to produce a state of shared fantasy. The other person acts as a screen blocking out the currents of scepticism which normally come in from other people, and the couple go on a journey into a space which they alone have access to. The effect which public fantasies have on us is conditioned by our recognition that they have intimacy as their secondary message. Poetry would hardly be recognizable without this effect and these recessed spaces.

The prevalence of identification as a means of art works against an idea of progress in art. The human subject has existed for some 100,000 years and the essentials of mutual empathy and transmission of mood have been around for that long, or longer.

Their trajectory was just large

Salt and the release of new poetry

If you search on the Web, you can still find stories about Salt giving up publishing new poetry (except an anthologies series) in May 2013. The coverage does not also cover their deletion of their back catalogue – technically, print-on-demand books need never go out of print, but Salt rationalised big-time. I don't have a date for the big deletion, but it was some time after the withdrawal from new work (and maybe 2016?). Chris Emery told the media

> For many years the market was static, and then it went into quite sharp decline, particularly through the traditional market of bricks-and-mortar booksellers. There has also been a massive increase in the number of poetry publications coming out. We think that's a good thing, but we can't commercially be part of it … As a very small, niche commercial publisher, we can't possibly sustain what we have done in the past.

It is surprising to hear that the volume of publication had gone up from (say) 2001 to 2013; the Worldwide Financial Crash had intervened, and people were talking about recession and a zombie economy. Salt had about 400 poetry titles in 2013 (according to their media statement) and deleted most of them. But it is unfair to record that moment without paying much more attention to the process by which Salt came to find and release so many books. Clare Pollard posted at the time "I mean, their list is bursting with talent: a whole, brilliant generation." I think they did roughly 200 British poetry titles in that time. I should make clear that Salt continued publishing single-author titles after 2013, and that they have kept many of their classic titles in print.

"The news that their poetry publishing will now be slashed to a single annual anthology is terrible for British poets." Pollard said in detail: "I mean, their list is bursting with talent: a whole, brilliant generation. People like Luke Kennard, Antony Joseph, Mark Waldron, Chris McCabe, Katy Evans-Bush, Julia Bird, Siân Hughes, Melanie Challenger, Simon Barraclough, Jon Stone, Kirsty Irving, Amy Key, David Briggs, John McCullough, Tom Chivers, Antony Rowland, Liane Strauss, Amy

De'Ath, Sophie Mayer, Tamar Yoseloff, Tony Williams, Anna Woodford, Abi Curtis, Rob A Mackenzie, Andrew Phillips* and Tim Dooley (to mention just a fraction)." (*Possibly Andrew Philip, a Scottish poet who did two very good books with Salt.)

While I am aware that I haven't read most of these poets, I am quite open to the idea that this was a generation and that Salt was an open door for the best young poets in that time frame up to 2013. The narrative shows us winsome young poets in distress and as we grasp the identification handholds the clip comes to an end. There is an infrastructure and it is left invisible by this foregrounding. Perhaps there is an unheard narrative which foregrounds the infrastructure. Could identification be what traps us in illusion? If Salt did 400 poetry titles I think there is a story to be told here. How did they get from zero to one hundred? Clare mentions 27 names, but Salt apparently did 110 debut volumes over about 12 years. I have never heard of most of them, and I think it's regrettable that Salt didn't do an anthology to showcase this group of young poets. The last annual anthology was in 2015 so that may also be when they deleted most of their titles.

Western Australia has extensive salt deserts. Salt spun out of the Australian magazine *Salt* and was set up by John Kinsella, who edited *Salt*. I do recall a meeting with John in about 1995 – Simon Smith will also remember this – and I think there was some publishing activity around then. In fact, I have a Rod Mengham book from Folio/Salt (address given as Applecross, Western Australia) dated 1996 – it was re-issued in 2001. The early Salt list included many Australian poets but also many Americans, because John was a frequent visitor to the USA and in touch with many poets there. If you have that depth of involvement to find terrific books that don't have a publisher, you are in a prime position. The pressure to exploit what you know is strong. So Salt ramped up very quickly, due to these contacts. At some point Chris Hamilton-Emery took over, or was in charge of the UK operation, but I don't know the details of this. That pattern of featuring numerous poets from Australia, the USA, and Britain, evidently came from Kinsella's connectivity, his personal geography you could say. I think Chris did all the technical work, so bypassing a typesetter to prepare a digital file which went directly to the printer. At some point the idea of using Print on Demand came in. Traditionally, small poetry publishers have limited capital and it is tied up in their stock. If they have one, maybe two, books which don't sell, they no longer have any capital to pay for printing the next one. Sour stock, congealed money. And the melody comes to an end. With PoD, you can have a very small initial print run. You can survive titles that don't sell. And in this way you can climb, up and up, to 400 titles in the end. This was revolutionary. Salt did publish 40 titles a year at one stage, and you have to have taken part in this kind of hands-on publishing to know just how tiring and (over-)exciting this is. A book deadline every week? That is like being dangled out of an aeroplane once a week. Personal opinion.

The element by which Salt will be judged is the quality of the poets whose first books they published. The Collecteds of so many of the great Alternative Poets of the late 20th C certainly draw a lot of attention, but getting in amongst poets in their twenties and divining which ones have real talent is the difficult part and so, logically, the part people admire most. Salt began with almost nothing (a magazine with a home in Applecross, hardly a big footprint) so they were not the first choice for unpublished poets in, say, 2002. They gambled on a gap in the radar of existing publishers. First volumes are risky, you are abidingly likely to lose money on them. So in that window starting in, say, 2001, you have an awful lot of young people producing terrific first volumes and looking for a sluice to release them into the high seas. If you have a firm which has realised that you can use POD to minimise losses, and that you can achieve economies of scale by releasing one title a week, you have the opportunity for a wonderful synergy. It's a historical Goldilocks Spot. This is where Salt seems to have found itself. If we look at Roddy Lumsden's 2010 anthology of new poets, *Identity Parade*, we find that, out of 84 names, 16 had published with Salt. 16 is a pretty massive score.

Roddy was announced as taking over the role of poetry editor at Salt at one point. The website records "In 2010 he became Commissioning Editor (Poetry) at Salt Publishing, with a remit to introduce new first-book authors to the list." He co-edited a *Salt Book of Younger Poets* (2011) with 50 names included. Salt may have been concerned about the lack of reviews for their poets who as yet had no reputation. Reviews generally did not catch up with the huge amount of books coming out; this wasn't a problem native to Salt. Because they wanted the poets to be teachable, I understand, they launched a series of Salt Companions for mid-career poets and also an in-house magazine for reviews, published on their website. This has been described as the online arts magazine *Horizon Review* (Salt Publishing), and ran from 2008 to 2010. I did read it once but I was disappointed by the low intellectual standards. Of those 50 "younger poets", 24 turn up, six or seven years later, in our PBS list (but they were too late, in almost every case, to get books out with Salt).

There is the question of whether Salt went down-market with their "novices" after pursuing a line of literary excellence in their first few years, albeit picking up poets in mid-career to do that. Several people, poets published by Salt, expressed to me a belief that a Salt showcase event in late 2008 was announcing that the firm was going down-market in a big way. They quite simply felt that Salt was no longer a home for their work. My impression is that the alternative poetry scene didn't read the young poets discovered by Salt. Salt evidently covered a broad spectrum, the inherited distinction between "underground" and "mainstream" had broken down by the time of their most intense activity, and it is not credible that they were simply trying to be a variant on Bloodaxe.

Victor Tapner, *Flatlands* (2010, 69pp)
Born in 1950, Tapner is of an older generation than most of Salt's debut poets. His website says that when he started on *Flatlands* he "had little idea that I was embarking on a poetry project that would take the best part of seven years – more if you count late stragglers. A cycle of poems in three 'movements' set in prehistoric East Anglia, *Flatlands* was published in September 2010, but, like the region's terrain, its way was often marshy and fogbound." He describes his poem 'Thames Idol', as "essentially the poem that sets the overall metaphorical theme". It refers to an object known as the Dagenham Idol, a battered pinewood figure that has been radiocarbon dated to around 2,500 BCE.

> The setting of the final poem, 'Blackwater', is an Essex estuary where the voices of the cycle, which at the start are embodied in the literally earthbound flint miners, now dissolve 'out of sound' into the sea and sky.

This sounds like a great idea, but one which quite a few other people have thought was a good idea. The flat bit is because he is living in and writing about, an alluvial plain – the basin of the Great Ouse, roughly. The sites are in Essex, Suffolk, and what used to be Huntingdonshire (outside Peterborough). The poems offer people in the deep past whose voices have been effectively lost and whose cognitive schemes and social lives were radically different from ours. It is fair to point out that Tapner has no interest in archaeological theory – it would get in the way of what he is doing, in fact. He has a costume drama in mind, with a lot about landscapes rather than just human scenes. Empathy tends to cover up the gaps and reduce the invincible alienness of the past. Tapner is not writing a poetry of ideas and this is an old-fashioned view of archaeology.

The stripped-down style belongs to the present day – the age of Hughes and Heaney. It is close to the objects which have survived from the past. It is not reasonable to suppose that Neolithic peasants spoke in a verbal style resembling "tough nature poetry" of the 1960s. So check this out, 'Arrow Maker':

> I straighten hot hazel
> scrape the nubs
>
> fix white feathers
> from a goose's wing
>
> with wax and sap
> I bed the tang
>
> nettle string binds
> the slotted head
>
> I run my finger
> from tip to quill
>
> sealed in the shaft
> the cry of the kill

This bears out what Tapner says about bareness. But, it's so evocative. The minimal verbal fabric opens onto a much larger reality, one of the imagination. The poems are like objects released by the earth's mouth after 3,000 years, they are worn but authentic. The volume works like one poem – amazing generosity, wiping out any problems from flatness and bareness. (I believe the reference is to "steamed hazel", you can straighten a shaft of hazel when it is hot.) The nubs of wood would slow the shaft down, in flight. The shaft screams like the animal it is going to penetrate. Tapner's poetry is inspiring. The style is as he says, sparse – like the relics which he is looking at – but taken in quantity it opens the abundance of the world. He is working on a plane of the essential, a kind of darkness where every phrase sears your eyeball.

Peter Larkin's *Terrain Seed Scarcity* (2001, 199pp), subtitled *poems of a decade*, was one of the early books put out by Salt. A statement goes as follows: "*Terrain Seed Scarcity* opens with a selection of poems in which the concern for scarcity as a speculative edge first surfaced, and is followed by six sequences arranged in short prose clusters or stanzas, sometimes with verse tail-pieces. Four of these focus directly on trees: under the aspect of addition as a branching diversion rather than a dispersal; the co-forms of forest evoked as edge, line and verticality; plantations as parallels to a re-covered, stretched centre; a lean, denuded outcrop of trees better served by what wheels around it than by what it fails to contain. Some of these sequences are accompanied by brief essays as sideshoots or offshoots. Other poems work through the sourcefulness of an environmental sink figured also as recess or protection, and there is a set of minimalist sententiae which rework 18th century landscape aesthetics. The collection ends with a cycle of syllabic poems, 'Spirit of the Trees' derived from a once popular anthology."

This is convincing in setting out why you would either like or dislike this rather technical poetry. Larkin actually began with prose influenced by the *nouveau roman*, and the idea of eliminating the human voice in order to release flat descriptions of objects unimpeded by human subjectivity is important to his poetry. The stress on geometrical shapes fills the gap where the movement of human eyes, or a body carrying eyes, is missing. I suppose that in about 1960 the *nouveau roman* looked like the new and severely intellectual thing and something which English writers could only aspire to. The *dernier cri*, in fact. It had limited entertainment value. I have inner questions which the poems never answer and so the rhythm of sense does not work for me. I recognise that this is partly because the point is to record a non-human state of being and to suppress the human projections in order to find what is really forest. The theme is often trees and this relates not just to an admiration for Heidegger's *Holzwege* but also to the author's youth in the New Forest and to specific stands of woodland in Hampshire and Somerset. Scarcity is a key and relates forests to a need for shelter and to feelings of dread about deforestation. Scarcity appears as what is rare and precious, which certainly applies to old-growth forest in Britain, and maybe to welfare in a degraded realm. As we become compulsive about scarce substances we realise that what is necessary is also scarce.

Anna Mendelssohn's *Implacable Art* (2000, 136pp) was published by Folio-Equipage rather than Salt. Folio has an address in Applecross, Western Australia. Equipage is a key small press publisher in Cambridge. This confused the market because previous work by this author had come out under the *nom de plume* of **Grace Lake**. Mendelssohn (1948–2010) had served a number of years in jail for crimes committed with a Situationist bomb-throwing group. The government found her guilty of finding the government guilty. Vaneigem had defined Situationism by explaining that in the future there would be an unlimited supply of material goods, so that the only real problem was how to spend leisure time. All the work will be done by somebody else. It appears further that the Situationists had no interest in things like resolving conflicts, allocating scarce resources, placing people in roles: the traditional problems solved by politics. All those problems could be solved by someone else, too. So it is not clear that Situationism had anything to do with politics. Of course, they had discovered that everyone else was caught in illusions – the Spectacle. Lake's poems exhibit infantile spontaneity as part of being free from work or function.

> Fitting compasses across the entire stretch of the ballroom floor. Yes well don't. Eyesight.
> Heave. Compare a digestive to a B brown mishap (eyeshadow).
> And above my eyes night.
> Don't you ever get **ng. Broad horizontal intervenience, don't Shout. Not now.
> (Buttercup) Lawyer, I know. Stars have hopped back into the boles of quercus leaning
> (from 'Naturalia')

It is possible to hear a voice in this, actually a flaky one. The boundary lines are psychedelic kitsch and the dissolution of the ego. Because government defined itself through being rational and accountable, Lake defined herself by being fickle and evasive. Relieved of function, language became a set of disparate decorative elements, a bag of beads. She was extremely good-looking in youth, and it is common for such people to think that everything will come without working and that people are hanging on their every word because they are so clever. She did not have a facility for putting words together, and the poems in *Implacable Art* do not express spontaneity very well. There are some good ones in the pamphlet *Bernache nonnette* – 'Dour', for example. It is possible that after coming out of Holloway and facing a life in the welfare system her natural feelings were of anxiety, and the insouciance of the poems is not really spontaneous. The stigma followed her and incited her to non-sequiturs. The vagueness of her logic is also the feel of society erasing the traces of her.

Rod Mengham's *Unsung* (123pp), a selected-collected, came out from Folio Salt in 1996, with another edition by Salt in 2001. There is an episode of a 1967 Granada crime series in which the villain gets away at the end – to a villa in Tuscany. This disables the usual end run and the gratification of winning. It leaves a puzzle and a frustration. Granada were ahead of all the other drama producers at that time. This gives us insight into Mengham's poems; evidently the act of divining what the poet is saying gratifies the reader. The poet is rewarding the reader for getting there. Evidently the poem which does not offer a feeling for us to empathise with withholds gratification in this primitive form. This expresses dissatisfaction with existing social arrangements. It may incite us to detachment and to abstract thought. Mengham (1953) edited (1981–91) the magazine *Equofinality*, with mainly Cambridge-linked poets who, generally, shared a scepticism about hippie ideals and Sixties poetry (even Cambridge poetry). The voice is singular also in its lack of loyalties. The pattern is the only thing, no factional allies seem to be available. This mood became more common in the colder economic climate of the later 70s – although not everyone was pierced by optimism and hedonism during the Sixties. It just depended on what parts of the scene you tuned in to. The collective high of 1968 had an ensuing collective hangover, and with that there was a visible collapse of the post-war settlement during the inflation of the later 70s. These processes created new patterns unobserved by those participating too deeply. The loyalties were actually dimming people's view of the newly emerging patterns. Individual fluctuations disguised the operation of the silent rules.

Leaving out the conventional comforting tones – the poet as soft furnishing – made room for a wealth of unusual and interlinked patterns. These deal with economic relationships and the fate of individuals in a heartless and uncontrolled network of power. Poetry had intimacy and empathy as its central dogma, but there was much more scope outside those constraints.

Mengham's later poetry is more genial and less preoccupied, as is true of several poets active in the Eighties. Writing about other subjects,

Polish art or the archaeological past, allowed an escape from conflict.

Anna Woodford's *Birdhouse* (2010, 68pp) was her first book, following pamphlets *Party Piece* (2009) *Trailer* (2007, Five Leaves) and *The Higgins' Honeymoon* (2001). I mention Five Leaves because it is the local radical bookshop here in Nottingham. Named after Nick Drake's song 'Five Leaves Left', I think. A book *Changing Room* followed in 2018. This is conventional poetry. It uses that "reality effect" whereby the most banal language is the most real, and must be true. But banality may be deceptive and prevent you from realising or noticing essential things, because it numbs you and shuts your brain down. The poems about family history are significant to the poet but probably not to people who do not belong to her family. The title poem deserves more attention and is a much better poem.

A review quoted on the cover says the poems "open out almost imperceptibly from their domestic premises, into a subtle exploration of the tension between stability and cliché." This must be sarcastic – "imperceptibly opening out" must mean "it never goes anywhere".

Michael Ayres (1958) is a prolific and advanced poet specialising in the impact of the visual-technological. He has been associated with other poets (born in the 1950s) as exponents of the New Pictorial Economy. These poets had in common that they missed the revolutionary cultural upbeat of the 1970s, except as students and consumers of art; were sorely at odds with the New Right hedonism of the 1980s; have largely been ignored by criticism; became very prolific, perhaps reacting against rejection; explored large-scale forms; do not perceive a vital 'high-low' difference between poetry and rock music; and that they are fascinated by the new pictorial economy which fills streets and homes with images – and by the processes which developed those images, as cultural messages with overt and covert content. Ayres debuted in the alternative magazine scene at the end of the Eighties and Odyssey did his first book, *Poems 1987–92*, in 1994.

> We meet almost every day now
> in buildings of paper, by broken columns,
> in streets of ambiguous proportions:
> we meet in Fake Tombstone
> where the saloon doors swing on their tarot hinges

> and the origami thesis of a colt trots by
> in a dust of print which covers the ground like ash
> and which old tortoise eyes have secreted
> dreaming their journals of tears:
> we meet in a folded city and a closed town
> topped by a papier-mâché acropolis.
>   (from 'Marshal')

'Marshal' is my favourite Ayres poem and is, we now learn, one of five poems, planned as a book, from the early 90s, the other four of which were 'Pool' 'Idyl', 'Sad Captain' and 'Nosferatu'. 'Marshal' concerns a US marshal, a cattle town gunfighter from some classic and forgotten Western, come to face down and seize the poet for an unnamed crime. The scene is one from some lost Surrealist film, of lovers chased by malign authority. The Marshal is Tom Mix as the 'taxonomic loco' who reduces the wild lands of the West and the psyche to miserable, apathetic order. Of all Ayres' poems, this has the most brilliantly changing images, like shards of glass flying apart just slowly enough for us to see.

> "The plump sun of a segmented tangerine burns on the saucer by the side of the pool: that taste is fire slowed and synthesized, stored in batteries of sugar, and the rays bend now into Lexington handmade paper 622 x 800mm, burns later in the suicide's blaze, where one dies of life, unable to continue: one, water dripping down back, buttocks and thighs, feels the bones enter the terrifying medium of cancer, now watches lover whipping a tethered dog with a leather lash, the greyhound eyes, the shivering physique, eyes of a Mary, a suffering Madonna, watches and does not intervene.
> (…)
> One pounds a piano, a hefty grand, a lacquered beast, beauty from blood, sonata from carcass, the smile of teeth, pounds, pounds, pounds, titillates, pounds, caresses, a rippling smile, moral grandeur with a yellow label, Deutsche Grammophon, a cubist crocodile fed on fingers of Schoenberg, and opens the jaws like a yawning patron on the void of boredom, one's private disease, an ivory throat yawning, and yawning – first fear, then fury, then melancholia, then despair."

'Deposition' goes on like this for 6 A4 pages (of *Grille*, #3, 1994), imitating the visual imagination of advertisements, taking on the MegaVisual tradition (in Peter Fuller's phrase) and excelling it. The poem stages a self-love-nest of commodity fetishism and climaxes with a quote from the Sex Pistols, a flashback to Situationism. Later work is expansive in the tradition of extended dance mixes, luxuriating in variations. Salt published *a.m.* (272pp) in 2003, and here the stylistic preferences include the optical; the opulent; and the surreal, so that images are juxtaposed to cause surprise. The images are new and we need time to take them in.

The poems tend towards the static, not just because it takes a long time for the complex visual effects to develop, but also because their purpose is to avoid the moment of loss: to create a still image. The length, 270 pages, suggests a loss of scale, in which we are asked to acquire slower scanning patterns and this overload is the source of pleasure. The balance of close detail and great scale is disorienting. Between digital image detail and the loss of the self in alien physical scales, the camera offers too much and the eye's resolution fails. We lose ourselves in the allover brilliance, the lack of boundaries or of patches of shadow. Slowed down and filtered, the flow of optical information is hyper-vivid, over-produced. The poems are picture perfect, and like a series of stills, in which surreal compositions of objects linger. It is not obvious that there is a line moving forward through the successive poems, and the lack of such an axis makes us lose orientation. The paths head us back into the book, not towards any outside or close. The soundtrack tends to be music rather than dialogue. The colour effects seem to be produced in the laboratory, startling and unrecognisable.

> Gneiss, granite, basalt – the petals of tulips –
> fall into the depths of the cornea, into which
> we, too, are falling. And like the rapid blossoms of irises,
> our glance falls into the depths of words.
>
> You turn away from them– what else can you do?
> They follow, and call after you – what else,
> in their turn can they do?
>   (from 'Zeiss').

Zeiss were a famous maker of lenses and optical equipment in Jena. The acoustic link *gneiss-Zeiss* is typical. Gneiss is a mineral which sparkles and so alters and returns light, in a way.

In 2002, **David Kennedy** (1959–2017) published *The President of Earth* (116pp), new and selected poems, dating from the mid-1980s onward, according to the jacket. This presents a variety of ludic poems, not representing a personality or convincing situations, but insouciant and amusing. It connects with the Sixties but this kind of thing isn't as original as when George MacBeth was doing it. The list of British poets who have used the New York School is interesting, but are they significant when compared with the originals? As usual, I hark back to a café I used to go to, which perpetually had tapes playing Blue Note recordings from the 1950s. Always 50s jazz, every day. The soundtrack to where you aren't. The second part is a kind of avant-garde pastoral, based on programmed repetition and recombination of inherited lines, which gets nowhere at all.

Mark Waldron (1960) published *The Itchy Sea* (66pp.) with Salt in 2011. The poems are parallel to each other but very self-contained and like films of an object lasting about a minute. There is no personality overlapping several poems and no running situation. (An exception is four poems about a character named Marcy.) The poems explore these closed worlds and do not shift the basic assumptions or cognitive framework. They are not aestheticised or part of a conventional line of scientific investigation. They seem like fragments of another world as well as just verbal toys made from fragments of our world. An example is a poem about seagulls which turn out to be taking off from his blood-stream. The hidden but true idea is that our blood reproduces the salinity of the ocean and is part of it. The poem itself is not true, but it is unique. The fabrication is remarkably solid, almost perversely realistic. When Waldron writes about 'The Life Cycle of the Fly', this is really the best poem about insects one can imagine. It is not about the way flies really are, but is "super-realistic" – perfectly visualised but autonomous from the world we know. The shared element of the poems is perhaps a state of mind: of curiosity, a phase in the inevitable cycle of perception when our eyes are open and conjectures are drifting around in a pleasant way. The poems always stop before we can become habituated. Consider 'Of Course, We've All Seen this Kind of Thing Before':

> The missile is decorated in thick paint which depicts
> an eighteenth century hunting scene.

> The intended effect is a frisson of irony
> that might move through consciousness
>
> in a ripple resembling a fading chuckle. In flight,
> the paint's bumpy embossments trouble the air editorially,
>
> as the pins in a music box's turning drum trouble
> the steel comb's tooth (those pins which are like men
>
> on a cylindrical world – men who play always their singular note
> according to their position). […]

Of course there is no such thing as a missile with an 18th C painting wrapped round its flank. It might hunt a target. The poems remind me faintly of Peter Didsbury. Waldron may have written a lot of these. This is a really forceful project. I wonder if a workshop might be commissioned to make some of these objects, as models for a future economy.

Giles Goodland (1964), published *Capital* (123pp) in 2006. He undertakes systematic poems, building up to huge projects defined by initial rules and specific means of capturing data. One could start from the near-fact that music or visual art have taken in digital and programmed techniques in a big way, whereas poetry has remained at the level of what was in the reach of Renaissance poets. So poems are still made from straw and river mud. This isn't quite true, for example Goodland records (in interview) that text blocks within a single poem were "quoting from *Aviation Week & Space Technology,* from the *BBC Summary of World Broadcasts* which was running a translation of Ma Wenrui's speech on the Shaanxi economy, from the right-wing American *Heritage Foundation Policy Review,* then *Business Week* and then *Time,* for the years 1978– 82." We are bound to think of Tristan Tzara's recommendation, in the First Dadaist Manifesto, to make poems by cutting up newspapers. The outside world is captured without losing its integrity and shock effect, and yet the raw flow is spun into new and overarching patterns by the organising processes used by the poet. Most of the words are not his; we relate to the poet by seeing how he navigates, correlates, links. We see all his eye movements. The poet said (in the same interview) "My collage is not aleatory, these are not 'found' poems but researched poems. The poetry is in the research. In these poems, collage is an attempt at social critique, using the tools of the dominant discourse: empirical, verifiable statements. I would like these poems to be taken as academic papers from which the literal layer of argument has been stripped, leaving the substrate of supporting quotation and apparatus." Goodland has produced a string of large-scale works. This is some of the most ambitious and successful of contemporary poetry. *Capital* is a set of 30 poems drawn from a huge text database with certain constraints: each poem is composed of one quote drawn from each of around 31 (up to 2006) successive years. Not every poem starts in 1976. Each poem has a theme and the quotes are connected by this theme. Thus

> the insect cloud's passing overhead was defined as the occurrence of 50% of the night's maximum density
>
> on the back of a sexual sublimation much more concentrated and intense than in the West
>
> to cope with the rigorous dream code, spicing it up with coloured veils, makeup and
>
> geometric solids can be animated and interactive. by putting these together, you can build
>
> dye-sublimation, wax thermal transfer, and ink jet in descending order of capital cost
>
> genitals smeared with black pigment, looks visionary a quarter-century later, when law enforcement officials
>   (from 'Dream Capital')

– so the theme includes both dream, night, and imaginary, but also sublimation (which Freud attributed as an activity to dreams) and vision. (I guess the geometric solids passage comes from a description of imaging software?)

The result has features in common with the output of GPT-2, which we will see later. The aesthetic effect is new and hard to fix, but part of it is like the feeling of being in an aeroplane, so passive and perfectly secure movement over a visual field where we can see everything and soar over obstacles. This is an effect which all poetry aims for. It is a kind of ecstasy.

The absolute steadiness of the journey, the lack of any emphasis, add to this effect. Despite the themes, the level of predictability is extraordinarily low: another effect which poetry aims for. The text blocks, all 900 of them, are not spoken by a voice; they are the unconscious of the world economy, the neuroses of capitalism. Each poem is named "capital" with different qualifiers. Everything flows through this channel of unvoiced signal; thus I am fairly sure that the string "Girls who meet in a mysterious collision of emptinesses. It's the dream of the American wasteland" is from a review of a film, *Three Women*, which I saw a scene from on TV in 1977 and which I saw in its entirety in 2022. The constraints are important; one could write a history of constraints.

The start point was clearly a crisis of capitalism, with the commodities boom followed by the oil price hikes and uncontrolled inflation, but the project stops the year before the crisis caused by adjustments to the pricing of sub-prime mortgages. The compound phrases follow the model of Bourdieu's coinage of "cultural capital" and "symbolic capital", which he deployed to describe the statistically established (but mysterious) shortage of working-class youth in higher education: places not directly paid for but assured to the offspring of the middle-class by tests sensitive to qualities which they had. The phrase type is thus a description of unfairness and the thirty titles Goodland uses may all be placed in that category.

The book contains the legacy of documentary, an aspiration or romance which British poetry has had intermittently since the 1930s. It has the tracks of an unwavering gaze, not directed by the unsteady impulses of a living eye and its underlying fluids. The subject is a large scale entity which is not systematic because of its huge instability. Each lower layer is stabilised by mechanisms which eliminate variability outside desired parameters but the whole has nothing external to regulate it and is staggering under the kicks of its own outsized limbs. The various energy flows affecting it are not a system because they are not controlled by anything except exhaustion or death. It is a catastrophe machine. The book ends with 'Zero Capital':

> its absence from the financial statements that they are called on
> to produce is a potential source of concern
>
> as they predicted nothing such dreams did not require the service
> of a dream interpreter

Zero, the twisted rubble and mass grave of where

necessary to obtain fluidity, and when this is removed by drying numerous empty pores result

the list of specific meanings included the following: time marker, empty of meaning-symbolism/ value, political exigency, resignation, hope

The very last word is pleasant but the others record some dire disaster and the prophetic dream is showing a nothing when everything has burnt up and come to an end. The poem follows no. 28, 'Waste Capital', the accounts of a waste land. We can interpret the *pore* line by bearing in mind the title of zero capital. Fluidity is a pun for liquidity. The business is not paying. The sources of recourse to liquidity are "twisted rubble". If we bear in mind that oil is sometimes (not always) found in porous rock, the idea of empty pores turns into dry wells and used up lakes of resources. The pore is like a zero punched or counter-sunk into three dimensions. The pores are actually holes in the balance-sheet. So this, and indeed all the text blocks in the poem, bear out the same theme: zero capital. If we were to plunge into the Crash of 2008, two years later, and gaze at the trading position of Bear Stearns, we would find exactly this: dry holes in the balance sheet. Capital worth less than zero. The bondholders get some percentage (and the shareholders are wiped out). As Giles points out, the citations are not "found texts", they all make sense, fitted to a smooth and incredibly long curve of meaning.

The book has some resemblances to a 1970s poem by Paul Evans which was constructed out of phrases taken directly from a French textbook of natural science dating to the late 19th C. Evans did not compose the lines but did fit them together. The poem however looks back to Dada collages of the period after the First World War: Ernst's *Une semaine de bonté* is the classic, a book of hybrid pictures fitted together from illustrations to late 19th C works of enlightenment, with engravings of singular precision and realism. The way in which a Dadaist tradition thus meets the documentary tradition is curious. Goodland's text database is full of precise language and so resembles a set of engravings.

Chris McCabe did *The Hutton Inquiry* (159pp) with Salt in 2005. The poems have numbers up to #1174 but I am assured that these are a count of the days of the Hutton Inquiry, which looked at the quality of the intelligence which led to the decision to go to war against Iraq in 2003. McCabe wrote one poem every day while the Tribunal sat, and part of the point of publishing the Hutton poems, while the tribunal was grinding on, was to remind people that it was taking an incredibly long time (and the public had forgotten what the issues were by the time the final report came out). So the poems are instantaneous and not all about British policy in Iraq – maybe 30 of the poems relate to that. The technique is imagistic – you get a lot of primary detail and not much syntax or interpretation. I think the avoidance of interpretation might be saying that if you get involved in the symbolic meaning of things you are heading down the path of consensus and exclusion of awkward acts which leads to something like the Second Iraq War, the Occupation, and astounding levels of violence. The poet does not use a phrase like "elite consensus" but I think it has to be that, the foreign policy making process was secret and to a great degree non-democratic. McCabe writes about commuting, observing fellow commuters, pubs, being in love, starting work in an office (actually a library). These are experiences familiar to many many people and interpretation would reduce the appeal. There may be a point that ordinarily people are sunk in their everyday experience, tired and distracted, even fulfilled, and that this is the context in which politicians can do things which almost the whole electorate would say No to if they knew what was going on. It happens that the disclosure to a journalist which led to media headlines about the "dodgy dossier", of rigged evidence about Iraq's capacity to make war in Western Europe, took place in a hotel which you can see from the building McCabe was working in. He records the expenses claim for refreshments consumed during that meeting – a reminder I guess that the elite are banal from almost every angle. The book can be seen as part of poets getting into real politics, abandoning their tender and ancient artificial models of what they thought should have been happening. The poetry is mortgaged to the State's flawed decision process – mortgaged to reality, I almost said.

Emily Hasler, *Natural Histories* (2011, 22pp)
The announcement for Hasler's 2018 book said "Emily Hasler's debut collection *The Built Environment*, published this month by Pavilion Poetry." So at this point she was setting aside the pamphlet she did with Salt, as not being a real debut. OK. You can make a debut many times. If I say that X was making a debut, it may not actually be the very first

debut they had made. This isn't a very good pamphlet. It's striking that all the poems are on one theme (birds), but the delivery is superficial, if well-mannered.

Salt put out **Andrea Brady**'s *Vacation of a Lifetime* (130pp) in 2001. Brady comes from Philadelphia but has been in England since the mid-90s. Brady is a political poet interested in the full complexity of human behaviour as pressurised or magnified by different strata of social and technical organisation. Her style believes in a monumental clarity where if every element is clear then adding 100 elements still ends up with clarity. She has published also *Cold Calling, Cut from the Rushes, Mutability: Scripts for Infancy. Wildfire* is a total documentary including a whole file of documentation on the history of phosphorus as a substance of war, adding up to an unwavering focus on the effect of a burning chemical on human flesh. The poem explores why the USA banned the use of phosphorus on human beings, why they used it on a large scale in the second battle of Falluja, and why they lied about it. The depth and seriousness of this work point to a belief in reason as the guide to human conduct. This is unusual in the Alternative world – normally the conclusion is taken as the start, so that the evidence does not need to be recited (and would induce tedium). *Vacation of a Lifetime* actually is a walk through the evidence, a journey over the surface of the world, an attempt to break the tyranny of the horizon. Take this poem, 'Hard on Soft Fatal *(for Madeleine Albright)*' –

> Count out this woman, set down
> finally what she knows. Her eyelids catch the rose
> petals she strews over bungalow couch-beds;
> she papers the toilet with a pale odour.
>
> At the juice-bar where she prosecutes horny
> Juries notice where her head flops against
> her shoulder, doubles for lip. Mini-mover, do you
> feel her and feel every inch a man. Do you lick.
>
> In porta-paradise the inmates all crawling.
> Toast her good luck, her teary mental,
> her damask proposal and breast-breast diaper,
> for life this close to feeling is fraught with

> dangers: what's that screaming? where are they
> dreaming, childhood, keyhole miseries?
> Fables are half-full of her talent; and feel
> you so useless– she'll certainly make you [.]

Albright was Clinton's Secretary of State, planning and justifying ceaseless operations to promote the overseas wealth of the American corporate world. She wrote a book of memoirs of her favourite jewellery (*Read My Pins: Stories from a Diplomat's Jewel Box*). The poem gives endless sensory details, moves in a permanent present like TV. The details seem to come from a TV ad, perhaps for air freshener. But the issues are all abstract – Albright as the croupier of the world-casino, rigging the outcomes, unable to feel compassion, only to get close to it. Damask and diaper (toile d'Ypres) are both high end fabrics, associated with table linen and high occasions – but diaper in American now means what the baby shits into. If Albright is wearing one across her chest (where the decorations go?), that is putting the unavowed stuff front and centre. The screams of the suffering in some sponsored Third World conflict come over on the soundtrack like the crying of a baby who will demonstrate to a TV audience the familial powers of the star of the ad. The stink that needs to be covered up is certainly American foreign policy. Brady has dissolved the burnt-down, unusable nodules of ideology and discovered a great range of information flows, each of which is interesting. This is really the opposite of ideology, the paths are leading everywhere. In fact, the unexplained part is how much information is flowing in all the time, as if there were a hundred camera teams bringing back the raw footage. This is the era of cheap information, but only clear heads can make anything of it.

Eleanor Rees, *Andraste's Hair* (2007, 71pp)
This is very subjective poetry, recognising human feelings before anything else, and a thematic description is difficult because the action is not about the objective world. The poems are long and drifting and come purely out of a mood. The tone is one of excitement, lyric suggestibility, anxiety, ideals soaring up and being threatened by reality. It is moving at a deep level and overcomes resistance. It reminds me of Keith Jafrate (cited in the foreword) and T Glynne Davies. (Davies? – Rees is somehow Welsh but I don't think she is Welsh-speaking.) The scene is Liverpool and the place is seen as a site of floods of aspiration and despair, alternately or

simultaneously. A lot of the energy comes from the fact that the poems are not about the past, or familiar works of art, or an argument. They create their own space and sound. Here is a poem called 'Night River':

> East to west, west to east,
> wetness crawls
>
> the promenade wall.
> Oil and chemical, salt and tar:
>
> the night is in my throat.
> I consume distances
> at the edge of the river,
>
> three a.m., solitary
> held only by the rain and the sky.
>
> The wind's touch is courageous.
>
> The stars are stags,
> antlers pointed at each new shore
>
> sailors discover
> far from here, in some sunny waters
>
> I open to it like a mouth
>
> and sense her shining
> full height on the horizon,
>
> as if the horizon is a ledge
> she balances upon,
>
> and hovering I rush to her,
> her starriness, her electric pulses
> that beckon, she widens:
>
> I immerse myself in her thighs.
> Her whiteness, her size.

> I am her: the sea is a boat.
> We ride until the dawn.

This is one of the significant debuts of its decade. I don't think you would classify it as 'alternative', but most English poets don't write about emotions so this does belong in a realm of the unconventional and anti-academic. The line is based on projective identification: the descriptions of the river seem to be descriptions of how the speaking human is feeling, and vice versa. Evidently this is the process which takes place to swallow the reader up in the poem. The characters in the poems seem to be in a permanent state of suggestibility, instability, excitement, and this has a profound effect on the reader's mood. The goal is not recording the names of streets or rivers, but evoking a state of mind. The chemicals and the tar are preset as symbols of squalor, in some accepted English poem-pattern, but Rees unwrites all that: they come out simply as physical traces to tie the poem to a specific moment and place. The river flows both ways, depending on the tide, and this self-referentiality becomes almost a fling of subjectivity, an extravagant *volte*.

Google says that when fleeing Boudicca invoked a Celtic war goddess named Andraste. Boudicca undoubtedly spoke a rather old form of Welsh, so this is part of being called Rees, I suppose. Source is Dio Cassius. The poem 'Andraste's Hair' is another extended mythical poem with realist elements, the characters like humans but not really human.

Although subjectivity apparently belongs to all of us, in poetry it is also apparent that some people can't do it. Rees has a sort of perfect pitch for writing subjectively. That might be felt as simplicity or simply as being talented. Not everyone can make the object world sing. But, if you can't write subjective poems, aren't you in the wrong business?

Melanie Challenger, *Galatea* (2006, 65pp)
Challenger was in *Identity Parade* and was one of the best poets in that anthology. Galatea was the lady who was originally a statue carved by Pygmalion, the one that came to life; an epigraph goes "We felt /a stone heart quicken, a deep fault made whole"; but she appears here also as the wife of the author Nikos Kazantzakis. The style is literary and over-educated, lost in the worlds of antique texts. The question is whether this represents freedom, the freeing of language from irrelevant bonds, or a kind of idleness.

The poems exclude an "I" figure, in a certain sense; they are constructed around a bizarre optical set-up, a studio arrangement which does not leave room for a personality as well. They are as if written on objects of a very particular shape, say a wrought-iron figure of eight, with everything eliminated except what clings to that curved surface. I am thinking of baroque paintings, especially ceiling paintings, where everything is depicted from a precipitous, dramatic, and distorting angle. They are not literally like paintings, of course. But take this poem. A note on it says "In 1901, an experiment was conducted by Raymond Dodge and Thomas Cline to plot the motion of a person's gaze by attaching the flake of a mirror to a cornea", and part of the poem runs:

> In the glory of limitless reflection, he gazes
> Through a fraction of her caste
> At the hilt of his beating mind; there it lies
> In the dark like a trap in the heart—
> Wood, reconstituting by memory the cold regent of the sky
> To a Hall of Mirrors where, by a single shard
> His image builds itself infinitely
> To the insatiate small shards of him, cut by a vanity
> That is itself and reins itself with pitiless patience.

So, sight itself is made visible – as beams that can be tracked on something (a sheet of paper). (Perhaps light-sensitive paper?) The words are caught in figures as the light is caught by the traps of the experimenter. The "her" is presumably the beloved, his view of her body dissected by endless shards of narcissism. Like baroque paintings, the poems describe extreme experiences. The previous page (also part of the sequence called 'The Service of the Heart') runs:

> He was a god disbelieving his own ability
> To be extinguished; anointed by the wounds
> Of her kisses, he said *I cannot die,*
> Blood from his mouth like briar-roses
> Each with their own tiny voice,
> He tried to silence them but the roses
> Found their tongues, *Oh Kay,* they said,
> *We have been in the earth where*
> *The dead are.*

> Now the corpse of light converses from its graveyard
> Of unmade bedclothes, culvert, clenched fist,
> Teasing the mirage of daylight from the menisci
> Of snowflakes – as if the looking-glass of the sky
> Ruins itself to bathe us in a thousand fragments
> Of the world-soul.

This is thematically related to the cornea/mirror poem, but I am embarrassed to explain how the parts of the two large sections (34 and 24 pages long), which the book is organised into, connect. They are 'Service of the Heart' and 'Galatea'. The parts seem disparate in date or setting but linked by theme. I think that the image of broken-up glass, so that every separate piece records the same image, could be a description of how these two super-long poems are designed. One theme is the story of Pygmalion, in which stone is turned into living flesh, and another is the turning of flesh into stone (by the gaze of the Gorgon). It seems that the book contains series of propositions and of repetition with variations – that it is made up of them. There are two disparate layers of the text, the modern interest in optics and the myths, which presumably bear traces of a Bronze Age origin. The poems are temporary décors, even if large-scale and dramatic in context. They seem to be moving on stilts. So if light pouring from the sky breaks up as it falls, calling it a graveyard is disproportionate. Light does not really die or evoke mourning. This is actually a trick of the light. The paradox of having light be buried is dazzling but evokes no feelings and is of momentary validity. There is such a thing as desensitisation through weirdness. A strange angle of visibility reduces identification or the feeling of reality. The poet is missing from the poems, but perhaps the idea is like saints' lives, as shown in paintings: the events shown transcend the possibilities of a body, or a faculty of the mind, and are recorded solely for that reason. As miracles, they are available for anyone. They are impersonal in the same way as superhuman.

Anointing (as coronation?), *wounds, kisses*: these images hardly belong together in a real experience. The sentence is over the top. But it fits in with opera or Baroque or Mannerist painting (or some poetry of the same era). These are big-scale forms of art, they lasted for centuries, many people like them (even if they don't suit most contemporary taste). I like them, actually. And this is poetry like an opera or a palazzo, conceived on a more generous scale than what is around it. But the literature about Mannerism includes people saying how unnatural it is, how it is hyperbolic and dissatisfied.

It is fair to say that these poems are unlike anything around them. That is almost unheard-of for the present crowded scene, and for a first book. The great majority of her contemporaries have the rigid idea of writing in everyday language about everyday, personally relevant, events. That vote does not make the idea good or interesting. Challenger is following the opposite route – the one which leads to undiscovered territory.

I am worried about the word "caste" in the quote, it would make much more sense if it was "cast", as in cast a reflection or a shadow. "a fraction of her cast", from a flake of mirror, sounds like the set-up. I am not sure snowflakes have menisci (meniscus is the surface of water in a tube, slightly curved). *Meniskos* means "little moon", so a crescent shape. Salt's website reveals that *Galatea* is still in print after 15 years. So, people are still buying it. But the poet has not produced a follow-up book, although a pamphlet did come out in 2016.

Siân Hughes' *The Missing* (2009, 53pp) came out of a poem on the death of a child, which must have seemed like a sure-fire idea but which also suggests embarrassment and non-participation. It was broadcast on Woman's Hour. The radio does not like ambitious language. The book seems to say, if I break the banality barrier, something must happen. If I use colourless language, it must be true. If I only use words a child can understand, I must be innocent. Instant recognisability is vividness.

Tony Williams, *The Midlands* (2014, 83pp). This wasn't actually Salt – it came out from Nine Arches, in Rugby – but I do have a copy of it. (Williams did three books with Salt.) Even buying this was something of a giveaway, and it isn't really about the whole of the Midlands, a vast and daunting domain, but the bit of the East Midlands that I come from. I am surely the target audience here and I really enjoyed this. He evokes certain travellers –

> Who are not lost and can't be found.
> Who gouge the fields like the swine.
> Who broke the branch and drew a line
> through every page of statute law.
> Who happened to be there, and saw

> a cheap arrest get made, and laughed.
> Who burned the harvest of the croft
> and spilled the pail, like infantry
> in the ugly rush of victory
> lit by the glories of the west
> and freed the young, and shot the rest.
> Who daub their lords with axle grease.
>   (from 'But Tell Me…')

The subjects are users of rights of way, which some people want to be suppressed. The reliance on rhyme and preset line lengths is rather unfamiliar in these days, but is native to Williams, whose combination of the power of the imagination with rich social detail is consistently satisfying. Nobody else could have heard these poems before they existed, but everybody can grasp their sound once they have been written down.

Antony Rowland, *The Land of Green Ginger* (2008, 70pp). The Land of Green Ginger is a street in the old part of Hull. Rowland (1970) has clearly read Ian Duhig. The idea of bizarre displays of weird erudition with a burden of whimsy and of unrespectable, smelly, narratives about the past is recognisable. Rowland divagates into the world history of haircuts, and into regional eating habits (via scallops, chocolate, parkin, cucumbers, pies). He specialises in exotic and recondite words. There is a touch of folklore. This is a pretty good idea, but I didn't like *Green Ginger*. Something hasn't put down roots yet. The words are dressing up in some kind of costume drama. They taste of dandelion and burdock. There is too much re-enactment food and not enough about character or ideas. The mockery is vague and not really malicious enough. But "The small pigs which carry happiness convey a feeling to everybody", what a great line that is!

Salt's bet on publishing great numbers of titles represented a belief in the abundance of poets around. They won this bet, and it seems that the era we are living through is one of the strict regime of abundance. Huge numbers of poets are writing and huge numbers of books are coming out. It is the critical reception side, possibly the retail side too, which are not keeping up.

   The books examined don't confirm the idea that Salt were "dumbing down". On the contrary, they leave me with the disturbing feeling that I should read all the 110 Salt debuts. As an aside, I still feel that Salt should have done an anthology as a showcase for their poets – this would still be interesting. The excellent *Salt Book of Younger Poets* (2011) is exclusively poets working towards a first volume – so excludes every published Salt poet by its definition! Amazing! Does reading 10 of the debut books get me to the core of what Salt did? Hardly so.

In the scene as a whole, the number of significant debuts over a ten-year period was probably several hundred. One source would be the Carcanet series of 'New Poetries', which certainly captured a number of terrific young poets. I mean, maybe they weren't *all* terrific, but if you look at those books it surely emerges that the idea of defining a generation takes more than just delving into the archives of Salt.

Postscript. In October 2022 Salt announced that the Salt Modern Poets list was being re-launched. The first authors were Aidan Semmens, Alexandra Corrin-Tachibana, and Ken Evans.

Cultural Asset Management

If we want to achieve balance in discussing art, the most obvious request is that we should consider right-wing attitudes towards a style or a work. Recent years have seen a notable buoyancy of the right-wing vote, even if split between UKIP, the BNP, and the Conservative Party. Without having read thousands of pages of arts coverage in the right-wing press, what I *have* read consistently takes the approach that the Left wants to destroy art and only the well-off are truly detached and truly in love with art. This wrong-foots the critical theorists, and the only way to make headway in this dissenting conversation is to be determinedly pro-art. There is a question mark about the validity of all critical approaches to art.

The scene is homogeneous. This is certainly odd in the middle of a society which is so divided politically. A hot button phrase in discussion is a "left-liberal bubble" in which modern art apparently is sheltered. If you look at the quality newspapers, the ones which demand high levels of verbal skill at comprehension, most of the copies sold express right-wing views. That is, the *Times*, the *Telegraph*, the *Financial Times*, and so on. It is hard to avoid the conclusion that most of the educated people are right of centre, and this is what voting figures suggest. Evidently it is quite possible for a banker or lawyer in the City of London to read reviews of theatre and ballet in their lunch break. Examination of the culture pages, for example of the *Financial Times*, suggests that up to half of the people who buy new poetry are inclined towards the Right, or at least not inwardly committed to the Left. So it is unrealistic either to decide that everyone who reads poetry is an academic or that everyone who reads poetry shares the Left/ radical bias of the poets. As for the poetry, it is mostly not about politics. It is different when we come to the discourse around poetry – when that is about politics, it is within the realm of feminism, identity politics, Green de-industrialisation, sometimes anti-capitalism. Conservative views are not expressed. If it is very difficult to find right-wing poetry of the last 50 years, it is even harder to find right-wing statements by poets. Evidently there is no bubble-wrap preventing left-liberal ideas from leaking. However, there is a mismatch between audience and poets, or perhaps between what poets say and how they think.

We hear little about the rather broader distribution of the informed audience. I can point to Andrew Lambirth's reviews of modern art, fascinating when collected together but originally commissioned for the *Spectator* magazine. *Spectator* readers also like to look at pictures of landscapes. The conservative view of culture (as opposed to political essays and columns) is that it should be non-political. In practice, you can find entire anthologies which fit into that and do not provide provocation, contradiction, awkward evidence, etc.

My impression of the silent rules in these newspapers was, first, guilt-tripping is *verboten*. Writers are not allowed to attack the social position of the potential reader and make them feel guilty. Even this wasn't altogether true, since there was plenty of feminist material – from the point of view of women in the professions. Archaic positions of male supremacy are being exposed and demolished in what would seem like a left-wing way. Guilt is not easy to outrun. Secondly, there is no interest in dumbing down. Culture is meant to be complicated and this is part of its role as a cultural asset. Poetry too is expected to be meritocratic. Owning the very best modern poetry is like owning a fast car. Thirdly, the poets are expected to have wonderful experiences. It is not about developing a critique, or having a knowledge of the sociology of poverty, it is about sensitive people having experiences which are wonderful because of that sensitivity. The stress is on gratification, and this receptivity to delicate experiences links to fantasies about a perfect childhood – the poets are expected to have gone to the best schools and universities and encountered other superior minds. Fourthly, there is a dislike of theory. It is too linked to left-wing philosophers. Poetry which develops philosophical ideas, or quasi-religious ideas, which could affect the distribution of power, is discounted before it gets started. This area is taboo – authority has already had its say. The receptivity does not extend to abstract ideas. Fifth, poets are defined as champion consumers. Expensive experiences are more wonderful when the soul is free to enjoy them. The sensitivity of the poet is supposed to enhance their receptivity to things like travel, fine wine, pictures, etc. which are widely enjoyed by affluent people in general. One has to wonder if ideas could, for this purpose, be redefined as objects of consumption.

I am only going to quote one such story. It is from *The Times* of October 20, 2022 (as the Truss administration was collapsing, excitingly) by James Marriott and headed "Art with a history lesson dulls the viewing" and is about the text of some art exhibitions. "Misplaced discussions of colonialism make museums less, not more, interesting." That is what you would expect. But he also refers to "the bad old ways of art history

– the Great Men at their easels purveying "universal" truths, the blank ignorance of any civilisation east of the Adriatic, the serene disregard of politics – were themselves rotten and boring." This is a pure left-wing view, and demands more attention. It looks as if the ideas which were radical in 1975 (when I went to university) are now so mainstream that you can recite them in the *Times* and not even expect to be shouted down. Evidently the point of creating those ideas was for them to become consensus, and not to remain rough-cut assets of a low-rent Bohemia. Does it not also follow that there is no left-liberal bubble? The universities are attended by future right-wing journalists as well as anybody else, and books, documentaries, even poems, are circulating as the consumption of a whole group which is motivated by cultural curiosity and not by sectarian politics. My impression is that if Marriott reproduced attitudes which were after all quite current in 1975 (is he not implicitly referring to Kenneth Clark, a TV star at the time?) then *Times* readers would find him impossibly illiberal and unreconstructed.

You can't spend an hour reading this right-wing press without realising that conservative women don't want to be dominated by conservative men, and that they want to hear feminist cultural positions even if they would reject the Marxism of the first wave and even the "feminism" word. But if you see those men as consistently selfish, you already accept most of the Left positions on how the job market runs.

Analysis of thousands of pages of this stuff would produce a more complex result. Considering Simon Heffer's writing in the *Telegraph*, for instance, shows a different set of attitudes – but isn't there a product differentiation here, that Heffer is not offering the voice of someone aged about 30 (like Marriott), but the gruff and stalwart voice of someone aged 70? Heffer is offering a nostalgia trip – where one can try out the pose of someone unreconstructed and unrepenting, like an old building which one could spend weekends in. Heffer isn't really as old as he makes out, and the construction of a past in which there had been no Labour governments and no left-wing artists, ever, is a sort of nostalgia weekend. That is surely because he is part of the culture section, where fantasy is protected and even stimulating. "He's been dead for years and he still won't give an inch to long-haired intellectuals and their pink ties."

After saying that there is no right-wing poetry (just as there is no right-wing rock and roll), I can go on to say that it would be hard to identify such poetry because it would accept all the radical assertions of the 70s Left which are now being reproduced in the *Times*. The cultural coverage in the right wing dailies is apolitical. This may not have been true during Thatcherism, but there was a new understanding which locked into place during the Blair years, and the Right rebranded itself on the way to taking over chunks of Blair's voters. After 1990, making the link between Left criticism of class inequality, and the Soviet dictatorship, became less fashionable and less interesting. This obscuring of politics is benign in the sense that it de-emphasises differences within the audience. It is better being in an audience that is having the same feelings. Art stands to benefit from a slightly mellower mood among the people sitting in the same rows of seats. Another closely related point is the interdict on guilt-tripping.

You may ask what is the connection between childhood and assets. The fantasy of childhood with unusual gifts and access to enrichment is basic to this collective story. The logic of a certain kind of poem is to display the faculties which one hopes for a child to develop and which are also the most vulnerable. I say beautiful feelings because that demands certain cognitive skills and is an exhibition of them. The beauty relates to a pervasive anxiety about depleted development of a child you are attached to and this is hardly separate from a residual anxiety about the childhood you lived through. There is a chime between the faculties which academic tests measure and the faculties which beautiful poetry exhibits in flower. However, it is because exams ask children to reproduce knowledge that the creation of original patterns is even more admired than exam passes. Creativity, insights, invention, patterns that cut across disciplines – these are rarer assets. They expose more and exhibit more. The arts pages are proximate to pages about the performance of schools and universities and to schemes for the transmission of wealth between generations.

British poetry has been extremely successful since some point in the 1990s. I don't have to write a searing critique of the poetry world, because it is attractive to a lot of people and its social workings are allowing talented people to reach the goal and write good poetry. It seems possible that the basis for success was the dual eclipse of the Left and the Right, in the cultural world. The Left had just watched the disintegration of the Soviet bloc and was still watching a torrent of exposures of just how tyrannical and corrupt the nomenklaturas had been. The legacy formulas of demanding flattened egalitarian language and numbingly obvious propaganda lines in poetry were out of action – at least temporarily. Meanwhile the New Right had hit a turning-back point, it was exhausted by its victories and had repeated itself too often. Its tunes were worn out, its crass economic simplifications had been exposed by being put into practice in too many countries and corporations, and the electorate was turning rather massively in a centre-left direction. The Conservatives just clung on to power in the 1992 election but were not in a position to bully and brag. In this conjuncture, poets had a unique chance to think about poetry and escape the patronage of cultural commissars eager to subjugate it (to assert its heteronomous status, in Tillich's terms). At this point poetry was ideally equipped to resolve outstanding problems, to create new and eloquent works, and to draw in a new generation who found the new freedom simple and natural.

The cultural tradition embodied in poetry

Culture counts as one of those valuable objects left over from the past which wealthy people acquire in such abundance. The Right is evidently not in sympathy with attempts to abolish the art of the past, or even with people who don't understand the art of the past. Writing a poem may involve use of an inherited pattern which is of obvious complexity, although not so complex that an individual brain cannot master it. Obviously, this rich language plays a central role in the indifference to poetry of much of the population and the failure of much poetry to embody what people like in poetry. This becomes a major political headache if you reason that inability to manipulate this battery of verbal and conceptual patterns is significantly located among people who emerge either from the lower classes in Britain or from non-British families, and missed the acquisition phase. Poetry could be unfair in just the same way that access to higher education is unfair – it is more there for income class A than for income class E.

The ability to enjoy a valued process is one of the things which affluent people compete over – obviously you haven't really acquired an asset if you don't know how to enjoy it. The actions carried out while enjoying poetry are implicit and I am unable to define how some people don't enjoy it. Asking what the content of collusion is is like asking what the information content is of implicit information. Everyone knows that most of the information in a poem is implicit. Everyone knows that culture is a shared game and that the people playing it know the rules of the game. But squeezing that silent but intelligent mass into daylight, into the audible world, is endlessly difficult. I suppose that all the people on the inside grasp implicit statements and retain them and that some portion of the people on the outside have difficulty in doing this. They have difficulty realising that implicit information is being broadcast. They can't hear it. The implicit knowledge is acquired by reading messages which ask for it – however, that may be an incomplete concept, as vital parts of the transmission may happen during face to face interaction with older speakers. If you live far away and know poetry only from books, the way you read the books may not be enough to let you grasp the message. Eliot was preoccupied with the idea of this Tradition; it has become deeply unfashionable among later strata of critics (employed in an education industry which is instructed to deliver social mobility and so to make tradition packageable) but this may inhibit them from seeing what is actually going on.

If we accept that there is no code in use, the turning point may instead be the capacity to identify.

Work and pleasure

I was at a day-long conference on a drop-out poet of the generation of 68 when I heard an academic say, *Close reading – there is no other kind.* This is odd, because I don't think anybody close-reads poetry *except* academics. People who spend Sunday morning reading a book of poetry are not close-reading it, and that is not the basis on which poetry is bought and sold in bookshops. Part of the academic atmosphere is that art becomes work. This is in contrast to people who work all week and have art as a form of pleasure. So the people who read the culture pages of the *Telegraph*, the *Observer*, etc., are mainly not academics. The culture pages are mainly there at the weekend because that is when such people have time for culture. If you do not see art as a source of pleasure, it follows that objectivity becomes a high priority, and you develop an interest in access to art, fairness in cultural management, or other impersonal issues. In fact sociology can be seen as the denial of individual wishes– that is its start point. If you work all week, it is credible that you have been carrying out other people's wishes all that time, and using accurate knowledge of their wishes as your primary intellectual value. The weekend is different and this is likely to include something rather more indulgent and directed towards the ego.

Weekend knowledge is biased towards a culture of consumption where there are a vast range of commodities available, let's say foodstuffs, and the value is distributed over the whole range of them, and relies on differences. Gratification leads to empiricism – the domination of the senses over general ideas. Poetry too is expected to be diverse and specific – like the menu of a high-class restaurant. The corollary of hating theory is that you invest in sensation, say of a particular squid dish at a particular restaurant.

Reading such newspapers is a cultural goal on its own. It is a pleasure – and has reached millions of people. The Sunday newspapers, in particular, are a core part of British cultural life. The question is whether poetry has something unique which you cannot find in the pages of these Sundays (which in the course of a year might extend to 5000 pages, perhaps). Political critique, social reportage, accounts of desirable things, intimate interviews, accounts of exotic and beautiful landscapes, voices from foreign cultures – all are present, and I suspect that the realm of poetry mostly overlaps with these areas. Journalists who write about food, or travel, or interior design, offer their sensitive reactions, share feelings with us, ply us with specialised information. It is credible that poets are making a similar offer and that one's attachment to a poet at least *resembles* attachment to a gifted journalist. Shared pleasure is a powerful thing. Poets expressing views on political events are not in principle different from columnists or interview subjects expressing similar views on the same events. It is not obvious that poetry can develop material about collective experience and political activity which is possible only in poetry, without then ceasing to be collective, and part of politics.

Part of the answer is that the Sunday newspapers are reliant on advertising for expensive leisure goods and so the journalism has to have a pro-consumerist slant. Part is that poetry really has a separate domain, a depth which prose cannot travel to. And part is that poetry is not unique, but part of a wider verbal world which everyone concerned moves fluently through. But, just as poetry is divorced from music, so it is also divorced from photographs – a vital feature of the culture supplements. Poetry has a special something, modern poetry may even have evolved to exploit the limited area which the newspapers leave alone, but poetry is mostly *within* this generous area.

I think there is a right-left division to do with precision and abstraction. Wealth is partitioned, wealthy individuals only own a fraction of the possessions that exist, owned in severalty and enjoyed in privacy, but the Left is abstract, idealised, flawless with equity. There is always a problem with adding detail to an ideal. A dinner I eat was eaten only by me. It is rich in detail but is not shared with other people. It is also a problem to propose an object-free future. Abstract thought does without objects but the future is not going to be abstract any more as it turns into real time. Objects are like meals, they are unique to a time and place and their essential features belong to their local nature, the way they feel in your hands or on your shoulders.

The most convincing anti-left cultural argument is nothing to do with poetry, in fact, it has to do with tower blocks. These included masses of highly monotonous living spaces because they came directly out of abstract speculation and that speculation was on a large scale but was missing detail. It was plausible that abstract thought functionally lacked differentiation. Perhaps it acquired its grandiose scale and universality by washing out details (in favour of massively replicated cells).

Why is modern poetry so in love with intimacy? Is there an intellectual reason for it? Or is it because of the over-presence of cultural journalism and singer-songwriter records, offering intimacy and freedom from theory as their stock in trade? Perhaps the key is a symmetry – the search for uniqueness reflects a fear of uniformity and featurelessness. This is one axis along which poems are propelled.

Poetry seems preoccupied with personalising processes. Perhaps we can describe poetry by describing its opposite: a map of depersonalisation. We can stretch personalisation out to the point where it becomes transparent. When we see through it… it becomes narcissism.

Refugium: a safe place

To go back to the 1960s, a favoured theme of the Left at that time was the complacency of the Western audience and their inability to understand population groups who weren't part of their privileged world. Much was said in the first wave about the invalidity of the bourgeois viewpoint, or the white male viewpoint, in writing about art. This was a way of winning arguments about committed art (of which a large part was rigid and unpleasant and unconvincing, even if not all Soviet or East German art was uniformly bad). So a large part of New Left discourse was explaining how uninformed the bourgeois' appreciation of art was. And how wrong he was even if he enjoyed it. Of course, this cognitive shortfall also summed up what formal accreditation and academic study had to offer to someone who already enjoyed art.

It looks as if critical theory as we have it came out of the sector of French theorists who adhered to Marxism. That is, they believed that all non-Marxist opinions on literature, or indeed on society, were invalid and self-interested, as a matter of doctrine. The *nouvelle critique* was straightforwardly a product of this, with the differentiation representing the dissent with the Communist Party of various other Marxist groups who did not accept the "Moscow line". The idea that the literary opinions of everybody else were invalid was never questioned. Without the Moscow Line the whole thing would never have started. So it is not surprising if people react to Parisian-style theory by questioning its relevance to the appreciation of art. Because critical theory takes literary response as the object of attack, as being prone to bourgeois subjectivism, collusion, class consciousness, etc., they cannot also regard aesthetic response as having any validity. This means that the only benefit of reading poetry is nugatory. You think you own your reactions and your memories and indeed your experiences, but once you enter the domain of critical theory none of that holds. *They* own it. Your feelings are the waste material which they will remove and shred in the process of reform and re-education. If your feelings are yours, the critics have no purpose.

So the Right has a taboo on guilt-tripping. Poetry stands to benefit from this since few poets actually want a sector of the audience to explain to everyone else that the poems on offer are based on neo-imperialist fantasies of power and any pleasure they supply is strictly illusory. Because a theory is constitutively a generalisation, a theorist can only deal with a single text after a process of defeaturing in which the parts of it which are different from other works of art are stripped away, to allow the generalisation to be asserted. Meanwhile, poets are aware that they are competing with each other, and give much of their conscious effort to differentiating their work and producing, by a process of creation and experimentation, the very features which the theorist is preparing to draw around and discard. Poets are not fond of theorists.

We have to go down a side road at this point. The UKIP analysis of the misgovernment of national affairs erases the distinction between left-wing post-structuralist academics and globalising City bankers. Both are swept up in a blunt category of educated metropolitan mischief-makers, which they have to share with bureaucrats and politicians in Brussels. Anyone else can see a strong distinction here, but the populist Right makes a point of erasing it. This is their charter moment.

The *refugium* we are speaking of offers a shelter in a place where nobody can make you feel guilty for being what you are. This can include the illusion of a social compact such that the working class and ethnic minorities are tired but happy at the end of their day's work and never thinking about improving their position. As a variant, and because modernism has so often been used as a way of attacking Englishness and dismissing the kind of art people enjoy, the *Refugium* offers shelter from modernism. A favoured narrative (and Simon Heffer seems to offer this every week in differing forms) is of an English artist of the 20th century who didn't get Modernism and was socially awkward and diffident, received scathing reviews from flashy young modernists who could speak French, but who plugged on undiscouraged for fifty years... and who can now be revealed to have been Secretly Talented all along. "Arthur Thruppeny-Codger was never nobbled by the modernism racket."

You may think that Parisian revolutionary painters, musicians hanging out in Darmstadt for the summer school, and bureaucrats in ugly buildings in Brussels, are three discrete groups. But, from the point of view of the *refugium*, they are actually the same person. The doctrine is that all bad ideas are French. Or French-speaking. People who can't compete, culturally, want a *refugium* where they are protected from losing. The idea of *refugium* applies even to literary academics. I think quite a few people accepted that the gurus, first of all, (later, the "post-structuralists"), were brilliant and opening new worlds but they personally had no ability to do that and wanted a safe place where they didn't have to encounter these radical ideas. What I am thinking is that the anti-feminist line in modern culture fell into this category; they knew that liberality and generosity were attractive qualities but knew they didn't have them. The conservative response to the new Marxist-based criticism which copied the *nouvelle critique* was shame-faced. They certainly wanted to undermine the people who saw connections between ideology and literature, as acts of the imagination. But the concept was not to vindicate the writers who got into fascism or imperialism when it was lucrative to do so – guilt was not being denied. The emotional appeal of refuge culture starts with guilt and is a way of soothing it.

Literature is, to generalise, about shared feelings displayed through symbolism. We have been talking about feelings which are inside the cone of silence, which were not shown in shared symbolism, which were private and to some extent shameful. There is another category, of feelings which were shameful but which are shared, which are the material of an alliance which can affect public life, and which are perhaps the inexplicit content of symbolism or the content of inexplicit symbolism. I am using the word *refugium*, which emerged into print as referring to a piece of land west of Britain which supposedly was dry land during the last Ice Age and so allowed various North European species to survive the ice. The sequel was that the land of Britain, as it thawed out, was not simply colonised by organisms from Africa or south-west Asia. The *refugium*, as a cultural fantasy, has by charter a complete lack of theorists and post-structuralists. The idea is that artistic pleasure is only possible if these people are directed elsewhere in the building, perhaps to a secure waste storage area.

Conclusion

The Right looks at modern culture through what is apparently a high-tech lens, made of special glass. But as it turns out a lot of what pretends to be lens is actually opaque. These ninety concentric areas of blindness tend to corrode and allow light through – unless expensively maintained.

The right-left axis is not a path which gives productive insights about poetry. There is no culture war taking place in Britain. Why is poetry not aligned with the power structure? I don't know. I think contemporary poetry has rushed into one quadrant of the graph and left the others empty. It has issues with wealth, power, technology. I am happy to find poetry where it actually is – surrounded by zones where it isn't. It is very hard to express right-wing values in poetry as we have it. In any case, the critique of the wealthy and powerful is very precious. Maybe culture is something they don't own (opinions are divided on this).

Verticegarden

We have considered a central genre of the privatised, but we evidently have to add something outside it: the avant-garde, and especially the radical wing of it. This domain is neither banal nor sublime. In a cultural milieu where people agree on so much it is helpful to go to the vertices, for example Peter Larkin, Nat Raha, Paul Green, Niall Quinn, Adrian Clarke. If we go to the edge we can see another terrain over the edge and stretching out into the distance. (*Vorticegarden* was a 1974 pamphlet by B. Catling.) Nat Raha began with a pamphlet, *Notes on Tauheed* (2009), and edits *radical transfeminism*, a zine. I think it is helpful if we talk about the body image for a bit before starting. When, many years ago, I was researching the culture of the Third Reich, I read a Nazi book on Greek art which identified the idealised physical figures of mature Greek sculpture with Aryan blood, so that not only did images of gods resemble people you would meet every day, but also those physiques were directly linked to the mental powers which produced democracy, philosophy, poetry, Greek colonisation, and the ideal of self-perfection. The author had noticed that some images showed deviant bodily forms (what you could call the grotesque) but attributed this to individuals of non-Aryan blood. So he had not only missed the point that Greek sculpture showed exaggerated and idealised forms, but also connected that artistic apex with a racial theory which meant that the statues were virtually German. We can put the thing in context by considering Roman sculpture, which derived from the tradition of keeping images of (distinguished) ancestors within the family home and was typically not idealised but realistic portraits. Part of the Nazi phenomenon was the use of new media, such as radio, amplification via public address systems, and newsreel, for which society had not yet developed layers of defence. People learnt scepticism, later, and the mass enthusiasm was not repeatable. When many people are united by bonds of an intense group feeling, they are likely to use that group feeling to isolate and attack deviants. This is what acquired inhibitions can guard us against.

One of the breakthroughs in modern cultural history is the realisation that a number of nuns and saints were anorexic and that it is possible to understand real-life anorexics by studying the first-person accounts of the spiritually starved. The history of representations of the human form cannot finally be separated from real human forms, from clothes and adornment, and from the imagination of the human form which preoccupies people so much. Perhaps experts in art history should occasionally put down that volume of Wölfflin and read about anorexia. It can be defined as a search for beauty.

Looking at magazine covers in a newsagents shows an apparently endless series of images of beautiful people, ones who fulfil conscious standards of beauty. We can reflect that consciousness consists of a series of schemas of physical positions and movements, of the self or of others, in an ever-continuing series. A disturbance to this faculty, so that the schema cannot be made satisfactory and successful, is likely to take consciousness over altogether. Maybe there is something non-visual and non-social behind that series of displays, but what it is is a mystery.

I used to work in an area of the education industry which involved me in reading accounts of bullying and also reports on teenage suicides, for my working day. I was made aware that in the view of professionals there was an epidemic of mental illness among children. I was contacted by a parent whose child was showing suicidal ideation and had been referred to CAMHS (children and adolescent mental health services) to be told that she could have an appointment in a year's time. My impression was that the State was defining good government apophatically, that is, it was everything which the State was not doing. CAMHS had previously had the capacity to deal with the volume of referrals. My supposition is that the combination of social media and the internet is presenting young people with a radical change in the data intake which society has not yet developed defences against. It is not correct that body dysmorphia, promoted by bullying by other children in the peer-group, is the only reason for the anxiety of adolescents. If they suffer anxiety and depression it is certainly also because they see bad things happening to their parents, in an economic crisis. But the sum total is that neo-liberalism has made a society which terrifies the children who are supposed to grow up and maintain and continue that society. The media show them things which they profoundly desire and also persuade them that they cannot have those things because they are flawed. Children are sick with anxiety. This is now very high on the political agenda even if politicians do not yet have solutions.

An ideal can be compared to a real body in terms of flaws: you are failing at this point and at this one and at this one. The failures just spiral and this turns out to be abusive idealisation. Raha's work in the magazine *radical transfeminism* is connected to this question of visual abuse, but her poetry is not usually following the same line. *Octet* (2010, 54pp) is a lyrical work.

>our serene consumptive upon this westbourne culvert,
>mooring amid cormorants signals bemused guisal,
>luminating directives of cranes
>for long water. has this land-calming
>mutated hir isoset, associating this lakebank
>to 18th century *wonders* of landownership, note:
>fishing vacuole, convecting moon phases
>& an invocation of recorded image
>sheds glare upon our self-observed menagerie.
>
>humour to consume gestures, iridescence flutters
>proxim of collar:: tailors mascule projection
>to fabric, & replacing headwear colourcodes
>your brow to my locks. landscape
>this youthless centrepiece
>muted from public frolic

I have grave doubts about paraphrasing the poetry or selecting passages which I can translate and which are in that way atypical. The gestalt of the work, the first impression, is an incredibly refined auditory imagination and an inexhaustible variation of emphases and ripples. My suggestion is that we go with the flow and accept the audible qualities as the ones we should pay attention to. *Hir* is a non-gendered possessive pronoun (borrowed from Middle English). The cover has a blurred photograph of what is probably the Serpentine, a lake in Hyde Park, with a boat and a green shore. The grey texture of the lake is expanded to fill the whole back cover. In the passage quoted, a number of words place us on the banks of water, with water birds. Bourne is spring and there is a west bourne stream in West London, which higher up is called the Kil burn, and which provided the water for the Serpentine. This is probably the *boating lake* just mentioned by the text. The party enjoy a landscape by water and wonder if this associates them with landscape painting commissioned by the owners of the land. The reflexivity, the *self-observed* footage, is typical, I think. This does remind me of D.S. Marriott and of the Jeremy Reed of the *Isthmus of Samuel Greenberg* and *Saints and Psychotics* period. It is dandyish, intricate, recondite. It is highly designed and has a sense of being at a distance from the world around it. Isoset could mean "a category of equals (with a boundary line)". The lexical choices could be part of membership of such a set – the sound of intimacy. I wondered about the title and the simplest explanation is that it refers to a group of eight people. So, eight people in the same boat, by a boating lake. A passage about "arms adjoined to hall/ half-past, slipping. seven siblings & exit, prepopulation. Alexandria/ bellows through flittering levels" may identify the eight. Perhaps they are all sitting beside the Serpentine. The word occurs in three contexts; "there's/ an octet waft spying on tinnitus", "octet marks metafilm", "our lookout on octet symphonia".

The text avoids pronouns and the copula. This has the effect of effacing the difference between I and you; the conduct is autonomous but sociable, musings of characters from some neglected volume of Proust or Pater. A passage at p. 22 offers a sign which has a value in externally available frames.

> the rest conduces visionary:
> earth-tones & verdance backspacing wallpapers
> along the longspace & your pierced additions,
>   (a near-dozen drawn needle-like: triangular series
>   on a lobe-to-shoulder hypotenuse,
>   tangential to cheek.)
>   smirk outfit, drawn red
> on forehead w/ drip / spatial contrast.

The first two lines show a view through a window, behind the wallpaper. The description is then of a person in the room, with piercings (and garish make-up). These modifications had associations with punk style and then with the gay world. To use this as an analogy, the other moments of the poem may also be describing gestures of the characters in the poet's world, adornments of the surface with secret implications which could be reflected by someone with similar preoccupations. The lexical choices suggest fields of great depth, almost deep enough to be submerged in; a crystal held up by the implicit. The level of detachment from conventional classification and purposes decides everything and suggests that *Octet* may be an idyll, a record of an experience directed by the subject's own values and preferences, miraculously detached from intrusion and overruling. Something so delicate and intricate points to the removal of recurring constraints.

Where do these verbal depths come from? The movement reflects a space full of people and the ellipses reflect the interventions of those people. The stylised and intimate quality of the language may record the trace of many conversations in eight voices. The conversations we don't hear are the water which shaped this landscape with its refinement, rarity, luxury. The dispersed crystal forms a pattern with vast gaps where a matrix sense shows us passages of gold and glass, the mirror motion of mutual esteem. Another passage runs:

> sultry heat title tired braze in idle
> hands, feeding frequency direct:
> authority blind to neglect / douse
> soaking conscious: we support only
> so many masks.
>   arboretum chokes the nitrates.
> burn photosynthetic. specificity
> of use-times sold by the seat claims.
> sun block + pollen toxicity. consider
> the cloud density –
> consider the capitol feeding this –
> start by throwing matchsticks, heat
> to perpetuate

This gives us variations on a theme of urban overload, the city as a lake of waste heat emitted by furnaces. The basic condition in the city starts with the skin, plunged into filthy and active air. The poem seems to have dissolved the language and started a new one but it is full of concrete details.

[of sirens. body & faultlines] (33pp, 2015) is very political work, of protest against police activity and urban living conditions. (There are two books with this name.) A siren has a deviant body image and can be a trans symbol.

Disaffection and conformism

The politologists Ford and Goodwin analysed disaffection in correlation with educational level. They found that the percentage of people with no degrees who said "yes" to the question whether the system was basically unfair was about 40%. Among graduates it was about half as high. (The question was actually "do you think that people like you have no say in the system?" and the count was of "strongly agrees".) So the educated are largely in favour of the system. The exam system validated them and they are now, relatively, affluent. The idea that the universities are pools of dangerously left-wing ideas is a favoured myth of the right-wing press. The more true it becomes that the educated are affluent and conservative, the more the press has to claim that they are seduced by extremism. Ford and Goodwin's research was aimed to explore the motives of BNP and UKIP voters. It also suggests that the literary world, while integrated with the educated part of the population, is not very radical and has difficulty with writers who combine formal knowledge with disaffection with the system. (To be exact the authors noted a shift, recent in 2014, where 40% of the working-class respondents were disaffected and only 16% of the graduate respondents were.)

It may be that the common opinion which is represented by (say) the *Times*, Radio 4, and the LRB leaves a part of the opinion spectrum off-stage and off-mike. It is true that this common opinion is fascinated by evidence, asks for correlation between evidence and conclusions, asks for assumptions to be explicit. But it is problematic if radical poetry scraps all those rules of political debate as conservative. With this poetry I often have difficulty working out what propositions I am being asked to assent to or what the link between the evidence and the propositions is or how the language on show can be mapped onto states of affairs outside language. One line of radical analysis is weakened by its acceptance of a Marxist basis. None of the people on estates in decaying towns want to live in East Germany. But even if you withdraw from this naivety and ignorance of history, that does not reduce any of the disaffection. If 40% of the working class respondents, in the British Social Attitudes survey figures, think the political bodies are not listening to them, you can't theorise that away. We live in an actual country, not in a beautiful verbal construction.

Consensus is a powerful force. If you read poetry aloud to an audience there is an internally rising pressure to move away from extreme positions and towards what will offend no-one, to disarm criticisms and to swim towards harmony and approval. This is true even if there are only ten people in the room. The consensus has to move forward occasionally, even if that happens only once every ten years. If you accept that it was the link to the universities which took the formal impulses of Modernism and reduced them to "academic modernism", then it is possible that the new disaffected poetry represents in sociological terms a return to Squatland, to a drop-out, bohemian, debt-ridden, way of life, and so to people who are non-corporate. This would represent an overthrow of the walls which had hidden modernism for five decades or so, and the original sound could be heard again like some collection of vinyl jazz.

We can propose that there is a group which is intelligent but not docile, that is they do not become educated because they dislike the educated and so dislike being in a classroom or reading an educational book. Docile means *teachable*, literally. So the process of acquiring culture would lead one to approval of culture, and apparently leads you to approve of the party system of politics, but there may be a cohort which fails to pass through this process. It may be they also write poetry. Where you hear something reasonable and well-modulated, you need to bear in mind that some people can't hear speech with those qualities without becoming enraged.

It may be that vehemence is the feature which the audience drawn from this group most want, and that they will reject anything which does not have this quality of excitement and momentum. But it looks also as if that vehemence were interchangeably similar to the rejection of reason and measured debate. I think that political discourse involves considering other people's feelings as well as your own. To set this constraint aside shows a loss of the polarity between the private and the public.

If we explain these subjective styles as probably a reflex of such a collapse, we point to the incongruity of their parts; this mismatch is part of a wished-for shock and dissonance effect. They are attacking the consensus as such. And tacitly claiming that the familiar is conservative. The poetic style records a train wreck where two realms impinge on each other and are superimposed in the same space. It plunges into a landfill of damaged norms.

The dream of sullen poetry is that it would channel the sullenness that everyone else feels. In doing so it would make a new society visible – free of the frustrations. The flip side is that it may evoke the breakdown of society, mirrored in the breakdown of shared symbolism.

Haley Jenkins, *Nekorb* **(2017, 40pp)**
As I mentioned, I used to work summarising complaints about schools, and I read thousands of letters from parents who were unhappy with what happened at schools. Next, it is part of this poetry that the author is autistic, "on the spectrum". A high percentage of the letters were about

autistic children. My impression was that orthodox schools were hostile to such children but that this was also a source of knowledge that was going to equip them to deal with a *slightly* less hostile adult world. Next, that there was a pattern in which other pupils teased the children on the spectrum and learnt how to provoke a crisis, a "meltdown" (I really dislike that phrase) which led to the autistic child being sanctioned and written up and missing out on things. The letters were essentially about how vile the other kids were, not so much about autistic life *per se*.

Nekorb is a tale of finding every day life crushing, of struggling to preserve psychic coherence and hope in the face of serially negative experiences. The cover shows images affected by jagged, broken, panes of glass. The title is the word *broken*, which may be connected with the (possible) mirror of the cover image and connected again with the phrase *broken mirror*, used by Uta Frith to describe a postulated failure to mirror other people's states of mind, in autists. *Nekorb* is the mirror image of *broken* so the title may be a rejection of the classifier used by government and science. It may be the label as seen by the contents of the jar. The cover has three faces, each with the eyes removed: *eye contact* is not available. The text is divided into three sections, 'Neurojumps', 'No Thunderstorms' and 'As the Nurses took a Coffee Break'. The first is about the autistic condition and reactions to it, and the second is about the poet and her grandmother. The third part is the most paraphrasable; it is dedicated to the eleven patients in the original paper by the Austrian Leo Kanner, who collated observations to define a condition later called autism. The other founder was Hans Asperger, but this was during the Third Reich and euthanasia, viz. State murder, was the fate of a number of his charges. How far he identified the incurables to the relevant branch of the SS is a matter of controversy. The dedication includes the 5-month old baby who was the first victim of the T4 eugenic murder programme (lethal injection "while the nurses took their coffee break"). The poem says

> a loss we continue
> the world make you like everyone else
> you who tikkun olam you who drumbeat
> you who rattles banners at charity races
>   have you heard of our neurotribe?
>   to create concrete Utopias
>   drill it like cars or copper
>   unconscious need to be created

>   in mid-walk
>   at the end of each trip
>   you get back to dream-work
>   us shall continue on we're always walking

Neurotribe refers to neurodiversity, it contains the idea that humans are genetically divided into different but stable neurological dispositions. This defines the difference between autistic people and the "neurotypical", the majority. It embodies the idea that there is no cure because there is objectively no illness here. *tikkun olam* is a Hebrew phrase meaning "repair of the world", so a charitable act, involving restitution, subsidy, amendment, etc.

The poem investigates Kanner's original paper and the history of understanding of autism:

> he was not learning to ask answer questions   yet
> pertained to rhymes   she ate the leaves and drank the water
> a pleasing physical symmetrical smile that translates shouts of high
> mental metal   primitive faces of caves hunter-gatherer smoke
> blood paint   these are not
> spectrum – once you know what to look for, you see it like water like
> an everywhere music a splintered glass beer   paused aloft she
> warehoused on the wards beat ideas into plasterboards iron-barred
> let's be honest
> all the managing are ill   all the managed are free
> living in aloneness   obsessive running counting we love

This is an astonishingly dense evocation of a state of mind and a political relationship. The "spectrum" is the one in "autistic spectrum disorder", ASD. Frankl and Cameron describe a girl who was in a flower arranging class but "ate the leaves and drank the water". (I can see a dozen quotes from the classic papers on autism but of course there may be others from papers I haven't seen.) "Warehoused" is a pejorative description of an older method of institutional care as "people warehousing" and would be the opposite of a pattern where some adjustments to housing etc. and special education, and some public awareness, would allow people on the spectrum to live independently, successfully acquiring education and carrying out jobs. This is an ideal, not what we actually have. The splintered beer glass is an image for a condition you find everywhere, a pattern as self-reproducing as a broken glass scattering and the beer spilling along with it. Once you see that everywhere quality, you acknowledge that the State needs to set up institutions to provide properly for this large minority. People say that bullies just haven't grasped the rules of social life, but it is equally possible to say they are carrying out a simplified imitation of adult social life. If you look at how the tabloid press works, or at some areas of national politics, you see the isolation of victims, their depersonalising, and the gathering of a mob to torment them, as basic parts of the vocabulary.

The text is organized around affirmative clusters, with grammar and lineation being neglected or treated in an unconventional way. I want to quote another poem to show how much stress the language is taking and how expressive it becomes:

> virtual, we vibrate back
> in slate, echo-lalia
> dis guarded
>
> we go to echo-sing
> repeat wound sound
>
> filled up dictionaries
> fine feel of no
> reverberation

Without going into detail, this refers to a state of being dominated by other people's words; serenity is a promise on the horizon. Being without *reverberation* means autonomy. The words in the poem are also echoes, phonic echoes of each other. Slate means a blank slate that anyone can write on, but also rhymes with, that is echoes, echolalia. Reading poetry is directed at empathy, but it is possible that autistic people do not want to be understood, rather they want their specific requests to be honoured and for articulate, popular bullies to find out that the rules apply even to them. Collusion tends to replace rules and collusion favours some people over others.

I wanted to comment on the factor of learning how to administer people because it is a fact that teachers and civil servants (of various kinds) are a big part of the poetry world. Undoubtedly public servants are worried about the difficulty of dealing with people on the spectrum, ethnic minorities, victims of abuse, gay people, amongst others, and undoubted failures of the State are concentrated in these groups of citizens, so that more knowledge is helpful. I think it is a problem if poetry gets taken over by what is logically part of vocational training. I have to note that people not employed to look after others may have much less interest in sociology lessons. However, for me curiosity is a big part of the literary experience, and I found *Nekorb* fascinating partly because I wanted to think about autism and about my own incomprehension. It is not true that learning about someone's personality is something outside the domain of the aesthetic, rather it occupies a central place there. Poetry is strikingly an activity which creates a social interior with much intimacy, and yet which is concerned with outsiders, the rebellious, the nonconformists, the under-achievers. That is a generalisation, for the poetry we have now, but I suspect this is much less true for any poetry before the 20th C, so it might also serve to define historical peculiarities of the poetry we have. Jenkins is palpably finding self-awareness through the activity of writing.

For contextual reasons I suspect that the poet has a history of not being understood and so has developed a plain way of delivering emotional information. This is more effective than a lot of aestheticised poetry which regards self-expression as crude and out of date. These poems are extremely direct, and moving for that reason.

If you want my advice, to fix bullying you have to fix society.

Insignificance;
or, Structure Engulfed by Surface

Raphael Samuel's last book, *Island Stories*, left unfinished at his death, describes the decline of drum and trumpet history (with wars and nation building) in schools in the 1920s and the increased popularity of lessons about the everyday, often using the Quennells' *History of Everyday Things in England* (volume 1, 1918) as the text to study. I am looking at the picture of a farm waggon which Laura Carter reproduces in her excellent *History Workshop Journal* paper on the Quennells. Clearly the person who hewed the wood, made the waggon, loaded and drove it around, was not part of the upper class. Clearly the object in sight was part of work processes and not display of some kind. This is important. No doubt in 1920 primary school teachers, the surviving ones, did not like patriotic history; they chose a realm of the typical, changeless, and almost featureless, partly because it was not part of a military narrative. What interests me is that people writing banal poems about ordinary people today think it is an incredibly new idea, whereas that sort of history had mass extension in the 1920s and was actually there in the eighteenth century. I think we are still in the era opened by the changes of the 1920s. To start with, this faith in the everyday and typical must be the basis for thinking that you can write poetry in banal and everyday language and still be treated as a poet. The loss of continuity with the poetic methods of the past (the Great Tradition, I suppose) can be dated to the post-war period; if the chronicling of the Army, the Fleet, and the Empire involved an investment in all English poetry as national poetry, then the loss of faith in generals and politicians soon after the war, in the hangover, brought with it a loss of the tradition, which had been tainted by association with nationalists. The arrival of university-level study of English literature simply sealed the rift: young people were to do close reading of poetry as a way of avoiding being intoxicated by it. Continuity was torn away, just as continuity with the *fights for the flag* poetry of the period 1890 to 1918 (roughly) ceased to be possible. We seem still to be in that historical moment, where modernism, banality, and academicism meet; facing a crisis of poetic language, and acquiring a deep inhibition about using verse drama or narrative. The attitude studies of UKIP voters show they still possess the aggressive nationalism which poetry had in

1905 or 1915; the least educated are the least affected by shifts of opinion mediated by print. The cultural situation was quite different in 1930 from 1917; I don't know who carried this legislation, but I don't think they had their seat in Brussels.

It is depressing to think that the ur-model for several common genres of poem is the lesson plan. I certainly wish that people were less influenced by the history they studied in primary school and more by the data structures which you encounter doing a degree in History.

If we could spy on writing workshops we would hear this exchange so often: "my poetry is important because it's unimportant" with everyone else in the room retorting "*au contraire!* Your poetry is unimportant because it's unimportant". It is quite reasonable to think that getting away from the display art of the royal family and the upper 1% to see humble lives for a bit would be a relief and desirable. Another common exchange would concern whether someone writes about personal experience because the collapse of the sublime is a kind of habitat devastation and people have withdrawn into the personal as a last resort. Poetry may be what was abandoned, its only location in realms from which we have withdrawn. Of course someone can retort that they write personal poetry because signals from close by the sense organs are unattenuated.

Seeing links everywhere is one of the cognitive enhancements that paranoia brings. But if you can't see any links at all then you can't write a significant poem because the connections are what give it weight and value, to unlock the symbolic tier. At mid-century people could site poems inside theology, or Marxism, or patriotism plus the Empire: giant webs of powerful transmission belts. But all of these webs were in trouble by about 1956, where there is a general satiation with propaganda as the age of commitment has burnt out and discredited its faithful writers. This satiation is still in force.

There is a specific response to it. We can approach it through the discipline of history. David Lowenthal (in *The Heritage Crusade*, 1996) has described a new market of the 1980s: "Modern preoccupation with heritage dates from about 1980". Clearly, the project of describing history as a process where the rich oppress the poor has won. Everyone can see it is true. It has lost its force. Moreover, it is divisive and the new middle class do not want to hear it. The government, especially, does not want anybody to hear it (Lowenthal mentions Reagan and Thatcher, in that same sentence). As a project, it is being replaced by a leisure industry approach to the past, where the central thing is tourism and a torrent of new museums is offering the past as role play, as a sort of costume drama. Historians are trying very hard to write stories that don't re-live the old right-left oppositions. Heritage has replaced the history of the poor and of struggles over land-ownership.

We do have public debate in this country. One feeling is that everything which had been the subject of argument has become tired, vexed, infertile. But what people argue about is what is important. Withdrawing from it is a trip into insignificance. If you have a poet who has been writing away for forty years and never said anything about feminism or masculinity or role acquisition, they may have avoided the vexed areas but they have also chosen not to articulate what matters to people. Privatised poetry moves towards a pose of being merely decorative and tangential.

In parallel, we had the new genre of micro-history. The key works are *Montaillou, village occitan de 1294 à 1324* and *Carnaval à Romans* by Emmanuel Le Roy Ladurie. Both deal with history in a very confined time and area (one is 14th century and one 16th century). That is their force. Paris is over the horizon. The stories are completely new – escaping the acquired tedium of clerical-secular, republican-monarchist, etc. struggles, that have lasted for hundreds of years. The idea that a political dispute, in 1580, between two class factions in a small town in the valley of the Isère, could produce a great book (also a best-seller) was bizarre.

Poetry, since 1980, has repeatedly tried to reproduce the success of *Carnaval à Romans*. It has escaped the genuine lines of history. If you follow the tangential and provincial path, eventually you reach the domestic realm and regard that as success. Religion too is a lost centre. People have been writing micro-poems, which eagerly lead us to the periphery of being – even if that is where new sensations are, logically, found. They seek out the tangential. This uncontroversial poetry is quaint, detail obsessed, peripheral, unfamiliar. It does not get beyond the status of trinkets, jingling and twinkling. Such poetry deals with sensations, to the exclusion of ideas and arguments. It is determinedly original, offering new fabrics or fruits. It is (tacitly) affluent, because it offers situations where compulsion or want do not exist. It asks us to be collectors of sensations. Because disconnected, it is un-insistent. It does not answer any questions you have ever wanted to put.

Bourdieu writes about something called social reproduction. Society certainly does reproduce itself, and this process is decentralised. Children acquire the rules of society mainly through face to face interaction, which means that the people who are actually there are the influences and that they are agents of social reproduction. It follows that a writer recording the daily life of ordinary people could capture this key process. Questions like "how is it that children in families of two different ethnic groups acquire ethnicity and deploy it in everyday life" or "where does the difference between the behaviour of men and of women come from (and how can it be changed)" could presumably be answered by detailed observation of the life of children. I must say that I have not seen any poems which have much to say about these processes. I am doubtful that poetry can work as sociology.

Everyone agrees that insignificance is a feature of contemporary poetry. The line where significance is parted from anecdote is not always easy to draw. But a convincing theory of the inconsequential, pleasing, and uncommitted would be consequential. This theory would tell us that our lives must have moments of significance in relation to our lives, their other moments. Significant poetry would deal with behavioural rules and not just farm waggons. Because social structure is stored in our heads, not in buildings or rules we don't understand, you do not need to go to the capital to find it. Rules are decentralised and would have no bearing on daily life if that were not so. The rules we are looking for must be small enough for individuals to learn them and apply them. This means that poems about everyday life can expose part of the structure of our society. Norms do not apply to an ego as an isolated and contactless thing but to groups of at least two people. So they are collective even if a unilateral attitude invades them. Poetry comes out of face to face interaction but there may be collective rules which organise such interaction and push it down predictable channels.

Poets who simply want the reader to like them and listen to them end up proposing themselves in intimate surroundings so that the reader thinks the intimacy is offered to them. They have noticed that ideas excite people and raise divided opinions so they are very keen to avoid ideas. They end up with domestic anecdote.

It is possible to think that the definition of a role comes from the practice of envy and imitation. The role is separated from the whole person because someone else wants to take it on, to put it on. In poetry, the part played by envy and imitation is large. Successful models are a focus through which poets construct what they want in the form of standing and esteem. The process of self-criticism is one way in which reflexivity can be reached – at the end of a long path which most people do not follow.

Laibach

We are going to consider the influence of Denise Riley's poem 'Laibach Lyrik: Slovenia, 1991', published in the volume *Mop Mop Georgette* in 1993. The poem originates at a point when there were wars in Yugoslavia and the topic of nationalism was on people's minds because there was no other reason, apparently, why nearly interchangeable population groups were fighting each other in the south-east of the continent. Denise went to Ljubljana and hung out with various Slovene Hegelian-Lacanians. Laibach is the German (or Austrian, obviously) form of Ljubljana and the city was known to a wider world, during the Austro-Hungarian Empire, as Laibach. Riley was attracted, earlier on, by the kind of philosophy which Maurice Merleau-Ponty wrote. One line of this was a separation between what was in a public record, like a famous text, and what happened locally, in individuals. So he separated what an academy knew from what happened in the cognitive world of an individual. They only knew what had been in the room with them; it was all local. What they acquired was less stacks of facts than distinctions – categories which limit each other, along the lines of intersection.

It was possible that if you could record all the moments of becoming of a person then you could explain what kind of person they were and why they had become that person. Riley applied this to the dark area of national identity. In the poem, she imagines herself going back to the state before the self and thereafter having experiences of becoming which made her (or, would have made her) a Slovene. This evoked a special type of category, one which categorises human beings. It had rules for determining what was inside and what was outside, like other categories. By setting out the steps of acquiring self-perceptions so clearly (and with all distractions erased from the text), Riley exhibited a process which you could imagine in reverse. Of great interest was the thing which was changeable but which forfeited the ability to change as it acquired distinctions; some moments of acquisition were one-way gates.

I don't know why the poem is called "Laibach Lyrik" instead of "lirika v Ljubljani" or something. All these years later, it occurs to me that it might refer to a blank page. "Laibach" is a form which precedes a Slovenian republic, arguably precedes a Slovene identity. The word Laibach arguably represents a blank slate, when the area of Carinthia was a Hapsburg fief with no constitution, no awareness, and no official documents (except those in German or Latin). Moving out from the word Laibach could therefore stand for a blank page – for the extreme lower left point of the graph. Exit from the Hapsburg aggregate was a forerunner of the moment of exit from the Yugoslav aggregate.

The last line of the poem includes the words "I am Illyrian", and the *lyr* string repeats part of the word *lyrik*. Illyria appears as a non-existent country in Shakespeare (next door to Illusory) but also, around 1809-14, the Illyrian provinces were a part of Napoleon's Empire which included Slovenia. This poem supplied a poetic model. Many poets have written about these moments of becoming. This has not always gone well. I am sure this poem has been influential. But I could easily dredge up thousands of poems which weren't influenced by it. At the risk of losing focus, I can use this as an illustration of how hard it is to write literary history when the apex has been widened so vastly, and the number of poets to be considered is so high. Should I locate a hundred significant models and list the poets who have used each one?

My impression is that something philosophical like "Laibach" silently defines a large number of poems which have no philosophical merit at all. It is obviously not enough to record any old memory from childhood and think that it opens any kind of intellectual space at all, let alone uncovering the mysteries of becoming. This is not surprising, since most poets are not intellectuals and their poems are unlikely to record abstract processes which are not going on in their brains. For me this is a question of status anxiety. Poets are not content with being excitable and narcissistic, they want also to be intellectuals. That would give them more status than other excitable narcissists. But this must be a mistake. Evidently most poets aren't intellectuals. But what they are is more admirable than their aspirations.

I have to ask why "Laibach" starts with a beautiful evocation of a landscape with birch trees. I feel that the validity is dual; first, that you can't say which country these trees are in (and that nationality is an overlay on trees as much as it is an overlay on young humans). Secondly, it is when the lens opens and very bright light falls on it; the sensory vividness of the landscape poem is the stimulus which makes the mind available to do philosophy.

We don't only know what impinged on our skins and nerves, there is also public knowledge. As soon as you can watch TV, locality doesn't apply across the board. Noticeably, it is meaningless for someone to decide they are Slovene if there are not 1.8 million other people (roughly) also deciding that they are Slovene too and so giving the category a substance.

Poets want brief moments to be significant because they don't have the linguistic and intellectual equipment to write about long-term processes, which are certainly what build up identity (at a millimetre a day, or 1/10 mm, or whatever). However, 'Laibach' actually was a defining moment for British poetry.

Home Front and domestic anecdote

We see a difference between a preset social role and the exercise of freedom as the basis for behaviour in the social realm. People experience this difference at moments when they say, because *I am a girl*, because *I am the youngest person in the room*, because *I failed my exams*, my choices are restricted. Sometimes people also experience this as a honeycomb of rigid cells which they can move through without being able to construct a cell of their own with rules set by them. Sometimes a poem is seen as a space without constraint where the parts of a scene are soft and open to freedom of choice. It is possible to think that history can supply a timescale and factors for the development of these roles and that anthropology can supply a comparative account of them.

There is a contrast between the importance of the household as the place where children acquire roles, and the banality of most poetry being written. If the household is important, therefore central, then domestic poems should be more interesting than they are. The same applies to child-care centres, schools, and other face to face interactions.

I find the history of this problem to lie in war aims. In the 1940s, the country was submerged in propaganda against Fascism. The war was alleged to be a contest between two ways of life, a claim which involved a cellular uniformity in Britain, with every family behaving in the same way, and that way involving fairness, equal rights, tolerance, and so on. This was what was under threat. The home was worth fighting for because it was non-Fascist. There was a reaction against propaganda even in 1943, but the stories carrying the message were very persuasive and even seductive.

After 1945 the propaganda was discontinued, but there was a massive media push to support the Cold War. This was a war on the Home Front in two senses. First, nuclear war (the proposed event once the USSR had developed atomic weapons, so from 1949 on) was going to destroy the civilian population. Secondly, the perceived difference between Communism and the Free World was in prosperity, not for the elites but for the average household. Thus the proposal was to win the Cold War through household consumption, and the new genre of TV adverts was the image gallery showing the Free World winning. So you have less propaganda but you have lots of advertising which looks like the same thing.

So when someone wrote about a family (the favourite subject of 50s popular art) that could include the issue of nuclear war through the threat to this family and especially to its children. The point of view shifted to be that of the children, and simultaneously a search for origins was taking place. When the undemocratic values of 'the other side' seemed basic to the nuclear problem, the 'democratic values' seemed to have a geographical source, in the West, and a temporal one in childhood. Critics repetitively probed the work of poets for "values" and the poets complied by exhibiting these. The difference between *showing values* and *propaganda* seemed important at the time but tends to vanish in retrospect.

In America, the family poem evolved to become the confessional poem, where the poet occupied the role of the child in a family whose tensions supplied the drama unfolding in the poems. This genre was inspired by psychoanalysis and often had to do with divorce. It offered a way of writing about family structure which could be used by feminist poets, whose disagreement with social roles naturally led them to look at primary socialisation as what happens in childhood.

This set of conventions became familiar to poetry readers and at length gave poets a sort of household appliance with which to construct domestic poems. Thus, moments from childhood could be read as significant 'moments of socialisation' which had an effect in adult life. A scene from the life of any family could be written as a critique of the family structure in general. The idea of *family structure* allows us to conceptualise a mass of face to face interactions. The domestic machine generates nationality as well as gender roles. Its results give us a definition of ethnic belonging: it is not to do with fighting when the state makes war, but to do with the roles which are carried out within a family and which a family inculcates. In fact it is the contrast between people from different cultures which allows 'family structure' to emerge into daylight as a concept which we can carry out mental operations with.

I can imagine an account of British social structure in a million pages. It would be like printing out the programs on the hard disc of your PC. I am going to avoid doing this – to economise the million pages. My interest is in detailing how some poems make social structure visible (without writing it out), and some fail to rise above the concrete and private. Autobiographical material could be given a value beyond the purely individual and ask us to think about how things work. Of course this was hard to manipulate, and could turn out to be dull poets simply recording trivial moments from their lives and hoping that a meaning would somehow attach itself. I am not claiming that recent poetry has achieved this programme in large quantities. It is an ideal. You are being asked to think that in thousands of days of childhood a single scene was triumphant and overwrote all the other scenes. This is not very credible but modern poems prefer single moments, single images. If I could make a generalisation, it is that all poets think that all their poems about domestic moments are the foundation for deep consideration about the meaning of family life; whereas for the most part the way they write prevents the reader from thinking about anything. So a key question when criticising poems is 'which concrete features of this verbal assemblage *prevent* thought, theorising, critical reflection, etc.?'

Piling up a catalogue of detail actually makes the conceptual moment invisible, it chokes the possibility of theory. The ideal is there to offer a way out of writing domestic anecdote – a genre which most poets practise and which most readers agree is numbingly tedious. Poetry which is merely surface is of little interest. At the risk of leaving a thousand issues unresolved, I am offering an explanation of why people think domestic anecdote is a potent genre and why the bulk of poetry being written (but not of the good poetry) belongs to this genre.

Domestic anecdote

There is some doubt about who originated the term *domestic anecdote*, but anyway the prevalence of tedious realist poems about ordinary life is a feature of the scene. The extraordinary feature of the era is the number of excellent poets, not the number of people scribbling away without an idea in their heads. When we see so much banality, though, we are bound to connect this with problems with accessing the elevated or sublime manner of speech. We can put this in schematic form.

> *Christianity.* Has special elevated language. Unavailable to poets today due to loss of belief.
> *Classical poetry.* Has special elevated language. Unavailable to poets today.

Legacy of great English poetry. Has several different special elevated languages. Unavailable to poets today. Tradition has been rejected.
Marxism. Has special super-generalised language derived from Romantic idealism and from Greek philosophy. Unavailable to poets today.

It is quite possible that banal poetry is prevalent because there are style/status problems with the right to use any of the available elevated styles. The problem may be with anxiety about power; the claim to power is unacceptable because of the lack of standing of the poets– they seem not to have aligned themselves with any source of authority. A lawyer has to cite laws that actually exist. Poets actually seek unofficial status.

It seems that there has been a distinction between prose and poetry here, namely that prose still has access to the sublime, in ways derived from Marx or from Hegel, for example, whereas poetry does not. A role is played by theory in contemporary literature and this relates often to status anxiety. A statement with a high theoretical component is felt to possess high status. In the education system, people internalise this ranking by seeing how their essays are marked and how books are reviewed. This is problematic when it involves assertion of status: *me anthropologist – you native*.

Clearly there is a modern way of writing ambitiously which has shed all the furniture of Victorian poetry. Does this relate to modern theory, as the institutionalised set of linguistic patterns, valid or not, to which it refers back? No. Theory has a limited role in the poetry world because the technique which poets use for writing is very dissimilar to the theory you see in the bookshops, being noticeably intuitive, improvised, all-over, egocentric, and resistant to analysis. That is – it may be a theory in the sense that it gives you rules of decision which let you write bad poems, but it is dissimilar from what is academically legitimated. A lot of poets strive to remove abstractions from their poems. This may cause the style to resemble the speech of 7-year-old children, which also has few abstractions. We could ask a lot of questions about this convergence. Fear of abstraction is one route by which you can make poetry trivial and anecdotal. Do poets want to sound helpless and in need of protection from adult life? Do they succeed?

Poems on Communal Wellbeing

Keith Jafrate, *Songs for Eurydice* (2004, 136pp).
Jafrate is an original writer. He doesn't fit into any of the self-promoting groups and seems to have made a career mainly as a jazz musician. His poetry is led by a sense of emotional identity, a cultural style, rather than one internal to literary history. His base since 1987 seems to have been Huddersfield and its region, and his publishers have mainly been in a tight geographical space north of Trent. If face to face interaction is a key, maybe there is a geographical aspect to taste because waves of formation and identification attenuate as they spread. His line is organised to keep the eye moving, it doesn't want to reach flatness (a dead halt) or a generalisation. The goal is not knowledge, as an asset, but to seize the next moment of experience, the next frame. It follows that this poetry is not interested in the educational assets of abiding knowledge; rather its goal is within itself and its centre is close to the goal. What I think has the jazz touch is its serenity – the writer is perfectly at ease and the poem generates its own time. There is no feel that we are moving towards an end, but there is never a sense of time being short. This is what a musician in unscripted music has, I guess, that the music always is in the present. This lets you feel free; it pushes you into uncertainty, perhaps risk, but also makes verbal routines fall silent. The title page kicks off with a quote from Buenaventura Durruti, not a poet but an Anarchist military leader (in Valencia) during the Spanish Civil War. *Eurydice* is a long poem (135 pages) with a remarkable sweep.

> here is the body without language
> weaker than a bird
> colder than a bell
>
> the body pretends to wait
> somebody moves it
> the body dances
> shivering and waiting
>
> dead names the size of buses
> pass the body traveling
> from continent to continent

take a Tom Cruise
use a Madonna
smoke The Whales
Coke washes whiter

the body rolls in fire
execrating curtains
gates and climbing plants
telephones the talking clock
and curses it

the body savages cities
writhing like a fish in the dust
somebody locks it up
somebody finds its language
to sentence it

This is from section 9, 'body lyrics', about the consequences of incarnation. The body is given language as an aperture on an abstract world which turns out to be filled with pervasive and trivially egoistic messages. Eurydice was the wife of Orpheus but the poem doesn't so much have a plot as a series of emotional centres around which clusters of images form. It is divided into sections, so that part 1 is about the love of a woman (possibly the Eurydice of the title) and 2 is the descent into the Underworld, showing the rooms of Hell. Part 3 is 'a little song of rain', four is 'bird song', 5 is 'at Cerne Abbas', six is 'ghost tribunal' and is about fear, about the environment being hostile to human life. 7 is the 'song of Orpheus' and is about flowering. 8 is 'by the fire'. The serenity of the movement, the beauty of the tone, also contain an instability, as Jafrate is deeply discontented with the society around him and its compromises of any organic life, and the natural reaction of the poet is dissidence and revolt. A key sound is vulnerability, the speaker wanders around the world, exposed to it, and reacts with immediacy and vividness. The poem descends immersively into the rooms of hell and their measuring scientists, into the tracts of the human-ruined landscape, but is perpetually moving and hoping. The political dissent isn't based on abstraction, on books consumed in solitude, but on life being lived, and on the contrast between authentic existence and the compromised version which he sees around him. *Eurydice* says:

Poems on Communal Wellbeing 141

   madness of numbers
   madness of tongues
   un stylo the children whisper
   m'sieur un stylo
   give me a pen
   to unlock the stone
   the builder imprisoned by percentages
   the house on a wave's hill
   your face its lamp

   in this poison land
   on a humpback bridge
   alone with the cooling towers
   sieved acres
   coffee-dark and black
   gulls and bulldozers
   chunks of water left in pits

This is from part 4 and the theme is apparently how the creative are not free as birds but must offer their creations to the corrupt and soulless, the ones with the money. The "poison land" is hostile to birds. If political change is going to debouch into a new life, it has to start with knowledge of a life that we can actually lead (and not an abstruse book by Adorno). Part 5 must refer to the Cerne Abbas giant, a hill figure set out in chalk. We can usefully compare this to Jeremy Hooker's *Soliloquies of a Chalk Giant* (1974), a sort of poem-myth about the same figure. The giant may re-appear at the very end of the book. I want to quote from this part 5 to illustrate the difficulty of paraphrase:

    soft motioning space bigger than a dream of ocean
    dark inside darkness
    that has consumed all forests
    infinity of wheels in collapsing green
    honeycomb inside honeycomb inside honeycomb
    sleep flight into surf
    containing every change contained by change

You may say, right away, that this doesn't relate to anything outside itself. But I am guessing that it relates to the green downs around Cerne Abbas, infinite because they extend to the horizon. The sea may be present because the chalk was formed as tiny shells on a sea-bed. The infinity is also the giant's perception, fixed in space but transcending time. The language starts from the death of the ego and makes self-restarting cycles visible. The grammar is mainly paratactic – it does not use syntax to make plain an argument, a set of relationships, which are nonetheless present in the fabric of the text. He does not draw conclusions at the end of poems. Emotions are also not signalled, for the most part – the whole flow is the emotion. The text addresses us with whorls and peaks, glides and swoops; frame shifts, refrains, turns and returns; flare-ups and coolings; spectrum shifts. The *way* he writes is outside time but belongs to a moment in serial time. Actually, it is because so many people in the Seventies, or in the time after 1968, felt in a certain way about politics, alienation through work, the distribution of wealth, etc., that Jafrate does not have to explain himself formally – he shares in a "solidarity within dissidence". If he dissolves causality, that may be because he wants to go to a place at the edge of socially agreed coding and overlay, where there is no knowledge. Freed from finished explanations, we can start to construct new causal patterns – with fewer institutional hindrances. The less the poet offers categories and judgements, the more space there is to think about how society came to be.

I am going to quote from the piece in *Tears in the Fence* 32 (2002), which has not appeared in any book:

> how to push sun along these hills
> that is trapped in tiny chambers used
> to hammer levers that turn gears in
> tiny repetitious detonations
> of wealth
> like mountains of pennies of energy
> burnt to gas to
> tiny grey
> unseen shrouds erased shadows
> falling
> hoards we cannot gather
> cannot spend
> how to unravel the meadow of work
> woven into any machine
> again

> how to begin again
> life for life
> to each according
> to need
> from each
> according to ability
>
> a boy passes through the graveyard walking two greyhounds
> the high trees fill and seethe
> clashing dancers armoured with fish
> the wind wants to shift everything
> lift everything

(title is 'neither created nor destroyed', which is presumably a definition of 'energy'. Work is what energy does, and is the theme.)

Toby Martinez de las Rivas, *Black Sun* (2018; 55pp)
Black Sun is said to be part two of a trilogy of which *Terror* was part one. *Terror* (2014) already includes the black dot, as a printer's ornament. It would be irrational to ignore the title of that first book: a carving on the lintel, presumably. There is a problem in assessing the work before the third part has been published. Martinez has made a provocative statement: 'perhaps the truly radical now would be to see a deep political shift from the left to the right, or the substitution of a committed neo-Georgian ruralism for a (de)constructivist urbanism in the halls of innovative poetics.' He was talking (in an essay in *PN Review* in 2014) about two forgettable poets, Clemo and Sisson. He has a specific problem with a kind of avant-garde Left poetry. There was a small brouhaha in which the black sun symbol was claimed as a claim of Fascist sympathies: Ira Lightman described this as "a horrendous bit of clickbait gotcha". It was based on poor scholarship and this interpretation of the symbol is wrong. If he had substituted the word *Angst* for the word *terror* he would be much more in the swim. Apparently people whose stock in trade is a critique of the modern world are indignant that Martinez has a deep unease about the modern world.

Black Sun presents as a series of personal poems in which the central experience can be reconstructed, with the help of interviews, as divorce and separation from his wife and child. The poems are about isolation, doubt, regret. It is where a duet turned into a monologue. The key structural decision is to have 55 parallel poems with similar structures – this is a drama about attention span. Evidently the work acquires force by persisting, it is more like a tree root, stressed by the weight of the whole tree, than a bird. What Rivas likes least, we suppose, is fantasy or theory – the intermittence which some people take for freedom. The meter and syntax stress continuity, every moment joins up to the others without (modern) jumps or interruptions. The emotion is also continuous – a steady signal for a steady state. He is not trying to be entertaining, as in a conversation, by moving rapidly from one idea to another. The time sense is of very long spans and this is why the language is grave and massive. He assesses his own worth not as a charming companion but as an ancestor, aligned with the forebears of several generations whom he invokes. A poem is labelled in a marginal note as "Allegory of the Church/ Hanged Owl" (which is a title according to the contents list). He describes how in a high barn, up at the top where there is permanent dark:

> an owl revolves, strung by the neck in rings
> of wire. A gorgeous ruff now mocked with blood,
> one claw hooked through the noose, one wing let fall[.]

The poem goes on to find the black sun motif in the owl's eye. The bird's sight is described as *glimme*, which is Middle English and is like our word gleam apart from the vowel quantity. Because it is swinging, and because we hear of a breath ('gauzy breath'), it may still be alive: it can see, and turn its neck. The symbolism may be that the church in modern times, or at least now, is like a pinioned owl: beautiful, but noosed. What could see in the dark is now just seeing the dark. *Glimme* may be a faculty, like glimmering; a glimmering of the truth. The owl was associated with wisdom. A barn can be like a church, with a hall shape and a high ceiling where the air is dim. The owl is like a monstrance, or like the suspended trophies, in certain churches, known as achievements.

    Each poem describes a concrete moment and each is continuous, written in verse which expounds feelings throughout. Frame shifts and montage are avoided. The feelings are not those of a moment, even if they are ones which we wish would go away. The different occasions of the poems are presented as tests. Of feelings which he is, probably, unsure of. Their memory shows the constancy of those feelings. Also, they are halfway towards the symbols which are so important to the poems: the memories say something is true and the symbols say something is true. They are sensory objects but record truths about the emotions and relations between humans. Martinez trusts his intuitions far more deeply than most contemporary poets. One could almost speak of the others undertaking risk limitation in this regard. He is not concerned with taking primary pictorial thinking and reducing it to analytical propositions. He wishes instead to sink into the picture and let its thin integrity bear his weight. The power of his image complexes is obvious and has attracted more attention than his contemporaries.

Rivas cites, in two poems, a few words from a song by Peter Hammill recorded in 1973. If we listen to 'In the End' we may imagine Rivas' poems being sung by that voice. We note that it is an introspective monologue, a full seven minutes simply about the singer's feelings. It is strikingly bare: Hammill had a band, but this is just piano and voice. He is using language to speak about the exit into silence. He is almost using sensory deprivation to promote introspection. The few surviving sounds are very strong, like the rushing of a river in which we immerse. The poems are like ashlar, stone cubes; they are massive and seem to have endured much time. It is reasonable to think that they embody suffering by embodying time and that as far as they are cyclic they sustain the hope of resurrection. They are static, in a way; we do not see anxiety coming and going even if this is its nature. Each one records a moment, a day perhaps, and a visual and tangible sensation vivid enough to disperse dark ideas and fantasies. There is a scheme of half-rhymes which adds solemnity; they give extra weight to the ends of lines, which actually slows them down. The hope is that these scenes are not evanescent, as in some *symboliste* idea of consciousness.

Martinez says in interview that he wanted a printer's sign to separate the four sections of the book. "[...] I was toying around with images and motifs. I sketched a much larger circle into a document and infilled it with black, and I was suddenly aware of it as a presence separate from me; or as the objective expression of something intimately mine. Staring at it, it seemed to stare back at me. I found something terrible about it, about its featureless, even, dense nothingness. But I sensed some kind of glory in it, too. I imagined a world turned upside down, a black sun rising over it. [...] In some sense, then, the book was a mere adjunct to the symbol, an attempt to elucidate what it meant. And I can only conclude, from the text, that it means many things." Attributing a propositional meaning to Martinez's symbols is almost like breaking a hole in them: we are being asked to respond affectively and with our physical being and not to analyse. It is immediately obvious that he is describing a state of deep misery. This exposes certain feelings about the modern world in which his capacity to feel is being nourished. He might be a character in a Peter Davidson poem; the Jacobites enjoyed a state of political misery which sought a Late Baroque expression. Just as the noon sun sheds radiance which illuminates the whole of the visible world and lets us distinguish shapes and colours, so the black sun, as its converse, sheds a dark radiance which reveals a whole world of dark and indistinct concepts and sensations, an eclipse of equity and truth. It seizes a planet as its fief and under its glow our senses give false reports. But the sun moves with celestial rhythms; it is likely to rise and to shed sunlight again.

He mentions Melanie Challenger in the preliminaries of the book and it may be that there is an affinity here. Not that either of them is literally writing 17th C religious poems, but that the shapes of those poems are at the back of their minds. Scenes of martyrdom and what has been called the dramaturgy of light in Baroque churches may be models for the words. Martinez says that the state is a body:

> across the State that is only
> an image of the body inviolate,
> the nation that extends through all time & space.

I find this problematic, since both States and bodies undergo metabolism, that is repeated changes, and they could only be inviolate under special circumstances. However, Martinez wishes to use bodies as vehicles for metaphor, and here he is setting up a human body to make statements about historical questions just as he uses birds to make symbolic statements many times in the book. He has surrendered to his intuitions, and frozen their external symbols. This is the intensity of the poems but also a breaking point, where we may not follow him. The State is not literally a body. But we are not here to find a way out of the poem, we are here to explore its path as far as it will sustain our footfall. If we search for a double of the hard word *inviolate* we might find *impassible* – sensations being transitory God could not feel them (cf. J. K. Mozley, *The Impassibility of God*). But as a man he was passible and suffered a *passion*.

In interview he mentions kenotic theology: "If *catharsis* might be translated as 'purification,' then *kenosis* would be 'emptiness' or 'emptying.' In the New Testament, the word has two applications. On its more technical level, it refers to the extent to which Christ fully becomes man, emptying himself of divinity, while on a more general level it refers to the will toward self-sacrifice in the service of others, an emptying out of self-love and self-regard" (interview, with James Brookes, in *Prac Crit*). Kenosis refers to a word *ekenosen* used by Paul (Epistle to the Philippians, 2, 7). The Authorised Version says "and took upon him the form of a servant", but the Greek says 'emptying'. Charles Gore, an Anglican bishop, made much of this topic around 1890. If Christ was still the Logos, he would have known he was going to rise again; he could have suffered neither pain nor fear on the Cross, so there was no sacrifice and no redemption. Christ 'kenotic', having forgotten his divine nature, is the only valid foundation for Christian myth. If the Christ had foreknowledge, his faith was never tested. If he didn't have foreknowledge, he wasn't God, who is omniscient. The literature on kenotic themes is huge. Martinez mentions the Georgians and it is credible that the loss of divine knowledge was connected to the loss, in the same decade or two, of the sublime measures of poetry, the ornaments and the poetic words, which led them to write so plainly. They were not talking Greek to God, or Prussian to Hegel. They wrote much about the rural poor, which has not been a feature of poetry coming after them. Christ needed a body to feel pain, this puts a stress on the body, which reflects on those who do physical labour, and connects also to Martinez's imagery of a body transcending. If God can sink into a human body perhaps the State can too. It is inviolate only in a deep way, battered at every other level of its being by ruin, disease, asymmetry, dissent.

The black sun is the hot sun after being emptied. Its rays are made of the anti-sublime, the darkness. The moment of redemption is that moment when the sun went dark, according to the Gospel. This is the unbearable moment of sacrifice; Christ suffers death and leaves the world. The dark sun represents the ignorance in which He is plunged because all men are in it, a noon of nothingness before the Resurrection on the third day.

I find Martinez's interviews very illuminating, but that just sharpens the perception that he is like a painter: the pictures belong to all of us and later accounts are good as responses but always incomplete. The pictures have to be interpreted, they shed meanings as the sun sheds beams, but they are not simply concepts coloured-in. We need to move towards the mythical pole of the linguistic realm in order to get any purchase on the poems.

Simon Jenner's long poem *Winstanley* (36pp, 2021) is a re-creation of the past. Gerard Winstanley was a reformer in the Civil War period who set up a commune near Weybridge in Surrey where people would work the earth and share the product with each other. He is famous less for this than because he was a great writer, issuing voluminous broadsides where he attacks the selfish and un-Christian basis of a society dominated by ideas of property, and suggests how life could be led if we accepted that individuals are not self-contained entities relating primarily to their property, but social beings relating primarily to other similar beings. His works were re-published by Penguin but their message was familiar in Britain mainly because of the writing of Christopher Hill, who along with EP Thompson was one of two historians essential to the Left of the late 20th century. I had to read their work (some of it) in the sixth form, as no doubt did many other people. Of course there was a hinterland of Left historians researching, for example the whole set of contributors to *Past and Present*, but those two were most likely to be in a bookshop. The long view of the past was necessary for forming a view of where you wanted society to go over the next, say, 300 years. Jenner's narrative poem, or series of monologues, pitches us into the middle of Leveller life:

> Immanence isn't naked, nor truth sheathed.
> Clarkson my antipodes you lode me, cold
> to leaden my opinion. Flamed licence –
> drossy surf of Birmingham – forged swords
> in your loud sheaths of air, you breathe
> your angles of misrule and retching housewives
> refting babes and ditching new ones
> for a fart of Heraclitus burning your bushes yet.

The poet has confirmed that it should read *angels* of misrule. Laurence Clarkson was a Ranter, an enemy of Winstanley and arguably much further Left. Hill's description is that Clarkson opposed the idea of sin, considering it to be "invented by the ruling class to keep the poor in order." *Refting* means snatching or robbing. There is a tension between recording concrete human beings in the 1650s, immersed in the horizon of the 1650s, and writing a poem primarily about life in 2021 and its people occupied with the future. Theological ideas, of beautiful visions and redemption, provide the vocabulary common to the two eras.

(I) ... try not to dwell on joys delved in a rising year.
I drave it in meeting, the silence, the spaces
we won forever, those absences between hedges,
those short hard breaths of scried ecstasy. These we take
on the slim trusts, words are invoked in quiet.
Elements burn this frail alchemy – in love
I mourn and celebrate the treasury of air.

Treasury of air is a turning of Winstanley's famous phrase about making the earth a common treasury. The treasure of air is breath, life itself. Winstanley was popular in the Seventies partly because poets saw the quality of attachment to other people, respect for their feelings, and rejection of fantasies of power and wealth and autonomy, as being the qualification for writing poetry. Winstanley had written a kind of theory of this. The language of the poem, slightly awkward, reflects the rhetorical style of English Nonconformism, soaked in the Bible and imitating its perpetually concrete images: the struggle to bring the concrete and the divine, the ideal, together in direct utterances is a record of a wider effort. Jenner's characters started with an ideal and then notched up a series of real years lived out under its influence; this gives us a place in which to imaginatively live out how our ideals could work out in a future (but real) time. The community came together around land and together insisted on working the land; burying seeds in the ground became a symbol of idealism, waiting in serenity for the eventual flowering of invested effort. The root of *equity* is a word meaning flat; the Levellers were so called because they wanted to level the inequalities between people, removing lords and bishops and the institutions which guarded them. This was also a way of referring to preparing the earth to bear: the effort of clearing all kinds of scrub, stumps, and stones to make a smooth field which the plough could be dragged over.

Jay Bernard, *Surge* (2019, 58pp)
In February 1981 a fire started at a party in New Cross in South London. The party was on the upper floors, it was hard for the guests to leave the building, and thirteen people died. In 1977 and 1978, fires had started at the Moonshot Club and the Albany Empire, two venues close to New Cross Road, and these fires are often regarded as being racist attacks on (respectively) a club with some Black clientele and a theatre which was a focus for anti-racist activities.

This is a series of poems relating to the 1981 fire and memory of a phase of Black activism in around 1981. Youth riots took place, also during 1981, and the word 'Surge' is a description of the riots as an insurrection (as in *in-surgent*). There is a whole doctrine involved here and it means rewriting history considerably. Some of the later poems are about being gay and about some reactions to the Grenfell Tower fire in 2017.

I read a newspaper story at the time (around 1980 or 1981) where a fire brigade senior officer interpreted many night fires as parts of a deliberate plan. All the fires were in houses occupied by ethnic minority families and all started in the dead of night. He regarded them as arson and complained that the police did not accept this interpretation. He thought it was more effective to catch the culprits rather than to let the fires happen and send a fire appliance once they had caught. I couldn't find a reference to this in an Internet search, but someone did see a larger pattern in events, rather than disconnected dots and strokes. The pattern trapped the shape of individuals sympathetic to the National Front, that is racialists, although it was not established who planned the series.

Bernard treats the New Cross fire as arson, but two inquests in 1981 and 2004 reached a different verdict. The text does not mention the inquests. A peak is certainly three poems describing dead people, presumably victims of the fire, conscious as if they were still alive, listening to people talking over their cadaver. One returns in a fourth poem.

My suspicion is that Bernard is writing about events 40 years ago because events today are too complicated to produce unambiguous conclusions. However, the reason why 1981 appears to be simple is that all the details have slipped out of view and Bernard is retrieving them very selectively. This simplified poetry works if it reaches someone who knows less than the poet.

The sentence structure is very simple throughout. It offers a semantic model with few elements. This can be interpreted as "voicing" the thoughts of simple people or else as making every other possibility invisible so that the explanation offered by the speaker is the only valid one. The approach is like talking to a child; every statement is made very clear. The link between restrictive language and a reductive view of events is embedded. The poet dislikes abstractions so that some of the poems are written in a sort of sea-shanty style. Some of the poems delve into states of grief, rage, and recalcitrance. The poet seems to hate London, only feeling secure in very restricted and predictable places and scenes; to distrust the English language and the substrate of people who inhabit it.

Some of the commentators were Marxists who expected that a revolution would occur, sooner or later, through a popular insurrection. Insurrections did take place in other countries, for example Iran in 1979 and Afghanistan between 1979 and 1994 (roughly). One did not take place in London.

My perception is that the riots in 1981 were direct responses to a deterioration of conditions, and to abuse, they were kinetic and reactive and there is a striking symmetry between the impact and the reaction. They were necessary and even part of the process. They were mirrors in which the government could have seen its true face, had it wanted to. The events started in the main streets of the towns, like other gatherings. These were also main shopping streets. The shops were full of display windows with luxury goods and it is plausible that the riots were there to display poverty, as a state of constant craving and self-denial, as a break from the high streets and the media constantly displaying luxury and consumption. No-one was spending a billion pounds to advertise poverty. In a town like London, riots are never segregated, and it is likely that the rioters were animated first by youth unemployment, secondly by bad housing, thirdly what is now described as "the breakdown of the post-war settlement", with politicians and most of the media denouncing people for being poor. Bernard does not mention any of these.

The poet is shown as spending time in an archive. Archive time is good, but the nature of the archive is as the output of Black nationalists and one has to ask if information about the history of London in 1981, and preceding years, is actually there, or if it just reflects specialised interests. If it was propaganda when written, it still is. Problems with Bernard's poem may connect to use of selective sources, which is the problem historians usually face. The documents compiled by a pressure group may reflect their policies and be altered by the pressure itself.

To reduce the events to milestones in the development of Black nationalism involves a very selective camera. It also involves a kind of piety. The belief must be that simplifying a set of events makes it more relatable, more literary. To identify only with a section of the population is attractive, but it is noticeable that a lot of people in London are either white or Asian. The proposal is that it is wasteful to identify with people of a different colour than you, and this is part of erasing the past in order to turn it into literature. It may be that all literature involves such processes, at one level or another. Bernard does not regard 1981 as a real thing, with real people. Politics is *all* about context. In a city of 8 million people, taking part in politics mainly involves learning that other people don't think the same way as you.

1981 was a peak year for unemployment and this fell disproportionately on the young, who had never had jobs and had no work experience or acquired skills. They had no money and their friends had no money. The riots persuaded a large number of people to start voting Conservative. The people who took part in the riots in July 1981 did not return, after the second day or even the first day. They were dissatisfied with the results. The media described them, afterwards, as people who liked to fight and loot. It became unattractive to have such people as employees and so youth unemployment came to be seen as a solution rather than a problem.

For each of these poets the interest is in public affairs but the impulse towards the personal limits the discussion of how society has been working. Perhaps a key scene is the movement of the Levellers to St George's Hill: an exit from the site of central power (occupied by other revolutionaries). The Levellers shrank their field of vision down to avoid disillusion. Equally, it would seem, poets draw bounds around the personal in order to protect the poem. There is a problem with scalability.

Local Knowledge

Part 1.
Elisabeth Bletsoe, *Birds of The Sherborne Missal*
(Shearsman, 2021)

"Sherborne Museum is housed in what used to be the gatehouse and almonry of the monastery once associated with the Abbey." The pretext is illuminations in a missal of c.1400 AD, once held in the Abbey, which show birds (mainly local); as there is a touch-screen version with replicas of the bird pictures in the local museum, and Bletsoe has worked there for a number of years, the images are a part of her daily experience. The book offers us 20 of these birds. A dozen of them have appeared in anthologies, but it seems that the final count is 20 and they are all here, also this edition has the pictures of the birds, in living colour – so it is clearly the one to get. The poet has remarked that "The Japanese haibun was loosely employed as its form is well suited to nature-notes and the similar sized blocks of text were visually pleasing […] The accompanying haiku allowed for brief word-sketch of the bird or its surroundings, which literally illuminated the whole", so each part is in prose and has a 14-syllable, elliptical, poem at the end. Loosely employed—we can hope that isn't like a zero hours contract for this venerable Japanese genre, often autobiographical and animated by a Buddhist sense of the ornateness and transience of natural creatures. So, the block prose in poem XI, '*Tayl mose*, long-tailed tit' is:

> Outside described as the colour of breath condensing on glass; the chill amnesia of fog. Instances of clarity & fading as if from radio interference. Shuttered sentences. Fur-gloved fingers of magnolia buds poke through submerged etymologies of such words as "garden", "enclosure", "boundary wall". Interiors hollowed by absence. Cross-quarter days herald the cessation of old land-tenure agreements, the lost chartulary of the town mapped by street-lights still tied to winter circuits. The inclusion, here, of a "decorative motif" enlivens the depopulated margins of the written page. A series of short, restless surges, inverted landings in the leafless branches of the Judas tree; *Jack-in-the-Bottle*, bottle tit, bum barrel. Hedge mumruffin. Elsewhere in

time, conversation alights on the two thousand six hundred feathers lining the nest; additions or subtractions made by researchers prompting immediate readjustments in favour of the preferred number. Dichotomies occur between the elaborated shapes of speech & an unarticulated persistence of the image within neural connections to perceived shifts in cloud strata. A moment of absolution among the accessories of horticulture; moisture droplets ringing the patrimonial bird-bath. Cursory insectivorous questing. Scarlet eyelid-wattles.

– and the haiku is:

> recall of tiny
> doll-sized memory   upswing
>   of an empty branch

where the core sensation is of something not being there and this moment of transience is the Buddhist part. The rebound just underlines the poignancy of the brief clutch of the senses – the memory is only doll sized.

We can start with a link back to the *English Intelligencer* (TEI) group, from 1966 on, with their conscious attempt to develop the basis for a new mythical English poetry, with the formula of 'Myth Geography Landscape'. One of the minor participants was Chris Torrance, who moved to south-east Wales in 1970 and later taught a creative writing class to think about myth and place – as laid out in his work *The Magic Door*. Torrance added an emphasis on performance. Bletsoe made contact with Torrance, in the late Eighties – and performed with a cabaret troupe, Cabaret 246, which led her to write the performance texts of *The Regardians* (1993) and *Portraits of the Artist's Sister* (1994). The troupe was named after the room where the writing class was held, and the ideas were also influential for Graham Hartill, Mark Williams, and Chris Ozzard. The angels of *Regardians* seem to like hanging around Cardiff; they also fit into warm New Age notions of personal guardians and guides. I have seen a photograph, possibly on a piece of 17th C English slipware, of a naive image where angels have the same body plan as birds; the Regardians sing and have wings, and we are allowed to think of them as analogies to the birds of the new book. Bletsoe also trained as a herbalist, and an accumulation of botanic detail was a step towards evoking landscape through dense, writhing language that, as it were, plunged several feet deep into the ground.

The poetic drama, the visible predecessor of the poetry reading, had scenery, even music. The solo reading offered up a poet isolated from anything except their text. The human figure everywhere is in space, and isolating the single figure of the poet actually made the space containing them more important. Shorn of rights to painted backdrops, poets could evoke space by verbal means. So there is a line of "live" poetry which describes spaces, taking over the space which surrounds both reader and audience and filling its neutrality. *The Regardian*s is a series of urban poems describing different parts of Cardiff – not obviously a theme for performance, but in fact this is a technique. Graham Hartill also writes a lot of poems about places.

An accident led me to read, just now, Günter de Bruyn's autobiography. As a librarian, in the communist part of Berlin, around 1948, he was weeding out unapproved literature but took most of it home. Something he especially liked was *Wolf Solent* (by J.C. Powys), of which, as I checked, a German translation came out in 1929. Dorset is also part of world literature. Thus encouraged, let me quote from *Wolf Solent*:

> Wolf tried to visualise the whole course of the Lunt, so as to win for it some sort of coherent personality. By thinking *of all its waters together*, from start to finish, this unity could be achieved; for between the actual water before him now, into which he could thrust his hand, and the water of that tiny streamlet among the mid-Dorset hills from which it sprang, there was no spatial gap. The one flowed continuously into the other. They were as completely united as the head and tail of a snake! The more he stared at the Lunt the more he liked the Lunt. He liked its infinite variety; the extraordinary number of its curves and hollows and shelving ledges and pools and currents; the extraordinary variety of organic patterns in the roots and twigs and branches and land-plants and water-plants which diversified its course. While he was thinking all this he had turned his attention away from Gerda; but now, glancing up the river, he was struck by a gleam of living whiteness amid the greenery.

This may be the source of the landscape poetry we are talking about. Perhaps everyone is pursuing a personal cult in the way that Powys likes to evoke, and landscape poetry is the unpent flow of religion once theology and the church corporations have dissolved. Stone was the churches' organ of corruption. This is not so Bletsoe-like, and we certainly have to admit to Bletsoe's high pulse rate – Powys is slow in comparison, and of course this heart rate is like that of the birds she is describing. The poems move quickly because they are about birds. Using the word *extraordinary* twice in one sentence is not a thing you can get away with in poetry. Anyway, I like that line Hardy – Powys – Bletsoe.

Bletsoe moved back, and wrote a series of poems, no longer about Cardiff, but about Dorset landscape. She wrote narrative poems with a strong dramatic element in which a central figure spoke, telling their story through an evocation of spaces, Dorset settings. She used Hardy heroines for several of these.

We can cling to the folk wisdom that to write about landscape you have to write something which works simultaneously as a statement about the landscape and as one about the ego which projects itself into the landscape. Work on delineating the self, projecting itself outward, creates a grip for the mind, tenacity which sustains the flooding in of the greater reality of land and space. Flowers of the field, birds of the air, are the organs of the landscape which stand in for it temporarily while a verbal equivalent for mass and distance is knotted together. The included detail allows the poem to include emptiness and space rather than being empty. *Birds* is strikingly closely stitched, a thousand concrete details about birds, folk artefacts, old land boundaries: it is intricated with reality, and with that part of Dorset, at every stitch. I just want to say that wroth silver is probably an old spelling in a source document, and we would write *wrought silver*. I don't think the silver waxed wroth at being drawn and hammered, it is a noble metal and was quite serene. "Wroth silver pays homage to the branched god, resplendent in deciduous velvet[.]"

Bletsoe's faith in the creativity of folk language, *mumruffin, jack in the bottle*, is astonishing, and the poetry is handed over to that vein to some notable extent. This just raises a question about merging with the source material, a dream where you can actually own that folk creativity and what you reproduce is going to be as exotic, concrete, warm, organic (etc.!) as the word *mumruffin*. I don't want to be too definite here, although I think you can see Bletsoe moving over this idea – lightly, someone walking on water. If you use the "capture method", the junction points between your (21st century) material and the source words are going to be sore and sticking out. Some process has taken place, probably over a long term, so that there are no starting seams in the Sherborne missal, no stumbles.

I wondered if the method of piling up motifs could be compared to collage, something which we did in primary school and can be called infantile. It also connects to crazy quilts, which are asymmetrical and made from patches of disparate material. And also to what we learnt in sixth form, that montage is a modernist method and heavy stuff. This is not yielding much in the way of descriptive accuracy, but my conclusion is (a) crazy quilts are not radical modernism (b) a rapid succession of ideas is not infantile. Editing is actually where intelligence comes out – as here, every junction is surprising and every sentence is fascinating. Arguably, the sheer number of patches is what makes the junctions acceptable and inconspicuous. I was interested by this one:

> conversation alights on the two thousand six hundred feathers lining the nest; additions or subtractions made by researchers prompting immediate readjustments in favour of the preferred number. Dichotomies occur between the elaborated shapes of speech & an unarticulated persistence of the image within neural connections to perceived shifts in cloud strata.

It feels as if the two sentences are mirrors of each other, in an incomplete symmetry. The stability of the ideal nest (so that the bird mends it if anything is altered) is like the stability of the cloud. 'Neural connections', of cells in the visual cortex to the sky, mean that a brain state is like the cloud; if the sky changes the neural network mends itself. So we can imagine the cloud as being made up of 2600 feathery objects (which give it buoyancy). Identity apparently changes as rapidly as the changes within speech, many hundred phonemes within a minute, but is stable at a deeper level. The juxtapositions are subtle but rich; they use the inexplicit to give a glimpse of the unknown. I am wondering if the motif is longer, so that "chill amnesia of fog" is related to the perception of cloud, and the lingering shadow memories of old land-boundaries (in the "chartularies") are related to the conservatism which makes the bird mend the nest: features that define place.

The missal points to the rise of lay literacy. There was an earlier stage when the congregation simply followed the service by hearing it, lost in communion. Having a missal you can read allows you to leave that moment. Because it is an object, you can take it home and read it on your own – we are seeing the start of privatisation here. That is the schema, not working so well if the missal belonged to a Sherborne monk, who by rule had few possessions and was an obedient part of a community. Is there a link to communities at a poetry reading? to performance arts? How do you keep the audience from breaking up again?

Moving on to 1966, it may be helpful to recall that one of the early influences on the TEI project was Ed Dorn, a friend of Olson, and Dorn was keen to say that "our poetry is bigger than yours because our territorial space is bigger". The link between the boundaries of the ego and the boundaries of the State was thus put on the table at an early stage. The point of the "myth geography landscape" project was partly to create the intellectual basis for an epic about England to be a riposte to *The Maximus Poems*, and partly to study the components of Englishness so as to catch up the poetry deficit which was much on people's minds around 1966. The thesis was that English poetry, as represented by Larkin or DJ Enright, had reached a null point in the early Sixties and had effectively ceased to exist. *TEI* was a research project to re-equip an industry, based in archaic craft practices and captive markets, whose goods had become unsaleable. Planners felt that local production might simply close down.

So the search for knowledge about the past of the territory was also a search for the origins of the components of the personality – actually a search for the reasons for creative inferiority. The external and internal factors were inseparable. The idea of spatial poetry is key for the 70s generation. Jeremy Hilton had also taken part in the *English Intelligencer* project, and edited a special issue of *Joe Di Maggio* (#11) on the theme of place, published 1975. He wrote, in a follow-up responding to criticism: "I do think it is significant that the five books which in my view gave our poetry the most important push to an exciting presence around the 1974 period" – he cites work by Allen Fisher, Ulli Freer, John Temple, Owen Davis, and Chris Torrance – "however different they were, had all very much a geographical energy-source." Hilton cites also Mottram's *1922 Earth Raids* and Sinclair's *Lud Heat* as place works that came out just after his anthology.

Clearly the geographical line in poetry had reached a peak by 1974. My understanding is that TEI did solve the problem, opening an era where, arguably, writing about landscape and its past was the dominant motif in British poetry. How someone whose grandparents are "not from round here" takes this on is not clear to me. Interrogating the components of national identity now involves comparisons – not certainly favourable ones and not certainly involving feelings of transcendent beauty and community when faced with, say, Avebury or Southwell Minster. If you want to say "this poem is your poem" you also have to say "this land is your land", and there is an inevitability about that. Because 40 people took part in the TEI project, and the alternative sector was so small at that time, it is easy to suppose that all radical landscape writing in Britain since then has been indebted to the *English Intelligencer* development work. But is that true? I find the links between different "spatial" poets are like a vast cable duct and even when I am in the duct I can't trace all the cables. Did TEI influence everyone? from those 40 participants, its ideas flowed in every direction, but maybe they didn't reach every floor? I don't know.

Part 2.
Tim Allen, Norman Jope, Mark Goodwin:
Portland: A Triptych (Knives Forks and Spoons, 66pp, 2019)

Bletsoe, while living in Cardiff, published her first two books with Odyssey, based in Somerset. (One of their editors was Tilla Brading, who has recently published landscape poems in the anthology *Edge of Necessary*, for example.) At a certain point in the early Nineties, I found that I was mainly preoccupied with poetry magazines from the south-west. So, *Odyssey, Tears in the Fence, Memes, Terrible Work, 10th Muse*. I have family links with the south-west, but I was living in London at the time and mostly people in London are only interested what happens in London. Why was it all happening in the south-west? I never found out. Asking "why" searches for a level of reality which the surface phenomena are wholly silent about. Jope and Allen were part of the "Plymouth Scene" in the early Nineties (as described by Steve Spence in TITF #73).

Portland is an island in Dorset which contains stone quarries. Bletsoe wrote that 250-line poem 'strandloper'; it is about Chesil Beach, the strand in question, and this runs for 29 kilometres with Portland at one end. Some passages of the poem are specific to Portland, "much to the chagrin of the islanders/ a high-minded race of phoenicians", and then we have a volume of works about Portland by three poets, Tim Allen, Norman Jope, and Mark Goodwin, none of whom (IMHO) is Bletsoe. So why do we have four people writing extended works about this tiny area off the south coast? Tim Allen grew up there. There are rumours that the Isle of Portland is really a peninsula, I keep an open mind about this.

This work was launched, if I recall correctly, at the Stourpaine festival in 2019, where Allen and Goodwin read from it, although Jope was mysteriously absent. I find it almost impossible to review, because the poets are so different from each other, but also that this is the drama of the book, that the shared subject matter and shared space make the contrasts even more highly visible and even more challenging. My problem is that the three poets are operating in different verbal universes, the book belongs to none of them and the contrast throws up difficult questions about the presuppositions, the buried decisions, which give rise to their language. The unconscious is forced to the surface and proves no easier to bring to terms than a geographical region.

Goodwin's work is interspersed with Allen's and consists of fragments of language, where the focal point is a disorientation where the direction in which the print runs and even the colour of the ink are varied. Our line of attention is dislocated. Syntax and grammar are dissolved, decentralised, and we are left with a scatter of gleaming fragments. A theme is the *oa*, the tiny fossils which form oolitic limestone, actually the shells of coccoliths. The tiny shells of language may even be a reference to these.

I am aware that Goodwin has also created sound sculptures, taking the raw acoustic material of poems and dissolving or expanding the system that binds them together. Sound and visuals. When someone sets aside the rules they actually foreground them – a mountain of rules structuring language, structuring cognition, which rises as if a great tide had gone out. *A Portland Triptych* does a lot of negative foregrounding (if I can say that?) and it is almost too much. A fourth part is drawings, by Susan Duxbury Hibbert, which seem to start from a flat, maplike version of Portland, and to mutate the textures of the map (18th C and helpfully reproduced on the cover, I think). "Drawing" is probably a misleading term for the visual processing by which these images came to be. Portrayal of the moon and its phases may refer to the influence of the tides on this coastal island; the cover superimposes what I guess to be the original map on the moon. Another theme is a spiral, possibly one of the petroglyphs mentioned by Tim Allen.

I guess that the place-writing of the Plymouth school was influenced by Sinclair, writing a mythology of London, because Sinclair was being read so much around 1990, when the Plymouth thing was being formed. Is this true? I don't really know. Anyway, Plymouth is an old city with a lot of social differentiation in its geography, which leads people to associate behaviour patterns with a locality rather than with individual character. The re-issue of Sinclair's *Suicide Bridge* ("a mythology of the south and east") includes a section about J.C. Powys, left out of the 1979 edition. Torrance's early books were published by Ferry Press or by Sinclair (Albion Village Press). We are seeing things fold onto each other here. Norman Jope published 'Tors' in 1990, which is already going out from Plymouth to the landscapes around. His work 'Veästa' mentions a fabulous beast spotted in the sea off Portland, but is for the most part an elusive narrative about a not closely identified character travelling to various ports: Aden, Valletta, Gibraltar, stages in the metabolism of a navy. The story belongs much more to Plymouth, the naval base, than to Portland (which, confusingly, isn't a port). The story evokes a whole political structure as its background, without being too specific, and sets up a series of enigmatic scenes as foreground to it. You can work out for yourself what you think about world power and its implantation.

> He strides, with an orange in his pocket
> and a stash of olives in his hand.
> He is parasite, he turns the world
> to scribbles in a battered notebook,
> destined for the archives.
>
> And even the hypogeum cannot hold him –
> spirals, hexagons, red ochre traces,
> swirling patterns and the echoes of riddles.
> The Sleeping Lady's face is as white
> as globigerina limestone,
> as coralline limestone,
> as oolitic limestone,
>
> as this creamy cloudy halva of limestone
> that is ghost-rock,
> moon-rock,
> papyrus of indelible silence.

The "he" may be either the Veästa monster or a travelling writer. (After this review came out, Jope emailed me to say that he wasn't thinking about the Royal Navy at all. So Plymouth, Gibraltar, Valletta, Aden, but it's not about the Navy.) The Sleeping Lady is a clay figurine found in the

Hal Safleni hypogeum, dug around 3000 BC. This is an underground chamber, part of the megalithic culture on the Maltese islands. (Sinclair mentions the hypogeum and Tarxien in *Lud Heat*; finding its design echoed in a machine-gun bunker near the River Lea in Hackney, re-designated as an "oracle chamber".) Thinking about landscape logically brought people to write about journeys. The landscape became a thought object only in its absence. And journeys may be the original stories. *Veästa* is fascinating by its juxtapositions, does not reduce to a neat summary. I can say that in

> Across the limestone plateau,
> the Potala of compulsion squats
> where pig-eyed window-slits
> conceal the crew-cut brethren

– Potala is a royal palace in Lhasa (and the building is a prison).
Tim Allen's piece 'Pontoon' includes this passage.

> The waves scrape Europe from the air. Coffee in your tea.
> England – an aquarium built for Leviathan but full of sprats.
> Sling your hook at your exciting desk you little bugger.
>
> The properties of the stone were a ghost's property.
> The proper way to speak earthed Earth to the dead real.
> Rich soil was some poor soul not a stone tonal everyone.
>
> The island refused any superior being's arbitration.
> Vindicate all then arrest the lot. Cogently petroglyphed.
> Asinine that religion is not plunged into its balmy doom.

A moment of explanation. If you start with a preset object to write about, such as a personality or a political doctrine, then over (say) 20 lines the poem will become more and more predictable, as it reveals more about its fixed intent. But if there is no such set object, line 20 of the poem can be as unpredictable as line 1 had been. The point is divergence. The line of predictability never inflects. There is no mood, no external object, which would lead the lines to curve back on themselves and repeat each other. Instead they march out into new terrain.

To put it another way, context disambiguates statements. Coherence sets up a context. Ambiguity is similar to unpredictability, and so coherence is very similar to predictability. But 'Pontoon' also includes recognisable autobiographical material. The subject matter is human beings, rather than the land poeticised as if there were no people on it. This is not what we expect from Allen. What we see may not be autonomous language but a cloud of childhood memories arranged to look like it. So "The experience of being/ surrounded by the sea can be compared to looking at radio" is the description of a memory. It may be (roughly) 350 lines in 'Pontoon' are all parts of Allen's past. "The proper way to speak earthed earth to the dead real" could mean that "learning to speak deferentially (and insincerely?) stabilised property relationships and helped us to memorise a state of affairs which we were no longer able to transform, so that we lost consciousness". Does it mean that? yes, probably. The line about "stone tonal everyone" somehow means that the good soil is the product of organic remains breaking down, and everyone else gets the stony ground (and has to hew and carry it for a living). The relational frame jumps in almost every line. This can cause perplexity, but its goal is to stop us from getting bogged down in a habitual pattern. This is an autobiography, quite unlike the rest of his work or any other autobiography. It raises the question of how his other work relates to his experiences, to his feelings about the world. Maybe the predilection for autonomy is a way of breaking out of insistent and over-loud patterns imposed by the outside world.

I glanced at the Knives Forks and Spoons website and saw what seems to be 120 volumes of high-octane small press weirdness. OMG. WTF. XXX. Undoubtedly I should have read all of them. But I haven't. Somehow I feel weak and overwhelmed. *A Portland Triptych* is full of innovative and unfamiliar verbal processes.

I suppose that we can see radical developments of language as being a way of getting away from the mundane, eternal love triangles, boy meets girl, cat meets dog, etc., and that this is also the initial motive for writing about landscape: that it gets away from the human. Language habits, behavioural habits. We go to extraordinary lengths to make our situation familiar and comfortable, this works best for what is within feet of us, and this is why art has to go out to a middle distance where this control breaks down and the unexpected can happen. Why set up your art in the one place where surprise is excluded?

Conclusion? The story of English, or British landscape poetry since 1966 or so is labyrinthine and not easy to memorise. Lines certainly lead from Powys, Olson, TEI, Sinclair. However, if you want to get with the English poetry scene, it is the heart of the matter. It is more exciting to list works than to refine rational propositions, so *The White Stones, Between the Cities, Lud Heat, Suicide Bridge, Metronome, Soliloquies of a Chalk Giant, No North-western Passage, Stane, Berlin Return, Lines for Richard Long, Hen Ddawns, Cennau's Bell, Brixton Fractals, In the Elements Free, Landscape from a Dream, Flatlands, The Face of It, Else, In the Assarts, Continental Drift, Tender Geographies*. The history is hard to trace also because hundreds of people are doing it – which is also why we want to find a few basic lines. Most landscape poems aren't very good. Paraphrasing a dictum about Dylan Thomas and the 1940s, writing like Bletsoe's is the best possible idea and trying to write like Bletsoe is a dumb idea that everybody else has. If you set out on a country walk with the idea of reaching a pleasant fatigue, and of going blank as troubles of the working week disappear, then the resultant poem is also going to be blank. The less you want to get anywhere in particular, the more the poetry starts to become vague and circular. Calling in drone-delivered drops of psychogeography, archaeology and ecology is just a way of evading the hard questions. The loss of the ego, hopefully temporary, raises the question of what language is for and what it relates to, in that situation. Space is by its nature passive and blank. It is indifferent to what shapes fit into it, and it forgets them. Poems, it follows, cannot simply take up the nature of space. Agreeably bumbling in the direction of The White Lion does not make for a poem. It is premature to speak of a Landscape Poet Monoculture threat. The poetry ecosphere has taken a lot of abuse but it is still resilient. The waterways will recover. The firebrats will return.

So much of the shared memory of the poetry community is in landscape poetry (and in landscapes); reading this poetry gets you closer to what insiders know. Also, the crisis that people perceived in 1960 or 1965 has dissolved away. Anxiety is not a precise mode of perception, anyway, but the objective problems have either gone away or are no longer persuasive in their claims.

Devolution and Disassembly

Devolution

In 1999 devolved assemblies came into power both in Wales and in Scotland (only the one in Scotland is called a parliament). In neither case did the change start a new area of literature, although it is reasonable to say that new funding streams brought a degree of comfort to local literary endeavours which had not always been there. There is a time shift effect whereby writers and intellectuals intensely lived devolution (or independence) during the years when it was withheld but had used up its possibilities before it actually arrived. Enthusiasm for new governmental arrangements was certainly there both in Wales and Scotland, but peaked long before 1999. Thatcherism certainly brought a peak of criticism of links with England. Some kind of anti-climax was inevitable after the emotional intensity of politics in those years. It is too easy to accuse Blair of decentralising in order to make life boring and free from conflict, but to a large extent decentralisation was rather boring and comforting and I suppose that the purpose of politics is to make crises go away and restore calm and routine.

Nationalist parties might seem to have more of a stake in arts funding for literature, especially in minority languages, but in practice the other parties don't want to get accused of not being national enough, so that devolution means more interest in arts funding (often seen as a way of encouraging tourism) from all parties.

As for the devolution, voices asking for it to be reversed have been inaudible. It is now a consensus arrangement; although one has to qualify that by saying that roughly half the Scottish electorate, and a bit less than that in Wales, want more of it. It posits the most substantial widening of the apex, as State power is given to a few hundred more people. National politicians always wield more power than local ones; the question is whether there is an illusory aura to it all, whether they are laden with power but make wrong decisions much of the time. Devolved politics involves less pomp and aura but better decisions.

New spaces for the Scots language

If the SNP has no language policy, then books about politics are not going to talk about it. The agenda is set and there is an emerging, or yawning, space of things that just aren't on it. I am recalling articles in the magazine *Lallans*, about 20 years ago, which drew attention to the lack of a question about the Scots language in the 2001 Census and suggested that there had been such a question but it was removed because admitting the existence of Scots would oblige the Edinburgh government to spend money on it. Later probes found that there was no interest in Scots among the SNP, officially, and that they didn't even have a policy on it. The website of the Scots Language Centre confirms my memories: "In 1994 the Aberdeen University Scots Leid Quorum was formed to campaign for a question about Scots language ability in the Scottish Census. By 1996 the General Register Office for Scotland had been persuaded to discuss including a question on Scots in the 2001 census. However, in 1997 the Scottish office rejected that. In 2000 MSPs debated a motion to include a question on Scots in the 2001 census. The motion was defeated. In 2001 a campaign group 'Forgotten Folk' was formed to campaign for a question on Scots in the census."

The SNP was thus the only nationalist party in Europe which had no interest in encouraging or reviving the national language. If you look at the relationship "Scotland is dominated by England" and then "Scots in Scotland is dominated by English" then you might continue to say "a Scottish nationalist movement would reverse the English domination both politically and linguistically". The reasons why that logic was never applied are quite interesting.

The new governmental class in Scotland has little interest in the language, and an accented form of English is what is spoken in Parliament and elsewhere. A bit of checking uncovered the fact that the SNP now has a policy about the Scots language. It was developed between 2010 and 2015 and is now enshrined in a policy paper. 2011 sounds a bit late, when the party had its first breakthrough in the 1960s, but the government they run is now funding a range of Scots institutions, including the Scots Language Society – which runs *Lallans* and was responsible for severe criticisms of official-nationalist approaches to the local language at around Devolution time. As the Scottish government website says, "The 2011 census included a question on the Scots language for the first time. 1.5 million people reported that they could speak Scots and 1.9 million reported that they could speak, read, write or understand Scots."

I have downloaded the Scots version of the policy paper and am very happy to see it. It starts "We wad like tae encourage ye aw tae recognise the valuable heritage we hae in the Scots leid and tae continue tae promote its popularity and recognition across sindrie aspects o Scottish life." Actually that is the third sentence. I put it there to show that the translation from English has gone wrong towards the end of the sentence, so it is really staying in English. The real start is "We are fair blythe tae be eekin on a cuttie innins tae this Scots Language Policy. We, in the Scottish Government, are continuin tae tak important steps tae heize the profile o the Scots leid." This has some inorganic moments, where official English turns into a register of Scots that doesn't currently exist (although maybe it did prior to 1603). The sound is a bit stiff but it is heartily welcome because this shows the old language growing taller – the creaks are the sound of new growth in an old tree. "eekin on" translates "appending", and "cuttie innins" translates "short introduction". (The same verb is spelt *eikit* later in the document.) A lot of word-creation has to happen, and Irish Gaelic is an example of how this task can be undertaken and brought to fruition. The Westminster government recognised the existence of Scots in 2001. Only 400 years after the Union.

The prevalence of Lallans follows socio-economic class – it is concentrated in income groups D and E. Within Scotland it does not signal "Scottish" but "lower class". This may explain why the SNP did not identify itself with it. If the early SNP spokespeople had gone on stage and delivered their ideas in broad Scots, they would not have been taken seriously (i.e. even less seriously than, in 1960 or 1965, they actually were). A lot of people who spoke Scots were strong Labour voters and a lot of early SNP voters were middle class and spoke English all the time. A version where the SNP would have sold itself through the Scots language and sent out its propaganda or policies in Scots is entertaining, but counter-factual. I am on a website looking at someone holding a banner which reads "Dinnae haed yer wheish. Haed yer ain", a great slogan, but although it is anti-English you can instantly see it isn't an SNP banner. Any policy directed at 1.9 million people is going to cost a lot of money. Helping Gaelic is a different question – the number of speakers is so low that almost any policy is inexpensive.

My trouble with the magazine *Lallans* was that the material they printed was too oral, too simple, not literary enough. Of course the strength of Scottish oral tradition is also important, and it is a larger part of Scottish heritage than the equivalent is in England. I am sure that having affluent, articulate, attractive people go into Scottish classrooms and speak broad Scots to the pupils is a terrific idea. The idea that Scots is not a failed attempt at English, but a language without a State, is something that should be shared with every child. Primary school pupils need material which is close to the oral style, and other material has to be newly written; after all they are not going to read William Dunbar. If you change the life of 5- to 8-year-olds, you will eventually produce a new country.

I don't think poetry in Scots is in a very good state. Radical new poetry in Scots was exhibited in *Sharawaggi* (by Crawford and Herbert) back in 1990, but that was not followed up by a long train of Scots poets. I have an anthology of young Scottish poets (2014) which is 189 pages long and only has 2 poems in Scots (with Scots traces in a third). I don't want to guilt-trip people for not belonging to income group D, this is just an objective count. I have seen good poems in Scots by Andrew Philip and W.N. Herbert. If I look at a recent anthology like *The Smeddum Test* (2013), in which all the poems are in Scots, what strikes me is that the features which the poets identify with the Scots language are precisely those which in my view make for broken-down and generic literary effects: avoidance of abstractions, avoidance of speculation, inhering in a concrete time and place, recall of familiar poems and songs, de-emphasis of individuality in favour of group solidarity. The association of Scots with specific sectors of experience – childhood, the past, folklore, the old neighbourhood – gives the poems their solidary powers but is unfriendly to new associations or cognitive frames.

> Scotland the teacake, frae Uddingston tae Duddingston
> I'll praise ye, the lave can haud thir wheesht.
> Whiles I'll sing ma hame, Embro, heroic toon,
> Whaur sonsy Shug the Scaffy gangs his roon
> An orra spuig, a Jambo frae baldy pow
> Tae pirnie taes, in galluses an nicky tams,
> Clearin dross frae roon yer feet as ye wait oan a tram.
>   (from 'Edenburg' by Alistair McDonald)

The style is copied from 18th century comic-realist and mock-heroic poems. In fact a poem in Scots belongs to a genre and the audience are unwilling to hear Scots used in other genres. The dialect dictates the

Devolution and Disassembly

personality which the poet must present. Other languages are mediators of the global project and its data streams, Scots can only represent itself, in a circular way. It is more like a costume than a language which has all the powers which an intellect uses and needs. So the English language is the most important area for literature in Scotland.

New Gaelic poetry

I will start by quoting some Gaelic:

> Bha bardachd na sgire tric a 'nochdadh gaol do theaghlach, agus gu h-araid urram agus meas do mhathair. Bha iad gu cunbhalach a' moladh deag bheusan nan daoine.

This is just to disillusion people who think that Gaelic is just a dialect of English.

The Famous Five

Celtic scholars are outnumbered by the material, surrounded, and in deep trouble.
  Donald Meek's talk on Christianity in 20th C Gaelic poetry has some generalisations which will be helpful: 'of the bards who put, as artists, the old bottles [viz. conventions!] behind them, and even faith itself. In this sector we are thinking, so often, of the 'Famous Five' who put Gaelic on a new course in the twentieth century – Sorley MacLean, George Campbell Hay, Derick Thomson, Iain Crichton Smith and Donald MacAulay.' *(trans. AD)* Generally these poets provided the material in Donald MacAulay's bilingual anthology *Nua-bhardachd Ghaidhlig/ New Gaelic Poetry*, 1976. Meek clarifies that they were raised between the two world wars. But, he goes on, 'there is another generation or two coming to honour after that time: my own generation, which is represented by poets like Angus Nicholson, Catriona Montgomery, Myles Campbell and Fergus MacFinlay. And there is a generation that is younger than that, and the voice of the women growing ever stronger in its midst. Meg Bateman and Anna Frater are a part of this generation.' Generally these two generations provided the material in Christopher Whyte's bilingual anthology *In the Face of Eternity*, 1991. I don't have an anthology to show

post-*Eternity* but that pattern has been replaced by the annual volume of *An Guth*.

Arguably, one could describe the 'modern' poets as literary rather than oral. Meek started that section of his talk by saying 'We need to remember that the traditional culture (*dualchas*) was behind everything, and that there were spiritual bards in the neighbourhoods all through the century: poets like Eachann MacFhionghainn in Bernera, and Catriona Domhnallach in Stamhain.' The ground rule for the anthologies we just mentioned was therefore that only poets who wrote in modern, 20th century, 'European' ways were included. Another anthology, *An Tuil* (The Wave) ignores this rule and includes a mass of work by the poets of traditional or folk style. It is a large-scale book. This may indicate a growing acceptance of folk arts by the reading audience.

The unique thing about Rody Gorman (1960) is that he writes in both Scottish and Irish Gaelic – being Irish. Anyone coming in from outside and learning the language properly is welcome, but perhaps the point is that where he came from never was outside, the division of gaeldom into two is imaginary. Yes, they are dialects of the same language, but this has been obscured by several centuries of history which many of us might want to obscure. Gorman starts each poem without preconceptions, only as a site for dazzling wit and formal invention. This does not leave much space for scholarly comparisons with Gaelic tradition – it's like comparing a spaceship with a bus – but his work is simple enough to be taken on by learners with a limited vocabulary. The book I got hold of is called *Zonda? Khamsin? Sharaav? Camanchaca?* (2006). Exuberance and love of modernity are not things we hear much about in the Gaelic.

He teaches at the Scottish-Gaelic college in the Isle of Skye, and edits an annual anthology of poetry in both kinds of Gaelic, *An Guth*. Helpfully, this includes translations of some of the poems (glosses, on others) for the benefit of people who speak the other language. A mercurial poet, he can be compared with Edwin Morgan. *Zonda? Khamsin? Sharaav? Camanchaca?* has many translations from Chinese or Japanese nature poets, and Gorman resembles these rather than the Gaelic heritage. Three of the four words all refer to winds:

> In the dead calm at Camas Darach,
> The waves breaking on the shore
> And rubbing and returning,
> Was I not disappointed

>   When Morag John had no name for the wind
>   Blowing around her from Morar
>   When Morar didn't exist.
>
>   *Zonda? Khamsin? Sharaav? Camanchaca?*
>   *My blessings on them!*
>   (from 'Suathadh Eile')

The word for "on them" (*aca*) rhymes with Camanchaca in Gaelic. Camanchaca is a wind.

Chernilo (2006) is a large selected poems. Chernilo means 'ink' – in Russian.

The connections between modern folklore and the older formal literature are a great theme of Gaelic scholarship. Folklore gives us the imaginary, not reportage. There is the past of the imaginary, and the real past. There is the imaginary of outside writers, English or German perhaps. There is present-day Gaelic reality. And then there is the diaspora, returning to what remains lost. Of Whyte's chosen eight poets, three had learnt Gaelic as a second language. Gaeldom is being stormed by 'returners', Scottish people whose concept of education was so energetic that it involved acquiring an entire language – naturally an ancestral language. This act of piety (a reverse scatter or unskailing) is distinct from nationalism, which after all involves ideas about the State and expansion at the expense of other countries which do not feature in the Gaelic scene. Ideas about conserving the Gaelic show the most analogies with campaigns for conservation of nature and the countryside. William Gillies has set out two themes of importance, the first being "the reality of Gaelic tradition had to compete with powerful but alien images of itself which became current in the second half of the eighteenth century". Secondly, "the critical tradition is defective: some key aspects of the main body of pre-modern Gaelic literature are not given due attention[.]" Further, an image of the Gael was set out which had set racial characteristics, rather than individuals exhibiting the full range of human possibilities; and the literature was asked to exhibit these not very real "characteristics". Gaelic matters, the history of the outer north-west, have been hidden behind the abundant projections of outside scholars and mythomanes, hailing from the inner, metropolitan, north-west of Europe. To reach the truth one has to get at the original voice. Studies of folklore and word histories are promising as a basis for a purged understanding. I was intrigued by the phrase *ceithir ranna ruadh an domhain*, a fairly common modern idiom for "(from) the four corners of the earth" "all and sundry". It means literally "the four red parts of the world" and I wanted to know why they were red.

An essay on 'cosmology' of the Celts (by Gearoid MacEoin) picks up a phrase from the huge mediaeval (10th C) Irish poem *Saltair na Rann*:

for bith ché chethairchair glé

This is translated as "on this world foursquare bright". It is clearly the forerunner of *ceithir ranna ruadh an domhain* (four red parts of the world). The lexical choices have changed but the slots they fill have remained the same. The phrase has reproduced itself and retained its shape. The colour adjective belongs with *world* and not with *parts*. 'che' means this (world), presumably in contrast to the world beyond, heaven.

It is very interesting that 'glé' [bright] has been replaced by 'ruadh'. This suggests that the primary meaning is "perfect" or "magnificent" and that the 'red' quality is secondary. Red is the strongest colour and so *ruadh* can mean "saturated" rather than a tint. "Glé" means "white, bright" but has also been generalized to mean *very* – so *glé mhath* is 'very good'. In the end we have a 20th C idiom which has clear connections to the elevated language of a 10th C religious and cosmological poem. This is a fragment but if we can gather a thousand accurate fragments we will be closer.

A recent advance in recovering the heritage was *Leabhar Liath*, an anthology of (Scottish) Gaelic erotic poetry. This came as a great surprise to me, but it should not have been unexpected that the Gael were preoccupied with sex. After all, there was already in O'Finnerty's book *Léas Eile ar ár Litríocht* (re-reading Gaelic literature) a praise-poem to a wonderful vagina. He attributes the poem to Andreas mac Cruitin, around 1740, but eschews commentary. He does say "Edna O'Brien did not fall from the sky". Whyte writes gay love poetry in a rather Renaissance style, giving their shared feelings a serene and courtly setting. I would say this was pioneering, but for all I know there is an ample store of Gaelic poetry about gay lords, Jesuits, and outlaws, removed from view by the delicacy of editors. Gerard Lyne has shed light on this. Progress in study shows Gaelic civilisation to have included all the human possibilities rather than being a picture where each part is like every other part, which can only be the effect of distance and sentimentality.

Devolution and Disassembly 173

Ríona Ní Fhrighil in her book *Briathra, Béithe, agus Banfhilí* (on two Irish women poets) reports the suggestion that when Paul Muldoon titled his 1992 book of translations (from Nuala Ní Dhomhnaill) *astrakhan cloak* he was making a play on words (imeartas focal) on the word *aistriuchán*, 'translation'. (This word does not exist in Scots Gaelic.) A translation cloak, made of dense lambs' wool, is not transparent, it cloaks what is inside it. Translation from Gaelic does not work: you can go there but you can't get there.

Janette Ayachi, *Hand Over Mouth Music* (2019, 53pp)

> Rumour of thunder in my throat, hoarse as a helicopter's
>   rusted propellers
> still eager for its flight of kamikaze tricks. And I sit in silence
> as the owner shouts through to the kitchen from the bar,
> makes shadows of chef's repeat orders, her fingers joining the
>   dots in the air,
> and a constellation of waitresses drop palms full of cutlery,
> apologise to each other then everyone else in the room…
> St Andrew Square – building inflamed by the stammer of their
>   last words.
> A fuss of torn cables hammer the air like ruptured arteries,
>   then fall limp
> under a cargo heap of scrap metal, a landing ceremony of
>   mutated stars.
> The death rattle dismantling of walls – each brick a sentence
>   I lost,
> each spinal tap sound of steel plunging at colossal planes of
>   glass compensates that loss
> as this is the best kind of collision: high-dose, full-throttle,
>   alchemical and driven by pulse.
>   (from 'I Laughed So Much I Lost My Voice')

The distinctive feature is the tune, a set of vivid experiences and intuitions running on from each other as verse lines filled with sense soar across the page and rapidly give way to other lines to build verse paragraphs with as much grace as force. The public apparatus of syntax and line structure is used in a way which exploits their traditional virtues to create a forthright and irresistible melody. The individual moments are familiar from the streets of Edinburgh, or any other city, but are sewn together with an optimism and rapid curiosity which reminds me of a *nouvelle vague* film: the camera shows things which were already there but the overall pattern of the information is lyrical, fresh, buoyant. Astruc spoke of *caméra stylo*, the camera as pen, and the acquisition and sequencing of the flashes of urban experience add up to a melody which expresses a state of mind.

The poem quoted is about the poet losing her voice ("the world's laughter that first kidnapped my voice") even if the text shows a joyous flow of words, and this state gives the volume its title. There was a real incident where a helicopter lost power and crashed into a bar in Glasgow. Helicopters do not have propellers but they do have vanes that propel them. The shift of images and conceptual frames through the poem is more complex than seems possible for a 65-line poem. The inversion where a collapsing building turns into the words the poet cannot speak and they turn out to be buried under laughter is dizzying and reminds me of a Mannerist painted ceiling: in its painted perspective, the building appears to be falling down around us but is not, even if we appear to be falling through the ruins of the building. The collision is "alchemical", so made of chemistry, and involves impulse and pulse speeding up: it is presumably falling in love. The alchemy comes back 50 lines later as "before the chemicals between us/ turned to glass". A shock broke the ice and knocked the walls down.

The events are often drawn from a love life where the other person often wears perfume and is described using the female personal pronouns. The poems evoke the desirability of a shared moment; that is their force of persuasion. They evoke the elusiveness of the other person and that is their nimbleness, the energy of their mobility. What I find is a lack of perverse effects. The verse line is very positive about the experiences which the poem submits to. We are not being shown critique, so paradoxes, ambivalence, disaffection, disillusion. This is the traditional area of poetry but it is unusually effective when presented with such serenity. Neither language nor experience are fragmented, dissonant... postponed.

Some of the poems evoke a family background in a country which based on the jacket information I presume to be Algeria. The poet includes several poems about her mother and these poems have the tonality of deep and rather immovable emotional patterns while the ones set in Scotland show liberty, improvisation, the pursuit of happiness. A disapproving father-figure appears in certain poems and we can suspect that he makes unavailable the role of oppressor which is usually filled, in

Scottish poems, by Westminster and the English in general. The whole volume thus fulfils an old rebuke or groan of Scottish poetry critics, asking a poet to stop writing about resentment and loss and start writing about the present, pleasure, benign experiences in Glasgow, and so forth.

Molly Vogel, *Florilegium. Poems with a glossary.*
(Shearsman, 2020; 120pp)

Florilegium means a collection of flowers – the Latin counterpart to the Greek word *anthology*. Another word would be posy, and one implication is a section from other people's work. This is slightly puzzling. One epigraph says "I have gathered a posy of other men's flowers, and nothing but the thread that binds them is my own." In fact, every poem includes plants in one form or another. The cover has a repeating floral design in strict symmetry, looking rather like a Delft tile.

One poem starts:

> As a girl, I dreamed
> of cotton. The inside
> of the boll shaped like a tiny
> skull would grow moist,
> malleable fibres, which would push
> out from the skin
> of the newly formed seeds
> like strings of pearls. As the boll
> ripened, it would turn a barren
> brown. The fibres would continue
> to expand under the sun's warmth
> until finally, they would split
> the boll apart and the thick cotton
> would burst forth between the shell
> like grey matter from the head. I would awake
> startled by this image in the dead
> of night, a slight pressure
> behind my temples, in between my ears,
> deep inside my belly. I imagine
> the whites of my eyes as cotton ground to a pulp,
> chalky as crushed bone, the kind you can taste,
> the bitterness lingers on the tip of your tongue

>   like phosphate, like a
>   sharp tooth.
>   ('Antonyms')

This poem is simply where I want to be. It is tranquil, richly detailed, intricate. It promises deep time. It is not even narcissistic. The issue moves away from whether it is great or not and towards details like "can I prevent this from stopping?" and "how is this integrated into a longer literary whole so that it does not simply end?". (The poem is "Antonyms" and the white terrestrial substance of cotton is the antonym of the black terrestrial substance of coal, in part 2, where the speaker remembers her father falling down a shaft 150 feet deep, into a vein so deep that his blood ran black. I doubt this is literally what happened, and the fabulous story about the cotton boll dream may also be a fiction.)

So we have a complete book of great poems, and the last 43 pages are given over to the Glossary, recondite facts in the style of Notes and Queries which often have a bearing on flowers and on the poems (although they are hardly necessary to understanding them). Several of the poems were printed in Carcanet's *New Poetries Six*. I certainly recommend the Carcanet series of showcases for new poets (some of them deliberately old-fashioned), although it can be a bit nerve-racking seeing which ones progress to full-fledged books. The poems appeared there without any glossary at all – the glossary is a sort of fern garden, ornate but unnecessary.

One of the notes is about reeds and grasses and advises us "*Canna*. From the Latin meaning 'cane' or 'reed' though the Scottish island bears the same name presumably from the Norse for 'kneeshaped'. Earlier Indo-European origins suggest 'bend' as a possible root. (The walking stick is born.)" *Can-* was borrowed into Greek from a Semitic language and is a Semitic word, widespread in the Middle East. Hence canon, for 'what is straight'. Or sugarcane, for example. Reeds have noticeably straight stalks. *Kné* is Indo-European and means "knee". So a knee bends and a walking-stick does not. We can bypass further ramblings to observe that these Queries have no point. But, they evoke a world of perfect security and unimpeded leisure, in which we fiddle with tiny intricate details because we are wholly serene and there are no conceivable time constraints, and pursue etymology or the history of plant names because the pure exercise of leisure demands subjects that make no possible difference to our well-being. If the topics were more exciting, they would only provoke disagreement. So the artistic intent here involves waves of security and serenity, as if we had wandered into a Victorian vicarage garden and our bus were not arriving for another several years. The effect of this "Plant lore in the works of Vogel" is curiously reassuring, it prolongs the poems after all their energy has exerted itself and returned to tranquillity, persuading us of continuity of impulse: our sensations will stay with us and will cherish us in much the same way that a Victorian gardener would cherish a tender plant. Instead of brief contextless thrills which dissipate into impatience and frustration, we are offered a welcoming sense of time. The poem creates a realm of sensation, and scholarship curates that realm and keeps its fragile but precious contours in being. The Glossary contains indexes of where the glossed plant appears in the poems. So, nine entries for "canna". I traced one of these:

> I have bridled my whole heart, a golden bit among apple orchards
> on holy grass sweet the tall hierochloe is a bride, white throats
>   pushing
> up from wet stones in mud; dawn has two faces.
> I have bridled my whole heart; on your left thigh a mark,
> a basin creek at your knee, I have seen the long way your body
> comes in from the rain, a great stone in bed, perhaps you exist
> best sitting on a picket fence, a long line.
>   (from 'The Child Dreaming in a Poet's House')

I wanted to quote this because it is beautiful. The poem is credited to "after Seferis", I can't find the Seferis poem, but it sounds a lot like Vogel. Hierochloe turns out to be a plant which grows a reed-like stalk and a head of grains. It is familiar because it is also known as bison grass, żubrówka, and is used for flavouring a Polish vodka liqueur which you have surely tried. European bison died out because they spent their days in increasingly world-weary and idealised pursuit of the banks of waving bison grass. (In America, it is *sweetgrass*. Hieros is holy, so *holy grass sweet*.) *Bridle* is like *bridal*, and *whole heart* is a phonetic echo of *hierochloe*. Do the ninefold appearances of canna's reveal a further, subterranean, layer of symbolism? or are they just by-ways of leisurely scholarship for the botanist-antiquarian? Let me just quote one of two 'verse-riddles':

> Silent is my dress when I bow to earth; pluck me
> for pleasure and watch me blush; witness the birth of neither

nymph nor satyr. I am barren with seeds; watch me dismantle
my own throat. Who savours me pressed in wind? My vellum
pinion spews life. Shorn, my woolly husk unfurls
like a mollusk. I stand singular with many, mimic of mimicry.

I can't identify the plant, but the process of exploring reaches of semantics and botany is fascinating. Luxury in poetry has to do with an altered sense of time. The detail of the perceptions speaks for valuing human beings. It moves us away from the brutality and instrumentality of so much in modern life. The altered sense of time is tangled up with intimacy – the loss of impatience. Really, the impatience comes out of me. My bad. Switching it off is quite an esoteric act, although it seems perfectly normal when it is happening. I find most of the poetry I read pretty irritating (as in: "Don't you have anything faster, like Metallica?"). She takes certain desuete American writers and, instead of sending them to Oxfam, treats them with love. The process of tenderness, patience, refusal to give up, tells a tale of time never being lost and impulses never fading. The writers cited could be just clutter, but the care they are given suggests possibilities of constancy and stability which are truly inspiring. This is the explanation for the "other men's flowers" puzzle; the incredible transience of sensations is picked up by the permanence of the symbolic tier.

Stewart Sanderson, *The Sleep Road* (2021, 66pp)
The cover shows a moorland plant fixed into the shape of Scotland by sticky tape. Contextually, it has to be heather. The core is a kind of nationalist piety in which series of knowledge are presented because they evoke the matter of Scotland in forgotten or unrecorded areas. This is a strong idea. The weakness is a relapse into list structures when the material does not allow for processes or human subjects. Almost none of the poems presents the poet as a subject but he is present as a reservoir of curiosity and frustration. So we get four poems which are inventories of Scottish lichens – notoriously old organisms which have archaic and unusual names. We get poems glossing old Scottish words like *tynsale* and *bone* (= boon). We hear about a tombstone found on the Antonine Wall and dated to around AD 140–165. It marked the grave of a Roman soldier who died in Scotland and came from the Brigantes tribe, so either from Scotland or from the north of England. He is a tangible moment. He was called Nectovelius – perhaps the first element is that found in Nechtansmere, a battle dated to 685, the Pictish king Nechtan, and in

modern names like McNaughton. That would be a long continuity. The stone has words but is propped up against a huge gulf of silence. Poems on stones with early mediaeval Ogham inscriptions choose the ones difficult to read:

> Even
> the lichen
> tricks us as it
> etches away and so
> confounds
> us till all
> hope has been
> erased of our
> translating half
> these stories lost in stone.
>   (from 'The Lunnasting Stone')

The short lines express difficulty and lost information but do not develop much momentum or abundance of reconstructed context. The wish is for acuity at the edge of extinction. Reading an inscription requires comparative forms which could be abundant, and speculation which could also be abundant. Neal Ascherson wrote in his book *Stone Voices. The Search for Scotland*: "Scotland [...] is a poor woman with little flesh between her skin and bones. Everything done on that thin stony ground from the beginning – from the retreat of the ice to the advance of the motorway – leaves its scars or its pocks on the surface. A cultural landscape is very much what Scotland is; something showing marks from all periods and land-uses of all kinds, an artefact whose art is human and inhuman at once[.]" This is surely a key to Sanderson's poems about lichen: Scotland is a gallery of marks on stone and the lichen are creatures which mark stone. This is an example of scalability. The fantasy is that the North is all rock and the South is all alluvial.

> One of the iron-tongued annalists records
> how James the Fourth, who knew nine languages,
> grew captivated by the silences
> in which the secret origin of words
> lies hidden from us. Listening to the birds
> whose speech comes closer to the deity's

> than ours, he asked the wind what language is,
> obsessed with glottal stops and voiceless surds.
> (from 'Inchkeith')

(If I am correct, all surds are voiceless; from French *sourd*.)

We hear "Anemones utter/ *aicill* underfoot"; aicill is a technical term in Gaelic versification, arranging for the last syllable of a line to rhyme with a word in the middle of the next line, and also called Irish rhyme. I am not aware if any Scottish poems have this feature, maybe some of the old bardic poems do. Because the consonant agreement works through classes of sounds, rather than identical ones, *under* could, almost, rhyme with *utter*. I bought this book because of a poem, 'Photograph', in an anthology called *Aiblins*. The poem evokes a meeting of Scottish nationalists around 1960, a generation before the poet's birth. The photograph captures a moment of becoming, a group imagining the future although they were going to slip into the past almost without notice. The piety is rigorous and in its patience evokes also the condition of Scotland as subsumed in an alien state and deprived of formal memory or agency.

The poem which contains the title: "smooth waters run deep/ walk with me on this road to sleep" is based on three songs from a manuscript of 1620. The sleep theme occurs also in 'Sleepwalking', a collection of proverbs or glosses that may contain a prophecy about politics:

> the harper's sleep | the road to insanity
> the propaganda of truth | the multitude of dreams
>
> the smoke of heather | the silent consent
> the state and the parties | the white hound and the deer
>
> the flee on the gridiron | the activity of the mob
> the pride in necessity | the direction of the wind

There is a new wave of Scottish poets captured in the anthology *makar /unmakar* (edited Calum Rodger, 2019, 156pp). This is a relief as the first modern movement in Scottish poetry for thirty years, that is since the Informationists. At present there seem to be similarities between Daisy Lafarge, Tessa Berring, Maria Sledmere, and Callie Gardner. The introduction evokes a Scottish avant-garde genealogy in terms of

Devolution and Disassembly

Hamilton Finlay, Graham, and Forrest-Thomson. However, the poetry is unfamiliar and not a legacy. I doubt it is avant-garde but there is an original tone of voice here.

> liquidity, quicksilver, singing
>   the undone gossamer hum
> comes towards dawn   is easy   lucky
> free   (maybe)
> a luxury bristles, syringes the silt of the sea
>   till ever metallic backed down and feeling
> navy, gracious, a pear cut in two by the sun
>   (from 'Object Sheltering' by Maria Sledmere)

I can't find a theme in this poem but it does have a feel. The tone is distantiated, unpressured, yet luxurious. The fabric is delicate, intricate, inconsistent, rapidly shifting frame, non-projective. A lack of core and focus makes the periphery of the text significantly stronger. This is a sense of liberty as much as passivity. Naturally there are patterns but they are subdued. What is visible so far is a shift of time sense so that the poems are like textiles, not moving in a set direction but with a soft and relaxing texture, a sort of low-key euphoria. An interview with an editor of *Spam* says that the new thing is recording "digital ectoplasm", the flow of social media, emails, etc., and that is why it sounds different. Actually when inhibitions break down it is the nature of what was inhibited which matters (not the medium). So the conversation which is released is only interesting because the speakers are interesting people. The thing is presence and intimacy rather than transfer of information. The poems do not stop, because they are mending tiny fluctuations to stay in the same state. Lafarge is the most exportable one – her poems deliver the qualities of being intelligent and dégagé, which is probably what eight or nine of the poets included want, or possess. With Lafarge there are fewer subsidiary patterns clouding the message. Her poems are not at all obvious or familiar but their intention is clear by the end even if they are not affirming the predictability of the world. The sound is luxurious, but Callie Gardner has published a poem 150 pages long which says very little, in a sort of benign twitter. An interesting poem in this manner is in a different anthology, *the weird folds* (co-edited by Sledmere). It describes the poet looking at a jellyfish and being taken over by the animal's form – acquiring the body image of a jellyfish. Of course this refers to anthropomorphism, the failure of humans to understand Nature as a thing separate to themselves because of their unfailing ego-projection. This connects to Gardner frequently writing about food, as the absorption of biomass which belonged to something else but becomes part of a human. Humans are felt as aggressive, not respecting borders. This poetry is a way of responding to eco-disaster in the domestic range.

Scottish poetry has a past of being plebeian and aggrieved, so it is striking how cultured and unemphatic this poetry is. It seems that the ambiguity and uncoded quality are part of an emotional detachment from a set of social expectations felt as impostures and aggressions. There is a legacy set of ways of expressing nationalist feelings which the 21st C has jettisoned just as there is a set of ways of signalling *I'm gay* which the new generation has moved away from. I think we know those tunes too well. When there were no Scottish institutions, writers were forced to stand in for a State. What does music for a new country sound like? It might take the form of a rhapsody, meaning successive improvised clusters of notes that don't add up to a tune. Its tentative nature would be a way of being open to the tunes other people were making up. When the fixed melody emerges, that might be a source of regret. The best poem in *the weird folds* is a 'Musée de la chasse et de la nature' by Alice Tarbuck.

> Everyone's gun is always with them, carried by a valet
> who stalks, pleasantly unremarkable, awaits
> some analysis of himself as anti-pastoral,
> as an economic marker, as an incursion of rural selfhood
> across the scene. The museum is full of the dead,
> the forest is full of the sun, silts the trees with gold on all
>   their brown
> and the faery-king sinks down in the saddle of his most
>
> expensive horse, whose back is lean, whose flanks
> are testaments of breeding.

Serial

Central to the reading of every literary work is the interaction between its structure and its recipient. Therefore an exclusive concentration on either the author's techniques or the reader's psychology will tell us little about the reading process itself.
—Wolfgang Iser, 'Interaction between text and reader'

Anyone looking at British life is going to conclude that television and supermarkets are major features of the scene. This is where we look at the media and ask if national preoccupations like anorexia and obesity also apply to our cultural consumption. If consuming culture is a formative experience, then it drags us apart from each other. I want to recover some of that network of routes and this is the point of this chapter. The marks of transformation may get us close to what happens inside a poem.

Evidently poets talk about the influence of the media on the population, and beliefs about how symbolic experience affects people affect the way poetry is written. We have to record some of the views on this. Access to the media is more unrestrained than it has ever been, and the variety of filmed fiction available makes it implausible that this media input has a consistent effect, or one that is not temporary and where the components do not contradict each other in the most obvious way. All the theories about this confused and self-erasing experience are vague, but poets commonly see the media in terms of the undue influence and control of people they disagree with, and the desire to seize more influence for themselves.

Episode Two of *The Perils of Pauline* (serial, 1914) climaxes with our heroine, in a runaway balloon, crashing into a cliff and being suspended there. This is where we get the word cliff-hanger. Naturally, the sequel was millions of impressionable young women climbing into balloons and crashing them into cliffs. Or was it?

I used to work with a British Asian guy who used to identify with the victims in TV shows. As a result of playground bullying, probably, he could only identify with marginal figures who, in terms of the plot rules, were bound to lose. He wanted to occupy a niche, say at 9:45, on a national clock face, and could identify this clock face and niche within any narrative space, as a universal schema. Maybe we are all trying to locate our time slot in any story. He rejected the designated identification figures for reasons which were, in a sense, political. He didn't mind sympathising with villains because other factors were, in his view, more central. The rules also meant that the figures he liked never got enough screen time – he was in permanent dispute over that as well as rewriting the story to make his characters more virtuous and more hard done by. He certainly didn't want to stop watching TV (or films via TV) and his personalised use of this only semi-collective fiction was satisfying to him, up to a point. Presumably TV creators design the stories so that there is room to manipulate them in your head. I was more impressed by the level of bullying (at a secondary modern in Kent), and the ability of aggressive individuals to manipulate opinion against someone from a minority, than by the negative effects of TV.

It is true at some level that films express the fantasies of the audience they are addressed to. When there were films directed at a teenage audience, the adult characters were complete idiots who got in the way. This is presumably how teenagers see the world, and one could extend it to fantasise that film oppresses every social group by not showing their fantasies in full feather. It is more credible that finished cinema scripts represent a compromise between the wishes of various groups (as interpreted by the scriptwriters). This compromise may even reflect a social compact between different politically vocal groups. The idea that you can launder film so that it starts to show reality is much in question. Cinema is certainly good at staging fantasies for the collective pleasure. Edgar Morin in the early 1950s produced figures comparing the number of car crashes in films with the number in real life. Apparently we like to watch car crashes. Morin, affiliated to the French Communist Party, wanted cinema to reflect reality. Cinema had other ideas.

I am intrigued by the idea that a traditional hero, in a British story, has the qualities of a bully (and is just unavailable to the wishes of someone who has been bullied). This is probable and withstands criticism.

Another line is the presentation of behaviour patterns, in collective fiction, which some of the spectators resent. This gave rise to a gay claim that Hollywood is propaganda for heterosexuality (possibly also to the idea that heterosexuality is unnatural and would collapse if it was removed from the TV screen). Some gay people were very fond of going to the cinema while also feeling a certain anguish at the happiness of blandly mixed-sex couples on the big screen. A similar argument was made by feminists, observing male-female relations as showed in, say, a thousand Hollywood films and finding them unrealistic and misleading. I have yet to see an argument that disproved this; the only line available has been that Hollywood knew what women wanted to watch and made films with them in mind.

Someone with personal problems may be like a figure trapped in a balloon and drifting on the winds of highly organised fantasies. It is plausible that only someone neurotic would be much influenced by watching fiction films, but evidently some fraction of the population is suffering mental illness at some level, on any given day over the last hundred years, and clearly their instability makes them vulnerable. People in two minds do not feel these impulses to be under their control and are likely to associate one set with a powerful external voice, so "society" (or "the patriarchy" etc.) or the Media. Anxiety usually involves doubt and both conditions are quite common. The issue is less about the media being abusive and more about the prevalence of doubt and a "weak sense of identity". Very strong media images become aggressive if your identity is weak. What's that – poetry is entirely the product of the volatile, the hypersuggestible, and the angst-ridden? Say it ain't so.

My impression is that many poets are exercised by the idea that the media are unrepresentative, but very few of them actually write propaganda poetry. The audience are not responsive to this kind of thing and the liberal-cosmopolitan bias of the poetry audience makes them quick to detect propaganda. So the rather large volume of argument about the media is not matched by a body of poetry that we could see as counter-propaganda.

A belief that the way the media work distorts your personality and builds up to internalised oppression may persuade a poet to write in a specifically cold way. This does not lead a child (or, reader) in any direction and so leaves them freedom. It does not create illusions. It does not sympathise with the characters – because identification is seen as a form of alienation. It does not show pleasant experiences because that makes political change less attractive. It does not show concerted effort as purposeful because that would tend to support the position of those in authority, who have made decisions which made that success possible. It does not show relationships as being successful because that would tend to support existing forms of relations between people, which are being reformed. All this is carefully reasoned but I don't want to read such poetry once it has been written.

If only neurotic people believe in the temporary identity of a film or TV programme it follows that reforming the media is not going to make any difference. The problem is in the way people consume the media and if you take that as a given then changing the stories will not have any effect.

Filters

A poem presents an inside which is different from the noise ridden data flow around it. It must have an inside. We spoke about a clock face, representing the visual field, where someone would respond to a 15-minute segment and ignore the rest. A poem presents an inside– this sounds like a strength. Selectivity is important in the poetic process.

For biological reasons creatures seek stability and predictability in their immediate environments and in their inner environments. If we see poets as creatures living in a data environment, their activity could be seen as not producing the basic flow but filtering it; with the goal of stability. We can see their styles as results of filtering.

The word ideology has negative connotations because it implies imposing pattern on a rush of data which exceeds the pattern. But we ask poets to impose patterns on reality. There is a procedure which makes the patterns clearer and discards the inconsistent data, and we recognise this procedure. It is almost as if we are all seeing the same turbid flow of primary audiovisual data, and the poet is someone who has an integrated circuit for altering this flow and making it coherent.

One has to admire a poet like Browning who can take anything in, and who has no recognisable theme because he does not accept limits. But in general selection and exaggeration are basic to the development of artistic style. The more variation is restricted as a key part of artistic form, the less unpatterned variation, from the outside, can be permitted. The work of art is directed at stability in the same way that a creature drifting in the ocean is.

There is a risk involved in filters, that they can reject important data and accentuate the initial bias; so the subject accelerates down a slope and as they descend they take in less and less data. Self-correction falls over and the input of new data is so distorted that it makes things worse.

I don't think poetry works without this acceleration, the self-reinforcing spiral. At a higher level, poetry is the product of a very long-term process of acceleration. If I have strong feelings about poetry it is because I read so much of it when I was 23 and that was because I was reading a lot of it when I was 16. The further in you get, the more you understand of what you see. The outcome is a wall between the poetry world and the rest of the culture scene. The gap is what shows the existence of an inside. I want, not just a poetry world which is not run by people who dislike poetry, but poems which have a deep inside and compose a world in themselves, impossible to confuse with the world around them.

I suggest that the demand to identify is something which is made, not just by advertisements and art, but by the world of signs in general, and that refusal to identify is a key factor of the personal worlds that people construct. At this point we should return to the theme of anorexia and obesity which I broached at the beginning of the chapter. Identifying is a core activity and is subject to all kinds of distortion, or loss of proportion.

The core issue is obviously how much people identify with the rich and powerful. This is the area most likely to go wrong. Poets can see that having a critique of the management, of how things are run, could make their voice important. That is because the audience *want* to hear this critique. But there is a distinction between refusing to identify with the people who run something, a school a corporation or a department, in the way that you dislike the people in the next town and their football team, and having a critique based on thought.

Jon Stone named a poem and his book (2012, 78pp) *The School of Forgery*, arousing the image of fake versions of profoundly beautiful and ornate things. Quite indicative for Stone's work is his interest, in a series of poems, in dōjinshi; described by him as amateur re-creations of comics, drawn to realise fantasies never permitted in the official comics, and often involving same-sex relationships between the beautiful and energetic heroes. So the idea is of artefacts which are kitsch by nature but also highly developed in a way which reveals deep desires and in some way recaptures the domain of the imaginary. Stone seems to prefer inauthenticity, but this allows him to jettison the apparatus of realism and moral seriousness, so that the poems have a wonderful lightness, bursting like fireworks.

> We came to. Soi Fon, prostrate before Madam Yoruichi,
> was tensed for the smack she'd been earning through weeks
> of unctuousness. Madam let the promise hang like a cherry
> then lit the nervous bulb of her protégé's cheeks.
>
> We came to. Love had broken out in the Seireiti,
> sloshed into the parched alleys as if from an overturned

vat or cauldron, a broth once-stirred intent to stir
the phalanxed hearts until each was hopelessly churned.
   (from 'Dōjinshiworld')

(Seireti is an imaginary city in the Bleach manga cycle. Sort of sword and sorcery plus Buddhist cosmology… *roughly*.) My favourite poem is the one about ray-guns which is made up of direct quotes from 1950s SF texts about guns firing rays. The text is torn diagonally so that much of it has not reached print: sentences are incomplete but we get the impression of a world beyond the page. The tear gives it its local energy riding over the worn but highly coloured texts. This probably is a flashback to being 7 years old and wanting to be a spaceman. He seems to have uncovered how the mass media actually work, with rapid change and overt fantasy being vital assets. 'Death daydream season' presents six poems, each of which displays the silhouette of a star character on TV: so the poem on John Steed, a character in spoof-sophisticated 60s TV show The Avengers, depicts in outline his umbrella and bowler hat. (He took the visual motifs from a 1939 film called *Q-Planes*.) It would be nice to think that my generation wasn't formed by watching TV as children and that a large part of our life energies hadn't been poured into that low-energy activity, where we swam through fantasy and got closer to everyone else watching the same absurd and populist shows, but I know that is what happened and we always watched TV together. Roughly half of the poems have Japanese themes… partly because recalling old bursts of British culture would be nostalgic and too dominated by reaction patterns already fixed or congealed. Japanese popular culture is western-influenced while also being uninhibited to an extraordinary degree.

   The tendency to start the poem within a work of art and make the characters play games reminds me of George MacBeth. Humans are breaking up into ornamental motifs, like prints of tropical birds. The detail is not kitsch but a special kind of pastiche where the richness of colour and the informality of the image work at a pre-rational level to open a box of delights. The poet has gone inside the logic of a game where the characters have no psychology but an altered and divinely aroused physiology. Taking the pit a pat metabolism of a bird to a new length, Stone shows us creatures made of light who can create shocking neon-pop photographs but have no bodies – they live in flashes. The poems are moving towards flat panes of bodiless colour.

We recognise *dōjinshi* because it is so familiar from British life. Perhaps a bronze and stone monument to gay life could be sensibly replaced by a series of TV episodes where the characters and events had been replaced by gay versions of what they should have done (and how they should have dressed), since this is so central to the idler parts of gay social life. TV is beamed into their living room in order to programme them, and they are quite serenely and intently reprogramming the TV footage.

One poem presents the narrator sitting helpless in a cinema in Bucharest watching a show where one reel of *Rashōmon* leads on to a reel of *Jaws*. I seem to have seen this Max-Ernst-like film in a poem by Mark Ford. The message is clearly that life is like a film where stories are never completed and consequences have no visible causes. Comfortingly, it is not our fault (but, if we could ever catch that scriptwriter!). So Japanese comics are derived (partly) from American comics, and gay Japanese fans draw their own *dōjinshi* versions of the comics, and Stone sets his poems inside imaginary *dōjinshi*. This is an example of how poets set up the material of their poems.

Disentitlement

Britain did not have the highly coloured, heroic, self-referential fantasy world of manga, but it did have Stalinism. John Berger began as a Stalinist and wrote in praise of Stalin. He put his objections to Western art across in the 1973 book *Ways of Seeing*. His introduction to his reprinted work of the 1950s is distorted by his wish to renounce Stalin and his unwillingness to accept that either Stalin or Berger was wrong about anything. Of course the rejection of Western art since the Renaissance was orthodox for a Marxist, it was a mainstream position. The links with capitalism and individualism were too obvious. Contemporary cultural anorexia is on a small scale compared to the Marxist purging of art history. As the truth about Soviet prison camps emerged, it was tempting to abandon the Soviet Union without abandoning the stance of judge putting European art on trial.

Consider a hypothesis that if we, our society, were the product of a tyranny which had wiped out opposition, then the public realm of that society would be full of deception aimed in the first place to cover up the wipe-out. Suppose that Hitler had won and we were living, in 1980 or 1990, in an evolved Reich, reading the history books which that regime permitted. Suppose next that Berger was right and the West, in 1970 or 1980, were such a regime, the tyranny of bourgeois civilisation. Where only Marxists knew the truth. And surviving records of the past would be full of anomalies that raised doubts about the common-sense version, and a caste of people would exist whose job is to paint out anomalies, to wipe away traces and lines of disjunction.

A response is to withdraw into a rejecting and blank state. Miasma spreads uncontrollably; all attachments are ejected. A spiritualised subject has its skin stripped off and desensitised – it cannot represent the feelings of other people & is occluded under tissue filled with pain – but devoid of knowledge. It is infinite but without information. The inability to identify is like the inability to eat. A sore mouth. The sore area may be very small.

We can call this project for annihilating cultural privilege Disentitlement. Where the self regard of an artist is taken as guilt. Where collusion is taken as conspiracy, even though all art is based on collusion and it is the core of art. Where all non-Marxist knowledge is error, a trap.

Understanding is not even desired. It cannot represent non-finite quantities. A feeling of total lack of autonomy is the basis for unlimited blame of (featureless) authority. In a fantasy of infinite weakness and infinite deprivation, authority is seen as the source of all wealth and abundance, which it must relinquish. It is a container, to be ripped open, emptied, and discarded. Assiduous grievance collection is related to claims (of right).

This position of depression and blockade is occupied by a wide variety of people for a wide variety of reasons. This state also works for someone who regards the whole West as post-imperialist, a collaboration whose immediate past is a cluster of colonial empires where the great majority of the population were reduced to shadows of the ruling races, where collective memory was corrupted by the sect in charge of writing and printing. Where Britain is not even post-imperialist but a continuation of imperialism by other means, with other faces presenting a surface of affluence and good manners. Where culture is part of money-laundering.

If you accept that 20th C poetry was possessed by greatness and possessed greatness, then it follows that the people in charge of the industry had succeeded, and that they derived from that a certain right to be in charge, and to speak. So, if you want to reject those rights, then you would need to reject the poetry also, and there are many ways in which you can do that. This is where collusion breaks down. We can see this as a kind of cultural anorexia. A food that makes you ill. That would connect it with kinds of renunciation in the history of religion, where natural appetites were switched off by some current or other. If fasting is holy, starvation is very holy. The logic seems to be that fasting brings you spiritual power and rejecting the collusion of culture brings you power to judge. The people we are discussing are not indifferent to culture, rather they want to seize power over it: by discrediting the body of bourgeois art appreciation they create a vacuum which they intend to fill with irrevocable judgements.

The claim to right of some section of the powerful is their mastery of technology, producing food and useful objects for huge numbers of people. If someone is interested in pollution and devastation, the motive may be to allow them to denounce technology and so annul the claims to right of the people who organise technical endeavour. So the whole history of increasing power over nature is one whose climax is in global warming and climate disaster. Fairly obviously, the people who reject the authorised in this way also reject the whole history of culture and so the creators of contemporary culture. They depose authority in order to claim total juridical or theological power. An apocalyptic view of the future serves also to discredit the government and any other institution. Miasma becomes a means to self entitlement.

The natural voice of this position is a whine. It is unpleasant to listen to. It would feature in poetry primarily as a sampled texture – something which you hear for five seconds as part of a musical landscape which has a wide palette and deploys such samples. You can't write poetry from within this position. All the same some people may have entered this position, left it again, and then worked out how to write poetry.

Capture of time

It is logical that a work of art which has had a great deal of time built into it is valuable. Eventually, the construction of art is the construction of wealth, and art is wealth. Pursuing this theme of time we can argue that young humans are in a basic state of frustration and hyperactivity and serenity is a refuge from it. The word discipline is a key. It is a misused word, since the root simply means learning. *Disco*, I learn. *Pul-* meaning "child". Discupulus, discipulina. Even a text is a thing which is taught and learnt: the transmission of information is the life of the text. Serenity offers an exit from anxiety by displaying large amounts of time, lived steadily and allowing the attainment of goals through the mastery of ego, the repression of incoherent and superficial impulses.

Any intricate work of art is the product of prolonged stability. This must appeal to conservatives. The conservation of information in a text is, after all, conservative. The idea of intricacy, of creating an ornate work of verbal art which embodies contradictions in order to still them, which preserves multiple mirror images of a basic pattern in order to rise above change, is analogous to creating an *objet d'art*; the sort of thing that can become a valued possession, to be exhibited and curated. Such an object soothes basic anxieties about loss and erosion, about the destructive work of time; but it develops in analogy to wealth, to technical skill, to stability of institutions, which also defy chaos and the dissipation of information.

Often contemporary poetry concerns itself with older texts, pleasing because the poets felt pleasure in learning the patience and empathy to deal with such elaborate and alien products, as students, and because they show completeness and fulfilment. As concentrations of highly ordered information they attract us, almost as if these were the calories, the saturations of minerals and dense cellular fabric, which the poets fed on. This is language of high status and it attracts the attention of many people who are fascinated by high status; which may actually be true of all humans. A love of the past embodies key, if ambiguous, sounds in a society based on hereditary wealth.

It is inevitable that such values provoke rage in those whose hatred of authority they contradict. Art is not found only in order and patience but also in spontaneous and destructive acts, where calm is achieved through *austoben*, the energetic externalisation of rage and frustration. Art is obliged to support an anti-authoritarian function in the same way that music is obliged to support dancing.

High and Lonesome: Daniel zur Höhe/Anthony Mellors
Winter Journey (2022; 124pp) with photogravures by David Rees
The book presents as a translation from the work of a reclusive, even fugitive, East German poet, departing from the 1824 work by Wilhelm Müller which was set to music by Franz Schubert as *Die Winterreise* (1827). The 24 parts of zur Höhe's work correspond to the 24 poems of the 1824 'Winterreise'. They fill some 43 pages of the book, with the rest being extended notes and commentary by Mellors on the allusions in the text and the difficulties of translating it. So the work is to this extent an exposition of the difficulties of identifying with art in modern

times, and of making public statements of emotions. The prose is framed by admissions that the text can't be translated – if not, that we can't understand our own deeper feelings and the self-contradicting flow of consciousness. At another level, there is no German text, zur Höhe doesn't actually exist and the risks are self-imposed failures by Mellors. The name actually comes from a character whom Thomas Mann used twice, first in a 1904 short story and then in his 1947 novel *Doktor Faustus*. The character is widely agreed to be based on the "kosmiker" Ludwig Derleth (1870–1948), whose 1,900-page chief work was not published in its entirety until 1971. The name refers to the prophet Daniel and to exaltation – zur Höhe means "on the height". Derleth's feet rarely touched the ground. As for the notes, one runs "&. first use in the cycle of the sporadic ampersand, a tic of the so-called Cambridge School. zur Höhe is a fan of the poet John James and occasionally emulates his louche, faux-discursive style, as well as striving for the garrulous maleness of his poetic milieu, but the effect is about as convincing as James shifting from Château Grande Cassagne and corduroy to weissbier and regenhose."

Schubert's song-cycle is accepted as one of the classics of the European repertoire. The lyrics almost touch kitsch – they describe someone losing a love and setting out for a journey in a bitterly cold winter, to an unspecified destination. The style of the poems is very close to folk songs and the work has that quality of deep and simple affective states which folk songs sought for. Both Müller and Schubert were learned men, but the songs evoke primal states of emotion and the touch of play-acting does not get in the way. Schubert did not compose for the concert hall but for small intimate rooms where, it is claimed, most of the people knew each other. One can see this withdrawal into intimacy as a reaction to the state of Central Europe in the embrace of the authoritarian reaction which followed the defeat of the French Revolution. The cold of the winter journey corresponds to the bitter coldness and hopelessness of public life, and the residual warmth of a room full of friends. Of course that is debatable. Song 24 is about the hurdy-gurdy man, with the piano part imitating the rigidity and droning quality of this humble instrument; the imitation of simplicity and emotional unity is something which European art has been carrying out ever since. But how does zur Höhe hope to capture this quality in a unified and capitalist Germany? The introduction refers to "wandering, introspection, exile, and political repression." The 24 poems of the new cycle fit inside the 24 poems of the 1824 cycle, adapting them. For example, the loss of heat in the snow, in the original, becomes in the remake the personal waste heat which betrays your position to heat sensors:

> night & day there are ears on us
> soft coercion forty seconds to comply
> every movement full of junk snowed-
> in or snowed-under has little impact
> on the fantasy of staying frozen to escape
> the heat map pink TV cheval de frise

(*Cheval de frise* is an obstacle of counterset spikes whose shape is a descriptor for anomalous graphic wave forms on the screen which images what the heat sensor detects. This problem is known as snow. The *cheval* is associated with frontier defences.) I am told that Mellors was sensitive to the cold. zur Höhe dropped off the screens and disappeared after finishing this poem-cycle, presumably devoted to his own journey into the winter. From encryption to apocryphon. East Germany ceased to exist twenty years before the (attributed) date of the work. Of course the qualities of folksiness and authenticity are ones which the Socialist Unity Party (the Moscow Line ruling party) sought for over many years without ever possessing. Poem 11 says

> The illusory major invites parody
> empty eighteenth-century gestures
> stand out on a white ground –
> there is no religion for the frigid zones
>
> since all matter tends toward
> the lowest possible energy state
> denatured nature emerges
> as furred life on glass
>
> you see onto but not out
> eyes tight shut to sublimation
> the beating of little wings
> against the mental pane
>
> their colours their stain
> given to be seen the beating

> of a hidden ground
> detains the heart [...]

In this case the affective state dominates the text. But its sound is so permeated by ambivalence, harsh denial of feelings, by the sensation of inauthenticity and the tracing of its shapes. The winter is here the inability to feel. The prose apparatus can be seen as an attempt to subject that to a therapeutic repetition until it destroys itself. The citing of a hundred or so cultural monuments is an attempt to find something we can identify with and so regain a primal unity with the desired object. The reconstruction of context is a search for how we fit into a cultural object, how we could unify our biography and our fantasies in one healing act. If only we were dissident from a corrupt State, we could withdraw into the comforting smaller unity of a Bohemian pub room, its warm defensible space; and exit from this uncertainty. That was the promise of the East Berlin dissident arts scene, run though it was by super-privileged Stasi informants. Mellors gives a wealth of specific details:

> *if you like*
>
> clouds on the horizon
> vinyl with a skip in it
> corroded screws
> an elaborate hierarchy of suffering
> ashes hauled
> sentinel crows
> moping
> random seed
> balaclavas
> mischance
> Popol Vuh
> vengeful spirits
> peaked knees
> unharmonized half-cadences

– the poem goes on to suggest what you might also like, if you like these. *Popol Vuh* is the sacred book of the highland Maya and also the name of a progressive rock band from Munich (as favoured by German rock-*Kenner* and critical anthropologist Martin Thom). The level of detail about East

German daily life is impressive. To give just one example, when I was living in an artists' house in the South Palatinate I used to talk about East Germany to another writer, also resident, who had grown up in Leipzig. The one common point we found about childhood was watching *The Singing Ringing Tree* on TV, an East German children's film bought up by the BBC. Mellors offers significant details ("Bardot coiffure indigo fringe") about this film and does recover what a child in the 1960s DDR would remember. However, I do not feel that zur Höhe's emotional state is genuinely East German. It seems more like feelings about being English under Thatcherism, refracted in a way which both hides and tells the truth. The DDR ended *before* Thatcherism. Mellors persistently finds inauthenticity in popular culture, as a front for the culture industry; where Schubert found authenticity in folk-song forms, Mellors finds the drone of the hurdy-gurdy stepped up to a volume which deprives us of sleep or serenity.

Mellors says that the principle of the poems is encryption, related to fear of the police state of the DDR. He describes the atmosphere of the Austrian police state around 1827, from a book by Alan Sked, without mentioning that Sked founded the UK Independence Party (in 1993). I could expound the criss-cross of allusions and inversions for ever. There is a melancholy of scholarship where we accumulate matches and the biographies of patterns without being able to recover what was lost before the start. So the commentary records that "Princess TnT" (in 'Listening Post') is Gloria von Thurn und Taxis, a socialite and regular in the gossip columns in the 1980s. The Thurn und Taxis family had acquired wealth as holders (from 1517) of the post monopoly in the Holy Roman Empire. The whole book (of which *Winterreise* is part) is called "from the posthumous papers of a travelling horn-player" – the word is *Waldhornist*, he plays the *post* horn. The discovery that all the trees are painted does not alter the fact that our fingers and toes, once blue, are turning black with necrosis. Just one more – zur Höhe's previous book is cited as *Jedem das Sein: Conversations In the Beech Forest*. Beech Forest translates back as "Buchenwald", a concentration camp set up within sight of Weimar, the holy ground of German classicism. If we add one letter we get "to each his own", title of a 1946 film which caused many of us to weep, a while ago (dir. Mitchell Leisen, Oscar for Olivia de Havilland); but as it stands it means *to each their Being* and refers to disoriented Nazi philosopher Heidegger's lengthy *Sein und Zeit*, being and time. The Bauhaus was set up in Weimar but after the election of a right-wing regional government had to move to Dessau – home town of both Wilhelm Müller and zur Höhe. The skein of cited or sub-cited texts gives the work the complexity of a novel by Mann or a Prisma by Adorno – to the frustration of its search for re-unification, even in pure sadness. The scholia are like surveillance, a combination of manic and blank states with the goal of control.

Mellors (anagram of Müller?) died in March 2023, a little over a year before this book came out. In 1990 he began co-editing, with Andrew Lawson, the magazine *fragmente*, a renovation of the Underground of the 1970s, lost at that time, which both sought to recreate it and to redirect it towards a virtue which it had not hitherto possessed.

The only thing which can be compared to *Winter Journey* is **Wayne Burrows**'s *Eastern Bloc Songs. Party, Pop, and Politics* (2018). This contains cogent analyses of works like 'Tajga Blues '69' by Marta Kubišová, and 'Wala Twist' by Filipinki, who were the Baltic region's answer to The Chordettes. Eastern pop was a sort of mirror image of the Anglo-American industry. He may have started with a book from Peterloo (2001), *Marginalia. Black Glass* (2015) is a 'new and selected'. The thinking of arts officials has to do with events which they can promote, which are an "event", and which have a link with a local community. Burrows has thoroughly adapted to this pattern and is an important part of the public arts scene in Nottingham. This means his work reaches an audience that does not read poetry. So *The Orchard Sequence* (2011) has a link with the redeveloped Sneinton Market, in an inner city area of Nottingham, but is also a set of brilliant poems about apples (a Nottinghamshire speciality and obviously often sold on the market). Seireti is not in Sneinton. In *Exotica Suite and Other Fictions* (2015, 175pp), the title piece relates to a genre of music popular in the early 1950s, which was associated with the arrival of stereo for domestic use: using the widest possible range of textures and sonorities, revelling in exotic instruments, spreading well over the borders of kitsch. Burrows' website features playlists, the poet also functioning as a DJ: the promise of an evening of specialised sound evokes a shared fantasy. The poems too are as exotic as possible, starting from a level of pop-cultural erudition which is stratospheric. The total availability of media sources leads to their dissolution; so a 2013 poem takes announcements of a political ritual in North Korea and edits them to be an unctuous commentary on the funeral rites for Margaret Thatcher:

> The Group for Comprehensive Exploration
> of Lake Chon on Mt. Paektu
> and the Group for Comprehensive Maintenance
> of St James' Park,
> both announced it was the first time
> such a big noise was heard
> from the ridge of Janggun Peak and the lake,
> from the junction between Whitehall and Trafalgar Square.
> All the exposed film in our cameras turned white.
>   (from 'A Simultaneous Translation')

The title poem 'Black Glass' is about cinema:

> Images consume us when they embrace the eye:
> a white star in the hook of the moon,
> an empty tower block with one burnt floor,
> the red sun winching slowly down,
> thinning out across a violet sky.
> A woodland is garnished with milk-weak light,
> there is glass on a pebble, a lens in mud.
> Look again at these images the eye absorbs:
> *grains in a sugar bowl on a linen cloth,*
> *liquid sugar dissolving a fractured tooth.*

Reading a Wayne Burrows book is like listening to an Exotica album. I ask myself how a personality emerges from a snowstorm of exquisite and unheard of tonalities, montage dissolves, North Korean court ceremonial. The answer is obvious: Wayne is the kind of person who always has a new and revelatory piece of vinyl to play you.

Wayne certainly likes exotica. There used to be evenings of Exotica at a pub, the Bodega I think. The idea of a themed evening is to abandon your musical tastes and go into a shared fantasy state in which you all pretend to be the kind of person who would listen to that kind of music. So for Exotica, an Early Fifties guy who was affluent and trying to be sophisticated. I was once listening to a Les Baxter record and I felt sick. It was like travel sickness. This is what happens if you try to go all the way with kitsch. I bought a CD pack with 8 Baxter albums and one is "perfume set to music" where each piece of music is a tone poem meant to evoke a certain perfume. The name exotica was a marketing idea but it did refer to a cocktail bar of unfamiliar instrumental timbres which were used in Hollywood for evoking foreign countries. The use of theremin for the outer space sequences of Baxter's 'Music out of the moon' is an example. In some way this was the origin of space rock (in 1947). I watched (on YouTube) the original 1964 promo TV clip for 'Wala twist', which is set on a merry-go-round and shows various Filipinki draped becomingly over the chairs. Wala is Valentina Tereshkova, the first woman in space; the merry go round lifts the chairs in its rotation, which refers to weightlessness, and the circular motion refers to the orbits which Tereshkova completed. (Is that Berger, smirking in the ice-cream kiosk?) Another part of the book is a biography of Robert Holcombe, an English artist of the post-war era, whom Burrows invented and went on to create many artworks by. The Holcombe story is an incitement to invent our own lost post-war artist. Perhaps contemporary poets invent an imaginary artist and then become that artist? Burrows is lost inside his constructions, which themselves are made out of other texts. I don't know if this is effective as an example, because it has migrated so far into its own realm. But perhaps that is indicative, because when people consume a thousand moments of culture they take a thousand steps away from the centre, and so everyone is on the periphery.

Somehow both Burrows and Mellors break into prose when describing the more extensive cultural programmes which steered the biography of their fictional talents, Holcombe and zur Höhe. This is a litmus paper for how we see poetry in this time. Reversing the frame offers a rational truth about the heroes, not momentary, but also threatens to push poetry into a sort of lyrical grotto, chained by its own song and the splashing of the waters. What bursts into the world of the poem and brings the marriage of what is inside the precinct and what is outside? The inrush of prose is where simultaneously the poem breaks its own bounds, to acquire reflexivity, awareness and frame markers, and by leaving those sacred bounds loses its mobility and ability to move us. The Holcombe story is a prose narrative. The more we uncover the field the more our report acquires the static quality which possesses the field. Only the players have mobility and that only by forfeiting knowledge.

How do we classify Wayne framing pre-existing archive recordings from the early 1950s (and, probably, late 1940s)? What kind of aesthetic act is this? And don't poems often involve framing of objects and people? The framing could be of something quite outside the poem. Do words have substance beyond framing what has substance?

Conclusion

These are certainly temporary identities. But what do they say about literary centralisation? The cognitive preferences I have dredged up come out of people's concepts of pleasure and order, they are overwhelmingly linked to data sources which have nothing to do with poetry, and they have no obvious impact from the vocal individuals who run the poetic scene. Modern people have a formidable weekly intake of data in which poetry is only one channel. In fact, the individuals I have looked at do not feel bound by the text, they colonise it with compulsions which generate a deficit which constantly needs to be filled. We acquire the idea of a tier of leaders of literary taste because we look only at their outlets as the possible sources of fashions. Culture is a conditioning set-up in which we serially programme ourselves and move away from each other. So we resort to a club like the Bodega and listen to 50s music to recover a lost unity. We hear the same song and dream the same dream. The collective finds us and sings us a song.

British South Asian Poets

I have a database of reviews appearing in *Poetry Review* (it stops in 1997) so I counted reviews just looking for Asian surnames. The total was for the 1960s, 12; for the 1970s, 1 (*PR* gave up reviews for 7 years); for the 1980s, 7; for the 1990s, 42 (my figures leave out 1998 and 1999). It looks as if there was some hesitation about writing poetry in the 70s and 80s: doubts about both the English language and the implicit content of the poems, being British culture itself. It was hard to be sure that you were doing it right. Other arts had less of an implicit load. If you look even at the 1970s, there are very few South Asian-British poets publishing. Zulfikar Ghose had the most of a career, but gave up poetry for novels. In the Eighties, it is a bit better. David Dabydeen did very well; Mimi Khalvati makes a debut in 1990. The Nineties see a general advance of poets from different parts of South Asia. This implies that the inhibitions attached to a genuine state of foreignness, to people having grown up without speaking English in the home, and outside England. They were simply not present for adults who had gone to English schools and spoken English as their first language, a language natural to them.

When I say doubts you can also put the word anxiety. What were they anxious about? Simple xenophobia in various forms. I can't document poems that didn't get written and hostile interactions that left no record. The anxiety was probably well-founded, like other anxieties. To move forward, there is obviously a delay between people from various Asian countries being here, or their children being here, and people from within that population group emerging as poets. Optimistically, you could say that "individuals who had been to British schools and then a British university knew what the audience would like because they had grown up with them, and this resolved the hesitations". White racism was obviously a factor. Still, it wasn't because white racism disappeared that a large number of Asian poets began to publish. I read *Preparing Faces: Modernism and Indian Poetry in English* by Sudesh Mishra. Very interesting but I don't see it helping us much with British Asian poetry. So we could posit three theories:

— British Asian poetry is indebted to modernist, secular poetry in India, sometimes in English

— it is influenced by traditional religious poetry in India not in English

— it is influenced by local British literary traditions and has assimilated to these in order to reach the local market

None of these is very convincing and I would prefer a fourth theory, that the originality of the British Asian poets we are interested in is such that this sort of genealogy is useless, and that in fact we are lingering here because of their radical originality. I could suggest that the unexpected and bewildering quality of being an immigrant, even a second generation one, creates new psychological states and that these are what the poetry is impelled by. That is possible but I would prefer to emphasise artistic excellence as the motivation for the poetry we see.

Nuzhat Bukhari's *Brilliant Corners* (2021, 91pp) was arresting by its high degree of linguistic finish and by its extremism, the product of acuity of mind. There is a great variety of themes. The jacket describes the poems as anti-colonial and anti-capitalist, etc., and (by my count) about 15 of 43 have such themes, dealing with refugees, blood diamonds, the colonial past, Che Guevara. This message layer is the foreground, but to fixate on it bypasses the most original aspect of the book, the unconscious layer of stylistic decisions and the fine-scale design of language. These poems can be seen as martyrdom paintings: figures embodying suffering and nobility, in exotic landscapes which satisfy the eye by their detail, however harsh they are.

> Reflect on one man, one rectangle plot.
> By tombs of rubble, an artery of highway.
>
> Aleppo's nickname is *Ash-Shahbaa*
> a milky whiteness stirred
>
> with black. Lead missiles shred clouds,
> fling and sow demoniac seeds.
>
> Clipping or fingering leaves, he says:
> 'This is a hazelnut at the start of life,

> this a red-blushed loquat fruit,
> a heady aroma, acid to taste.'
>
> 'This one was hit by shrapnel,
> but is alive, thanks to Allah.'
> (from 'Last Gardener of Aleppo')

The poet refers to terribilità and does actually have this quality, said to be something which Michelangelo had (and others did not). The title comes from a composition by Thelonious Monk (released 1957). The image is perhaps that corners show the vertices of an object and so its essential shape; if the corners are dazzling then we cannot see the shape, only the shine. The poet refers to atrocity and offers an etymology of the word as from *atr*, burn, and *okw*, eye. This is a wrong etymology, in Latin *ater* means black (matt black) and *ox* is just an adjectival ending, as in *velox ferox praecox* etc. The solution the poet desires means *scorched eye* and this is significant in itself: certain of the poems (at pages 54 to 66) are baudelairean, full of spleen, seeking shock effects in a way that suggests desensitisation. Injecting etymology into a poem is prosaic but points to a belief that there is a pre-conscious world of meaning in the language we use and that it is important to uncover what is concealed, which leads to the shock effect in fact. A poem deals with *kintsugi*, defined as a "Japanese art of golden joinery of broken objects, in which fractures are illumined", and goes on to Bashō saying poetry treads "a middle path between reality [and] vacuity", then a lava field in which the freezing was abrupt and led to all kinds of plane edges caught in stone; then to Chinese oracle bones in which heat fractures allegedly form recognisable characters usable for scapulimancy, a kind of divination. "Scored on the edge of one resolute slate, mute for millennia,/ our first script on a sighting of a comet's delirious torch". The golden flaws may have a link to brilliant corners. The poet this is most similar to is Geoffrey Hill; 'Sappho in the Fourth Reich' must echo 'Ovid in the Third Reich'. A group of about six poems are based on works of visual art and their theme seems to be a sort of anti-narcissism: close attention to visual data is diverted from adornment or admiration and directed instead to horror, to what adornment represses, to hidden structures. This verges into the territory of Iain Sinclair, since this sort of effect has been brought to the public quite a lot in the past fifty years (maybe in the era since *Psycho*?). There is an anecdote about a nest of bedbugs in Chaïm Soutine's inner ear which I had read earlier the same week in a book of art history: these effects are avidly collected, they are charged, but also obsessively repeated. Several poems about explosives probably echo the interest in anatomy, with buildings being laid bare in the way that a dissected body reveals its structure. The dynamics of a blast probably echo the plane edges of the lava-field. Despite local flaws, the verse moment is compelling, developing large-scale paragraphs which possess mass, objectivity, coherence. This is from a poem which evokes Sparkhill, in Birmingham:

> They call it *hüzün, hiraeth, saudade, tezeta*; though it's illegible.
> A Welsh soldier-poet saw memories as pollen of unsung maladies.
> The émigré's larynx, a coffer of ghosted lingoes, muffled songbirds.
> Once Urdu was for princes, poets, a *laskari zuban*, warrior tongue.
> But it quailed in my ripening palate, paled in the North's palled
>   light.
> Outsiders say it as *Ur-du*; clip, unsplice its delicious aspirate purr;
> *Urrthu*, a birr sound of a dove's fanning wings as it flares for flight.

(*Tezeta* is Amharic, and apart from 'nostalgia' is also a genre of ballads. *Saudade* is Portuguese, same word as Spanish *soledad*. *Hüzün* is Turkish for "melancholy" and apparently is used in Sufism to record the distance between the soul and God.)

Four or five poems deal with etymology. So far as I can tell half these etymologies are wrong. We get a poem entirely about the derivation of the name Adlestrop. The trop is the same as thorpe or Dorf and so there is no *strop* element which could be, as the poem tells us, cognate with Greek *strophaligs*, 'whirlwind'. (The gamma ksi graphy is transliterated nx and records a nasal, so it is strophalinx.) It is unlikely that the people of Shropshire would give their village a Greek name if they could not speak Greek. Even the eccentricities of an important poet are important. These freelance word histories are like shadows painted on stage scenery that move by themselves: shape slips away and something formless starts to erode the apparently solid outlines.

The entry on stage of terribilità opens the door to discussing Mannerism, a word which occurred to me frequently while reading this book, dramatic, erudite, and highly wrought as it is. I reject the word, because it has that original implication of an artist who put their personal style, their *maniera*, ahead of the (religious) meaning of the picture. This will hardly do. Everything suggests to me that the research and experiment involved in Bukhari's style are there to reinforce the expressive element – which is also the ethical and political element. So her poem on 'Liberty', describes a statue whose right to stand in for a principle is affected by the corrosion of many centuries, beautiful skin replaced by intimate damage, and is fabulously stylised, its extent (of 50 words only) calculatedly laconic, but everything is forcefully directed to the emotional point: of a lost ideal. (I have a *feeling* that "Indo-reds/of a dying sun/// churn, trapped/ in her hoax torch" should be "indigo-reds".) Arnold Hauser's great work on Mannerism has the subtitle "the origin of modern art", and this is not just a narcissistic deviation from loyally producing propaganda art. He remarks that Mannerism (as painting and in *objets d'art*) was produced for secular tyrants, so free from the demands of the church; often erotic, and developing the nude as a subject; often over-size, and developing stylistic originality as part of the lords' competition with each other. It hung in palaces. It represented the loss of restraint. It accompanied the development of efficient tyranny, and the growth of spendable wealth, in the 17th C: Bukhari is writing very often against tyranny. So the adjective is not apposite to her. Bukhari has that ability to think through artistic problems in stylistic terms, and this is incredibly rare. The linguistic tropes, ellipses, and flourishes *are* the expression. At points the poetic task seems beyond her technical reach, but the overreaching is itself fascinating and dramatic. One key is the geographical imagination: the poems are set in up to six different countries, but there are minimal and telling details which orient us to the right place, just as details in a 16th C painting might connect us safely to the Holy Land and the story. This places a great strain on technique which shows itself to be adequate at every point.

Kintsugi also appears in a poem by Rebecca Perry.

Small Hands by Mona Arshi (2015, 53pp)

This is hard to describe because I do not know of anything similar and the classification words do not come to hand. We can say that it centres on a woman, also a housewife, and on a house and its garden. This offers a container for the poems. They are domestic poems. This surrounding offers an answer to questions about who is speaking and how she satisfies her needs. In a way this is there to remove the questions; the speaker is at the centre of her life and that creates a stillness inside which everything else moves. The writing has nothing to do with domestic anecdote. The title gives us a theme: the phrase occurs several times in various forms, and also it gives us, perhaps, a link to the other theme of birds, whose small hands are seen as giving them a grip on the rare substance of air. Perhaps also we can see this as representing finesse: as small hands are associated with the ability to do very fine work, fine stitching for example, small hands may stand for sensitivity and for a layer of interactions which rough handling causes to disappear and which might arouse delicate feelings in us. The font size is several points smaller than usual, which underlines the smallness – but the *poems* are not embodied in a font. We would not attribute power to these poems, but that quality is not necessarily present in all the poems we admire and which we wish to linger in. Take this poem, 'You are Not':

> You are not the ageing tortoise shell.
> You are not the pillows of my hands.
> You are not the metallic taste in my mouth when I wake
> (though you could be those threads running underneath my
>   tongue).
>
> I doubt you are the threads of hair which survive on my
>   windowsill
> (and are likely to have lost their film of neem oil).
>
> Though you could be the windowpane itself, which allows me
>   the view of the sky: the interesting birds.
> (You are not the birds.)

The rhetorical structure ("you are not" appearing nine times in the poem) is in fact rather explicit and is familiar in Western theology and known as "apophatic". (This is generally attributed to the Orthodox Church, so not the West, but has attracted wide interest in the West in the past two centuries.) The you addressed is not God, as it turns out, and is not a person. The poem reveals at the end that the you might be "that moment when the clouds ripen/ just before the rain": so a moment of perception, a neurological state which we can imagine as a tune, and which is evanescent: the moment disappears just as the clouds break. This is a transcendent thing which is yet within the grasp of the senses. It answers the questions of the senses, and is even domestic, yet it is elevated enough to withdraw itself from a named sensation, because the things which it is not must also be things which are similar to it, enough so to be mistaken for it. What is it? perhaps I can respond by a disclaimer – this poem does not give away to us what all the other poems are, and its distraction from the subtle and familiar and barely-named moments reminds me that I also can't name what Arshi's poems are like or why I like them so much. This poem (not the others) reminds me of a poem by Anthony Thwaite which also defines something, perhaps the glory of God, through a list of fascinating and beautiful sensations; Thwaite's poem is a rewrite of the doxology, part of the Anglican Sunday service in which the great achievements of God are listed. Thwaite's direction is very much to find the divine in the small-scale, not blasting the senses but adequate to their limited scale and range. This divinity is privatised and everyday. But, Arshi is evidently not a Protestant... and "You are not" is not really a doxology. In local terms, we can detect that in an era of magniloquent tyrants the achievements of God were magniloquent and displays of tyrannous power, and that as wealth spread to a large number of households (with limited political power) the works of God were also seen as locally present, ordinary, and on a small scale. This is what the small hands handle, the information which their network of nerves collects. There is a kind of inheritance process in which a big tyranny is subdivided between a million equal heirs and the outcome is the domestic scale.

Perhaps we can also compare the poems to paintings by Bonnard, which are domestic in setting and undramatic in theme, but which are agreed to embody daily life and in fact daily love, so things in which we find the human race (and we are wrong to look for them somewhere else). Perhaps the descriptive problem is that the poems embody serenity, delicacy, and tenderness, and I am unused to these feelings. This is a profoundly original book, a first in our collection, asking for a new room to itself, and it is better if I just wave my hands at it ("just look at this!") than try to classify it.

The Voice of Sheila Chandra by Kazim Ali (2021, 67pp)

Ali was born in Britain but moved to America and now defines himself as American. It looks as if I am cheating by including him, but perhaps I can get away with it. This is a poem of 34 14-line stanzas, dealing with important issues which chase each other without logical bonds. Sheila Chandra was someone who brought a trained Indian singing voice to the pop world in about 1991. She was interested in regional folk music and recorded a version of 'McCrimmon's Lament' with her voice taking the line usually played on bagpipes. I taped this off the radio in 1991 and I still have the recording, fabulous. So Chandra was someone who brought South Asian cultural prowess into and inside British music. Someone for British Asians to be proud of. But, the title also refers to her no longer being able to perform after about 2011: Sheila Chandra's voice is something you can no longer hear, and the poem is about what is missing, what is elusive and yet central. It deals with the bonds between the self and the universe but also with glimpses of non-being, the soul slipping outside the universe and hearing the silence. Take this stanza:

> Is the voice to know or to know
> The edge of knowing Muslims do not
> Depict or particularise God only gesture
> With blank spaces Ali Kazim does not
> Paint with a brush but pounds powdered
> Pigments right into the paper he compromises
> Masculinity by depicting a muscular
> Man with a flower tucked behind his
> Ear shaving himself with a straight razor
> He reinvents manhood as a form of
> The feminine texture of a voice breaks in 2007
> I saw a Catalan *Antigone* and at the moment
> Of her incomprehensibility the actress began
> Screaming in English

The poem has consistency in line and stanza length, there is a pattern which drives it forward and gives it unity. But the syntax is not fully logical and the ends of clauses mostly don't coincide with line ends. The key for me is the lack of grasp between the parts. The poem has that extraordinary impulse and conviction but that is a framework which holds it against an outright spontaneity and irrationality, where the themes chase each other and the links are purely personal. The poem is based on a coincidence: "Chandra/ Lost her voice around the same/ Time I found mine at midnight/ We went to swim in the sea so/ We could be in the dark and not/ Know the bottom". The issue is orientation; to accept the verdict of coincidence expresses a belief in the benevolence of the universe (and the weakness of reason), while the wish to be in a sea and not know its limits is an acceptance of forces outside the self, and of a realm outside the senses, opening onto uncharted passages and secret harmonies. Sewn between the frustrating data of the senses and the tantalising twilight of what does not give itself to the senses at all, the speaker is guided by a bodiless voice. The biographical events are urgent, transient, cluttered, distracting, because that is the nature of the sensory world. Another poem mentions "the old belief that God is found in abstraction and in sound say the Sufi teachers it is the physical matter of the universe made". This explains more about the choice of the sound of a voice as a cosmic theme in 'The Voice of Sheila Chandra'. (I think the phrase could complete *the physical matter is made orderly by divine sound* but also *the physical matter is made abstraction so that we can understand it*.) It also recalls a Neo-Platonist belief that God made the universe by the utterance of certain sounds, which endowed matter with shape. The universe was originally filled with bodiless voices. The idea of a beautiful silent voice is suitable for a traditional religious poem. It is like a cosmos of beautiful invisible forms.

The volume also includes a 17-page poem about a university caretaker smashing a stained-glass window as a protest, in 2016. The window showed two Black people working in the cotton fields and was stately and pastoral, but the protester saw a link to imperialism ("I shouldn't have to come to work and see things like that"). This one is also about David Berger, an Israeli athlete who was killed by Palestinian activists at the 1972 Olympic Games; it is called a "hesperine", so an evening poem, the opposite of an aubade. Addressing the darkness is a message to death, a murmur in the final silence.

Wolves of Kultur: *The Routines 1983–2000*. Khaled Hakim / Sister Ray. (Contraband, 2021. 110pp)
Bengal was conquered by an East India Company army in 1757 and fell under some kind of British government. At that time it was one of the wealthiest regions in the world. Today its population is 250 million – a much larger concentration of humans than Britain, and presumably (now as then) a larger section of world history. It is on a huge delta, where the run-off of great rivers makes the land (and even the sea) incredibly fertile. The silt, the fisheries, and the ports make it naturally rich, like the Low Countries. The fertility allowed for rapid population growth, so that an amazingly wealthy region could have a population who were individually poor. Dhaka is not Antwerp. Here is part of a routine, 'Gringo':

this is the part where poets introduce thr poem, like they do this explanation about where it comes from, to locate it in some special moment. & they do this genial preamble, where yr seeing them at thr most interesting. & then thr voice changes & y/ know theyr Doing the Reading.

Hi, Im a poet – fly me!

Do y/ want to help my cousin open a Balti restaurant in Halesowen.

And some more:

faling into th gravitacional feeld the hwile I chaunt th marginless tym in me hypotheticaly fricsionless rubber pants

porige granules on yr photospheer – matter becom subject
the academick selfhelp industry a crazed system that alows everything in

sumhwere owt dere is th real wirld. & if ye can rite it, maybe yu can make it

Therz sumthing, therz sumthing. There's somthing forgotten – poetri
pathological bullshit held in check by enjineering

critical rase theorie as religius incantacioun
depreshion is too litel Prozack in th braine
looking for the geenom for homelesnes
thire painstaking cartographie

a dezert ileland whare the uniuersals of anthropologie play owt th constant oppozicioun: th need to define selfhood in th trybe:

tribalizms conseruatiue economie of identitie
        ('Gringo')

The photosphere is the visible surface of the Sun that we are most familiar with. I am not sure if these routines are poetry. Clearly they are monologues in several voices, scurrilous, brilliantly comic, insulting, hyper-reflexive, often couched in stigmatised and sub-standard immigrant dialects. They are performance scripts and were written 20 or 25 years before reaching print. They include alternative wordings because they were delivered in different ways on different nights. Quite often the point of departure is a film, a familiar narrative in which the roles follow preset ideas about the ethnicity of the characters and how the events bear that out. They were composed, mostly, in the 1990s, but the author was unsure how to record them in print. Quite similar material from the same period (up to 2001?) is in *Letters from the Takeaway* (Shearsman, 2019) which is improvised letters to various cultural heroes, but reads like stand-up routines. I did actually review some of this material, about 20 years ago. I couldn't recapture the details of the routines – they were too quick, too full of rapid reversals, too startling, too verbally rich – so I did what any professional would do, and made something up. This wasn't a high point, and at this point I have the texts but am having difficulty in reconstructing how they worked in performance. What I did then was compare the performer to a Bozo, a kind of clown ("insult clown") who had no script but got laughs by insulting members of the audience. Quickfire ripostes to the heckles. The aggrieved customers paid to be given balls to throw at the plank the clown stood on and dunk him. A quote from the I-net gives us– "As Jackals and I talked, Patches got dunked at least five times. Water splashed out the back of the cage and dripped on Jackals. Still wearing wet clothes, he didn't seem to care. [...] The first thing I heard Patches say was, "Your sideburns look like old porkchops, and your hair's got more grease than two Chevys. Now I know why your sister left you, you dumb redneck." If you want to know more, the film *Carny* (it's on You-Tube) has Gary Busey re-enacting a Bozo. So Khaled's routines got voltage out of fanning the latent hostility between the performer and the audience, and within the audience. The comparison is relevant because a bozo has to give recognisable parodies of a real person's appearance (or it wouldn't be funny) and has to be verbally quick, irrelevant because Khaled's routines flicker between different themes so quickly and because there is also an autobiographical strand in there – "adventures of an Alt-cinéaste and the grotesques he meets at the arts centre", more or less. And this cinéaste is a Sensitive Chap. But he does *bring it out in people.*

I think the act didn't go over in Cambridge. The audience in that town couldn't even imagine that they were being mocked and just reacted with indifference. The thousand yard stare of self-regard.

A lot of the information is in the dialect and in code switches. Film history is so much shorter than poetic history, the components haven't been covered over by paint and vegetation yet. It seems like you capture the rules of the game by 'material' analysis of one sequence of one film. Poetry has too much of an implicit load. Start with assuming that someone who writes "yu kno" is ignorant. OK, so how do you construct someone's character if you meet them? maybe how you narrate social events is like the way film narrative is constructed? This is where Khaled's analysis of social scenes is more complex than poets usually manage. He thinks that analysing this is like analysing the montage of a scene in a Raoul Walsh film or something. Maybe it is, anyway the discourse here is about social value and it is very critical. The poetry world idolises Empathy, and so the injection of a cold view– *me anthropologist, you native* – breaks a taboo. At the same time it is the call sign of an academic, so a very high-prestige profession, and offers information about behaviour which is normally repressed – so it can be scurrilous. After all there are reasons why it was repressed. The shift between the voice of a Bengali waiter with bad English and the voice of an intellectual who says *me anthropologist, you audience* is the kick of the performances, you shift between superior and inferior and get seasick. Or high, I suppose.

In the poetry world, poems which fulfil tenets of Theory have high prestige. The more they implement the Ideal, the more prestigious they are. But these ideals cannot be descriptions of life as it is led, or poetry acting them out would not be so rare. The Theories are like the Arthurian tales of the high Middle Ages, which reflected the imaginary of feudalism but had no element of reality. A poem can only be Significant by acting out a moment of Grand Theory, because that is what all university graduates crave. Theory is more prestigious than just reading texts. Moments from Grand Theory do not occur in real life. This is how grandeur is protected. If it were practical politics, or understood by ordinary people, it would lose theoretical status.

Of the Letters, two are addressed to Stan Brakhage, one to Peter Gidal, and one to the Austrian Kurt Kren – all film-makers, and I then regarded Khaled as a *filmi* who regarded the poetry world with bemusement and was preoccupied with Peter Gidal, a theorist whose Structural Cinema forbade narrative, since narrative was the sign of commercial cinema. No, real films had to be structural. The *persona* who delivers the routines is not a cynic but someone preoccupied with making alternative films. Almost all the humour is about alternative culture, it is insider humour even if it mocks the people who are laughing. He finds his creative aspirations mocked by work at a takeaway in Cradley Heath. Khaled hung out at the Film-makers Co-Op in Gloucester Avenue a lot, found the poetry scene ridiculous but was already looking for comic material. Much as radical film was implicitly involved in a critique of narrative cinema, Khaled's routines are based on a critique of poetry. He was interested in the lack of narrative in poetry. One interpretation of this is that poets avoid describing people other than themselves, and avoid describing changes in the central character, because that character is the commodity. Poetry is apathetic because it is egocentric and has already reached the centre of everything. This may not be true, but the repressed returns as anxiety, so shapeless and content-free. This is comedy with a melancholic feeling of being the target of aggression. Harold Lloyd, Buster Keaton – where would they be without danger, disaster, the malice of over-powerful machines? Lloyd dangled from a clock at eight stories up, Khaled deals with racism. It is always there.

The dogma of empathy is that benevolence finds the Real You and criticism of any kind is error. So that the extremes of self-regard coincide with what the camera finds. Perfection is what intimacy reveals, and the poem delivers intimacy. If you want to back off from (mis)construing other people then you can say that the poem achieves authenticity if it describes only the poet's feelings. So you've just turned egocentricity into ideology. How great is that. Obviously the idealistic component of this is extreme, and the ideology of poetry includes a lot of repression of the facts. It needs hostile satire to detonate the self-idealisation. Khaled mocks both Theory and Authenticity:

> Sume kind of substitute lezhure activitie – for animizm shamanizm kabbala the magical alckemical, the healer musician legal scriybe oficsial tribal historian, to th ritual weeve
>
> I suppose I was drawn to those mythopoick or ritual modes lik all actual magicians to the trybe, coz it was a chance to dress up in womins clozs. I gess its the same for yoo.
> (from 'Sixth Routine')

I think there was an early performance role as "Sister Ray". Again, provocative and radiating unease. I think he used to wear the clothes on the bus on the way to the gig to produce insults which he could then add to his routine. Counts as research. Kind of! Exploiting locked-in ticket value. The good people were provoked into supplying spontaneous folk texts expounding their ethical principles. Execration texts, many of 13th century origin. The cover of *Letters* credits Khaled as the first Black poet (in the UK) to write experimentally. Since D.S. Marriott published *Hours into Seasons* already in 1987 (I have a copy, with a picture of Stendhal on the cover), this sounds unlikely. I don't think you can remember everything, it was a long time ago, but my feel is that both poets were widely ignored in the 90s and have been written out of the history since then. They didn't fit the marketing programmes. It's no good emptying vacuum cleaner bags to find trace evidence on this. Yes, something happened. Who knows if there were others– the underground was genuinely invisible. All kinds of things could just pass you by.

> For som tyme in the West, ther has been a notion that afluent damiged peple produce formal inovacion.
> If you are wite middelclass & educated, wat els can yu doo except becume invizible.
>
> As you grow older, th stars wil disappear.
>   ('Eleventh Routine')

The East India Company exported textiles to European markets and was later renamed Primark. 'Wolves of Kultur' was a silent film serial, circa 1917, whose plot is the subject of conjecture. "A Somali, a Sylheti, a Hazara, a Chelsea antiques dealer, and an accountant, went into a shisha cafe…"

Splendours and Chagrins

Chlorine Footprint

Will Harris' first book **Rendang** (2020, 83pp) includes a poem called 'Seven Dreams of Richard Spencer', which describes seven short narratives which appear to be dreams. The person who does not appear in the narratives is, or is likely to be, Richard B. Spencer, born 1978, who claims to have invented the term *Alt-Right*. He works for the National Policy Institute. He is a professional speaker and Internet voice for the non-traditional Right. He was part of the harmony voices for Charlottesville and Trump's 2016 victory. One of his enthusiasms is the ethnostate, a new zoning code in which the good parts of the United States would be for Whites only, and other ethnic groups would be penned up in what you might call reservations. This geographical plan would be applied in Europe too, as the only solution to the threat of multiculturalism. One of the dreams tells us:

> Once I was the chlorine in a public swimming
> pool and I flowed into the open gills of a woman
> I believed to be my mother, before it occurred
> to me that my mother isn't young and doesn't have
> gills. I turned into a macrophage and was able
> to see that the woman I believed to be my mother
> was addled with cancer, so I started to eat my way
> through every cell I came across. Not because
> I wanted to save her, but because it tasted good.

So, we have the option of not seeing any ulterior meaning in this. But, the shared rules say that the interpretation which accounts for more elements of the verbal whole is the better one. If we connect this to Richard Spencer, an alternative layer of meanings surfaces. The gills refer us to evolution, something which the Alt-Right see as what gives Whites the edge, while they are steadily denying its factuality in the cause of protecting traditional Biblical religion. In a swimming pool, we are weightless, and this is like the situation of the unborn child, suspended in the waters. But birth is a moment that Alt-Right speculations constantly revert to: the difference between races, which they hold to be the basis for every political value, goes back to birth, and is where White citizens acquire their birthright. The differentiation is held to be present at cellular level, a biological reality, and the poem gives us imagery of illness. Cancer involves cells proliferating and being not enough like the host organism; it is a common racist metaphor for other ethnic groups. The chlorine is a purging chemical used to kill swimming cells held to carry disease – and, in the recent past, segregation of swimming pools was a big issue for the supremacist Right (and for civil rights groups). Sharing swimming water with non-Whites was held to be a threat of disease. Spencer's attitude towards "other races" could sensibly be described as like a macrophage and like chlorine. Like, bleach the ethnostates, bleach the water, bleach the museums. How are we doing? Let's look at another passage.

> Once Europe was a market square and though
> it wasn't market day we had come to sit and drink
> hot chocolate and listen to the buskers, one of
> whom was singing Schumann's *Dichterliebe*, which
> for some reason you thought was *Bleeding Love*.
> *It's not*, I said.

This is relaxed and it could simply be an account of a dream. Imagery follows in a sequence which has no meaning, we are carried along by the effortless flow of figures. Or, the subject could be some other Richard Spencer. But, the idea of Europe is also key to Richard Spencer – it is the "birthright" which gives White Americans their special and unimpeachable right to American land. Schumann is ideally simple and beautiful, but classical music is precisely one of the things which, in the doctrine, Europeans have and nobody else does. *Dichterliebe* means "a poet's love", something remote from features like enclosures, cannon foundries, and conquest as parts of "legacy", but art has been so frequently used by Nazis and neo-conservatives as part of an argument for White supremacy that this association of ideas takes us in another direction. So, perhaps what we have is a serene flow of images, without any moments of analysis, admonishment, or argument, which is still criticising modernised racism. And maybe we have a pastoral, a sort of clip advertising a holiday destination, in which Richard Spencer is the dreamer, we are watching his dreams and seeing his Earth. It is hard to aestheticise Spencer, who has the complete porn stash of Far Right ideologemes, but it is credible that his thought processes are akin to aesthetic processes. Highly patterned scenes that dissolve reality – some art is like that. The poem goes on:

> The exhibits, on loan,
> had been replaced by photographs. Each time
> I tried to touch one, it moved. *You better back
> the fuck off*, said the security guard. I turned
> into a boy and girl who had lost their parents
> and we hugged each other, crying.

This could continue "waking" stories about museums as colonial booty and about deracination, of immigrants maybe. The blood in 'bleeding love' could be the idea that "European art is for Europeans". But anyway culture is all surrounded by bourgeois guardians (Roy Fisher's phrase), and the feeling of being the wrong sort of person is stored somewhere in everybody's memories about Culture. The first two sections talk about *cuckold* and *cuckoo*, an old metaphor but one proximate to fear of being replaced and fear of race mixing.

There is a deeper reason why you would treat ideology in terms of dream. If you accept that there is no factual or research content to Spencer's claims, you are left with the element of fantasy as his talent, his USP. I have a feeling that the distinction between ideology and other forms of thought is artificial. Ideology is how people imagine the social process, and this imagination only becomes problematic because of discrete flaws of process such as compulsive repetition, failure to adapt the model to evidence, depersonalisation of other witnesses, unresolved aggression, and so forth. Certain aspects of thought begin in subjective and insubstantial inner scenes very much like dreams. There is a later process of reality testing which goes well or less well. We are designed to go on adding more instances and more precision. That is why we read.

If you go back to 1950s episodes of *Dragnet*, you see a realist view of Los Angeles in which nobody is Black, Oriental, or Latino. (This changed a few years later, after the Watts riots in fact.) I say "realist" because that is the ethos of the show, semi-documentary. But they seemed to have a kind of camera which only recorded White people. And this is already like the ethnostate, an idealised landscape in which you only see White faces. The Alt-Right want to re-create the 1950s, with everyone having a job and living in neighbourhoods based on ethnicity, but actually they are thinking of 50s TV, not the 1950s as a reality, with sundown towns, slum landlords, loan sharks, the Korean War, and so on. The LAPD at the time were not only all-White but profoundly racist. It was the age of polio in swimming pools, I suppose. There is not much doubt that Alt-Right thought is a kind of collective fantasy. But this makes it easy to see the people who invented the fantasy as having a kind of creativity. People like Spencer put an emotional wish into sensuous, flowing, externalised form. That form may remind us of a 50s TV show, actually. So the point of describing a series of dreams may be to say that dream is endlessly creative, not bound by the limits of objects and other people or that whole zone of reality, and that the trouble with ideology is its bareness and repetitiveness – its self-destructive decline from creativity into rigidity. As culture becomes collectivised, it becomes able to fulfil its strongest functions, but is also exposed to the risk of *prestige model* status, becoming so attractive that everyone repeats forms, in a sophisticated rigidity and repetition. The original tier of dream fades away.

When Harris describes dreams, throughout the book, I don't think he is just recording what he happened to dream last night. His method is disconcerting, unfamiliar in its shapes; it is premature to have confidence about discussing it. I think one aspect of it is a critique of ideology, where someone like Richard Spencer is a significant other. The idea is that fluency in the language of dreams is bound to discredit ideology, as a failure to adapt to what the waking senses tell us –and we are all fluent in the language of dreams.

Fawzi Karim's ***Plague Lands and other poems*** was published in a translation by Anthony Howell in 2011 (114pp). Howell worked from an English text by Abbas Khadhim. Karim was born in Iraq in 1945 and left in 1969, and he has lived in England since 1978. He has written in Arabic throughout and, as the poems reveal, he is an Iraqi who happens to live in a place in England. The impression I came away with from *Plague Lands* was that I understood everything, with a lexicon of natural symbolism using familiar and everyday organisms and objects illustrating a political tale of dictatorship and State violence, where the destruction of buildings and landscapes is part of a prolonged campaign of destruction of human beings. But that may be an illusion; the translation may have been brilliantly adjusted as tucked in so that the gaps in translatability disappear under the pleats.

The afterword reveals that the book was published in Arabic in 1995 (in Damascus). It is therefore a direct response to the first Gulf War of 1991 and to the mass death of Iraqis in that war which was followed by further

Splendours and Chagrins

deaths in the military repression by Saddam of a Shi'ite uprising and the civil repression of the population in general. The political background is obvious, and by chance these were events which the Western media covered closely, so that we have some visual memories against which to set the texts. A long poem, *Plague Lands*, occupies the first fifty or so pages of the book. It depicts devastation and hyper-vivid memories of an Iraq full of peace and flourishing trees. Long stretches of the poem refer to exalted drunken nights, wrecked mornings, in Arabic cities, which must refer to the 1960s. The plague is the government and its wars, rather than something organic. The poem occurs in a permanent present tense; it starts with the river Tigris and the poet's birth (on the last day of the Second World War) and continues with a sort of frieze showing the river, war, drunken nights in Baghdad, farewells to deceased friends, going into exile, the experience of exile. Because the poem is in exile, devoted to memories, the time line is not literally fixed; we can easily attribute the fatalities to the Iraq-Iran war, a large-scale conflict which dragged on for ten whole years and only ground to a halt in 1989. The coup of 1958 involved the dismemberment of a deposed premier, in Baghdad: part of his body was burnt in a suburb where the young Karim witnessed it (recalled at p.16). Memory sees the pattern entire, not like a camera which sees a particular moment (and erases any pattern, leaving it out).

And poetry, shaven of pate, shepherds everything, high on a hill.
A rural man with a flowing gown,
How striking he looks, as the sun sets: one who enjoys his aloneness.
One with a view about everything just as he sees fit:
I am at one with the breeze, and this is how I am.
But poetry departs, when under threat, heads for
The snow-capped peaks. Poetry always departs,
Its shrinking silhouette ever decried as apathy.
Now I shall partake of the forebodings of Al-Rumi,
Enter the house occupied by the clairvoyant in the verse of al-Tayyib,
Lock myself into the cages of Abu Tammam,
And, orphaned, I'll tend prohibited fruit in the orchard of Abu Nuwas
While tearfully striking sparks from the *Saqt al-Zand*.
And I shall descend, with punters such as Baghdadi,
Into the dens of the poor who wear nothing but shadows
As Ibn Nabata would reel from the dens of Shorja
Enwreathed in the heady aroma of spices and debt.

We do not need to know details of the poets cited to grasp that these are very specific memories, mixed with fantasy because they are mixed with craving, of Baghdad or other places in the Middle East, and that they stand also for real people with whom a city is filled, and from whose number the victims of the Ba'athist government were generously drawn. Poetry is personalized here as a robust rustic, so a figure from before the city was built; innocent of the crimes which tracked the city's development. Shorja is a quarter of the city, the *Saqt al-Zand* is a text ('Sparks from Flints'). Remembering Iraqi poets from the previous millennium, or just at the start of the eleventh century, is a way of emphasizing the continuity of the Iraqi people and the transience of governments and their self-referential claims on history.

> So let us now praise exodus,
>   exodus *en masse*,
> Let us now praise exodus before dawn
> While checking inside the receiver
>   and under the car.
> Let us now praise exodus
>   as those who are exiled already
>   praise those of us who are exiled after them.
> Unto them let's advertise our attractions
> And publicise our qualities to disbelieving lands.
> Our travel songs are shanty towns
>   and the sun goes wailing through their slats.

Checking for hearing devices and bombs responds to the activities of Ba'athist police, who evidently did not halt at the borders of Iraq but engaged in their own self-exile. At one point the Arabic text repeats a pattern found in old Arabic manuscripts, where there is a poem on the page body and a different one in the margin, and even, in a sort of game, the two can be read both together and separately. This is possibly a point where the original resists translation.

    I have always neglected authors who live in England but write in other languages. They are a whole world, I admit, but the issue is really whether I can write anything intelligent about them. The way I like to go about it is to read 100 books from a five-year period so that any poem is heard against a really dense background. I can set German poems against a full context but can't really do it for other cultures. Karim's poetry is great, I can get that far, but I don't know any Arabic and he is the only Iraqi poet I have read. London is a city in which affinity is the real map and people construct a city in their own image following, and also leaving behind, dense scent trails of affinity. So I am sure that Karim found a London subjectively full of Arabic poets and readers of Arabic poetry. He has made a living by writing for two Arabic-language newspapers.

***Amnion*, by Stephanie Sy-Quia** (2021, 112pp)
Amnion means "a little lambskin" and usually the membrane which encloses the foetus in the womb. The OED has a 1627 quote "the inner skin that compasseth the child round in the womb". The Amniota, it also says, are the reptiles, birds, and mammals, so the amnion was an improvement on the egg of fishes which led to more protection and nurture. As a title it means autobiography, but especially one before birth: so the nurturing environment from which the poet was to emerge. The story continues more or less to today. I am not sure I could sum up this family history without mistakes, but I can say that it involves four grandparents from three different nationalities and that, unsurprisingly, this does not produce a divided soul, but one with lots of stories to tell. The first thing to say is that this already has classic status, to my mind; because of the tone of voice, which is persuasive and perpetually curious and hard to say no to. Something about the distribution of detail even in the first few pages persuades us that there is endless material and that we want to hear all of it; a promise fulfilled over the length of the book. I think her grandparents and parents lived in six different countries. The stories are about contrasts between countries, sometimes.

At one point we hear that her grandparents had a lawyer named Marcos, and that her grandmother had a notable number of shoes; and that the lawyer's wife Imelda got the idea of collecting shoes from his employer. This is the perfect anecdote, but in someone else's narration it would be merely an anecdote, and not part of a whole texture of vivid stories. The point seems to be the distaste of old land-owning families in the Philippines for the new rich.

Each curve of words is intriguing and then satisfying in itself. This set of family memories amounts to a new memory itself. The book develops a pattern which is completed by developing Ms Sy-Quia herself and the parts develop a pattern in which the arranging pages are completed by becoming the book.

In a previous existence, my job was to summarise complaints about schools; so that I have read a few thousand of these. I am not eager to read one more complaint about an English schooling, but this one is palatable because Sy-Quia is such an interesting narrator. The schools, and fellow-pupils, do not come out of it especially well, but Sy-Quia is always curious and always able to recall details, so what we relate to is her emotional and intellectual capacity rather than a set of grievances. When she turns up at a Church boarding school in or near Canterbury, the first thing one of her (unnamed) fellow-pupils asks her is "are you rich?" Much as we might fear that being socialised in such company is going to produce deep misery, and we are going to have to read through it, it is clear that children acquire a notion of social value, even if drastically simplified, which often grasps the basics without successive screens of deception and disguise. Yes, if you are thirteen the basic question is whether you are rich. The education system is a result of the answer, I would think.

The unifying thread of the book is certainly one person, which might have produced an egocentric result. However, reflection shows that many of the stories are from before the birth of the author and must reflect not just the occasions of relation, but actually the speaking voices, of older family members. The poet may have recited these stories to herself, as part of defining herself, but they are other people's stories. It seems likely that relatives told her them as a way of explaining to her how she came about; and also that some of them had passed through two or more generations as stories.

It is hard to quote from a flow, but this passage may show how this is poetry but not organised in conventional rhythmic lines:

Student nights with their divine time of bells and the blood beats of other bodies.

I saw the sum of love my parents came from, and wanted
       a piece
            of that

Catchment areas, not pertaining to rivers. Lotteries, not pertaining to winning great sums. All that money lurking in the walls of houses. We were casting around for angles of oppression to cling to and be perpetually enraged.

> Postcolonial
> Postcode
>
> (lottery)
>
> post imperial
> We were learning, with great viciousness, to unzip one another
> of our illusions.

The "postcode lottery" was a shorthand of the time to refer to geographical inequality of housing, healthcare, life expectancy, education. The argument was that government should level up and bring equality everywhere. The "lottery" is from the point of view of an individual, obviously poverty has a history rather than being the product of casting lots or pulling numbers from a jar. Obviously, inequality is *the landscape* and not an illusion. The catchment area refers to the district in which you have to live to get into a given State school (possibly to other sorts of limited resource).

The epigraph is a Coptic phrase meaning "I am the utterance of my (own) name". This relates, I think, to a conception of magic in which the recital of names has mighty and non-human effects, on its own. In the book, it means more like "I am the sum of my past and the past is known through stories", I would guess. Administrators today have a pervasive feeling that they do not understand the children, and others, whose welfare they are charged to foster, and part of the interest in autobiographical poetry is to explain how biography led to a set of problems and needs, in an administrative sense. I am glad to say that some books are there to share experience and to give pleasure, rather than as part of some course in Diversity Awareness. I am still wondering whether Imelda finally copied the attitudes of the sophisticated with success, or whether she remained a parable of greed and insensitivity to context to the end of her days.

Jay G Ying, *Katabasis* (2020, 28pp)
A note tells us that the 2001 invasion of Afghanistan was originally known, in the planning stage, as "Operation Infinite Justice". Infinite is a large concept but justice is a larger one. Injustice too is a subject of notable scale. This is the perfect poem. The word *katabasis* means going down and refers specifically to the goddess Inanna going down to the underworld to rescue her lover. The reference to Mesopotamia (the story

is as old as the third millennium) is because the poem is about the second Gulf War; death in Mesopotamia is very much its central theme, but no-one will be coming back. Half the pages are given over to what seems to be a translation from a Sumerian text about Inanna, but probably isn't; we are at the origin of writing, 5,000 years ago, and the tone is of prophecy, advice on how to carry out saving actions and avoid fatal spells, to return to light from where you have descended to.

> Post-war I always remembered the gold coin counterfeit
> underneath my tongue would be the most useful metal.
> It is a communal affair to bless the newly dead, transfuse
> blood from a fake jewel in the maternity ward. On the path
> out of the humanitarian hospital, fresh veins of blue seemed
> to be the only medicine my ancestors sowed into miles of
> stone. The cyanosed baby's lips are the colour of lapis lazuli.
> ('Cursed Resources')

If we have visual memories of Mesopotamian relics, inlays of lapis lazuli (gives our word "azure") are likely to be the most vivid recollection. The stone is likely to be ancient Mesopotamian buildings, the origins of civilisation, often erased by explosives during the war. The "resources" must be oil; as an alluvial plain, the land between the rivers has few mineral resources. The theme is what we most fear and what reduces us to shivering naked creatures, souls and bodies stuck together with frail bonds; and the style is sublime, an exit into the mythological where every action is mysteriously vivid and concrete but at the same time evolving in mythical space, witness to the gods walking the earth.

> A colony of water rails skulk past the same common
> reeds of our house. I recall War's fingers taking it: one
> empty egg War clutched whenever our coast shrugged
> off its sawed yellow sedge; I could feel that water margin
> grow cold on me like a second skin. Singed splinters out
> of sight, ash on the lens of War's new black camera[.]
> ('Visible Waves')

The third element is that it deals with the State; the State we belong to was part of this war, our government played a crucial role in developing the lies which deceived the public and allowed it to happen. Does Hell exist? If it fills the stage here, it is because the Anglo-American alliance re-created it in order to punish the people of Iraq for a crime they were innocent of. They impersonated the wrath of God and carried out a levelling to bring about justice. This is sacrilege. Ying does not break the tension by allowing documentary fact to enter; we all watched the news as the war was happening, or read the follow-up stories which showed Iraqi society collapsing under the strains of "liberation", and we do not need documentary footage. Documentary is not myth. By believing in poetry he raises the matters of State from a hypertrophied archive of banal documents in banal language, including the key distortions that allowed false intelligence to become a political fact, and makes the government itself a sublime theme: inhuman but embodying a corrupted sliver, a live tissue sample, of our humanity, part of what we have to answer for. The state is sublime in the same way that a mountain is, because of scale; Ying does not allow the reduced moral and intellectual stature of so many of its servants to diminish the poem. The State walks through his great poem like a fallen goddess as much in love with mutilation as with the creation of new life.

The sense record throughout is like someone waking from deep unconsciousness and seeing a physical scene with hallucinatory clarity, shorn of prior memory; the scene is full of charges and warnings, elements of an event which altered the speaker's life irrevocably, which is still going on. They are on the way to being symbols but still signs, evidence by which we work out where we are and what the highest threat is.

Kata is a pair with *ana*; they are opposites. *Anabasis* is the name of a famous book by Xenophon, describing the journey home of 10,000 Greek mercenaries through the mountains of Anatolia to the Black Sea and ships home. Their start point was at the capital of the Persian Empire: in Mesopotamia, our Iraq. Their employer died and his contracts became null. Profit and violence were married to each other, already then. Their exit strategy was under-worked. Children are born with a sense of justice and adults sell military services to the highest bidder.

> Ghosts on fire swept past silvery
> cedar figures like a glue you might find if you, in foreseeing
> a surplus of blood, of credit at the turn of the century, slapped
> each foreign metal mosquito with your palm; and saw she
> had given birth to a stone child, eyes as quiet as lapis lazuli.
> ('Cursed Resources')

The poet is now publishing as Jay Gao.

Writing the Camp by **Yousif M. Qasmiyeh** (2021, 118pp)
In that empty reservoir cemented by my father I once hid hoping that at a certain stage I would drown alongside my image.

This is like reading a book of the Bible which you had never seen before. I can't see anything aestheticised, or even anything which would make you happy, but in compensation the degree of truth and of validity is off the scale. The author now lives in England and wrote the book directly into English, but he spent all his life, up to a certain moment, in a Palestinian refugee camp, Baddawi, located in the Lebanon, and the book is about a camp as the only human reality.

There is no moment of argument about what happened to the land which was taken away from the camp livers and whose absence confines them to such a narrow and barren ground. Argument is too traditional a human activity: we are inured to not listening to it. Astonishingly, Qasmiyeh is not interested in dispute; and this is why his book seems so true, because it does not enter into legal dispute, where there would inevitably be an opposite view. This would halve the force of his work. Law is always in dispute even when it is manifestly true; the courtroom is the natural home of deceit. So:

> As we walk, we remember: memories to me and the equivalent to her. We remember that those who watch are the ones whose traces are prior to their essence. They live. They die at the same time, to the extent that contracts are exchanged hastily, amongst themselves. They utter the same words in the name of the same thing. No time to revere the unseen. No time to lament the superfluous in sand. A camp, it is, sufficient in death as it is sufficient in itself not being a place to place.

> To my mother, it is through the old cemetery that women can reach the cheapest greengrocer, he of the roaming eyes and no sons.
>   (from 'An infinite outing; or the cemetery')

The book does not compare camp life to any ideal, hiding it behind a norm which we would instantly recognise, which we would prefer, which would make us feel more comfortable. That would reduce the density of his description. Comparison is an illusion. His work is as dense as stone, it seems to have turned into stone rather than simply being carved into its surface and hiding its depth. The stone is not just in itself. Justice is a sound we invented in order to cover up what we know, what we remember, the sense record.

This is a primary book in a sense that everything around it is not. Afterwards, it feels like part of our life rather than something we encountered in words, in anything as thin as sound. Comparison may reduce its density, directing our gaze away from its centre, but it does feel to me like a definition of the city, as a site of exaggerated human density, the catastrophe of human freedom and mobility, the explosive destruction of space in order to concentrate people where they can serve as cheap labour or as available consumers. The city was born not far away from the Lebanon and it was the extraction and grinding into dust of what humans had most loved up till then. Both living space and humans were subjected to a degree of symmetry which represented mindlessness and which made them available to calculation, to a form of knowledge which relied on the absence of mobility. It was a knowledge of the reduction of consciousness which was too much to be known or stored or reproduced.

I do not find any theology in this book. The subjects do not exit into a dimension of righteousness which would efface their daily lives. They do not exit into conformity with a divine law which would mean the silence of the compulsions of daily life and their rigidity, their reduction of human life to a piece of matter. Qasmiyeh is writing about being and time and so has been compared to Heidegger, a philosopher who was marked by recollection of divine life, but is much less theological than his model. Heidegger seemed at times to be reducing everything which was not experienced by an individual, and that is the core of Qasmiyeh's book, that he is looking at the other people inside the camp and not outwards at any other reality, which would attenuate consciousness of the real and the present. Rather we get a new sight of the books of the Scriptures, that they are moments of true narrative, of real experience, put into words by exceptional writers who were intellectually close to reality. The thousand layers of analogy came later and were only virtual planes, paper skins shed by the primary reality, the foundational story. Language is corrupted by analogy and speculation. The deeper layers of European culture, the moral strata which directed the geology, were imported from south-west Asia, and for thousands of years the local cultural experience was as a periphery where the core was in the East Mediterranean, and the sacred texts reflected that geography. *Writing the Camp* also reminds me of Yannis Ritsos' poems about life in the prison camps on Greek islands, (he was confined from 1948 to 1952), where Leftists who had taken part in the Civil War were imprisoned by the other side. One camp leads to another, an archipelago for sun-dazed sailors. Ritsos wrote many poems with almost no sensory or abstract content, direct efforts of consciousness in a confinement without paper or abstractions. In order to control many things and animals it was necessary to invent arithmetic and to pretend that they were all similar. This was a product of wealth. In the camp monotony amounts to sensory deprivation and the emptying of the senses gives rise to abstraction: the invention of philosophy. This is a product of poverty.

Anglo-Welsh

Ridges of Luxury: *Edge of Necessary. Welsh Innovative Poetry 1966–2018* (ed. John Goodby and Lyndon Davies. Aquifer, 2018. 342pp)
The design is to represent the non-mainstream, or underground, poets from the Anglo-Welsh world. The span of this selection is 1966 to 2018, and comparison is immediately possible with a 2007 anthology by Meic Stephens *(Poetry 1900–2000)* which covers most of the same span and is from the same small country. Visibly, *Necessary* is more or less the mirror image of *Poetry 1900–2000* – they hardly overlap, and this is the key to the mandate of *Necessary*. Out of 100 poets in Meic Stephens' selection, only 5 recur among the 46 in Goodby and Davies' roster. At the level of poems – only two recur. The depth of split is extraordinarily thorough. Wales is a small country. Actually, Meic's exclusion line guarantees the integrity of *Edge of Necessary* – as a cultural exclusion refuge. (He carries over fourteen poems from Rhys' classic 1944 anthology *Modern Welsh Poetry*.)

This opposition is the one between mainstream and underground with which I began my critical career, some 25 years ago. The mapping does not also give us the aesthetic quality of the anthology. But actually, it's great. And Stephens' anthology is a disaster, a kind of banana republic monoculture. After 850 pages, it feels as if the least creative poets have defined themselves as being the most Welsh and the most deserving of subsidy and promotion. How can artistic sterility be patriotic or Welsh? Was the composition of interchangeable poems by several dozen earnest people taken as the imagining of a classless society in which we would all say the same things at the same time every day? To sum up, the Goodby/Davies anthology is the first chance we have had to get a view of the last 50 years of Welsh poetry in English.

The book includes 46 poets which *pro rata* would equate to an anthology with 636 Underground poets from England. (Is that possible? The total count of Alternative poets is much *more* than 636. This is a valid thought experiment. We could call it *Hedge Fund of Inconsistency*. The volume would take two people to lift and glow in the dark.) It makes known the case for the unknown. So for example we have poems by Paul Griffiths and Heather Dohollau, who lived in France most of their lives, and who just don't feature in the surveys of Welsh literature. I find Dohollau's work (written in French) culture-pious, distinguished but not memorable. However, we need to know about it. We also need to know about Philip Jenkins, Ralph Hawkins, Graham Hartill, Harry Gilonis, Zoë Brigley, Rhys Trimble, and others.

 The introduction directs itself mainly at disqualifying the mainstream view as a consensus – an assault on the map which suddenly makes the other 80% of the landscape visible. Less time is given to describing the poets included, especially what might unite them. (A brief introduction locates each poet, within the text.) But any path you follow without turning back will take you away from the centre – these paths would not then get closer to each other, they would naturally lead you further and further apart, unless you turned, again, to converge. I can't sum up these 46 poets and that would only be necessary for a blurb, press release, etc., under artificial pressures. Does this make reviewers look ridiculous? Er. If I say that you probably won't like all the poems in *Edge of Necessary*, that isn't really a criticism. It is a classic anthology, if I am allowed to say that on publication, and there is a *frisson* at the start of each selection as you start to work out the poetological rules in force and their implications for the navigation of a self which changes its state every time the world impinges on it. I can talk about Elisabeth Bletsoe, someone who is surely writing some of the best contemporary poetry. Take this invocation of mid-winter in a poem drawn from folklore in which a dance might reflect the circling of the stars:

      Christ's mass
  light strobes through scattering pines
    hones itself on the earth's rim
        at the low point of the year
Milky Way a faint lactation
as rival groups of carol-singers in Severn Road
      set up a counterpoint
Plough hanging over the chimney
ladles great lungfuls of freezing air
      straight from the Pole:

  nail-star
round which the great world-tent
    revolves

>   demon-gatherer,
>   enemy of the Leviathan
>   on the last day you will still attend us,
>   a faithful spirit;
>   when the first three evening stars appear
>   the prayer invokes you;
>   I wait
>   on your circuitous arrival
>   and, like the door in the moon,
>   my heart stands
>   a little ajar for you
>   (from 'The 'Oary Man')

Zoë Brigley is also writing some of the best contemporary poetry:

> At night, I follow footprints, the five beans of each toe,
> and the long loaf of the foot. The war-flowers are stained:
> I follow the eye of each toe: the moon is the skull
> of a bleeding rabbit, its pock – all that these people
> have lost. I follow the flame of each toe, its branding
> of soft earth. That is all that they answer to our breath:
> they herald the moon's pock, the eye of a rabbit skull.
> They watch these forest-soldiers who hack the dropping eye
> of butterfly wings, who scrub the Z-like scar that bleeds
> the softened bark. When stars fade to breath, the sun races
> its blunt hooves through the wet forest horning and dappling
> the blinking dead in their long loaf of flowery death.
>   (from 'Day 8: Quarry')

(There is a tequila bar in Nottingham called 400 Rabbits and I think the setting here may be Mexico.) The comparison with Meic Stephens, who even after compiling numerous dictionaries of Welsh literature didn't know enough about John James to include him, is all in favour of Goodby and Davies. In fact, Stephens' anthology may still hold the title as the worst of the 21st century. His story is recorded in his autobiography (*Cofnodau*, in Welsh) and is roughly that he was a vigorous and gifted nationalist student, at Aberystwyth, who virtually invented Anglo-Welsh poetry publishing by founding Triskele Press (in 1967), and *Poetry Wales*, was on hand for the invention of Arts Council subsidy of poetry publishing, and from 1967 became a fragment of the nascent Welsh State, and subject to overwork rather than street demos. The text of his anthology (p. 877) describes him as having been "author, editor, and translator of about two hundred books." Very little of this was creative, or involved free critical interpretation. Most of it was trudging compilatory work. Much of *Cofnodau* is about his determination to grow old, and die, in the house in which he had grown up, in Treforest. Late in life, he wrote poetry, in the Welsh dialect of Treforest, recalling the 1940s – although as a child he had not spoken Welsh at all. This poetry is very good (the dialect is difficult). This was an obsessive journey into the past, a dream of circularity. Patriotically overworking, and becoming larger as the decentral Welsh State became larger, Stephens did not take on any new ideas in poetry after 1967. His autobiography becomes paralysingly tedious – as if he had given up on sensibility after taking on a job. Becoming the State may be a damnation, retaining unofficial status is a basis for creativity even if it means that ideas remain as vapourware.

Someone missing from Stephens' anthology is David Barnett.

> A child's death starts only
> their file to the she-
> earth among her sarsen stones,
> to a company
>
> of their guardians who'll shrive
> and move them when they enter
> this split in a settlement
> of oak and elder whose leaves
>
> are dyed for their sacrifice
> to her and whose produce
> bloats. Ducking fuss, she traces
> her scurfy hands across
>
> these few who lay upon her hips
> the shift to a green
> sleep beside the fire-issue
> from her flint feet
>
> and the aura from her stream,

jittery with dace.
  (from 'West Kennet – Long Barrow')

I find his integration of (originally) Third World mythological material into an English verse fabric compelling and virtuosic. I see an affinity with Bletsoe and Brigley – I just love poetry about myth, I admit it. I may be forgiven for going back over the border post to the Underground. The introduction uses the word *empirical*, a key-word for the Cold War Christian ethos in poetry. But is the new poetry recording things that did not happen? Take this poem by Peter Finch –

RNLD TOMOS (*vcl. hca. sme prse*) aka Curtis Langdon. 1913–2000. Gospel. Austerity tradition. Jnd Iago Prytherch Big Band (1959), gog, gap, bwlch, lleyn, tân, iaith, mynydd, mangle, adwy mainly on Hart-Davis race label. Reissue Dent PoBkSoc Special Recommnd. Concert at Sherman support Sorley Maclean (*gtr, hrt clutching*) sold out. Fire bomb tour Sain triple CD for D Walford Davies (*vcl, crtcal harmonium*) new century highspot. A pioneer of dark wounds and internal tensions. In old age bird song and reliable grouch. Stood, was counted, still no change. To live in Wales is to become un-assailable. 'An angel-fish' (Clarke). Expect retrospective, marvelling, and statue.

The subject is R.S. Thomas, a poet who regarded originality as the condiment of Gomorrah. Surely this is full of accurate experience, and Finch generally contains more information, and less filtered information, than conventional poets. (The poem is in both anthologies. The use of conventions from record sleeve notes may be a hint about the lack of entertainment in Ronald Thomas' work. He wasn't there to cheer people up. The "gog" bit is a sort of accelerated summary of Plaid Cymru clichés.) The difference is in not using a conventional perceptual rhythm – where every element is simplified to fit one route of flow control, and as we are knocked unconscious by a sermon-like Moral at the end the chance of developing new perceptions is suppressed. Finch takes on all kinds of information and has a high documentary content – but also sees information as a substance that can be channelled, recycled, inverted, mutated, and so on. This manipulation expresses the freedom of a self in a world made of sensations. Tilla Brading is clearly in touch with memory and sensation:

>   listen   stumble
>   on town brews
>   trespassing
>   stubbled vision
>
>   snuffing climbing
>   bills in the fire
>   climbing the hill
>   to scratch it alone
>   thistles pricking your work
>   mild cattle holing your fence
>
>   officialdom wears
>   paths through your Caebach
>   condescending accents
>   slice quaintness
>   bara of your warm kitchen
>   work it down
>   clean earth may cover
>   ('Movement from the Hills')

and this is true of Ferry Press-era Chris Torrance:

>   Strode out into the woods with
>   cat, axe & saw to bring back
>   mushrooms: Ceps
>   & Rough-stemmed Boletus: apricot-
>   lunged Chanterelle; pretty, intoxicant
>   amanita muscaria emerging
>   richly red from her
>   silky membranous fur. The
>   music becomes more insane, more unreadable.
>   Tea onto the compost heap. Empty the cats'
>   shitbox. & then, preferring "my ease
>   to my will" (Valéry)
>   nettle & marigold beer
>   trickles down my throat.
>   ('The Theatre of its Protagonist's Desires')

– it's all concrete details really. The primary component of the alternative poetry is documentary. The alternative style involves a dropping of barriers to all kinds of signals, relying on the incredible human sensitivity to human signals to reach an emotional effect. There is much less labelling and separation. Information is flowing in from many spectra. This poetry is not a flight from experience. If you go back to the famous bridge-blocking nationalist protest, against the use of English in the administering of the law, in Aberystwyth, on 2 February 1963, what happened was that the locals stopped to jeer and then began to beat the students up. ("'Do we keep you in college for this?', shouted one rabble rouser … A companion looked down at the icy waters of the River Rheidol 40 ft below and suggested: 'throw them all in'".) Why? The belief in progress out of poverty through education was basic to Welsh people, and the locals saw the students as playing truant and indulging themselves in airy fantasies, which were likely to break their parents' hearts and waste all the sacrifices of their relatives (probably over several generations). This urge to get on had, indeed, led to the spread of English. This part is not described by Stephens in his autobiography, although he was on that bridge. What happened then? The nationalists did persuade the electorate (by the 1997 referendum), and this occurred by putting over a simple and repetitive message which placed people in fixed and rigid roles. This became the way in which people thought about English-Welsh relationships. The poetry favoured by Stephens is not empirical but it does involve a very simple message, installed in very fixed and rigid artistic schemas. This manner obscures other possibilities, and asks all poets to write very similar poems, to reinforce the message. This is what Stephens' anthology documents – and I don't think *empirical* quite gets the measure of it. Goodby and Davies insist, in their introduction, on the English source for this manner – roughly, the hostility to the Soviet Union and to teenage culture in English Cold War poetry was replaced by hostility towards England and to English-language mass culture. Little needed to be changed, then. Basic forms repeated.

Stephens' resistance to the modern-style poetry in *Necessary*, over a 50-year period, shows a lack of artistic sensitivity and is not politically benign or open. I can see that deep diversity makes government more difficult, but the idea of a population with homogeneous feelings and thoughts strikes me as a nationalist fantasy. Just to pin this in place – many of the "alternative" poets are deeply patriotic, I think, and write persistently about Welsh scenes and about the significance of the Welsh past.

There is a match between the tightness of the bonds between Stephens, a small group of his associates, and their sources of patronage, and the tightness of grouping of the poets he favours. What is this? It looks like a map of the negative effects of solidarity. I'm not saying that diversity makes government easy – just that society became ideologically diverse in the Sixties, and that you can't put the water back in the pipe. I think the didactic and simplified version of modern existence might support a governing regime, but it raises questions about tutelage and policing of a consensus. Finally, the realistic/communalist poetry in Stephens' huge but narrow anthology just hasn't been very productive artistically.

Samantha Wynne-Rhydderch gets into both anthologies:

> Been under a preservation order for a while now,
> me and Dave Penhaligon, the Court Stenographer.
> Pillar talk with lemons. He was the one who painted the
> mural in Talybont. It was a get-out clause really.
>
> Before the war we drank in *Tafarn Jem*, enjoying a bit of
> quality isolation. Wensleydale and Bourbon,
> a right caryatid I was. They live for the *Jif*
> all those cariads behind the bar.
> The good thing about the plastic ones is that
> they stay yellow forever.
>   (from 'Deacon Brodie's Predecessors: 2. The Surf Report')

The rhyme of cariad and caryatid is just irresistible. (The pillars are also barmaids in this case.) As this would suggest, the landscape is continuous. I suspect that Wynne-Rhydderch does not belong with the "alternative" poets", but that does not say she is not an excellent poet. Sheenagh Pugh and Robert Minhinnick are also "mainstream" poets who impress as writers. From 2002 (with *After the Hurricane*), Minhinnick evidently lost all literary inhibitions and became an alternative poet – becoming a far better poet by this liberation. Paul Evans, early on an associate of Eric Mottram and the dangerous radicals, went on to write very conservative poetry – the only phase which Stephens chooses from. His poetry suffered a disastrous fall in quality. The analogy with Minhinnick is compelling – Minhinnick gets much better and Evans gets much worse. This would suggest that the innovative style has more to offer artistically. This is why an anthology like this one is an attractive idea. Minhinnick doesn't get into *Necessary* (don't ask me why), but his older poems are in *Poetry 1900–2000*:

> A rusted naval craft
>
> Gutted from deck to brine
> Filled bilge – while faint on the wind come sounds
> Of the remote city, the retreating tide,
> As the Channel shifts its immense cold acre
> A little farther from
>
> The shore, revealing a
> Tundra streamered with weed
>   (from 'Salvage').

The problem with this really isn't the physical description, which is excellent, but the smugly neat conclusion: "And there is/ No shaking off one's own defeat". The scrapped vessel is a symbol of defeated people, and the poet thrown out of a job. This isn't empirical but sentimental.

Wynne-Rhydderch's poems probably fail to be alternative because they are monologues pointing back to the poet, who is a character described by them. This is also why they are good. But the rule might be "you can't mortgage your poetry to a Self unless you're Frank O'Hara", and anyway John James and Paul Evans (both influenced by the New York School I guess) definitely write monologues that create a personality on the page, and describe autobiographical adventures. The definition of "alternative" is owned by the audience, a speech community, but they use the concept inconsistently.

One final point is about the definitive status of the anthology, whether it holds its ground against a complex and decentralised reality, and how it could possibly cover a field which by its nature is scattered and suppressed. One hitch with this, obviously, is that I can only review it in terms of what I know. Since it includes so many poets I have never heard of, I would hazard that it is comprehensive to a very impressive degree. The background is of consistent research efforts by the editors over a ten-year period, and (I understand) of fortunate meetings with very cooperative local dissidents who cling tenaciously to memories which the great and the good have told them to be false. This is the ripe product of a fragile project. *Ardderchog! dal ati!*

Cris Paul, *stenia cultus handbook* (67pp, 2010)
The idea of newspaper design is that people buy a paper which reflects the judgements they have already made and which, therefore, causes the least possible mental effort; out of multiplicity warm porridge. In poetry, too, you have a line which smoothly reinforces social roles and which shows brothers being brotherly, fathers fatherly, dogs acting like dogs, in a comforting way. Conversely, you have poetry, and Cris Paul's is a wonderful example of this, in which at every step there is a sense of shock and confusion at political arrangements and their everyday consequences.

> *The gorgeous simulacra, as seen from space, from the very launches of the ivory tower, or from TV, is so gorgeous, endless interplay, signs sighs and meanings, but close up and personal, pushed up the face and the daily brickwork, it seems patchy at best, a packed and stale air, dreadful superstructure[...]*
>
> *However, through the gold we could discern the earlier aggression of wretched men. Some spells and pacific lulls, immobile they bled, lashed and severed from themselves, hopeless as the war industry perpetuates itself, tattoos the figment of any particular blood to any particular soil, nations and culture or portable feasts, but not the means, or riches. This struggle. This writhing.*
>   (from 'Dream of the Rood, a translation')

Vandalising a Saxon poem is a metaphor for the saxonising of Welsh culture. The literary method has reading as a metaphor for 'reading' everyday life by means of its dominant rules. The fabric of the poetry is partly the uninterpreted, unresolved by set ideas, and partly savage rewrites of the over-interpreted flow of the media. The appeal of his work relies on a supposition that simply behaving exactly like your parents is not enough, and that the state of 'everyday life' is connected to an integral set of failures. Constantly a displacement of scale or speed disorients the text. Thus in 'Cas' we are presented with a shape and with a set of words made unrecognisable by leaving out the vowels:

```
p st che m s c
th  p st
 n th r  c  ntry
f st  n n st lg
 r s st nc  nn x d
```

This 'develops by exposure to light' into *pastiche music/ the past/ is another country/ of standing fast long/ resistance annexed.* The point of the abraded words is to make perception more acute: the recovery of the words reveals the presence of a threshold of response, decoying into awareness a level, a damp course, of suppression of response. The question of aesthetic acuity connects at once to the damaged nature of our daily world. The return of suppressed meanings opens up new political and social possibilities, the return of the aesthetic sense too. Previous poems have told us that the 'cas' in 'Casnewydd' means castle and described the castle as kernel of the town being surrounded by an unreadable jangle of urban motorways and underpasses. The shape reveals itself as the castle keep, a hexagon with jutting battlements.

I could deliver a story in deep time of what this was, starring a living stock of ideas in the London scene, the whole career of Peter Finch, the post-war European avant-garde which promoted sound and concrete poetry, Rio de Janeiro, Stockholm, Basel. Milan. Newport. This would be too comforting, since the continuity on view offers protection from that shock moment where we find that all our intellectual investments have been wiped out and that our acquired reactions are useless. *stenia cultus handbook* does not reassure because each part of it offers disorder and instability, where things are vanishing and beginning. The title seems to come from an Ancient Greek festival, Thesmophoria. A *Cultus* is a ritual act. The Stenia involved the exchange of obscene utterances, possibly related to fertility.

Keinc (2010) is the debut of Rhys Trimble, a Welsh-speaker writing avant-garde poetry in English with snatches of Welsh. *Keinc* means branches, so spelt in the manuscripts of the *Mabinogion*, which say 'the four branches of the Mabinogion' and so on. It means 'divisions', the 'logy' of 'trilogy'. The first section shows four poems based on *Mabinogion* characters, including the less than popular Efnisien. The work starts with a sweeping out of the inherited furniture of poetry, leaving a gleamingly empty space which is partly filled and partly evoked as the realm of freedom. The poems seem to be written not on a series of flat squares but on a more shaped and unpredictable object, perhaps in fact a spindle or multiple spindles. They are intricate, sophisticated, prolonged, and serene. The relaxed feeling about allowing Welsh phrases to drift in parallels the relaxed attitude to using free syntax and versification. There is no problem about hopping over walls. A taste for singularity and conceptual folds goes along with patriotic Welsh reading and going on walks up Welsh mountains. The pattern is often a journey, such as, in 'afanc' one by rail up Snowdon, in which the noted Glamorgan patriot Iolo Morgannwg is seen both as a beaver (the *afanc* of a certain folk-tale) and as an opium user:

*contra di*eselfuming with

erratics: a dead child's playthings
I breathe mist, exhale smoke
afancaidd, & aching enamelling
       raw & *blys y boncyffion*

Blys is *craving*, the *boncyffion* are tree stumps being eaten by the beaver but merge with the fogs of the mountain and Iolo's famous literary mystifications, possibly also with the dross of opium from his burnt-out pipes. The manner of meaning is both light and constantly original. For example the flower, in English bluebell, known in Welsh as cuckoo bells, clychau'r gog, is associated in another poem with the Gogs, short for *gogledd*, the North Welsh –

you get the gog
the north
walian, pure-slate eyes that
shine with
fall-in-love
potentialities

drawn here to this
bell of phrastic line, to these snare-
currents.

Trimble treats sounds almost like places, in his botany of sensations. If sharpness of perceptions and indifference to ideologies are indices, this is pure poetry. Looking at 'aros', the one poem wholly in Welsh, shows up the omission of conventional structures of language, the freeing of a feather from a matrix of stone. We do well to focus on the omissions, most extremely in the twenty words of 'goshawk', their virtuoso staccato furl, as they leave space for passages of density and opulence:

>   the same blue
>   the same green, heal
>
>   metamorphic, illite & mud slatted
>   siliconic-sills
>   ferrous, spheric
>   words azure & grey
>   left a party marked
>   scar-thumb
>   (from 'awdl pesda')

It would be a shame if his poetry became monolingual.

Robert Minhinnick (1952–) is the most gifted poet of his generation within the Anglo-Welsh tradition. He edited *Poetry Wales* (1997–2008). He began in the Seventies and his first phase is recorded in the *Selected Poems* of 1999. That volume virtually defines that local line of realist and communalist writing with its sociological accuracy; it also shows someone supremely skilled writing in a style which does not profoundly excite him. His later development left or re-invented that tradition. As we said, he took off artistically after 2000, on realising he could be a world poet and not just the best Anglo-Welsh poet. He moved roughly from 'communalist' to 'rustbelt poet' to 'magic realism' and thus became the heir to Dylan Thomas. I think that his really important work came then, in the two volumes for Carcanet: *After the Hurricane* (2002); *King Driftwood* (2008, 129pp). The transformation is of singular interest and the pressure to write in a pinched and empirical way was of geological force. He has worked in the environmental movement for many years and his unifying theme is the destruction of the environment. 'The Hourglass' is a poem about sand:

>   At Kenfig the fog
>   fell in a golden
> Götterdämmerung. The swan, the sanderlings,
> the conger cold as cistern-iron?
> The famished sand filched that feast.
> And the poets who practised there left nameless;
> well-drivers, grapegrowers, wolfwatchers likewise.
>   If any escaped

> they are unrecorded. Only the castle sometimes
>   is mistaken in the mist.
> How drunk was that watchman
> he missed the dune at the door?

This contains a reference to a Norman castle which was recorded by Leland in 1539 as having been almost buried by the sand, drifting in from the Bristol Channel. The theme of the poem is coastal erosion and it crosses three continents. The planetary scale of the environmental crisis is the hatch by which the poems escape into a boundless world of new connections. The arrangement of consonants (Poets–Practised–graPe-growers) reproduces *cynghanedd* but since the verse is not otherwise regular this is just anglohanedd. Or perhaps a special blurred sweetness called mumblehoney. 'To Those on the Promontory' describes a coastal town (probably Porthcawl near Cardiff) through the colourful characters who live there, seeing them in mythical terms. A touch of Jacques Brel, a touch of T Glynne Davies.

> Down Rhych Avenue I think it was
> I shone my torch around a cave:
>   isopods scittered,
> there was a tear duct in every gryke.
>   And that's where I saw them,
> the paintings the current had left
>   stick men and stags,
>   and our sun with its green helix
>   in a core sample of fossilised light.
> The sea's scrimshaw maybe,
> as if we lived our lives upon a narwhal tusk,
> this town where the road ends is ending now,
> where we are on the promontory.
>
>   Last night under the breakwater
> while the dark double bassists were sawing with their limestone arms
> and the conductor brandishing his pincers at the air
>   each wave was a white
>   was a white
>   carnation the orchestra
>   had trodden underfoot

> as Grace Williams with her book of children's psalms
> > drowned in a lobster-pot.
> > > (from 'To Those on the Promontory')

(The *helix* probably refers to a phonetic theme which will appear twice in the poem, once before this passage and once after: all hail helios. The Welsh for sun is *haul* which is pretty much like helios (IE *sowelos)). He describes a metal-detectorist: "NV has read of chariots unearthed/ with the skeletons of gold-corseted kings/ still holding the rawhide reins". I think the poet actually wrote "corsleted", but who knows. It is striking how much of the visible world of the streets and the pubs he evokes while transforming it all into myth. He is one of the most important poets now writing.

Short Strings, Polyrecombinant;
or, Raze the Seabed

It is a fact that a poem is a long string of sounds made up of short strings of sounds. The short strings have characteristics which are too small-scale to be personal: you can't own words or stress patterns. If you make the ego the centre of attention then all the text supports it and the shape of the text is both a reflection of the ego and lives at the highest level, the overall level. But if you look at the shortest text strings you get a different view. The text is decentralised and the overall level disappears. This non-conscious level is of interest to historians because it is where you can date a text. As you assign a poem to the decade in which it was composed, you find a stratum of verbal behaviour which is not individual property – it is collective.

Reading a poem involves submerging in someone else's patterns and publishing a poem involves surrendering ownership of patterns so they can become anybody's. The problem with plagiarism (there were some enjoyable scandals about this in 2013 and following years) is that it reintroduces ownership in a fake way. Arguably, poems aim to become everybody's. You can't get the scene without realising that at least one person has been awarded a PhD in Creative Writing for poems copied from other people. *Call the doctor, pretty baby. Tell him it ain't no fun.* The most effective plagiarism sleuth is Ira Lightman. Ira said in an interview "The feeling I was having before the plagiarism stuff was that nobody thinks there's any meaning or catharsis in my work: they think it's trance-like, comic, pattern-generated. That wouldn't have changed if I hadn't done plagiarism sleuthing, and possibly has changed now. There's a side in my early work that's very agitprop and protest poetry, and I've always wanted it there in my poetry. But maybe it's not my fate. I don't feel I've restricted myself as a poet because of the sleuthing."

Not only Ira, but also his friend Matthew Welton (whose poems were copied out by a copycat in another celebrated case), have an interest in procedures which can be used to generate poems. There may be a link between Ira's artistic interest in freely chosen patterns and a detached grasp of patterns which helps you to spot strings repeating in a new context. His use of patterns is related to detachment from coherence– with the idea that personality patterns are compulsive and so conservative and unfree. (Repeating stored memories is a loss of freedom.) Using designed patterns which can produce unplanned outcomes is a critique of ownership. It moves away from the idea that the poem is a sort of bottle in which the poet's personality is the wine, and that personality is worth buying because it contains unusual talent, sensitivity, etc. That theory of exceptionalism raises the question of how the poem benefits the reader, who obviously is *not* so special, chosen by the gods, etc. If you design a process which generates poems, it follows that someone else could run the process and generate a poem.

The more you get used to programs, not just in poetry but in business and anything else touched by computers, the more often you have a moment of suspecting that the brain runs programs and that behaviour is composed by numerous programs which are more or less complete in themselves and reliable because pre-set and fixed. In this moment, using explicit and declared programs to generate poems is a mirror to the mind.

AI generates poems

There is a long history of using programs, later artificial intelligence or "AI", to generate verbal texts. In 2019, a group of computer engineers was looking at the high-end text generator GPT-2 and I managed to get involved with their work. They were interested in finding out how the program worked, whereas I was interested in getting random strips of strange language which I could use in poems. The runs were extremely expensive in computer processing time. The main expense was in letting the program teach itself the input textual corpus: "Once I have the material it takes a few days/weeks to generate a model." Having learnt the ropes the program could turn out output in unlimited quantities, like many poets. Interest faded when the developer released GPT-3, although actually GPT-2 had not ceased to be interesting and unexpected.

Part of one poem ran:

> The roar of buildings shook the earth.
> The drums of flesh and matter shook the air.
> Agitatron crunched the Bible in his head,
> He worked in a false division of weight and depth,
> He called his pendulums mass and depth and mass
> And mass and division and division and division.
> His nine-headed clank shook the frozen earth.
> The streets were choked with voice calls.

> The fossils of the terrestrial earth shook the temperate earth.
> The mountains razed the seabed to make way for cities.
> The waterways choked with live fish and mammals
> Shone the earth of walkths, dead the metropolis of fishes
> Deaden my people from taking arms; slaughter my fish!
> Their slogans mocked my dominion; slaughter my mariners!
> Their slogans mocked my nations;
> Their slogans mocked my worms.
> Their slogans mocked my cities.
> Too many mouths for the known. Too few for the theiave.
>
> The roar of the factories made the graves of empires.
> Traitors to the planet's memory to ruin.
> Thousands lose their limbs and swamps are full of worms.
> The flanks of a toque of lizards smear free-falls.
> A sleeping tyrant crumbles to a tincture of lolling lizards.

I really liked this, especially "The mountains razed the seabed to make way for cities." Part of the appeal may have been that some runs were based on raw text which came from my early poetry. It produced patterns which deeply stirred me even when they had no meaning, and I recognised part of the reason why I had tried to set those patterns to words in the first place. We didn't get very far with working out how GPT-2 worked, but you could see that outputs like this sounded like myths because a program has no context, and myths are about primal eras when things are being created from nothing and have no past and, genuinely, no context. If you check, there are no adjectives in this passage; entities appear as if they were the only exemplars of their category, and this is also a feature of myth. (Actually, there is at least one adjective. I love the way in which *terrestrial earth* has such a ring even though terra means "earth" and earth is terrestrial by definition.)

There is a link between GPT-2 and the analysis which Ira carried out to identify plagiarism. Ira trained himself to recognise short but variable patterns, and to see only these while blocking out the overall poem – especially its emotional message, its reference to a (supposed) human being. So he could recognise short patterns when they recurred in other poems. The copyist does not copy a personality but only patterns of phrasing. The copying is literal in the same way that GPT-2 is. Isolating patterns allows GPT-2 to generate more or less endless variant strings of

words (but not to express a personality).
Another passage was:

The artist in me flickers, awash in ideals
lustring on the count of gold watches and fine apparel. But
the strong wind ruffling my veils draws me in step
and shouts at me in the rich, noble tongue
in the slow wind it shouts again,

"You must possess and rule this expensive corporeal
stuff, rich woman, and please your lover
with the figures and the ceremonies."

Each of these objects, each
is yours; each can be possessed and loved.

Each of these objects is owned by someone;

they lack personality: they are not things,
they are passions; they are not
love. No, you cannot possess such a thing.
Each one is yours in three ways:
to possess them as a jewel is to own them
as a possession is to control them.

We thought this might be derived from an advertisement, or from analysing advertisements. A colleague remarked that a certain GPT-2 passage sounded like a Prynne poem. I agreed. I would guess that the ring has to do with a dissolution of the "ego illusion", so that language is not reflecting the repetitive patterns of an ego/body. Then, there is a data intake of vast extent, flowing in articulated information of unmeasured diversity. The parts don't curve back into one shape, they go on moving out into a void, not confirming each other. Subjective feelings of similarity may genuinely be feelings of insecurity and cognitive incompleteness, i.e. that well up from our own body/ego and are not truly to be found in the language samples we are looking at. Prynne's texts are not reassuring. The generated texts are not the product of wisdom, depth, or even of experience. We have to ask if Prynne's texts actually have these assets. "Ego free" language may affect us like immersion in cold water – we are feeling something drain out of us. Insecurity may cause us to form hypotheses – a kind of productivity. Another passage I liked was:

Stone objects strike discordant metals; metals
Which are called knowledge or beauty or knowledge
Which the eye picks up in successive steps;
Which, seeing a dark blue, reveals a deeper truth;
Which eye sees a rich red, reveals a stranger soul;
Which language is the spoken language of men?
As in the quarrel the jealous eye has three part

wrath is a ridged channel found both in the planes of blindness
and in the coma of the eye
that channel is wrapped and protected by the
vertebral column

Sheared: a reticulate sound that pierces the motor cortex
as she slays matter.
Borne: a curved and fractured sound
lips through the viscera
 as it rushes through the built-up circulation
Sensation has no body, and no family; now comes

far, in the lofty cavities of the Chamber of Fine Arts,
where the novice glass making team
draw up an impossibly simple optical model of stellar motion,
far away from the workhouse.

The high temperatures of the High Bronze where the finishing touches
dry cast, the Model Tartu, an astronomical observatory
in 17 rooms in the Institute of the High Eight ounces of copper
wet in sunlight, in the flawless Q lens
that lets the Light enter into the Institution. The institute is an
       exchange for silver,
the slight exchange for knowledge, the
negligent and excessive exchange for favour.

Ira (1969) trained as a mathematician before getting involved in poetry (I know this because he mentions it in a letter from about 1991 which I looked up for some reason). I feel this gave him an unusual ability to focus on short strings of language and to see how a relatively small number of transforms could reflect and shear these strings and produce new ones. My feel is that this skill has let him identify hundreds of plagiarisms but also it helps him to invent procedures and to create hundreds of new lines following those procedures through.

It is easy to code up strings of sounds, writing began to do that 5000 years ago; it is more difficult to identify how a somatic basis, a body and sensory system, amount to an ego and animate a poem or a set of poems. The stored record of the poem is just a string of letters and blanks, actually the body and ego are not stored and we create them during the reading process, by projection. This is quite complicated and we can see that some people have difficulty doing it. Identification is the usual word, but this covers a serial process whose parts are undescribed and unrecorded. As usual poetry is resting on an extensive basis of theory that does not exist. How do you record changes in the implicit? There is an ethereal substrate which we only know by how it shapes words and tempi. An animation. A torso with organs but no substance.

Ira Lightman has worked as a public poet, collaborating with visual artists on installations and being in residence in towns apparently thirsty for culture. This has combined with an avant-garde approach – it seems that the traditional type poet has the personality as the dominant structure within the poems, and this makes the poem inherently private, and so not public. He has been interested in the minimal structures of language – the ones which generate utterances over repeated runs. This axis has been obvious to a generation raised on computers, aware of how simple forms generate complex ones. And, of course, of how small changes in the generative forms lead to staggering changes in the large-scale forms at the output end. The new language which arrives is strange – the poet can no longer hear their voice, but this is a drama about inhibition; someone insensitive to risk will plunge into the unmapped terrain and lead the readers there. In contrast, there is a collective voice of cultured poets which is static and a legacy and fragrant with authority and security. The more of a legacy it is, the more reassuring, and the more numbing. Lightman's language is childlike, that is where the game leads. I was especially impressed by *Duetcetera* (2008), which has two streams of language running simultaneously. The language overflows and we are in a state of unawareness, swimming through data which we can't assimilate.

<pre>
    REMEMBER the led better   DON'T know why with
                       life   inspired
                      next   steps
               to the good   tiptoeing the cartoon
             accommodating   clown
                  situated   vehicular
                     comic   transport
             less the brief   tickles in rigidly
       scripted and more the adult viewing frame of
        character if you buy reference no longer for
           enough to keep a   many who grown up
         float in the black and colourless half the time thus
           am I or have I ever been tortured by dizzy pacifiers
</pre>

This is an artistic effect, like surrealism, we are destabilised and as it were dancing. Intellectually, a point is being made about attention, how it misses most of what is really there (and which could be picked up by a camera or a microphone, let's say) and how we head for stability all the time – and are bored whenever we actually reach it. Neuroscientists speculate that the mind actually has multiple parallel processes, and the single dominant voice is an illusion. The swarming fragments of the poem *Duetcetera* may in reality be these parallel processes, running through the fields and off the road. It could be argued that art differs from reality essentially by being more consistent and self-reinforcing, allowing the ego to reach greater unity than is its everyday lot. There is an unconscious rule that more consistent language is better language, and one can observe more and more re-edits of a description making the prose more consistent; although it may also become less and less accurate as we do this. I am quite happy to admit that descriptions of poets which consent to the inconsistencies are more truthful – even if it sounds like I haven't mastered my material. Lightman destabilises us by temporarily abolishing unconscious rules like consistency. Lightman's style is the result of genuine and repeated risks, and it is likely that this is what allows his poetry to pose genuine intellectual questions, and that this is what people look for in modern poetry – as opposed to more and more country walks and old churches. The interest in language as something generated is significant to anyone involved with computing, as I said;

Lightman's poetry can be compared to works by Matthew Welton and Giles Goodland, I think.

Artistic procedures as developed in the 1960s resemble the non-conscious patterns which GPT-2 isolates in huge unsorted extents of language. Set procedures are mirrors in which we can see the real sequence of normal psychological patterns. We can see the dark processes only by catching them in mirror materials which mimic parts of them. This mimicry lets them be known. The line of conceptual art generally involved lifting out the archaic and spectral to run something concrete and conscious. But this limitation could also be challenged.

What if we see emotions as procedures, and so archaic blocks of code of fairly small lengths – and consequent predictability? If emotions are common to all humans, they are archaic – and so belong to the older layers of software and not the modern ones.

West-bloc dissidents: Alternative Poetry

The appeal of the Alternative cannot be summed up quickly but we can make some suggestions. Its suppositions may be as follows:

> That all the practical knowledge of how to live and have fun is wrong and surrounded by better ideas as if it were some wrong idea in mathematics.

> That the conventional knowledge of sociology, anthropology, and history is full of holes and human life is full of undocumented and repressed possibilities drifting off in a wealth of unknown forms.

> That language can be separated from representation and used to create endless new patterns, just as numbers can.

> That poets are interested in showing off their most attractive features at the expense of unfolding new forms the whole time as they should

> That psychology in poems is attenuated by this showbiz need to be personable and predictable.

> That language is made of conventions held in place by apathy and that patterns which seem improbable and deviant may work far better than the conventions

> That exclusively the wrong people are in power

> That every existing interpretation of what happens in any given scene of human intention is wrong and judgements made on human beings, relying on such interpretations, are all wrong.

How well all this works is a question too complicated to answer. There is no inspectorate of alternative poetry. There is an alternative sector and it is embodied in publishers like Veer, Sad Press, Knives Forks and Spoons, and Contraband. Strictly in volumetric terms, one could write a book on alternative poetry that dealt with nothing else. Separation is the thing that people argue about, I suppose, but the patterns of attention which this poetry demands are different and it is sensible to produce a book or a magazine that is *only* alternative, so that the reader is facing the right way. I admit that there was a period when I read only alternative poetry, and that I exited from this because I found sectarianism so unattractive (when directed at me) that I wanted to cover the broad spectrum. I suppose that the Alternative includes about 15-20% of the poets publishing. Figures are difficult because so many people are not completely inside or outside. Inside the Alt world the Alt world is seen as the apex of poetry. This is an example of a secret apex, because everyone else certainly doesn't see them as superior or more advanced. (I wonder what the *total* count of secret apices is.)

Imagine you are back in the 1950s and there is a theatrical impresario who is gay but declines to stage any play with a gay theme because of commercial worries. The reason why managers don't publish or stage Alt poets is not to do with ideological oppositions but with economic anxiety. They are worried about success. Whatever they are in charge of, whether a readings series, a magazine, a publisher, they want popularity and they are going to have a bad feeling if the customers stay away in droves. Their associates will blame them, and they will feel like failures. There is a very strong stereotype of a poet being someone who asks people to identify with them, who offers simple patterns of identification, and reassures the audience that they are having the same reactions as each other. The managers feel people keep coming back to secure the same feelings. Conversely, they are worried that Alt poetry offers abstractions rather than feelings, doubt rather than reassurance, challenge rather than comfort. So they associate innovative poetry with anxiety. If the audience drops from, say, fifteen people to ten, the readings will come to an end. They are worried about the resentment of disappointed customers who feel that they are being excluded. This attitude is not based on evidence, or not on recent evidence, and is not responsive to argument. It is quite compatible with admiring modernism (in any *other* context).

One way of looking at the Alternative is to say that conventional and conformist poetry is lumpish and makes you feel ill, and that, every day since about 1960, one person has said, *I've had enough*, made an exit from the central, High Street, camp and made off on their own. If they find other dissidents, later, that is because art is a social thing and you want company, at any time. I raise this as an alternative to the genealogical view of the Alternative, which suits the interests of older poets so neatly. I think it is quite reliable that young people will read Armitage, or Motion, or Kathleen Jamie, and think "Oh my God do I sound like this. Let me die". The idea that the dissidents also share something with each other is much less likely.

Discussion of alternative poetry in the abstract can be frustrating, so I thought to compile a list of 20 works which, among so many, state the case for not being conventional. Richard Capener, *KL7*. Andrea Brady, *Vacation of a Lifetime*. Sean Bonney, *Letters Against the Firmament*. Philip Terry, *Advanced Immorality*. Nat Raha, *Octet*. Peter Philpott, *Textual Possessions*. David Spittle, *B O X*. Luke Roberts, *False Flags*. Nancy Gaffield, *Continental Drift*. Mark Goodwin, *Else*. Marianne Morris, *The On All Things Said Moratorium*. Samantha Walton, *TTAGGG*. Peter Manson, *Between Cup and Lip*. John Goodby, *Illennium*. Maggie O'Sullivan, *Palace of Reptiles*. Oli Hazzard, *Between Two Windows*. Nicholas Spicer, *Lines on the Surface*. David Ashford, *Kharagmata*. Linus Slug, *Type Specimen*. D.S. Marriott, *incognegro*.

I am doubtful that the experimental poetry of the Seventies has much to do with alternative poetry of the past ten years. When students break out of the territory which the textbooks and anthologies are confined to, the cultural artefacts which they do accept may be post-structuralist theory, radical politics, rock music, conceptual art, classical modernism, and other things. These objects or records are much easier to find, when shopping, than British alternative poetry. Of which it is still true to say that "our history was written by our enemies".

I am putting forward the geographical view of alternative poetry which says that it is the whole of the spectrum (except the centre) and that this wavelength band has a geographical site which is abiding. Scotland is to the north of England, alternative poetry is everything which is not conventional and familiar.

The voiceless and surfaceless

Didier Eribon quotes a moment from a Foucault interview of April 1966. The question was "when did you stop believing in meaning", and the answer ran in part: [that] "meaning was probably only a sort of surface effect, a shimmer, a foam, and that what ran through us, underlay us, came before us, sustained us in time and space, was the system". [p.177] If the conventional poets produced ideas which were justified by reference to the poet speaking, and feelings which were justified because they took place inside that poet, that is an enterprise which was bound to grind to a halt when faced with a thinking person whose theory led them to regard the bourgeois subject as a phantom, a component of a capitalist state, a fleck of foam, a pretty shimmer on the surface of the real. If you find in a book of poems a couple of hours shaped by the presentation of a self, and offering a voluntary and finite identification with that self, that sums up what the anti-humanists could not believe in. It sums up also the motive for poetry as an activity. A different poetry could show involuntary movements of the body and subjectless action. It would be like a documentary, without a script or collusion. (Only in this sense does it lack meaning, as self-presentation.) It would be governed by processes, not self admiration.

Art is all about sight lines, directed attention. But it is possible to look at the silhouette and take that as the source of message. To detect the lines along which attention is directed and to direct one's gaze at every other line. To look at the wall rather than the picture (is that not the intent of structuralism? to gaze upon structures?). To plunge into the uncosmetic, unvoiced, controlled, incomplete. Is that not the journey which various idealists undertook roughly fifty years ago?

The ego is a barrier protecting patterns from information so that they can become pure repetition. Just as the skin is a barrier and the site of sensors, the ego lives in information but also fends it off. We can speak of the directed kind of poetry as based on self-presentation, so that the reader is offered an experience to repeat and to enter into. This involves qualities like suave and smooth. There may be a complementary distribution of self-presentation and reflexivity, such that they never appear together but take up structurally similar sites. The presentation is of the self but this involves social awareness, a welcome to the reader. The distinction between this smoothness and reflexivity, a critical attitude towards language and status, may be a key dividing line in poetry.

It is easier to describe what is in the frames than the frames themselves, which cannot be directly visible. It may be that the world of self-display is just a surface. But is it possible for poetry to speak once the surface has been pried away?

Structuralists wanted to recover large-scale, long-term, non-personal, coherent structures, whose parts conditioned each other and forbade those other lines of growth which we do not, after searching, find. They were a proposition which was not uttered by a human. It was a Grail quest. I can't guarantee that these large scale structures exist or that Alt poetry succeeds in exposing and describing them. It seems equally likely that there is foam all the way down, not some inhuman coherence. Alt poetry found zones of possibility which the orderly surface had repressed; it did not follow that those possibilities supported each other or were well ordered.

There is a fundamental difference between the view of a poet of someone who dislikes them and the view of those who like them. I can't write the history of the period by simultaneously describing the positive and the negative view. Would the superimposition of these images still produce a pattern? But both produce large drafts of information. Maybe we should ban the negative view. But what about that figure of 39.5% Oxford graduates? Isn't that also telling us something about the poetry scene?

Maybe structure would sound like white noise if you could snag a microphone on it. The idea that it would build a narrative has no rational basis. Narratives have subjects. The "market response" of other groups, the context if you will, did not accept the idea that Alt poets were free from illusion and self-projection. They detected arrogance, intolerance of other sectors of taste, a belief in a World Historical Mission. It's always a problem if you tell other people that their ego is too large.

Does this moment of rupture give us the gate into Alt poetry? Well, perhaps only for 5% of Alt poetry. Or for 5% of the events before a certain poetry started. It is not certain that this is the solitary source of anti-humanism even when that is the ticket which allowed a group of poets to set out on their voyage.

Generalisations simply do not hold for the whole terrain. If I can count 290 titles from the radical publisher Knives Forks and Spoons (in the catalogue of a certain library), we already suspect that those texts cover a vast artistic area. And, that they would not be saleable, after a point, if they all had the same points to make. We could surely count a thousand poets in the Alternative area. The Underground has continuity as a community of readers, but has certainly not remained stable in the cultural preoccupations and ideas of style which animate its projects. The continuity of individual poets, pursuing their personal style over several decades of productivity, only disguises a basic process of change which may be clearer if we just block out the dominant figures. A useful historical approach would be to examine vertical sections, defining moments in the advance of a column. I looked in early 2015 at the website of Knives Forks and Spoons and captured the names of authors they publish:

Tim Allen, Meredith Andrea, David Annan, Joanne Ashcroft, Alan Baker, Richard Barrett, Jeremy Balius, David Berridge, Michael Blackburn, Mark Burnhope, James Byrne, Neil Ambel, Joel Hace, Lucy Harvest Clarke, Adrian Clarke, Wayne Clements, Mark Cobley, Rebecca Cremin, Sarah Crewe, Sophie Mayer, J Crouse, Philip Davenport, Ian Davidson, James Davies, Peter Dent, Ken Edwards, Neil Ellman, Stephen Emmerson, Matt Fallaize, Gareth Farmer, Patricia Farrell, SJ Fowler, Kit Fryatt, Andrew Gallan, Peter Gillies, Rupert Loydell, Jesse Glass, Howie Good, Giles Goodland, Gavin Goodwin, Chris Gutkind, Trevor Simmons, John Hall, Peter Hughes, Dylan Harris, Daniel Y. Harris, J/J Hastain, Colin Herd, Lindsey Holland, Simon Howard, Sarah James, Tom Jenks, Joshua Jones, S Kelly, Ira Lightman, Travis MacDonald, Ann Matthews, Anna McKerrow, James Mclaughlin, Nicky Mesch, Geraldine Monk, Frederick Morley, Stephen Nelson, Bruno Neiva, D E Oprava, Ryan Ormonde, Lars Palm, Daniele Pantano, Bobby Parker, RT Parker, Peter Philpott, Stephen Pike, Evelyn Posamentier, Jay Ramsay, Kevin Reid, George Szirtes, Simon Rennie, Antony Rowland, James Russell, Ian Seed, Robert Sheppard, Marcus Slease, Ben Stainton, Paul Sutton, Todd Swift, Andrew Taylor, Nathan Thompson, Scott Thurston, David Toms, Rhys Trimble, Debbie Walsh, Tom Watts, Michael Wilson, Colin Winborn, Cliff Yates.

I hope this shows some of the fertility of the contemporary scene. KFS have a bit of a trawler approach, they take on a lot of books. Have I read all these poets? Certainly not. I have read *Eighteens*, the KFS anthology. I did this retrieval as part of an exercise to count the total of Alternative poets from 1965 up to 2015. I didn't complete the count, it offers some thorny problems. They just come along in swarms, my friend. This list could be seen as a picture of the scene in 2015. There are hundreds and hundreds of other Underground poets writing, but this is a view, something small enough to look at. The number of poets involved suggests how difficult it would be to find out if they all have something in common – and that they probably don't.

Peter Riley has said that the "British Poetry Revival" of the 1970s didn't really exist. Since there is a list of 36 poets in the essay which coined the phrase, and their work altogether covers maybe 15,000 pages, we must accept that there was such a group. Since Riley is on that list, his assertion implies that Peter doesn't exist – a claim we should not accept without further research. Since he mistakenly says that the term refers to the 1970s, we can guess that he is delegitimating poets younger than himself, as poets tend to do.

Dark Entries: Ian Heames, *Arrays* (collected edition, 2015; 95pp)

>it is a compound 1,000 times
>more bitter than loss
>
>the digraph
>the turn to encryption
>in its contextual form
>
>I need you to go back on
>to look at pictures of your face
>
>poetry, marble, onyx, email
>my you is a cadet misleading
>my they
>   (2.1.1)

It occurred to me that *email* could stand for French *émail*, which means enamel. A deeply buried memory led me to find this line from Théophile Gautier, author of *Émaux et camées*: "Yes, the work comes out more beautiful from a material that resists the process, verse, marble, onyx, or enamel." The poems define the edge of planes but do not fill in what would live on the planes. This reminds me of constructivist art. At this point we could think of a grid, which would be a kind of array. We live in environments designed with specific routes and outcomes by other people. We normally take the description of these routes as one of the basic processes of writing. Heames is declining that process and setting up alternative frameworks with uncertain outcomes – the uncertainty is perhaps the aesthetic dimension or an area where we can simply improvise. I had a feeling of warmth as soon as I saw a page of his work – there is after all a historical dimension to this reframing activity, and it reminds me of the sector of 70s poetry into which I was, historically, socialised. It is a feature of games that they can be played by many people and are a way of being social. The minimal nature of the frame components is exhilarating and in fact key tonal values in the book are warmth and exhilaration.

The value of the word *array* is to declare language as free data in the way that numbers are free and serial. That is, it sheds the shadow body which, in the archaic world, gave it content and fatal bounds. We navigate it through successive attention schemas – like a fish moving in a river. A fin flick and a loop, as it were. The self-rotation is the original frame shift. Helpfully for me, Heames actually uses the phrase, body image: "Intact RQ-170 Sentinel body image", twice. He qualifies this as "Exclusively peaceful metalloid cartouche butterfly" and this pilotless "single wing" spy plane made by Lockheed Martin for the CIA does not, indeed, carry any weapons.

An array is a data structure. I had forgotten the difference between an array and a matrix but have now looked it up. "A one-dimensional **array** can be considered a vector, and an **array** with two dimensions can be considered a **matrix**." Matrices are a subset of arrays. Heames refers often to computer games – so, in 'recall how/ the RCP-120 would lose/ ammo to go clear", the RCP could be a remote control panel, but I suggest instead that it is an automatic weapon made by Carrington Industries in the 2000 video game *Perfect Dark*. The game world which appears to the player as sequential states seems to the programmer like a static array of which selected parts appear as screen images. "[M]atrices are widely used for specifying and representing geometric transformations (for example rotations) and coordinate changes." The basis for representing a place on a flat screen is that you define space as a two-dimensional array (where the entries correspond, eventually, to pixels). Poets born after circa 1970 (I suppose) are so used to video games that they are likely to see poems as variants of them – language is, arguably, a way of addressing shared data arrays. The numbers ascribed to poems within *Arrays* can be seen as referring to entries in an array (with, apparently, three columns and an unspecified number of rows). The gameworld is something blatantly fictitious and yet immersive, able to yield insight into control environments of other kinds and, naturally, how to distribute stimuli so as to reach pleasurable states. *My left thumb is so sore from tilting those worlds*. The book opens with

> the right side of the butterfly
> sits against the idle ports (one
> right opposite the edge of the butterfly
> (
> as the right side of the butterfly opens

>   upwards and creates a venturi
>   next to these ports
>   (1.1.1)

Butterflies create a wing display by means of an intricate set of colour-bearers which can be considered as an array. The endpapers have a rather beautiful, originally painted, shimmering image which I at first thought was like a peacock's tail but which more likely is a reference to something optically similar, a butterfly's wing. The image, then, shows us an *array*. The description of a butterfly adjacent to the ports of a jet engine makes them manufactured objects rather than insects: like butterfly valves, maybe. The Venturi effect refers to the behaviour of a flowing substance when constricted or choked, but a *venturi* as a noun is a kind of pipe used as a gauge. In the poem it seems to be a regulator rather than just a gauge. This jet intake context shimmers and mutates into a flower, two pages later, as "orchid floods   butterfly// orchid floods orchid/ with butterfly [...] it was a butterfly/ orchid" – flooding is something we readily associate with valves, but the context has flipped over – shimmered. Plants, we suppose, use flow choking effects to draw nutrients from the soil and move them around internally. So we have a peculiarly rich set of internal relations, with a relationship to a world outside the poem tamped down.

The poetry is extremely non-didactic and yet has a heavy information flow. This leaves us with intuition as the director. The poem does not exactly mean whatever you want it to – but, it pursues a wish. So in "had had bliss from training/ had had bliss form/ seraphic droid epaulet" the bliss and the seraphic must go together. The training is undescribed – but an epaulet is a badge of status, which you might acquire by passing training. And, I don't need to know what a *seraphic droid epaulet* is to know that I want one. A set of six pigments, starting with "Omega chrome Blue", presumably specifies the colour of the epaulet. More colours mean more control, as we used to say about management graphics. A resemblance of "omega chrome blue" to "high pink on chrome", a 1975 book by J.H. Prynne, may be just a happy memory. To give an instruction which cannot be interpreted inside the currently valid framework draws attention to the framework. The successive propositions within one of Heames' poems definitely do not amount to a logical instruction; but they suggest that there might be a realm of some sort outside the screen edge and in fact outside the array we are programmed in.

> Modernism is not the same
> thing as love
> between two lines
> and the bureaucracy of the day
> (2.1.3)

A poet who has moved towards the Alternative is Nicholas Spicer. Spicer has released two volumes with Contraband which show a rapid process of change. Aspects of the earlier work which attached to a recognisable, conventional manner of cynical colloquial (even rancid colloquial?) cause a certain dissatisfaction, which leads on to the development: towards something which apparently breaks language up in frustration, moving towards something inorganic but at the same time profoundly transformed. It represents vast linguistic processes, even in the form of damage. *Lines on the Surface* (133pp) is subtitled *poems 2000–2009*. This dislocation of conventional appetites, to perceive or to speak, suggests a dissatisfaction with the state of the country. The cover is strewn with barcodes, and these are actually the lines on the surface. It is hard to determine what the content of this critique is, but it is more effective for being unconditional: the poet is angry, and this anger warms the poems, lights them up. The most ambitious part of *Lines* is surely the 'Three Odes' at the end, a total of 243 lines (or, 3 x 9 x 9). It starts with a description of intimacy, and although the other person is not the speaker the whole poem can be seen as wondering how the speaker seems to that other person and how their happiness is going to survive in the economic world. One stanza is:

> Easy, easy now. Bound to be bloody something
> stirring my pot, its obvious dreams the worst dream
>   destination: gamble on consent,
> the wine-dark sea with other rejectamenta
> bore Venus from a shell-game, emergent function
>   of ancestors in deliquescence;
>   asked for help who can't get
>   off those well-soaked pillows
> on your own but wallow away, I'm telling you.
>   (from 'Counter-turn' in 'First Ode')

Counter-turn is an English version of Antistrophe, a part of a Greek ode (related to choral movement of the reciters). The poetry seems to advance from one figure of speech to another, in each case messing them up in a way which suggests disillusion and irritation. So wording amounting to "that's another kettle of fish and there are piranhas in it" is close to worn-out everyday language, its adhesion to the ordinary and frustrating seeks to avoid escape into a false and idealised realm of the aesthetic. The following bit around "stripped to image" suggests projection into collective representations, perhaps ads or films, which are insubstantial; the "evidence of myself" is the presence of the subject as consumer, occupying part of the process but on terms which imply the frustration of his wishes (or perhaps the enticement of false wishes – false needs). It may be the style is influenced by Prynne of the *News of Warring Clans* and *Brass* era. It may also be that Spicer is an early shareholder in a generation under economic blockade, where the value of assets has risen quite insanely in ratio to the price of labour, and the economy seems to be locking a new generation out. His poetry may be a direct response to zero-hours contracts. So "wine dark sea" (a tag from Homer, *oinops*, presumably the worn-out stage of legacy classical culture) is the "dream destination", presumably the Mediterranean, where we go in search of that classic tradition. Venus does not emerge from a shell, on the island of Paphos, but from a "shell game", where fairground hucksters win your money by persuading you that you can see through their tricks. She "emerges", edited into an "emergent function", a capacity which arrives with increasing complexity, probably of an organism's powers of perception and data processing. The human hunger lunches out among leavings, this is an emotional outcry, perhaps the core of the poem, surrounded by scornful distortions and inversions to disguise its intensity. This poetry is hard to describe. I think the point is that he sets up his camera to show instability and oscillation. An Ode is normally a victory poem, and this seems to be a state occasion of some kind, perhaps involving choral movement. The frame shifts are like the turns of the chorus in their recital.

If we say that his poetry is about introspection and conflict, that also says that British poetry generally avoids these things. Generally it seeks a pleasant sound and tries to repeat it.

So, one description of 'Three Odes' might be that its direction shifts all the time. One version would be that the poem is a description of subjectivity – and of entanglement. As the outside world changes, the inner world loses what it had occupied: this is the point. How the arrangement of the social world, its urban layout, derelict buildings, collective excitements, affects the way we actually feel – this is a subject poetry can take on. But not if it is a commodity. We really are connected by so many responsive nerves to so many parts of the world, which do not keep orderly formation. The surface of the poem shows a dense set of frame shifts, not contradicting each other but vexing the line of sight we had just now. The fabric of the language is dissonant but also meticulous. With Spicer the point is to achieve consciousness – to be released from the grip of irrational compulsions, and flawed ideas, into real awareness. That is also a release from the state of harmony and serenity which poets generally try to put over.

Heather Phillipson, *INSTANT-fLEX 718* (50pp, 2013)
Instant-flex is a camera. I did a search on the assumption that it was the model which Lee Harvey Oswald owned, but no, it is an instant, and modern, so an appliance for amateurs which bypassed the whole connoisseurial labyrinth and gave an instant result. It is made by a Hong Kong firm called Mint. The "flex" titling refers back to the original Rolleiflex of 1929. I traced a TLR-70 (the tlr means "twin lens reflex") but the 718 is not a camera; it may be a video format (718 x 404 pixels per frame). The twin lenses are the camera's lens and the viewfinder. The book is a different size from other Bloodaxe books and this format may refer to a photo format. There is something dazing about this collection because it is so consistent and because it is how we would all like to be in social interaction, glib, witty, quick-fire, constantly seeing experience as it passes as full of contradictions but adjusting at improbable speed to that long rope of wrong folds. So many people see experience as something which they can get rid of to protect their intelligence, or are so slugged by what happens to them that they can only repeat it, mumbling, without the quality of swift response which humans have as birthright. Phillipson also works as a conceptual artist, so that the interest in the way people frame experience, shift frames, reduce it to order, drop out anomalous facts however blatant, is of interest to her and the analogues for this poetry might be visual art rather than poems. The interest of conceptual artists is, to state the obvious, less in pictures and more in the whole set of cognitive processes by which impinging light is translated into ideas, hypotheses, and experiences. Impinging is not a compound of pinging. I think we can get at these poems by evoking roomfuls of people discussing

hard and breaking free into a world of concepts. This is the key to each poem having a separate concept, and it is very hard to imitate. If you re-use designs for poems, it is much easier to write, but in fact that gets in the way of writing original poems.

The poem I liked best at first reading was the one with an ad for a box of memorabilia, title '1960s Monochrome Hollywood Paraphernalia ($47, collection only)' which on reading turned out to be the possessions of Norman Bates from *Psycho*. Listing the objects evokes the plot of the film (surely you've seen it? do I have to tell you everything?):

> 1 sizeable hoard of defunct birds (some deader than others). Includes an owl (unusually rigid) and anything else you would want to see in flight in spring (mounted, in a parlour). All come with tiny bones crunched into a museum of artistic poses (if you lean in you can hear viscera or sky curdle steeply). In addition, a period of hurley-burley just beginning.
> [...]
> Violin strings (lightly scratched) in upper registers. Blanched hair of a certain period. Tiny gloss eyes pinned in the middle distance. Miscellaneous beaks and a man's mouth, all in nipping distance.

There is a twist to this. Conceptual art jettisoned objects on the grounds that you didn't want a collection of objects which are complete because they only *allow* one reaction. Instead the complex of [object + reaction + visual procedures] was under investigation. It is a kind of pun if Phillipson makes a description of objects (in a box) which is then a conceptual poem. (Bernard Herrmann's scary string section is also in there, it is an unusual box.) However, I liked all the poems, try this passage:

> Danielese, Danielese, my coat's been stolen
> from the heap of party outerwear in your sitting room.
> If I drove the world's crammed bus, I'd brake and loot
> its side-pockets. A person has my coat
> along with the filthy history of streets we trod,
> my railcard and guarantee of sophistication.
> My personality will never be as pure-new-woollen.
> We must hunt for my coat, Danielese, everywhere between

the front door and the art students at full-throat
in your kitchenette, thrust in flat-pack cubbyholes.
(from 'The One Coat That Could Have
Made Winter Worth Living Through')

I can disclose that John Baldessari is a conceptual artist, one of the most famous, and that Xavier Cugat was a band leader in the 1940s whose work has been described as Amero-Cuban pop rather than Latin jazz. When conceptual art began, around 1960, it was the Cold War and the principals just wanted to stop identifying with the war propaganda all around them, to stop the flow. The focus then was not accepting that we are all immersed in advertising and the audiovisual media, and also that analysing how that works was basic to retaining self-awareness. So conceptual art became mainstream even while the Cold War was leaving the stage.

Triumphs and panics

The first thing is that I am worried about a stop-start quality in dealing with a couple of dozen volumes which are not visibly related to each other. You can't write a novel with three dozen characters who never meet each other. I usually make technique the central thing but that exposes me to criticisms from Luke Roberts about being interested in techniques but lacking in empathy.

Ephemeris, **by Dorothy Lehane (Nine Arches Press, 2014, 61pp)**
'Hemera' is day, 'Ephemeris,' is a 'diary' or day-book, and the Greek word of which the Latin word for 'diary' is a translation. Ausonius wrote around 380 AD a poem called Ephemeris describing a day of domestic routine hour by hour. One folio seems to be missing. More locally, it means an astronomical table for determining the position of a heavenly body on a given day. Swim-suit, space-suit. "seismic waves of deviance/ tongue-tied miasma", Dorothy Lehane's book of this name is an extended metaphor in which the course of a heavenly body through the sky draws after it shifting experiences, in an organism susceptible to the influences of heat and light. "Too many moonlight kisses/ Seem to cool in the heat of the sun", as Doris Day sang. The link, supposed by astrology, between subjective experience and astronomical events, is unreal – or perhaps not wholly, as our biologically given alternation between sleeping and waking is given by the day-night cycle, rather certainly linked to the geometry between the Earth and the nearest star.

'Solidarity' goes like this:

> try not to tamper
> with 'alone', sketch
> each comedown, note
> the dust-devil colour.
> sulphuric Venus rain,
> the sediment
> of skein, the downs,
> our lapping suburban hearts
> pushed to unfurl
> to give something back,
> how fabric life collects,

> it's not enough to just be
> cradled, regrouped, jerky nervous
> it's a system, a modulation spectrum
> adjacent window   traffic rise

The poem has a double sense more or less throughout. 'Comedown' is simultaneously something falling from the sky (dust) and an emotional state – post-climax. Charles Jencks, writing about post-modern architecture, described double coding, where a feature of a building has two functions, typically carrying out a physical function, part of the utilities, and referring to something in classical architecture which it is tailored to visually resemble. This was actually a sarcastic utterance towards purist modernist critics for whom ornament was crime. With Lehane the duplicity is probably to retain the secrecy which is necessary for personal life and to push us into a state of suggestibility where we think twice about the shapes we see and imagine new resemblances. Social contact slowly builds up into a social network: how "fabric life collects", it is like all that dust falling. The random events that build up to life are analogous to the ones that build up to a community. 'Modulation spectrum' may be a spectrum through which a given signal can be modulated (by various episodes); astronomers might know that dust is present because it modulates light that passed through it. This seems to be the syntax of the poems in *Ephemeris*; the two sides don't have a precise symmetry, because the stars have precise physical properties of location, rotation, colour, etc. which language can't render, and because emotions and feelings about other people aren't visible or precise and can only be set down on paper through analogy. Actually language doesn't do very well with emotions either – even if language was invented to describe them, feelings and words don't match in any exact way.

The poem on 'Stephan's Quintet' seems to be a description of this group of five galaxies identified in 1877 with their strange and perhaps revelatory characteristics, shock waves of molecular hydrogen and other brouhaha, reconfigured as a subjective image for a human interaction that perhaps is waiting to exist. 'Limb by limb, legless, kiss me combatant, are we brothers or are we bastards, bystanding is a sin for the fey.'

Apparently swimming around Tycho Brahe's island-observatory, the poet lays down personal feelings as myth, and links intricate though inanimate processes into a narrative. Impressive amounts of detail on cosmology, fossil microwaves, the origin of matter, etc. are combined with what may literally be a diary: a cycle of feelings, piercing, tender, and confused. "Stella by starlight", or a calendar of moments without proper names.

Lehane's project has to do with combining poetry and science. The two are intertwined in a very specific way here: objective knowledge separates projections of feelings and wishes from the information provided by the eyes, but here the idea is to interfuse them. Her poems are intensely personal and highly coded: everything profound loves a mask. In an ephemeris the sunlit vapour of feelings is fixed with huge lenses in their true position, which they immediately abandoned. The astronomical mask dissolves biography into a million parts, evolving into singular geometric figures; molecules forming on the beaches around a million stars develop into a million sensations, which the poet as sensitive wrack washes through at the mercy of the tides. I am reminded of some kitsch but wonderful late-Soviet architecture realising the illustrations to cosmic fantasies of 50s science fiction writers. It's Earth but it feels like out there in the void. The poetry-science project is likely to draw a great deal of attention in the next twenty years or so. It is quite hard to define what the purpose is; I think the core is the sense of opportunity, that there is a wilderness here, and that if you buy creative people time they will wander around that wilderness and bring back things never before seen. Part of the impetus is the wish of museum staff to have their holdings presented anew in visible or audible form. It's not that these works are putting scientific truths in simpler forms (like illustrations, maybe), more that after the arrival of a complete excess of scientific data mediated by instruments people have realised that relationships within those data can be made clear by symbolic depiction and manipulation in very very varied forms. All starts from a dial: the dial shows quantities in terms of a space, possibly also colour, but is a metaphor for the physical quantity it displays. Simply thinking about the metaphors is productive as it liberates scientists from the legacy graphic assumptions.

'Coronal Mass Ejection' (p.40) is an event affecting our sun (and perhaps others) where protons from the corona (the outer rim) are physically thrown out, rotary energy overcoming gravity: raising what is known as a solar wind:

> Inside the sun, veil, inside my heart,
> internal forces   bleached out childhood
> beach days in the thermonuclear

> compression of the convection zone
> boy, you sure are magnet, an engine
> from the chromosphere, coronal rain,
> filament matter lift me up like an arc
> like a bridge
>
> Magnets fight, we also fight over
> who misses who, turmoil rising
> solar wind, particles, ammunition
> into Aurora.
>
> Conquer national grids
> conquer national headaches

When the wind touches the atmosphere around the earth, it is visible as the Aurora Borealis, and its electrical charge can bring national grids down. The idea of a bridge between sun and earth is analogous to a link between two human bodies.

Star-gazing is a state of primitive wonder which is perhaps a stage before science. Astronomers do astrophysics to work out, for example, the mass and temperature of stars, but perhaps they are stargazing as well. In the poems, we are not doing astrophysics. The point is mimesis, a state of intense and profound attention that we copy and lock onto. The object which permits this state could be almost anything that is profound, not rapidly exhausted. Images of stars happen to be a good source of high-grade visual objects.

Astrology is wrong but it has been very productive in poetry. The product which is "Ephemeris" is not easily definable, in fact I am clear that it involves a multitude of different things, and they don't have proper names yet.

The publisher is Nine Arches, from Rugby. The *comandante* of Nine Arches explained to me that it refers to the arches in a certain railway bridge leading into Rugby and that a later count reached a different but less memorable result. There used to be a set of inhibitions or obstructions to writing poetry, a huge park of things like the old railway network, and the unmounting and demolition of these inhibitions has been a constantly progressing feature of the last 50 years. The dominant feature of the new poetry scene is accessibility, huge numbers of people are writing poetry and it just feels like an extension of talking or of being conscious. I just like the idea of a poetry publisher in Rugby, and I don't see why the English Language would work differently in Rugby than it does in Oxford, or London.

Dorothy Lehane can be linked to other poets doing science writing (and frequently collected in *Litmus*, the magazine Lehane edits). (So lit is literary and litmus paper belongs in a laboratory.)

Luke Roberts, *False Flags* (2011; 79pp).
In an earlier stage of warfare between states, some naval operations involved ships making an approach under false flags. In the modern world of covert operations, some (illegal) actions are carried out in such a way that they are not secret but attributed to a different agency or country. This would include (battlefield) electronic signals which imitate the emissions of a foreign aircraft, or mass release of social media messages which pretend to be from concerned US citizens but actually originate from shift workers in a room full of cubicles somewhere near Khabarovsk.

It is hard to overstate the appeal of this poetry, its wonderful variety of patterns and textures, the serenity with which it rides over constant change. It is a fountain of sound. It is also difficult and we can hope for light from his autobiographical prose work, *Glacial Decoys*. In it he says: "All of this, whatever it is, means nothing without the politics.
Bare minimum: hatred of authority, especially the police; acute intolerance of the very rich; distrust of fakes and fame; hatred of war; hatred of fascists; opposition to boredom and bullies. How all this works in the language is what poems consist of."

This does not seem to connect with any passages in *False Flags*. Or maybe it is a pin-up on his wall? Hatred is a very personal thing so the absence of a pronoun suggests that the emotions described do not actually belong to the poet. He comes over more as balanced, perceptive, changing from day to day. The missing pronoun is part of the telltale language which is how all this works. As a writer, he avoids conflict situations. *Decoys* may be a brilliant explanation of something but not of his poems.

The cookies at the Chinese restaurant say *Upper Egypt* and lower
      ascending tones,
perpetual triad logic. Increasing time pads creates bird versions,
      disfigured
as flames, reflex cloud versions, the quest for a perfect body swallows
      everything,

geocities of empty accounts gone outside to divert the monotonous
rivers & mountains of nouns, whole towns worshipping production.
       Surrogate kidneys
get swamped by the liver unfolding on streamed talk radio, it's artificial.
Disgust sweetened by the dilute scale, enthusiasts rush to the aquarium
under the cover of jellyfish tanks, obscure mourning procedures are
       observed
by those in the suspended globe. No-one will believe in each other's
       version
of events gone separately home. We hear as loud as you do. No you
       don't.
          (from 'Terraform lecture notes')

(Geocities supplied free personally owned Internet sites, or accounts, and was popular and pioneering at the time. It ran from 1994 to 2009 and the new owner asked users to pay, at which point possibly the biggest deletion of data in the history of the Internet took place.)

What we see in the language is a radical seriality, themes follow each other with great speed. The book is like an overture, where themes are stated but do not resolve. They do not provide the middle and concluding steps which we know they imply, thus keeping predictability down. The language moves swiftly, through n-way gates where there are many possibilities, and we go through many of these gates, at speed. The course is unconstrained at each point. Successive parts are not answering questions raised by preceding ones; they are serial rather than constructive. We can approach this intoxicating acoustic ripple through the idea of competition: people linked in are accepting information input at great speed and with easy access to fabulously diverse sources, so poetry might speed up in order to avoid seeming out of date. This disconnection suggests that political decisions normally have more outcomes than you can measure, and that a distinction between good and evil is infantile: this manner makes it difficult to believe in evil politicians. We are not seeing the consequence of actions and are not encountering passages where the poem distinguishes between truth and falsehood, so analysis of the news is not its main interest. Hatred is monotonous and requires stability, since it is based in closeness to the object of hate.

A time pad is a track with a reference tempo (and a faster tempo would be more birdlike). The contrastive symmetry of *upper* Egypt and *lower* ascending tones is exquisitely formalist. Upper in this case means south, as the Nile land rises in that direction; whereas lowering tones is a phonetic alteration. As reflections they give off a sort of glockenspiel tone. Even within those few words, the idea of lowering ascending tones is a mirror image with shift, since lowering the tone (of a syllable) is the reverse of raising it as it develops, which is called an ascending tone. Lowering the overall pitch is presumably a vocal inflection, a way of signalling some inner state. Terraforming is a fictional idea for reshaping entire planets to be like Terra, or earth, and so suitable for humans, but it could refer to engineering processes on Earth itself. Waste is a problem for Earth and this could be why there is an interest in the liver and kidneys, waste processing organs. The toxin is being released, dilute, through the radio (and this is a good explanation of what the media are like). I wondered if the obscure mourning procedures were being followed by the jellyfish, but a suspended globe is surely the earth itself. Jellyfish notably do not process waste through specialist organs like the liver.

Because an aquarium is a bounded environment special attention has to be given to removing excreta and refreshing oxygen, and it is therefore like a terraformed planet, which has also received such attention. I don't think the link between aquarium and terraform is conscious or explicit. I offer it as an example of how the poem overflows with meaning: it is all over poetry, never mind logical propositions. We are willing to recall Alexandre Astruc on film directors, talking about a *camera-stylo*, a camera whose moves reflect the handwriting of the director. Neurological patterns are heard as a kind of melody. Also with poetry there is an unconscious level of uncountably many minor decisions which are the substrate for the explicit level. In this case the underlying geometry is like a dance, the line seems to glide everywhere rather than decelerating or coming to earth. The manner is elegant, allegro, like a travelogue. The constant affluence of images removes any frustration by satisfying our most basic need for change and ideas.

The cover shows two copies of an image which looks like a world-egg floating in a sea with clumps or curds. An image inside the book shows Yuri Gagarin, in his space helmet and presumably inside his capsule, as the first man into space. This resolves the cover as an affective but unrealistic re-build of Yuri: the oval is the capsule, and the space helmet, and even his face. Didn't I once translate an East German poem about Yuri Gagarin? Gagarin s nami. Perviy polyot v kosmos. The most brilliant poem is about Yuri descending:

> Yuri singing on his descent, brain singing
> home, arms extended in a series of the sky.
> Lift off the space ribs, human noise wished
> for lungs, like living things of aerial desire,
> acting out gravity sung back to grass, and
> parachutes blossom with nameless users
> of oxygen, exchanged for tender colours,
> columns intercepted by fields persist, some
> of the world breathing out.
>   (from 'Interlude #2')

Kepler proved that the courses of planets were elliptical, or oval, so if you see the course of a planet you might perceive it as the surface of an egg. The cover has superimposed triangles which are coloured and which could be pennants: these could be the false flags. There is a mention of the flagstaffs erected, by Soviet and American astronauts, on the Moon; they are flags but they are not false in any way I can think of. They are notably declarative. The atmosphere in certain passages evokes Soviet science fiction of the 1960s, when briefly outer space belonged only to them. In the stories, you go to strange planets and the characters come from every possible culture: nationality has ceased to be a problem. But there are never Americans. The presence of *amerikantsi* would imply that Russia has not won the Cold War: you could go to jail for that so you just leave them out. In this world, America is *an error of history* that, er, rectified *itself*. Also, there are no classes. The continuation of class struggle in the distant future would imply that communism had not abolished classes and so that Marxism was wrong. Again, you would avoid saying that. So this science fiction is without the standard plots; it is unconstrained in a way which we can compare with being weightless. The stories are also travelogues. *False Flags* at least in part captures this soaring and unconstrained serenity of the Soviet space era: the end of conflict, the triumph of technology and travelogue.

There are so many motifs, but one ('Feast Days in the Desert') is about Utah and deals with breatharians. This is a group whose leaders claim, in Utah, to have given up food altogether and to be living on air (and solar rays, of course); their flock supply credulity. The text also shows Utah as a place for practising for the lunar terrain, as part of a space project which involves living on recycled food. This is somehow a mirror image of being breatharian (and is designed for a place where there is no air). A description of desert living may also refer to economising resources (and near-perfect insulation). Another poem brings back the lovely breatharians and has a passage about exploring for underwater resources ("Reagan with his iron fish maps the shelf,/ o hydrosweep, projectile vomit into/ continental scraps, with deep-sea fans/ tubes pointing at the sky") which is also somewhere where no oxygen is available. I think the fans may be an organism (a kind of tube worm) living near *hot smokers*, vents from deep in the earth, bursting out in the sea bed, which are especially rich in valuable minerals.

This reminds us how enjoyable this poetry is, how graceful it is at high speeds. That combination of deftness and exhilaration reminds me of Peter Porter. The mention of Haji Baba (p.27) makes me wonder if this is a reference to *The Adventures of Hajji Baba*, a 1954 film by Don Weis made a cult of, in the usual way of French cinéastes, by a group regarded by *Cahiers* as heretical. Ah, those rascals at *Présence du cinéma!* Adulating Don *Weis*. But no, this is just a coincidence.

Maria Stadnicka wrote the book *Somnia* (2020, 74pp). The word means sleeps or dreams in Latin, with dreams being the most likely sense. The poet is Romanian, and *somnii* means "dreams" in Romanian. The implication may be that Romanian is closer to the sources of civilisation than English. There was considerable hostility in the press about immigration from Romania when the country passed the test and joined the EU. The manner is rapidly recognisable as Eastern European and not English. It is hard to translate intuitions into correct description, but the signs are there in a poem like this:

> Tuesday with dust shining on jars
> and Clara piles memories in black bags.
> *Cleaning day* she says.
>
> Up and down the stairs, one-winged sister
> trips over my legs, keeps singing,
> the tune slides across walls, butterflies jump
> from her mouth on her head then out.
>
> I wonder what butterfly meat tastes like,
> if sliced with a silver blade; what mother tasted like

> the moment she released me – honey coated pearl.
> I smell the skin on my wrists: mother's hiding place.
> (from 'Spring Cleaning')

A sister is one of a pair but one-wing is one of a one. One aspect is the Aesopian language, where points are not made explicitly and we see simple organic images which have oblique symbolism. The background to this style seems to be the era of communist dictatorship, where poets could not afford to be explicit at any point, and also the regime printed vast amounts of folklore and wanted poets to use that imagery as part of proving that they belonged to the people and not the bourgeoisie. The style is like dreams and is almost infinitely flexible. The regime would have preferred poets to be modern enough to make explicit declarations of allegiance to the people's Leader and his Thoughts. When we say Eastern European that is not to be outside Time, the style was probably relevant from the 1950s to the early 1990s, at a guess.

Any narrative in that region, at that time, related to the communist party because of its monopoly position and claim to benevolence. If you went for a walk you were in a sense walking through communism. This made it easy for poets to define themselves – they always seemed to be Hamlet figures at the court of a relative whom they hated. It is different in Britain, where power is decentralised and it is not obvious that whatever the poet is facing connects with whatever the reader is facing. Writers are less important in Western Europe. The government doesn't even care enough to arrest them. Each line seems to be self-contained and to present a continuous present, in which a new visual image fills the screen as soon as the previous one departs.

> We inhabit the world's pipeline,
> picking up fallen apples. Friends
> who died of battlefield injuries
> turn into slow burning paragraphs.
>
> We inhabit churches and prayers
> floating from cell to cell,
> and damp kisses: our proofs
> that we remain enemies.
> (from 'Journal Page')

Every part is clear but I am hesitant about explaining exactly what the pictures refer out to. They stay in that phase of lucid dream. Maybe the way dreams, *somnii*, work is not to interpret experiences but to mutate them and move away from what they actually were.

This does remind me a little of the work of Nicki Jackowska ('The house that Manda built').

Ian Seed's essay in Jon Thompson's book *Encounter* gives us four discrete phases: early work in the Seventies, a 20-year gap up to 2004, a new phase involving verse, cut-up and collage (see *Anonymous Intruder*, 2009, *Shifting Registers,* 2011), and then from 2010–20 on a phase of intense composition of prose poems: *Identity Papers, Makers of Empty Dreams, New York Hotel, The Underground Cabaret.* He names nine writers who influenced his prose poems. Seed studied philosophy and it is credible that focus on very short sets of connected propositions, establishing their inner logic and removing superfluous phrases, had an effect on his poetry. Almost all the pieces are less than 200 words and some are under 100 words. The most important aspect of philosophy, of course, is its grasp of the unknown: a grasp that never closes but which can at least remain close to what it misses.

When I met Seed, and we had identified each other, in an almost completely dark Dorset lane, the first thing he said was "I was born in the same year as you". I couldn't respond, but on reflection this was a Seedian moment, with a minimal word-count, evocation of a whole biography, ambiguity (was this about all the experiences we had shared or all the ones I hadn't shared and now never would?). With any kind of minimalism, the question of what has been omitted takes us to the heart of the compositional process, without any guarantee that what we can say about the omitted is true. Seed's poems certainly don't answer all the questions we ask about the situation. Equally certainly, the omissions are the product of a very lucid intelligence and exacting focus. To arouse true acuity it is necessary to limit information rather than pour it out.

Ian McMillan says on the cover of *Makers of Empty Dreams*: "These are superb pieces that give us a glimpse into some kind of translated backlit European hinterland full of the music of menace and desire. I read them in my conservatory in Barnsley and I was instantly transported to a city that I half-knew, full of people I wanted to meet or avoid." On *Identity Papers* we have Mark Ford saying "Ian Seed is our most brilliant exponent of that most unBritish of genres, the prose poem. Hilarious and unsettling, his beautifully controlled micro-narratives genially induct us into a world that soon turns out to be as dangerous as it is magical." There are 300 or 400 of these pieces now; they are clearly designed for long-distance travel; they never repeat and you never get tired of them. That is partly because they are not broadcasting a personality – there is no self-adornment.

The core of the poems for me is surprise at being in any particular situation, the state of a mind after incomplete waking as it is just realising what the environment is. The limited information in each poem opens a gateway for the abiding uncertainty of existence. As follows, a fundamental power of the mind is to deal with this uncertainty, to orient itself and to distinguish up from down, light from darkness. The character in each poem is outside a cognitive frame and using the powers of cognition to work themselves back into a frame.

Chrysalis

> The creature came out from behind a dusty curtain. It was dirty and bleeding. We had thought it died years before when it shed its skin and became our beautiful daughter. Somehow it had survived. But what could we do with it now? We already had a daughter. And how could we tell her that she was this creature, too?

And here is part of another:

> I wasn't sure which station was mine. In my broken Italian, I asked an old man who was standing next to me. It was a good twenty minutes yet, he said, swaying with the motion of the train. He began speaking to me in a mixture of English and Italian, telling me all about Milan. By the time I arrived at my stop, I found myself not wanting to leave him. Now I would have to find my own way through the streets of a city I had never seen before.
>
> (from 'Chances')

(both poems from *Makers of Empty Dreams*, 2014, 74pp) The European setting is not there to contrast Europe with Britain, but exactly as a setting where the character who speaks can experience strangeness and form little bits of a cognitive map, like where to get off a train. The theme is basic strangeness so the setting could just as well be a foreigner in England, or an English person in the wrong city. The idea is not that Italy is strange, as it obviously isn't for Italians. We are getting a glimpse of home through moments when we are out of contact with a place. While the poems read like parts of novels, where notorious characters are set up in situations and we are thrown into, or dressed up as, them, this set of roles and frames was not invented by novelists, rather it was already present in the social process. I am reminded of a tale in *Gesta Romanorum* (12th C) where an emperor is bathing one day and on emerging from the river finds that someone identical to him in bodily form has put on his clothes and is now emperor and in full exercise of all his privileges and seat in life. He on the other hand is now an outcast, without even rights to his name. Seed's work is less didactic and thunderous than this, but all the same he too is asking what is a social identity? what is a situation? In a way that tale predicts the novel, which had not been invented yet.

Hannah Silva, *Forms of Protest* (2013, 76pp). This reminds me of a stay in Germany where the people I was sharing a house with were very keen on "Little Britain". I wondered about this, later, and decided that the point was a complete lack of nuance. The sketches translated into German without any loss of meaning because they had no refinements at the start. Totally excessive people were just as recognisable in Germany as in England. Silva's work has a complete lack of nuance. This offers space for emphasis and for simple momentum.

Some part of it takes the speeches, or radio interviews, of right-wing politicians and cuts them up, prints endless repeats of them, etc., in order to ridicule them. This surely has a big appeal to most people in Britain. It is curious how something populist can also treat language as material, a sophisticated technique. This is much like what the avant-garde does (Peter Finch, for example) and the conclusion is that a lot of avant-garde activity is anti-authoritarian in a way that could be populist. Silva does not wish to present counter-evidence and construct an argument; she simply turns the source into strips and distresses the strips. So these pages have no information content: they are more like imitating someone's walk, they are comic and drawn from life but not actual information.

Something so unmitigated raises questions about the nature of nuance. If we enter into multiple tiny variations of signal, do we have tiny selves that feed on tiny amounts of energy? Silva's work has a momentum that something more highly wrought, more rich in information even, cannot develop. As if its energy were used up by enriching its own surface and fabric and it could not then move again.

People do not always spend their time distinguishing a hundred varieties of garden or wild flowers, because they are too tired and preoccupied, and they may not have a sentimental attachment to the way they live because the external factors of wage rates, doing the job, rent levels, and buying food do not allow that, and they would rapidly move out if they had the power. Maybe they are not expressing a character because there isn't space for that to happen. Some environments don't attract sentiment, are not perceptually rich, are too rigid and bare to be moulded by wishes, are insensitive to human nuance. Aesthetic subjectivity is only possible under the precondition that the conditions which would prevent it are objectively absent.

Samantha Walton, *Self Heal* (2018, 85pp)
First, this is one of the best collections of the time and one of the best I have ever read.

It is difficult to analyse something which is allover, covering all parts of the visible text.

I thought to compare SW to John James. Also with James, there is an insouciance about details which leaves the overall feel of buoyancy intact and sweeps us along with pervasive feelings of serenity and joy. I was reminded of him because I had the same feelings as with the Welsh poet – but Walton's tone is really quite unlike his. I think this is an area which few poets venture into. Self heal is a plant but also refers, we would think, to wounds and forms of damage that heal up. In fact, one of the main functions of the mind may be to heal damage – experiences or information which cause pain. The mind is always mending itself. Impingent information can be seen as bending the nets which the mind is resident in – the nets are designed to change shape and to mend themselves. Arguably, the primary function of the self is to heal the self. The two terms are intertwined. The field dominates the details in this poetry – the implicit and overall quality builds up as the book goes on. Part of this effect is due to an indifference to details – they stay safely at the periphery and so the centre is placidity and serenity. The poetry does not have a thesis and does not deal with crises. That would disturb the overall feel.

Even though we can perceive a variety of things, the object most symmetrical to our personal self is another self. Since we are apparently all made of self, and the basic quality of our self is to mimic sensations that impinge on us, the most direct line for poetry is to represent a self which we can mimic. There are overall qualities which compose the self's successive states, they are like heat or light levels in that they are not momentary and do not change rapidly from moment to moment. What affects us most in a poem is not crises but the abiding qualities of the self which we are, at least linguistically, immersed in. These steady qualities covering the entire field are represented by overall and often implicit qualities of the verbal flow, and details may conceal them or block their effect. Conversely showing the profound and unconscious state of the poet's mind affects the reader's mind in the most profound and direct way, and this is an incredibly powerful effect.

Discussion of this state of harmony and profound influence generally talks about mis-steps, as small mistakes by the poet can have a great effect on the channel carrying it. I don't want to use words like perfect or smooth or flawless, not because they are inaccurate but because details are really not the most important thing and avoiding mistakes is irrelevant if the deeper values are unreleased and unimpeded. It may be helpful to bring on Ehrenzweig's Gestalt derived theory of art, where he claims that everything depends on deep gestalts (significant shapes which the mind searches for in its environment) and that because the mind detects wholes from partial signs very effectively (only for these significant shapes) then the artwork does not need much detail. Because the organism primarily wants stability the artwork should seek serenity. He talks about "the full emptiness of the scanning gaze" for perception in the middle of serenity. Stability allows processes internal to the organism to be carried out in a rhythmic way, and healing would be one of these. Is this helpful? Ehrenzweig had read careful psychologists but did not carry out any experiments to support his writing. It may be beautiful rather than scientific and unfortunately it may be soothing and rewarding without explaining anything. Perhaps we can take one detailed moment and claim that this might be thematic because it opens the section called 'self heal':

> Flowering in winter just once at nightfall
> as the cold snapped my filament & style
> I passed my life, trunk, soma, memory
> over to a collective hush, acquired tics still
> discharging down neurons to be bathed in
> the living body of the collective earth

> harmonic seed bed fed on jelly
> & black earth turned. We haven't attained
> light or transparency [.]
>   (from 'Winter Code')

One of the interesting things in Ehrenzweig's books is that he turns off the need for art to move: for him it is already there, just as gestalts are primal, even innate. Something well designed in Walton's work may be the transition between themes: how everything is discarded without a feeling of breach or loss –and concomitantly how every new theme is connective and not jarring. The poem is autonomous from its objects – they are on the periphery of something much larger and less explicit.

At this point I don't want to go on with the project, I want to halt and read more Walton poems.

John Robinson (1945), is a Yorkshire poet. *The Cook's Wedding* (2001, 126pp.) is a remarkable example of 'late Pop' work which has great charm and energy and never outstays its welcome. This is apparently his first book. The jacket says "he shovelled much of the concrete in the M62". The poems have no literary features at all, but instead have moral and emotional substance. There is after all a module of linguistic power which gives social fluency and solidarity with other people, as opposed to esoteric vocabulary choice or experimental improvisation. Some poems offer specialised experience, some acquire strength by venturing out across boundaries into more social scenes and contexts. So a trip to the Orkneys allows Robinson to give us 'A Speculative History of Theft', where the structures which devised stone circles were:

> Astronomic hypotheses and a social-religious value system
> Which was likely to offend modern sensibility
> Only insofar as it neglected to protest the borrowing of women.

In contrast, on the Isle of Lewis, at the same time, they had

> an abstract concept of larceny
> Which preceded any behavioural manifestation.
> However a vital flux of ideologies came about there
> With the abrupt intrusion of seaborne Danes and Goidels.

So they had the concept of gift but not of theft. He compares the gift customs to New Guinea.

How can I write out a theory that poetry is sprawling out in a dozen different styles without producing a book which is itself dissipated and disintegrated?

The Human Voice

In this section we look at six poets for whom the focus is certainly on the individual self. This is a way of assessing how well privatisation and autobiography work as themes for poems. I was blown away by Emily Berry's anthology *Best British Poetry 2015* because the poems were all of high quality and also because there seemed to be a new thing which meant intimacy about describing passionate experiences and the poem as a safe space where the most intimate things could be said and where we heard self-awareness rather than some conventional form of goodness.

It may be we can think of this new attitude by recalling the critique which was made, a few decades ago, of phallocentricity. This was held to found feelings of domination and confidence which occupied territory and bestowed political power. Erotic responsiveness made the world a source of delightful instability. A state of self-centred fantasy invested the world in layers of projection and wish-fulfilment. Despite the fantasy, heightened sensitivity also made perception of some parts of the environment sharper. The sound of the self was like some loud and repetitive music. This egoism constantly created symbols, halfway turning the material world into pleasure and display.

An early phase of feminine attacks on this self-projection gave way, we may think, to envy and to imitation or in fact occupation and take-over. The attitude involved geniality, relaxation and hilarity. *I'm bad... I'm nationwide*, we hear. In any case we are looking at a basic pushing-back of the limits to intimacy. Cultural space is to be filled with scent and sound and turned into personal territory. I am not sure this is a "thing" in the sense of a continuing and bounded poetic style. It may be more a concept which a clever editor had for a single anthology (which was sadly the last one in the series). There is a certain dazzle effect when an anthology which contains only good poems also focuses on a certain manner of writing. However, Melissa Lee-Houghton and Sophie Robinson seem to have written persistently in this way, and their work is substantial, at the same time as being highly subjective. Hannah Silva may also be placed with this grouping.

You gotta say yes to another excess:
Sophie Robinson, *rabbit* (2018, 80pp)
Most poets are defensive about emotional states. The zone of exact observation is set up as a defence mechanism against feeling, a way of diverting attention from its absence. How often do we hear critics praising precise observation as if it got us anywhere? It is hardly going to be as precise as a microscope or even a photograph. It never involves numbers even though measuring things is more precise. It is more as if there were a didactic intent of obliging children not to react emotionally and to observe things outside themselves as a way of winning marks. Poetry is going to get a lot further by accepting what is inside the poet and which is also inside everyone else. Tracking an individual consciousness in all its nuances is intelligent because we the reader are also conscious, and all issues of small scale fall aside because the poet is on exactly the same scale as us. Poetry like Sophie Robinson's, which addresses the subjective world without flinching or taking steps to reduce the tension, has a gradually growing effect which reaches thunderous levels.

The deranging impetus comes from the complete frankness, the constant self-assertion, the frequency with which themes change. Real rock and roll is not hyperbole because the energy is real and someone who can crank it up and knock it out for 40 minutes is not lying to you. They are hanging from the jet engine of showbiz like a tree from a mountainside. This is high energy poetry. For me, the key is that combination of unerring focus on self and the flickering needle of attention that jumps and shifts its weight every couple of lines. The reward of donning that role of diva is possessing that jet engine, being in the high-spec-alloy nacelle with it, and the price of doing that is frequent exhaustion and constant risk. In this case the self-attention is half self-doubt and the heightened perception is also self-condemnation. The poems stage intimacy and make one think that intimacy is the central poetic thing, the direction poetry has been heading in for the past 500 years. It emerges that when the poet breaks inhibitions so much the effect is to break the reader's inhibitions and material spills out of all kinds, simply anything that was held back. There is something about evoking the most basic states which removes them from the sphere of privacy and of accuracy into being exalted and unassailable, in the public realm, because everyone shares them and because they are not subject to reason. It is as if a poet needed to violate basic inhibitions in order to start up the flow of the feelings which we most desire, are most curious about, and regret most keenly. It is as if the realm of affect were also a non-secular building. I am thinking of a nightclub where the environment includes a solid wash of dance music, with singers pouring out high-affect call signs. In those rooms, the disinhibited signal is public and externalises passions from deep inside people – they may not even be there. This uninterrupted signal is what makes the passion impersonal. Paradoxically, they are not fickle – the same sounds will be there every night. They are programmed, in several senses. Maybe I dragged in the idea of rock and roll – the poet mentions Frank O'Hara and Tracy Emin. I am entitled also to think about Shirley Bassey. The poetry is circular in its returning to the same states of craving and yet evanescent, burning its context up as the energy to move onto the next line. Introspection is only possible when the lower layers of the self are not being held down by straps, and introspection is the fundamental thing in lyric poetry. Woe betide us if we reach eighteen with some exam results and a better knowledge of the absolutist policies of Louis XIV than of our own inner states, of the desires which we have neither formulated nor fulfilled, or of the mysterious desires of other people. That is what you would call a wasted youth.

This is not documentary poetry. At ease in a nightclub, it does not record the prices of the drinks or how the cocktails compare to the ones somewhere else in town. And that is hardly what we want to know. Poetry is more ancient than the retail nexus and has to fulfil other imperatives. Although the poems are about pleasure, the search for it involves bizarre affective repetitions and cycles. Increasingly, the landscape of nightclubs, living rooms, and galleries is saturated in a craving. The poet is caught up in a quest, and the narrative gives way to renunciation even if each step is also a fulfilment, a moment of knowledge. It seems clear that the craving is also on a scale small enough to be satisfied by another human, and that the writer is also capable of answering the cravings of that person. This is a small scale as viewed from Sirius but it is the human scale. The frankness is a problem for some people, but there seems to be an awful lot of experience which the rules of an older poetry excluded, and maybe it was just a phase, a form of damage caused by Christianity, even if it lasted for a long time. Emotions are no longer real at a point three feet away from the subject's skin; they are attenuated by a medium which is all around them. Even in time, they come to an end and they oscillate from second to second up to the end. Yet they can also climb up the slope of intensity. The fact that an emotion is no longer there when a person leaves the room does not prove that emotions do not exist. I have the sense that this projection of the ego illusion is the big thing in contemporary poetry and that a critical view which splits the self has been relegated to the background. The model could be pop music, dance music even, but that is unclear. The affective approach is just so strong. Endless doses of critique wash away in the launderette.

Rabbit turns up as a real rabbit: in 'Four ways to trap a rabbit', a poem about childhood in which, as expected, security is not present; the rabbit is shown as a creature with very many predators, an analogue for the insecurity of the child. In the poem, the family home burns down. That rabbit was not a symbol of affection invested and warmth, except maybe as a negative symbol of not having feelings, but re-appears ("Lit Moments") as an apartment-dwelling rabbit who is probably a symbol of the poet herself ("& the rabbit passed out from too much talking /& the rabbit passed out from too much tender rabbiting"). Late in the book the poet refers to issues with alcohol abuse. This is honest, although it puts an edge of bitterness into the flowing words. The sense of freedom is restricted, after this, by the compulsions. The poet is right to own up but this undercuts the feeling of subjectivity which is so strong in most of the poems. "Thirsty work", indeed. Missing out on this is like missing out on Billie Holiday. Holiday had certain issues, too.

Berry moved on to become editor of *Poetry Review*, the most-read poetry magazine in Britain. Did she follow up the high level of energy, not to say of damage, from that 2015 anthology? The answer is mixed, although a group of three essays appeared in the issue for summer 2017 on "offensiveness, risk, and the risqué". One of the poets in that stunning 2015 anthology was one by Lee-Houghton ('I am very precious'), which was quite apparently about sex. This felt like the borders of poetry shifting. Desires for autonomy and power over one's local environment could hardly be more simply realised. Lee-Houghton released a book called *Beautiful Girls* (2013) which kept up the pressure. It was set usually in a home for the mentally ill. One poem described two young patients departing the comforts of the Home for an evening during which they functioned as prostitutes in order to meet men and, apparently, to assert themselves. They earned some money and spent it on chips. The poems depict a community in which everyone is in the same boat. They are socially inclusive, for certain. A lot of the poems aren't about the poet (this is not wholly clear). I appreciated the aesthetic drive of the collection, but it was too even – it was hopelessly intense, you don't get that movement between strain and relief which is necessary for art. That just means we should be precise in identifying the poems which really work. It would be inexact to forget about these.

More blandness! now! The poems do not deliver the normal setting of poetry, as one of serenity, emotional stability, the calm sound of numerous stable friends, the sensitivity which follows security. However, if you acquire wealth and status, that may make you secure to a point where you are desensitised because nothing is getting through. This raises the spectre of a realm in which anxiety would be the basis of sensitivity and so of lyric poetry in general.

Berry published, in *Poetry Review* for winter 2017, another Lee-Houghton poem, this one called 'Heroin II' and evoking a tender scene of two people retiring to deal with love and heroin. The characters have gone through bad times and now at least one is going through withdrawal. The poem is volatile, involves a cocoon of warmth, reassurance, venom, and cleansing. The two are cut off from the world, in a boat surrounded by rushing waters. It makes me anxious to see two people with a such a dependency, even as they stride away from it. But that releases adrenalin which contributes to an artistic "high". In the punk style, people actually defined themselves through anxiety, and something similar applied to Goth and heavy metal. The reader cannot take a custodial attitude towards the poem.

Eleanor Perry, *Venusberg* (2015, 38pp)
In the folk-tale, the minstrel Tannhäuser went to live under a hill, the Venusberg, with Venus, the goddess of love, in dalliance. He came out again after 7 years had passed. The poet says:

> distortion which exceeds the very category of lust. A carnage implicit in the stark lunar zones. Cyanide drossscape, risen into ectoplasmic dump. Or multiple points of entry bleeding into hinterlands. It's like watching asexual products of precision-manufacture subverting integrated vampire technologies. For economy, the angle of the slagheap doesn't matter.

This is from the bad side of town, but I unconditionally like this, possibly because of my wasted youth as a rock fan. This works as rock music because it is high energy, it is about the conflict with authority, because it throws out norms, because it treats every event as if it had never happened before. The energy level is motivated by threats which may be imaginary but which elicit alarm reactions which work like drugs. The overall quality is the vital thing, a completely integrated image which we perceive in a flash. Analysing it is going to be like fact-checking Little Richard. The angle of the slag heap is a real issue, effort has been spent recently on re-grading slag heaps and china clay tips. They are like a lunar landscape (abiotic). Lust implies heat, and the product of burning is dross. Distortion anticipates the angle of the heap. There is this curious equation of metabolic processes and physical ones. "multiple points of entry" mimics the phrase "multiple independent re-entry vehicles", or MIRVs, but also the "six organs of admittance" defined as the basis of perception in Buddhist anatomy. The poem continues as "hallucinogens to pervade the bleak non-places [...] VFX motivational sales wracked with intergalactic hate-speech." (VFX – visual effects.) One poem says "why not slip comfortably into the cattle cult carnival, teased with the promise of a penislike eye". There was a Miss World competition compered by Bob Hope who really did refer to the *cattle show* at one point; the reference is to legs and haunches, amazing he got out alive. This leads on to the phallic eye, something which probably didn't exist outside 1930s surrealist erotica but which expounds a basic device of replacing descriptions of mental processes or of the outside world with a kind of alienated physiology. The density of organs is high. This resembles a room, or a street, full of photographs, so without words but rich with messages. The subjective landscapes may be coming from the media, allegedly showing the speaker what other people really want of her. The speaker is sucked in and trapped in an infinitely shallow, blindingly glaring, surface of high light; "pornosophical damage gone viral". This could actually be the Venusberg of the title, a prison filled with repetitive erotic compulsions. There is no mediation. The high affect is a description not only of the speaker but also of other people, seen in terms of the demands they make on her. "ilinx and voluptuous panic" refers to an element of Roger Caillois' theory of play, also used in George MacBeth's long poem *Lusus*. *Ilinx* is dizziness or ecstasy. Reflection is absent but we have serial states of high anxiety which may be its forerunner – decaying into self-control with a half-life of a decade or so. The 'penislike eye' is probably a quote from Bataille, who participated with Caillois in the Acéphale group in the 1930s. James Clifford has described Caillois' version of the sacred as "ritual expressions of primordial chaos, excess, cosmogony, fertility, debauchery, incest, sacrilege, and parodies of all sorts". We encounter the speaker of Venusberg as a participant, rather than an observer, in these rites.

It is a problem to translate the poems into rational terms when so much effort has gone into making them high-speed and melting away at every moment. The collection is completely consistent, blown away by a kinetic energy that seems to go on long after the last word. I fact-checked "Rip It up" and it's all true.

Caroline Bird writes poems with a deliberately simple vocabulary and syntax, which consist usually of self-contained lines rather than longer runs. They are all monologues dealing with domestic concerns, imitating the tone of a phone call with an intimate friend. They have a noticeable perfection, I mean that not only are there hundreds of them at a consistent level but also the level of finish within each one is astounding: everything flows. The jacket to her Selected (*Rookie*, 2022, 177pp) tells us that Bird published her first book (*Looking Through Letterboxes*) at age 15 – a fact hard to take in but correctly indicative of virtuosity which is also a sort of personal integrity, where the connection between the natural person and the words is unrestricted, and artificiality or calculation do not get in the way. While reading the Selected I thought of *commedia dell'arte* and of classic silent comedies; the level of skill is expressed in a fluency which can improvise new *lazzi* in the middle of a performance and without waiting to rehearse or rewrite. It is literally true that the monologue style is a boundary, or set of boundaries which join; there is a rule that no second person is allowed to speak. But we hardly notice this. What we hear is entirely natural and feels like a complete conversation. The voice is strikingly social and not self-preoccupied. Silent comedians literally did not speak, but in the middle of a Buster Keaton film, let's say, we simply forget this. The poems describe third parties and could even represent the self-awareness which comes from hearing someone talk about us in the third person. The poems are similar, as silent films were, but if the poet stopped producing them one can imagine a protest march to make her repent the decision.

In the silent era, highly verbal comedians made silent films. The era we live in is monotonously filled with monologues and with bulk details from the private and intimate realm. Bird takes these features to their natural limits, finding a territory which feels boundless even though we can see it is bounded; I get the impression that if verse drama were the thing of the moment she would write perfect verse dramas. By describing the domestic and natural tone of the texts one could give the impression that they are flat. But in fact the poems are accurate enough to show fantasy and the irrational as part of human behaviour, and we can see in them how illusions about the self and other people are part of everyday life and in fact a normal part of human behaviour. The quality one remembers about the poems is effervescence, fantasy, spontaneity. So take this quote from 'Flatmate':

> My shadow pressed a hot-water bottle
> against my ruptured side and tucked me in.
> Her mobile phone shivered like a habit.
> A shred of stocking caught in the flung door.
>
> My shadow dragged another shadow home,
> their eyes dilated with rotten sunlight.
> I slept under the bed with the secrets
> watching bed-springs flinch from their ghostly weight.

Even though we are hearing a stand-up routine in the genre of complaining about a flat-mate, the details are continuously unexpected and revealing. I am impressed by the willingness to display how irritating people can be, because poets like to put themselves on record as being kind and blameless. A flatmate who gets more phone calls than we do is objectively irritating, surely we have a right to complain. Finally, the poem is not certainly about another person at all: the "shadow" could be the speaker, recording how she has habits, repeats herself, might repeat conversations in the life of a shared flat. Take this, again, stanza 7 of the same poem

> You want to walk with redheads on the beach
> drink milk with men in white suits and smugly
> pride yourself on being ashamed of me?
> I fumbled the doorknob with my limp wrist.

What is the point of me analysing 100 poets saying "I am sensitive and egocentric and have a degree in English and cultural grievances" when Bird despatches them all in 40 words? I counted 10 stanzas in 'Flatmate' and they are all similar. But this repetition is rhythm, it not only makes each new stanza easy to follow but also highlights the differences. This highlighting bathes everything in a bright light; and the differences are intricate and smooth, they just shimmer as you look at them.

*

In British poetry the most gripping issues arising are simply bypassed, in the pursuit of serenity and order. There was something very exciting about poets breaking all that up and letting it rip. The anthology mentioned has classic status. What I found, when I read entire volumes by the poets whom Berry selected for it, was that the disinhibition related to individual poems only. The conflicted and compulsive level of existence is not where modern poetry generally sites itself.

Now we have two more poets, only one of them in Berry's anthology, who have developed a voice as the binding element for their poems. Mark Ford (1962), is clearly influenced by the New York School, on which he is an expert, and works in a world which is generated by language more than generating it. He sounds like John Ash, due to this shared influence. His manner is assertive and forthright, which makes it different from other poets in this tradition. The poems are high concept but full of banal lines. It is not always clear why he is writing the poem. *Soft Sift* came out in 2001 and had 49 pages. In 'Early to Bed, Early to Rise' he describes a series of comic mishaps based on cultural errors, so someone who confuses George and Zbigniew Herbert. So, in this poem about recognising the names of artists, the punch-line is the mistakes he makes. This could in fact be a parody of a New York poem, where the poet expects you to recognize hundreds of names and instantly get a brilliantly vivid memory of what they stand for. When he confuses names, the outcome is surrealism but also embarrassment – a basic mistake like putting on odd socks. To be carried by cinema into an imaginary identity offers freedom and detachment, but the poet does not want to follow up this offer, preferring to capture elements of disappointment and self-deprecation. The NY poets were glitteringly metropolitan and *au fait*, the reader could momentarily share that, but Ford spoils this by being interested in conversations that go wrong. Ford is not flamboyant or suave, and this puts him ahead of other NY School imitators. The language is genuinely mysterious, but there may be a lack of intent rather than a kernel of joy like a liqueur chocolate. Maybe this is the only way to be influenced by the New Yorkers – to remove the sophistication and sound like yourself. The poems record what may be a genuine disconnection. They are dandyish yet plain. He is still a bit cursory, inconclusive.

Sam Riviere has a tone in the way that Stéphane Grappelli had a tone, it was delightful even in a single bar, information simple enough to show up in that bar, by definition, but which you are extremely slow to get tired of. It is a manner, indolent, genial, easily bored, and I suppose the basic thing is that we want to fall into it, we want to inhabit it as if it were some photograph of a desirable and dégagé scene. He wrote a whole book of translations from Martial, *After Fame,* thus following up Porter and competing with him. Compete with Porter, *are you out of your tiny mind?* When something has been translated and imitated so many times, in the past 500 years, you need to have an excessive belief in the tiny gaps and pauses, the rises of emphasis, which you can deliver and which fifty other people can't, and actually didn't. This works for Riviere, he has a voice and it is charming. A certain anthology has emails between Riviere and a poet who notoriously overproduces and is proposing a long collaboration with Riviere, so possibly hundreds of pages, all his projects have a long train following them. Riviere simply provides elegant and not explicitly mocking reasons for not taking part. Why work when you are Hugh Grant on a bad day and Cary Grant on a good day? Somehow it seems as if this is Riviere in the pure state, the whiff from a glass after the spirits have been drunk and enjoyed, the qualities of negligence and *sprezzatura* showing up in emails which say *I'm not interested* without exerting the energy to say no. It may even be true that his greatest virtue is indolence, that ability to see through the pointlessness of almost anything people want him to do, to realise that conversation is not work and everything enjoyable in poetry is part of conversation.

Riviere has advised that three of his books roughly fit together as "conceptual" works. So that would be *81 Austerities, Kim Kardashian's Marriage,* and *After Fame.* The poems are like proposals for poems – he imagines perfect poems and then writes perfect poems. *81 Austerities* is apparently about the austerity programme of the Cameron government cutting public services to balance the loss of tax revenue after the financial crash of 2008, but Riviere's commentary says "suffer from paralysing yet hyperactive mode of boredom" leading to "its central theme is billed as the economic downturn that has negatively affected so many, but your existence, funded as it is at the taxpayer's expense, remains almost completely unaffected." He describes the process in a flow chart. Conceptual art classically needs project documentation, which can be thriftily recycled as a grant application. The Kardashian book (2015, 96pp) is the most interesting to talk about because it takes on inauthenticity full-on. There is one poem for each day of Kardashian's marriage. I should explain who Kardashian is. The key is that she was Paris Hilton's personal assistant, so trained in getting maximum publicity for someone of limited talent but boundless desire for celebrity. So Kardashian is the handler not the talent. And has no talent. So far as we know. She could put the risqué, the sleazy, the swaggering, and the fake on a spreadsheet. She takes part in a reality TV show about her family in which nobody has any talent and the events shown are shopping, doing make-up, and counting calories. This appeals to a wide extent of people who find following a plot too demanding, and there is a proposal to replace culture with "reality TV" altogether. Riviere does not deal with this red-hot tinsel by describing it or by analysing it. He avoids injecting a second voice which would contextualise it. There is only one side in this depiction – and it is the voice of the star herself. Inauthenticity is shown as a state with no borders and no way out. Every colour is a sort of shrill chemical enamel, so the sky looks like a painted fingernail and the pool has the tint of a cocktail. The point is emptiness and as every poem has a banal theme repetition is deployed as the way of depressurising perfect leisure, of showing a void inside it. The recurrence is intensively programmed, and curiously the source of the titles which repeat is Riviere's previous book, as if the avoidance of effort had gone so far as to use only recycled material, harmonised and sequenced in such a way as to drain meaning out of our world. (The 72 poems in *Marriage* are based on a grid of 8x9 themes, so 17 motifs altogether, all of which appear in the section titles of *81 Austerities*. The grid names sound like shades of some cosmetic.) The cover suggests that the textual material is drawn from a feed of Kardashian's make-up choices. The Martial book suggests analogies between reality TV and the moral decadence of early imperial Rome. The core of celeb reality TV is that they have personal brands of make-up, dresses, etc. and the plot of the show has them using these products, all the time, so that the whole thing is a commercial. Get rid of the programmes and reach the nirvana of TV, the end zone. Ancient Rome had nothing like this.

Go blank, envy, spend. It is hard not to see the Kardashian reduction of any information except the purely personal and transient as linked to privatisation in poetry. This analysis simply will not go away. The poets just discussed write in a highly personal way. To read them is to know them – and also to grasp the aesthetic point of privatisation. Even though you can say that their subject matter is small, the aesthetic returns for so much focus are large. A shift to the large scale would make these specific effects unattainable – they would be lost to us.

Pistachio Euphoria Sorbet

Nathan Thompson published *the arboretum towards the beginning* (Shearsman Books, 2008); *the day maybe died / (tributes and torched songs)/ Imagining China* (knives forks and spoons, 2011); *The Visitor's Guest* (Shearsman Books, 2011); and writes

> such a beautiful evening mist
> mucking the near sky   bags under its eyes
>
> my name is Angelina or it isn't
> I'm not certain this matters
>   faithful visitors
> concentrate our general existence
> punctuation's main point stop me
> if you've heard… conspiracy theories
> lie all around complete in their tatters
>
>   this manual is for the perfect organisation
>   of busked speech
>   the box is open
>   and all these things come out like voices
>
>   bent recording slowness
> (from 'the Texan with the instamatic') [in 'the day maybe died']

This is so much what it is. Do I need to write a review as well? Effort seems misplaced – the poem is laid back. Defining the poem is misdirected because the lack of definition is central and this is the feature you least want to lose. It's all about the spaces between the notes and the feeling escapes into your life through the gaps between the poem. The dedication to *Day* has "for Lee Harwood, an inspiration", and in the poem quoted above "manual for the perfect organisation" alludes to Paul Evans' 1979 book *A manual for the perfect organisation of tourneys*. Evans and Harwood between them define a Moment in English poetry, something which was open on one side to Pop music and on another to the avant-garde. That Moment was probably happening in 1967 and was strong in the early 70s, before louder music came along and meant you couldn't hear it any more.

I much prefer this poetry to Lee Harwood's. Lee always seemed to be wiping holes in a narrative he hadn't established, so that my attention wasn't seized and I didn't find an experience inside the poems, which were too nebulous. What he had, was a weak ego. He was interested in what you felt, even if you weren't actually there. *Day* itself may be a mismumbling of "the night lady died", a 1959 poem by Frank O'Hara about Billie Holiday, a singer from Baltimore. Juncture is the key stylistic device and I expect that looking at a hundred line junctures would teach us how this poetry is made. A key element (on the basis of reviewing Evans and related poets) is volume: the author turns down the volume on his own voice. What follows is that other sounds become more audible, and it's really about power in a relationship; the weaker voice allows for two voices to be heard. The boundary between two people gets blurred. Concord becomes more important than achieving a preset goal. The poem is permeable to everything around it, but cannot be weakened because it is receptive, it gets stronger with everything that does not make it lose that receptivity. Thompson is more interested in leaving a space empty than in filling it with assertion and territoriality. As for the juncture, the key is that none of the lines reach a point of exhaustion before halting: each one is evocative and tantalising. What it is, is readiness to turn into something else; a floating sound light enough to detect featherweight shifts and so receptive to the delicacies of other people's feelings. The goal is openness rather than knowledge.

Maria Sledmere, *Leave Bambi Alone* (Mermaid Motel, 2022; 79pp)
It is an object of conjecture how someone thought *Leave Bambi Alone* was a good title. The decision evokes a roomful of people dressed in paisley clothes, constantly agreeing with each other, twittering in excitement and mutual affection, oblivious of the outside world and unable to put their feet on the ground. The publicity actually refers to *Bambi* as "a bad poem": the implication is that it doesn't matter if the poem is bad as long as the sound keeps flowing and we are together and don't have to give up the mood which we love so much. In fact, it might be delightful if we accept our own naive wishes and realised that our absurd affection for a cartoon fawn was a helpful concentrator for our gushing affection for ourselves and indeed, for others. We find the constant sound comforting and it shelters us from everything bad in the world. This whole milieu is suffering from euphoria and a symptom of that is happily chattering away nineteen to the dozen and a part of that might be that nobody is too

worried if the burden of meaning is not heavy.

I took out another poet to make room for Sledmere because she has completely unfastened moorings to explore a hypothesis, psychological and linguistic. The hypothesis might be that we actually *want* to feel euphoric. The cover of *Leave Bambi Alone* has a colour scheme in pistachio and candy stripes. (The candy canes and the pistachio occur inside the poem.) It is enough to evaluate these colours thoroughly to reach a conclusion on how much we like Sledmere: they offer a window on a universe of pure pop (and so do the poems). If we check the poem:

> applying mascara in the bathroom
> mirror
>
> I wonder how many eyelashes
> glued to the planet Uranus your eyes
>   bluey-green are cute
> not hydrogen, helium and methane
>   as other places, you're always seeing beyond
>
> This Christmas,
>   leave Bambi alone!
>
> But don't leave her alone in the snow
>   as per the ethics of all huntresses
> I took the menthol sweet
>   a seed for all seasons.
>
> 'Cute, loveable, vulnerable'

(Uranus looks blue and its atmosphere contains the gases mentioned.) – it genuinely is pure pop. This passage shows that the literal meaning of the title is advice not to watch *Bambi* yet again, this Christmas. The film was released in 1942 and hard for children to avoid in the following decades. Bambi was actually male, in my memory and according to Wiki. Sledmere wants her friends to focus, get real, bite on the bullet, and watch *Meet me in St Louis* instead. (Menthol contains the word mint, like crème de menthe, and has a cool taste sensation, which links to the snow. 'preferable to the all-night café/ of my thoughts/ which are mint-to-sage on the coolness scale'. It occurs to me that the Peppermint

Pistachio Euphoria Sorbet

Lounge was so named because it was cool. Who could resist their song: *it goes like this/ the Peppermint Twist?*) Good pop offers a succession of brief bright stimuli rapidly replaced by others in a simple rhythm setting up a response pattern which it then satisfies; this could apply to *Leave Bambi Alone*, as well as 'The Peppermint Twist'. The poem starts at Christmas, runs for 1600 lines, and may have reached Hogmanay by line 1600. It has jaffa cakes:

> Break it softly apart
>   at the bark
>   and the gaps will be orange, ersatz
>   encased in paltry layers of chocolate.
>   This is a day
> studded with lights, sugar, lemon
>   and bitters
>   dissolving from the cube
> of your thought, which is an art gallery
>   of unsent images
>   in the general theme of fuchsia
>   looks for summer and spring.

Imagine the bubble bath/ of language from a bank of words: we quoted Foucault describing meaning as a foam. That is, everything personal, all the messages a self gives out about its internal states. If a self is large and doesn't weigh much then foam seems like the most likely structure. Maybe menthol foam. Scotland is surrounded on three sides by foam. To generalise, poets are good at empathy and bad at economics. Serious poems dealing with economics are mostly ridiculous because the poets are usually so hopeless about money and business and the real melody is, *empathise with me because I am such a good person*. So if poetry is good at empathy maybe it could try abandoning the realms of quantity, logic, and material restrictions, and advancing into the quadrant of sympathy and mood altogether. Sledmere is remarkably consistent and inventive at doing this, so she reaches a new and stimulating sound, and the question is more: how much do you like euphoria? how much do you like pistachio? how much do you listen to your own and other people's moods?

I was struck by the fact that, in *the weird folds*, there are 48 poems covering 240 pages. This distribution is really unusual for an anthology, and I think we are seeing a new time sense. The poem becomes a place rather than a sequence in time with a high point, a limit, and a conclusion. The edges of the poem vanish. Mood is everything and you don't want to leave. Texture takes over – like a fabric design which is continuous and does not genuinely have a start or a finish. Paisley would do. Pace is irrelevant because the end cannot get closer. Nathan Thompson has also developed a poetry in which mood is highly tuned and there is no particular sense of progress. He had worked this pattern out earlier, so ten years before *weird folds*.

Sociolinguistics

Any local statement in a language is conditioned by the social context in which the language is spoken. A poet can redraft their poem but the rules by which language is evaluated are stored in many places and put up stout resistance to reform proposals by poets. Any successful poet has a shrewd grasp of sociolinguistics and it may be that this is the engine driving poetry. Language signals status and will do so unconsciously even if the poet has a conscious wish to send a different message.

Daljit Nagra has written widely acceptable poetry and was poet-in-residence at Radio 4 for a year or so. In performance, he delivered in two widely different voices, one received pronunciation with a slight Indian accent, the other English with an archaic and very strong Indian accent, a *chee chee* voice, which would usually be heard as comic. This voice aroused many memories because it was so much a part of reality; although part of the past it was tangled up with many other things from the past. This code-switching was a provocation. Listening to it, you could not help feeling some unconscious hostility to the voice, and then realising what it meant to be the speaker of such a voice: someone incongruous and of low status. This was a shock. The feelings aroused were altogether too strong.

His first book was called *Look We Have Coming to Dover!* (2007). Dover is an entry port. The subject is that of arriving in England, evidently as immigrants, and seeing the event as momentous, visually exciting, memorable. The overt enthusiasm is uplifting, it makes us happy – but how long can you feel that enthusiasm before seeing something ambiguous about it, and recalling how many people in England weren't enthusiastic about immigrants and for some reason didn't feel happy that they were happy. These six words pack in so much of an emotional message. Nagra doesn't point out the ambiguity, he leaves the language as a live sound rather than moving on, or withdrawing, to reflection. The phrase would be utterly different if he adjusted the grammar. The poetry is not as interesting as the double voice. Part of the effect is of imitating South Asian norms of elevated speech by laudatory use of enthusiasm and many words with an overall low information content. This is meant as eloquence and deep politeness. But, English norms (since 1920, possibly?) are different. Again, the speaker comes across as incongruous. This is comic. But, at the same time, it is attractive because it is like naive art: it is enthusiastic, decorative, uninhibited. It lacks the businesslike qualities of caution and accuracy which we find so depressing and pessimistic. Also, it is full of information – it is a good description of what it sets out to describe.

This act is a satire on the prejudice of English people, making deductions far too quickly from patterns of speech. It points out the gap between outside and inside. But it also recalls a gap between two generations – the voice is one which nobody born in England speaks in, it evokes an older generation, the parents of people born after 1970. It can mean lots of things – it could mean a reflection on the things which the children had to learn, their innovations. It could be saying, I am part of a British tier of affluent professionals, exchanging intelligent remarks, but inside there is an immigrant with a *chee chee* accent (and unreserved enthusiasms). If I make the wrong move, I could be back on the outside, a figure of fun. It just takes one speech by a politician attacking immigrants to bring all these thoughts back. Code-switching, even if it is found in most human societies, points to an inner split, to a hindrance on natural expression. One possible version of this floweriness is that redundancy of syllables connects to honouring the person being spoken to – a sign of prestige. The flowers mean that the person speaking has much lower status than the person being spoken to. So its lack of coherence relates to a social situation based on deep inequality. This inequality might mean that the speaker is insincere – he or she fears the wrath of the person addressed rather than liking or admiring them. Nagra's verbal tactics evoke quite profound anxieties as well as displaying that rather high-calory surface of enthusiasm and excitement. He never explains what he is doing – my reactions may be wrong; but his use of language brings up all kinds of memories. I said that the pitch patterns of the more "Indian" accent of English recalled an older generation. It follows that the feelings wrapped up in it embody all feelings about a parental generation.

The title poem in his second collection (*Tippoo Sultan's Incredible White-Man-Eating Tiger Toy-Machine!!!*) described the wooden painted carving made for an Indian monarch around 1780 and showing a tiger devouring a European in a military uniform. The king was Tippoo Sultan, of Mysore, and he was engaged in a war with the East India Company. The impact is limited by familiarity (didn't every child in the Sixties get taken to the V and A and see that tiger eating Europeans?) but more interesting is the ambiguity. The style of the carving is naive – it seems to be aimed at children, and the word "toy" does belong here. According to the V and A website, a concealed handle "simultaneously makes the man's arm lift up and down and produces noises intended to imitate his dying moans." It was captured by the East India Company and was for many years in their museum in London. I suppose that when I was seven years old anything from the sophisticated areas of Indian art would just have gone over my head. If you ask why the guileless older Indian man is speaking a European language with a laughable accent, the answer quickly involves asking why a European power (actually, it was three powers) invaded his country and installed a new dominant class there. The carving recalls a war which instantly recalls the suppressed fact that the British penetration of India was not a benign spreading of prosperity and trade relations. The carving has a fairground quality, but it also offers the possibility that you as an individual could identify with the tiger, and local resistance, and not with the European.

The flowery and voluble word flow of Nagra's poems shows us frankness and spontaneity, qualities widely felt to be missing from English daily life. That is especially true of interaction with outsider groups. Nagra writes monologues which simultaneously hark back to Kipling's recitable poems and have the naive quality embodied in Tippoo Sultan's tiger. Nagra's poems are comic but full of information, they are reminiscent of Kipling's poems (based on music hall recitals). They spoke about people of other cultures in a broad and simple way and Nagra may be satirising this and saying that the English understanding of Asians living among them is cartoon-like. Yet again… if you are working with people without a common language then you may produce a version of yourself which brings about companionship and is broad and often non-verbal. The surface has that glare and deftness of a game-show but the voice expresses the wish to be friends. I can talk about Nagra's style but really it retains its ambiguity and resists simple translation. The speech patterns he manipulates connect to a thousand different things – bits of all those processes stick to them.

From 2003, **Meic Stephens** (1938–2018) began publishing poems in the Gwenhwyseg dialect (spoken in Gwent, from a Celtic word *venta* which means "market" or possibly "town"). When I first encountered one of these I was shocked because I couldn't understand it. It was a submergence moment – I was in the middle of language but I couldn't find the surface. The background is that Stephens comes from Treforest but grew up speaking English; he became an ardent nationalist as a student in the early 1960s, and learnt Welsh as part of that. He helped to set up the literature section of the Welsh Arts Council and produced an astonishing number of handbooks, anthologies, touring guides, etc. over the next 50 years. He wasn't a modernist but he helped put the infrastructure in place. Opinion divides, perpetually, into those who think any system is institutionally corrupt and those who think the infrastructure is helpful and necessary to an art. He chose to write poetry in the dialect of Treforest possibly because he had an extreme form of local nationalism.

Stephens' book collecting the dialect poems is called *Wilia* (Cerddi 2003–13; 2014, 122 pp.) which (he explains) is normal Welsh *chwedleua*, so it means "talking". There was a Celtic word *skuetlom* which produced both *chwedl* and Gaelic *scéla* (now spelt *sgeul*). The *kw sound turned into p in P-Celtic, except that *skw became chw instead. According to Wolfgang Meid, there was another P-Celtic language in which it became sp, and so *skuetlom* produced spell (meaning "speak") which was borrowed as the Old English word spellian (meaning "speak"). After studying a textbook called *Blas ar iaith Blaenau'r Cymoedd* I came to understand the dialect poems, and they no longer seem so strange. I think the correspondence of *chwedleua* and *wilia* shows the problems. The most disconcerting feature of Gwenhwyseg is calediad (locally *cletiat*) in which voiced consonants at the end of stressed syllables become unvoiced. So Tredegar (near Treforest) is locally called Decar. A pond called on the map Ysgubor Wen is locally Skipper Wen. And, see *cletiat*. Here is a flavour of one of the poems:

> On' 'r un mwya ithus, cret ti fi,
>   o'dd 'wnco manco, pwerdy Glan-bæd,
> yn natu am y dansher i'n cartrefi:
>   (from 'Wteri')

This is a memory of circa 1942 and Stephens as a child hearing air raid sirens (*wteri*, hooters). I have the impression that this resembles an English-language poem which Stephens wrote in about 1972 (also called 'Hooters'). Both poems compare the sirens to the hounds of Annwn which, in folklore, howl as they come to fetch those about to die. The difference between the poems is partly that the Welsh one rhymes ABAB and the English one does not rhyme; partly that the English one is more complex, with a three-level time scheme and interesting cuts from one scene to another. Poems in dialect are always simplified – this is sociolinguistics. The linguistic density of these Treforest poems is astounding but the poetological density is less so. Because of the industrialisation, there were more people and more Welsh-speakers in Gwent than anywhere else; Stephens in an afterword credits it with a million speakers at its zenith (*anterth*). It was the centre of the Welsh language community. In ways related to rapid development, rapid immigration, site nearest to England, and so on, it lost its Welsh with amazing rapidity during the 20th C. Arguably this collapse was the biggest event in the history of the Welsh language.

Gwenhwyseg was a dialect on the border of Welsh and English. It is possible that the loss of initial h, together with the loss of initial ch-, is part of the influence of spoken English, which locally also had no initial h. I drew a blank with *wnco manco* but a check reveals that it means *him over there* and that Stephens used it as his pen-name when submitting a poem (anonymously) to the 2003 bardic competition.

Obviously one has to imagine the past of Wales as taking place in Welsh, but it is only realistic to imagine it as taking place in dialect Welsh. Much the same is true of English history, I suppose. Standard Welsh actually is an infrastructure, one which enables messages to be sent from one part of the country to another without dissolving on the way.

The converse of sociolinguistics is a fantasy that one can exit from society and set up a blank language in which statements can be made with no experiential content. Poets are interested in controlled games where they invent the rules. If the rules are made of information, they are like language and can be redrafted and re-spoken much like a text. The evidence is that the rules, also, of collective poetic language change from time to time. They are not a literal reflection of the wishes of the audience – or, perhaps, those wishes can change from decade to decade. The idea I am working with is that what is revealed, was there. Style reflects social processes. But in a society given to self-reflection it is apparent that some writers will untether from this and have it that what is revealed, was not there. Some contemporary poetry is composed in a fantasy of the unconditional; or, language without experience. We have to consider some poets who decided not to normalise their linguistic experience but to retain it as something opaque, as the material of a poem.

Jasmina Bolfek-Radovani. *Knitting drum machines for exiled tongues* (Tears in the Fence, 2022, 58pp)
A key to the fabric of the text is that parts of it are in three different languages: English, French, and Croatian. I first heard parts of it at an

event organised by *Tears in the Fence* magazine which was dedicated to bilingual poetry. This is a challenging concept. I should explain that I can read French and due to knowing another Slavonic language I can recognise the Croat words, on a second reading. On that basis I can say that almost all the foreign words are glossed by the English ones; their effect is quite subtle but certainly includes reproducing the feelings of someone in a country where they cannot understand everything being said, and of recollection of being in different cities. The strange words are specific to a city, in memory, and embody the feel of it. They stick to the original moment of hearing them. So "I ask you again – Si je suis un heartcoeursrce ordinaire, what languages jezike langues do I speak?" – *srce* and *cœur* both mean "heart" and, obviously, "jezike" and "langues" both mean "languages". "flowfluxtok" similarly. The trilingual quality is not part of a city but of a human being, a subjective power before the languages but shaping them. The poems are about leaving or arriving:

> You place a paper slate on moist
> ground   measure
>   its resistance to   water
> It is possible to invent   a language
> in which   degree of wetness   means   degree
>   to which you belong. You can be long. So,   you
>
> be langue.
>   (from 'What is the colour of dépaysement?')

The cover has an illustration of a circuit diagram for a machine that knits, explaining the title; although textile looms were run by stored programs already in the 18th century, this one is fictional and has something to do with weaving feelings or states of mind. A poem with the same title as the book discusses rhythm as something human and more basic than language

> poetry of the mind
> ruptures free
>
> tongues, incessant beats of
> voodoo dolls

> weaved into the last chords
> of Coltrane's
>
> 'Blue train', melancholic
> sound textures
>
> muffled voices,
> knitting drum machines.
>   (from the title poem)

The heartbeat motif also takes the form of arrhythmia; one poem is 'potres', a tremor which affected Zagreb on 10 March 2020, seen as an event of the heart.

The poet is literally Croatian-Algerian (but has lived in quite diverse places). You get a couple of words of Arabic (I think it is):

> Houria, *liberté* weaves
>   her Arabic
> into the fabric   of French
> imprinted on the back of the girl's   mémoire
>   rougefoncé du sol de l'Algérie
>   goût
> du baghrir
>
>   jardin de   la maison   des Anciens

(I believe baghrir is a kind of leavened pancake.) The diagrams inside the book are labelled "tattoos" and the knitting needles of the looms connect to the tattooing needles used at least in some parts of the Maghreb: the tattoos carried significant symbolism. The blue marks are being equated with life experiences leaving marks on the memory. Themes keep repeating but they are like attractive melodies, we want them to repeat; the information content is not the main point. One them is the beating of a heart, evoked through arrhythmia:

> the beats no longer follow time, syncopated
> rhythms
>   take over city's homes, streets, workplaces
> many

>   are playing their tunes backwards; they
>   incomprehensible]
>   dance
>   to other people's tunes.
>   (from 'All that Zagreb jazz')

The registering of the *potres* on the paper of a seismograph probably involves needles again. Much of the poem is about dance music as an international beat; evoking again the needles of the level controls of a mixing desk. One moment evokes hearing Bowie's "Let's Dance", in Zagreb, in 1983.

The book is like one continuous lyric poem and its furls take us deeper into the emotions of a human being. It turns out that achieving emotional identification does not depend on having led a life similar to the poet but on the poet making emotion the main content of their message.

Da swittle o ideas: Christine De Luca: *Northern Alchemy* (2020; 93pp) De Luca has been publishing poems since 1995 (*Voes and Sounds*). We have to start with the nature of the variant English in which most of these poems are written. Around 1400, there was a West Norse language (we can call it Norn) spoken in coastal Norway, Iceland, Faeroes, Shetland, and Orkney. It was a little world. Distance made for rather rapid linguistic divergence. Between roughly 1500 and 1700, the Northern Isles came to speak a dialect of Scots, acquired partly from sailors and partly from settlers, and it is this dialect which is spoken today (while the genuine Norn died out by 1800). The disappearance of Norn from Caithness, the Scottish mainland nearest to the Isles, removed a vital social support from the language on the isles.

The poster phrase for Shetlandic is *dinna chuck bruck*, i.e. No Littering. Shetlandic is the most peripheral member of the English dialect continuum, and that is a kind of maximum. Of course this sheds light on how hard it is to write in dialects that are much closer to the English standard. Audio versions of De Luca's poems are available at www.christinedeluca.co.uk. Shetlandic shares most of its DNA with English, and that is why we can read De Luca's poems:

> On a shingly beach at Linga Grieve hed
> his wilderness experience; wrat his epic

at owsed da wash of culture, da swittle o ideas.
Only da stons apö da ayre wir irreducible.
Da briggistanes o Sodom man a shiggled
tae der very atoms wi da weicht o wirds:
wirds fae da skröf o sciences, geology,
an fae a teet at testaments, a nod at Norn
an odd conglomerate.

Man, I doot if dere's a raised beach
onywhaar in Whalsa. (*Da Nordern Isles wis
relatively droonded i da Late Devensian,
no raised. Wis glacio-isostacy a wird owre far?*)
Dy poem wid a hed mair pooster if du'd waeled
dy wirds, chukkit oot da ballast.

Fairly obviously, this is dialectal Scots and not dialectal Norwegian. The Orkney and Shetland dialects are closest to north-east Scots. This is part of the dialect continuum which covers most of Britain. (Sodom, a corruption of 'Sudheim', was the house MacDiarmid lived in while in Shetland.) This poem, 'Not on a raised beach', was printed in the special issue of *Lallans* magazine, "A sklent at Shaetlan". It is saying that 'On a raised beach' wasn't written on a raised beach. *Glacio-isostacy* is the rise of dry land up after being depressed down by the weight of ice when glaciated. *Ayre* is a gravel spit, a kind of beach (as in *Eyrbyggjasaga*, one of the classic sagas). *Pooster* may be from *posture*, as in military posture, anyway means "vigour". *Teet* is peep. *Skröf* is like 'scrape' and refers to the top layer of soil, so in modern usage "stratum" or "surface"; De Luca is suggesting that MacDiarmid only took on the surface of sciences; perhaps that he was more concerned to use knowledge to dominate than to bring illumination. 'On a Raised Beach' was written in English, and De Luca is getting back at MacDiarmid for deprecating "kailyard" writing, the most popular writing in Scots: when it fell out of fashion, it wasn't replaced by anything except more writing in English.

The poems are strongly Shetlandic, not Norse, and Shetlandic is not English or Scandinavian but peripheral. Being peripheral is a stable state, normal and a sound basis for culture. If Orkney and Shetland went back to being part of Norway, they would be more peripheral, geographically and linguistically, than they are now. However, there are quite a few Norn words lingering within the island dialect (and in the Caithness variant, too).

'Conundrums' starts with a jigsaw puzzle:

> At da cafe, someen tried a puzzle med o wid,
> a ticht knot. Takkin apairt wis aesy; piece
> bi piece, no bafft and brukkit tae a coose.
> (i.e. *battered and broken to a heap*)

The poem is a description of the Grind of Navir. My source says that *grind* means "gate" in several Scandinavian languages, and that "Da Grind o da Navir at Eshaness is the gateway in the cliff where the powerful action of storm waves forces quarries out huge rocks and throws them up to form large heaps or storm beaches fifteen metres above sea level. *Nafarr* means an auger or gimlet, a tool for drilling holes." (https://www.shetlandamenity.org/)

You can see the gate clearly in online photos: it compresses incoming waves and focuses their energy. The poem describes the broken rocks in their path:

> …But, my gori,
>
> whittan a backdrap! Da Heads o Grokken,
> Da Drongs: ootmarkers o fechts and spöllis.
> Da ocean here is wild, weel wint wi takkin
>
> gyoppmfoos; he's riven it sindry, tirled
> hulters headicraa, höved dem dis wye an dat.
> Maybe, in a tirse, he birsed da watter intil
>
> a cave whaar da basalt, brokkin inta blocks,
> offert her waekness.

(spöllis, *breaking*; wint, *used to*; gyoppmfoos, *double handfuls*; hulters hedicraa, *huge rocks somersaulting*; tirse, *high spirits*).

This is then an analogy for the jigsaw. It is hard not to see in the shape-forming energy of the ocean an analogy for this compulsively creative language. Shetlandic is not a language used in the classroom and the people who speak it may be unable to recognise their own words in written form. It is not a cultivated linguistic variant. It seems to be more work writing this in dialect but also the linguistic shapes which come out are more pristine and more evocative of the shaping processes.

De Luca excels at dealing with geology. I was really excited by 'Not on a Raised Beach' and 'Conundrums'. The other poems are like genre pictures and deal with love and endurance, often, or childhood, weather patterns. The islands contain clusters of human beings, one of whose purposes is to love and nurture each other, but are also three-dimensional masses of rock whose geometry decrees that they are above sea-level and whose site decrees that they are surrounded by the ocean. Two other poets using Shetlandic are Robert Alan Jamieson and Roseanne Watt. It is puzzling that there should be three good poets from this small community at one time, but I don't have to solve that puzzle. Watt's *Moder Dy* (2019) is about half in Shetlandic; the title refers to a 'mother wave', actually an undertow, which fishers locate, under the surface, to show them in which direction land lies. It is about the rational aspect of the irrational.

L. Kiew took part in the same *Tears in the Fence* bilingualism event and published *The Unquiet* (25pp) in 2019. The story is one of painful geographical emergence and I cannot track all the events. The subject is learning English while hearing a Chinese dialect inside:

> uà ài: gāt lèu dă: jek dă uẹ
> orotund   nullibiety   opaque
> smeasling   desuetude   spoilage
> uà ài: gāt lèu dă: jek dă uẹ
> minatory   plangent   deliquesce
> lutulent   sportive   grackle
>
> The words I swallow become
> feathers poking through my skin,
> I am fledging for the migration.
>   (from 'Swallow')

This shows the poet "overeating from the dictionary". The poet emphasised that this was not the national language (based in Beijing dialect). The name *Kiew* uses an archaic transcription, and *w* does not appear in the official transcription into a Roman alphabet. Lisa Kiew messaged,

"In reply to your question, the other languages I use in *The Unquiet* are Teochew, Hokkien, Mandarin and Bahasa Malaysia. Teochew is the one I write most across from." I don't know what the Chinese line in this quotation means. *Ibi* means there so I would guess that nullibiety means "not being there anywhere", displaced, and is the opposite of ubiquity.

I would not want to spend hours listening to poetry in a language I don't understand. Actually boredom etc. is not the sensation I had. I spent a lot of my life living in London, where you constantly hear foreign languages spoken, and I generally filter them out. Actually what I thought about was Yiddish, which I certainly used to hear in one specific part of London (and could more or less understand snatches of). Listening to the poems was like switching that filter off: and floating on a tide of words whose importance I could not assess. What I thought was that the real voice of London is one that nobody understands fully, because it uses 100 different languages. I don't know if there is a word for "a community that doesn't understand itself".

The poems are dense and seem to cover decades of experience. Kiew does not seem to have been happy about the migration (which I guess was from Malaysia to England). Part of the text describes sensations and food back home, poignant because they are lost. One moment refers to learning Hokkien in the playground, so not at home; the family might have been in a district that spoke Hokkien but have come there from somewhere else. After a point the message is more than we can take on, because the differences between two continents are too great to be grasped. We can imagine grasping them and use that as a stopgap.

Privatisation and Religion

The situation for English Catholics involved not just the humility of lay people in a church dominated by the clergy and by Latin, but also the suppression from public space entailed by the Protestant nature of the realm and its law. Catholicism was heresy in the British context. Lay writers were excluded from serious subjects. The marginal state of those who write about human affairs without being priests is equated with the monotony of suburbs where the original developer left out any central spaces. The rise of literacy led to heresy, but both literacy and privatisation were also features of Catholic Europe, and of Catholicism in England and Scotland. The rise of the vernacular is the parallel to privatisation, and the missing central space is the disappearance of modern Latin, the major cultural endeavour of the Catholic Church. The audience for this Latin creativity was small but we have to recognise its existence, and its resistance to French and enlightenment during the 18th century. This is a forgotten past. There may have been a kind of poetic dissidence which expressed recusant and Jacobite sympathies.

The most recent Latin poems I have seen are by **Peter Davidson** (1957), who began with a pamphlet of poems in Scots, *Works in the inglis tongue* (1985). His most celebrated work is *The Palace of Oblivion* (2008, 59pp). This is in English and, in a way which may be increasingly part of modernity, Davidson is the academic authority on the specialised area which he writes poems about. The key is defeat: he takes several wars of the early modern period and looks at the mentality of the unreconciled. The losing parties are mainly the English recusants, holding out after the Reformation, and the Jacobites, loyal to the Stuarts after 1688. I looked up on the Internet several exhibitions which Davidson was involved in: one of them showed the embroidery of Lady Helena Wyntour, religious garments where the stitching was an act of piety, and remarks that this is the most complex work of visual art made by a woman in 17th C England.

The title poem deals with the defeated in deep, permanent exile; as part of a series of ten poems dealing with different stages of political defeat, merging into a fictitious place, one you can never leave. The "Spy's Letters" deal with someone of ambiguous loyalties: 'My principals are dead or have run mad through the ruins of their mirrored offices.' Perhaps he is a Fascist (of a monarchical, Legitimist, strain), perhaps a communist. The setting may be the 18th or the 20th C:

And how would you suggest that I should live in England in this year
– and how should anyone live in England now?
(We raised our eyes from the systematic gardens, the classical villas, our black, encompassing water.)
As a spy. How else?
But how should I begin to think of it?
Especially where speech and writing are proscribed?
With invocation of rain, in fear of the Muses; the usual precautions.
   (from 'The Spy's Letters')

The *systematic* gardens must be in Europe because a wild garden is called a *jardin anglais*. The speaker is unable to live in England because he finds its government and sovereign to be illegitimate. The proscription suggests bans on the Jacobites, but is left open, as a malaise. The 'Palace of Oblivion' series covers dissidence from Tudor times onward:

There may also be moments of arcane or magical significance:
Rooms of unimaginable, praeterite splendour in once fine houses deep in the London slums;
Music-halls, with light striking up from the pit on coarsely gilded pilasters
And songs which lurch suddenly from innuendo into lucid, prescient despair;
And a master of spies, grinding the ash of a dead fire in his grey kid glove
Then sifting it about him on the floor of a high cold room furnished only with umbered mirrors,
This last as a pantomime of warning to the two heroes, a reminder, which they do not heed, of their mortality.
   (from 'A Choice of Emblems')

The music hall suggests a time after 1880. There may be a residue of Scottish nationalism in the design. But this is present as something which the poetry is apparently tired of – it has moved beyond inherited positions, even if its direction pursues theirs. Catholic aristocrats are not figures that most Scots, most SNP voters, can rapidly identify with. However, this is a key to the depth of the book, opening up a forgotten and eccentric world. The characters are usually Catholics; because the culture they were rejecting had a Puritan element, with stress on words at the expense of the visual, the sensibility which Davidson is recovering is heavily ornamental, tied to what was pejoratively called the Baroque. At least one poem is set around 1640 in the camp of the *Pfalzgraf* of the Rhineland Palatinate, leader of the Protestant cause, with his English wife and supposed links to the Rosicrucians.

This is not poetry about a country we hope to live in. Its sensibility is entangled with the perceptions of excluded minorities – life in a suspended ideology. The subjects are living in the wrong country. Arguably this is the precondition for being conscious of politics: you can think about what is not there but not, after a certain point, about what is there. It may have been the capacity to say No to a king or a liturgy that produced the awareness of the individual; like an object, it only came into existence by acquiring boundaries, which separated it from the social flow all around it. The individual says no and therefore exists. This disconnect, self-wall, may have founded 20th C literature, and may anyway bring unhappiness. A real country is shapeless and contains everything, but a kingdom that does not exist lends itself to schematisation and capture in visual or verbal patterns. Davidson starts with concrete objects, like Jacobite drinking glasses, and is less interested in social arrangements; this is part of the strength of the poems. The factions he is interested in were not proposing to redesign society. They were interested in changing the ownership of estates, and in different liturgies – and, to some extent, different buildings and ornaments.

Davidson has published extensively on unrealised architectural projects, which often came out of conservative religious minorities, unable to build and with enforced leisure. Another of his exhibitions included a building I had, by chance, spent time in, as part of a poetry weekend. This was a tower in Alloa (Clackmannanshire) owned by the Earl of Mar, who lived in exile for several decades after leading the failed 1715 Uprising. In Italy, he produced a design for rebuilding his tower which had a lake on the roof. Fish are nice, but this was a loopy idea; one has to accept that one aspect of the *avant-garde* derives from rich people who were out of power because they supported the wrong dynasty. His long-term frustration produced fantasy architecture, withdrawing into the unknown because it could not be realised. The plans are the link between the invisible and the real. Davidson associates these schemes with allegorical buildings built by Mannerist poetry, to visualise states of mind, of which the *palace of oblivion* is one. Such people still had the power of patronage, which was the basis for all serious art, but had lost interest in using it to reinforce the status quo. It may be that frustration actually stimulated these isolated families or networks to venture into the imaginary and to produce a more energetic culture than the successful needed to. Of course, that also implies that we are recovering a history of political fantasy, of a diminished sense of reality. Excessive belief in art may be a product of failed politics. Part of the reason for the success of the book is its originality, exploring realms of sensibility which historians have consistently bypassed and which a more affluent age has time to wander through and recover. There is no other book of poetry which is similar to *Palace of Oblivion*.

Sarah Law published *Perihelion* (2006) and *Ascension Notes* (2009, 75 pp). The point to start with is the crisis of Christian poetry, which was obviously there in the 1950s. Older forms of Christian poetry had just lost credibility. There were still a large number of Christians, and they were eager to find innovative ways of writing poetry – they didn't really have a choice. Law's poetry is hedonistic and individualistic, without being materialistic, as it is metaphysical and flying away from the earth.

So take these lines from 'Poetry, etc', from the collection, *Ascension Notes*:

> Like a gull's egg, very light – a blink's splitsecond.
> It's the dash that makes you human –
>
> Here is the mouth closing – holding its portion of silence
> in a pearly bite – a spark – a baby bird; the birth of myth. It
> feathers being, the flame of the games.
>
> By which ye shall know – for the sake of things unbidden.
>
> You learn to perform tricks with the pen – holding it loosely,
> *wave between finger and thumb* – that it seems to sway (((like a
> wand)); a willow inclined by its nature to grieve.

The symbols tumble over each other in a Quarles or Crashaw-like way. They are supremely light. This line does not include the pastoral side, the involvement with the welfare of the whole parish, including the poor. It does not enjoin morality or re-tell stories from the Bible. That is, it starts by rejecting all the elements of Christian poetry which the reading public objected to (during the Sixties). Instead we have a euphoric attitude towards the spiritual life, and a credulity about the presence of the divine in everyday life which is quite close to superstition. So a poem about "gemmology" records that in "alternative therapies" flawed gemstones are valued, because the way they seal up around the flaw shows signs of healing. This is superstitious, and puts the emphasis on the individual, who buys an object and carries it around with them. (The "Manifesto" also mentions "a clarifying gem". Surely amulets are part of magic – or Anthroposophy.) Religion has generally gone in the direction of the "New Age", that is putting the individual at the heart of practice and rejecting dogma in favour of an eclectic use of religious symbols. Religion is decentralised, the priest disappears and the individual ministers to themselves. Jung replaces St Augustine. What I want to point out is that Christians have also followed this route, they overlap with the New Age thing.

Geraldine Clarkson wrote *Monica's Overcoat of Flesh* (2020, 87pp). Clarkson was a nun for several years before quitting, and the themes of the poems consistently express what is forbidden to nuns by vow: attractive clothes, self-adornment, dancing, vanity, carnal thoughts. The contrast with the regime she was emerging from makes these things unusually vivid, high-relief, surprising. The exit from vows may also have broken certain inhibitions which poets feel about precisely these areas. The poet did not give up being a Catholic; a quotation on the title page has Meister Eckhart saying "A human being has so many skins inside, covering the depths of the heart". Eckhart was part of the group of writers known as Rhenish mystics (flourishing 1260 to 1330). They wrote primarily for nuns, who were supposed to be less educated, and who usually did not know Latin. They used the vernacular language and also did not use abstractions (which were less common in the vernacular). It is not rare for people who have had a prolonged period of sensory deprivation to experience simple things with great vividness and intensity after emerging. The result is characters whose view of life sees a very short time-span and who are perfectly happy with decorative surfaces. This appeals to a simple but universal level of human awareness, and that level is unusually free from thought and doubt. The poems are close to what we can see as a basic song-type: the character is preoccupied with self-adornment and wishes to be seen looking attractive. The poems themselves are very attractive and animated. When the present moment is complete in itself, we lose interest in problems. In the title poem a child dies and the overcoat is what unwraps itself from her soul; the body itself is just a skin, in an ancient Christian metaphor. 'For Our Extinguished Guests' shows a nunnery in Latin America surrounded by exotic animals and picturesque guerrillas. A less picturesque shanty town is near the cloister. A father's visit to his daughter (he "glimpses her/ three times a day through the grille") distracts her from the spiritual duties:

> The daughter, inside the enclosure, dreams
> of peacocks and snow. Rises earlier, collides
> with a junta of nuns who, as if playing chess, devise
> urgent sweeping, singing and scaling of fish;
> keep her busy. No visits. His ticket expires.

This triggers a decision:

> Soon after, she breaches the cloister-wall, arcs the desert-and-selva-
> and-mountains herself; returns to her father, November, fireworks like
> gunshots, brief birds climbing the night, and the original wall
> made of muscle and will.

In the dream, do peacocks stand for vanity and the snow for emotional coldness? I don't know. She "arcs… herself" because an aeroplane has done this in the previous stanza. The way in which young women put on a look, made up of clothes and so on, is comparable to the way in which a saint puts on a set of accessories, by which they are recognised in visual art (and in devotional poetry). Together they raise up an image of people as addicted to roles, with an unknown depth which is before any roles but which seeks to take them on. Perhaps poems succeed by offering the reader a role which is self-supporting and easy to grasp. This is an exceptional book in its fertility of ideas and its spontaneity.

We can compare Sarah Law and Geraldine Clarkson, because they are both Christians. This is a source of alarm, because they are so disconnected with traditional Christian forms of expression. Our society is so saturated with individualism that even people who subscribe to a centralised philosophy find original ways of expressing it.

Richard Skelton's *Stranger in the Mask of a Deer* (2021) is another kind of religious poetry. It is 150 pages long and deals with an existential issue, the life of humans in the Late Palaeolithic and Mesolithic and the difference between them and modern humans. As Prynne pointed out in the Sixties, the nomadic stage lasted far longer than settlement and modernity have lasted so far. It has a claim to be the fundamental human condition, over which other forms of ease and wealth are simply overlays. Poetry is made of language. We have no idea what people in post-glacial Europe said or sang. The semantic fields in which our language, or experience, is organised are not usable. *Stranger* abandons modern language without a serious attempt to re-create something that could have been said 8,000 years ago. The vocabulary is very, very simple, the inventory of phrasal structures is very, very limited, the simple words falling into simple patterns yield an astonishingly small amount of information. It was reckless to expand to 150 pages when the basic formal units were so weak. We make an exit from modernity and its excess of objects (and people?) into a cognitive blank.

The writer used to run a label issuing landscape-oriented music. This has a certain ring of the ECM label and what used to be called New Age easy listening. The music of Terje Rypdal and others was associated with landscape because it was so uneventful. There is a suspicion that *Stranger* is not a leap into the dark but a continuation of a genre which has already found its market and its set habits.

In the PBS list I assembled, four collections use the records of Norse pagan religion: *Bragr* (by Ross Cogan), *The Nine Mothers of Heimdallr* (by Miriam Nash), *Skald: Sword & Sea Cloud* by Ian Crockatt, and *Casket* by Andy Brown. (*Casket* is more about Anglo-Saxon paganism.) Their success depends on actually existing texts to work with – Skelton does not have these, for the Mesolithic. It is just too long ago.

A bibliography lists works with the results of anthropology, archaeology, etc. and shows that Skelton has thought seriously about the deep past. And the topic is so fascinating. The first dig of Star Carr (a Mesolithic site in Yorkshire with freak preservation conditions) yielded twenty head-dresses made of deer bone and antler and the second dig 50 years later found 12 more. Did this decoy craft relate to tales of man-animal transformation? The images are rich. Did this travesty, dressing up, relate to an awareness that humans had ceased to be animals although made out of animal? Great bibliography, poetry not so hot.

By Land and Sea

More nature poetry! More guilt-tripping!

Lesley Harrison published *Disappearance. North Sea Poems* (74pp) in 2020. This appears here because parts of it are excellent but also because it raises questions about the genre of "landscape poetry" and its popularity. I must admit that I see a lot of poems which do "landscape poetry" in the same preset figures of speech, usually with a bit of politics about pollution and extraction. The jacket text for this one says "… examine the coastline and our uneasy, unresolved relationship with the waters that surround us. Around the northern North Sea rim, the coastal margin is constantly being made and unmade by vast weather systems and currents that begin thousands of miles away. Drawing from archives, folk myth and cultural memory, these poems make real our sense of living at the edge of an older, sub-polar world, and the ongoing human process of negotiation with, of giving meaning and scale to, this unstable and ultimately unknowable space." Well, this sounds great. It defines something you certainly want to get into. But that just raises questions about how you can put the boundless into words, and whether something as monotonous as the North Sea is going to turn up as the model for monotonous and featureless poetry. One bit of the North Sea is pretty much like the other bits. There is a remark in Luke Roberts' *Glacial Decoys* which may be relevant: "We used to laugh at the ecopoets because it seemed that they were trying in dumb astonishment to bore us all to death." Saying that nature poetry fails to evoke our feelings in front of nature and great space is like saying that rock and roll is monotonous. There is a sort of piety in which rather wooden forms of words, familiar from much repetition, allow us to soar up towards conceptions of great spiritual value which our minds cannot reach unaided. It would appear, though, that not every Anglican poem ever written is a great poem.

The mention of giving scale gives us a way in. Evidently this relates to the body image (as described by psychologists from 1910 on). Neuroscience has picked up the body image (or body schema) idea and made it more elaborate and connected to an evolutionary model. The mention of scale proposes that we can only apprehend the sea through the archaic and inexorable knowledge-model of our own body, attached as it is to our ego. So projection is the basic process (and possibly the only way in which we can know the realm of the non-human). It is as if we had a triangle, in which the body schema, the ocean, and language were the three sides. Making them meet is a fraught process. Some of Harrison's poetry fails because the language falls down; it consists of lists rather than propositions, it has no grammar to entangle the scrap raw material into significant shapes. So grammar lets us apprehend the sea – but what does the sea have to do with grammar?

This theorising is not relevant to hundreds of other books of nature poetry. The variations are too great. Actually, the sea is very big… a human body image is incommensurate with the sea and has nothing to say about it. The sea has no organs and no ego.

I am inclined to mention **Julia Blackburn**'s *Time Song. Searching for Doggerland* [2019] which is also about the North Sea, but more specifically fragments that reach the shore from the submerged land of Dogger, which was dry land until 6500–6200 BC but then went under as sea levels rose with glacial melt. Actually, Doggerland is the North Sea. The name was given to it by Bryony Coles. While not strictly poetry, this is a wonderful book. When the sea yields bones of ancient herbivores, or tools made from flint and bone, these are tactile experiences, they can be held in your hand, and that grasp injects the body schema into the picture, making it so satisfying. Actually, such bones are the organs of the sea. People, mainly in the Netherlands, spent days combing the dunes by the waterline which eventually turned into years. Is this less interesting than spending years reading poetry? Er… not necessarily.

With **Jean Sprackland**'s poetry the idea is how polluted nature is. This unites us, but is quite a generic idea. Her prose book (*Strands*) suggests that most of what she has to say goes over equally well in prose. One can't disagree with what she says but language is not really yielding up its secrets to her. Obviously the poems are giving other people what they want, this is not the product of some personal theory or error of vision.

In *Green Noise* (2018, 52pp) the poems depict scenes of local dumping and damage. We see, not the sublime but a torn fabric. The thrust of the poems is about mending the rips. The scenes of scruffy and degraded, yet fertile, plots of land of a confused spatial pattern where the natural strives with the businesslike and the simply derelict, are profoundly recognisable and moving. The idea of healing it is instantly convincing and attractive. The terrain is closer to an overgrown garden than to an ideal landscape ready for grand schemes, as the home of grand poetic ideas, but does allow for the expansion of ideas too. Where I feel these poems are original is in their affection for the small scale – of course this allows intervention, restitution in fact. Nature poetry tends to deal with the grandiose (of great spaces) and also grandiose loss. A feeling of success is only possible where the conversation is dealing with a space on the scale of a single human, ideally something small enough for one human to clear it, sow it, or otherwise attach themselves to it. There is a Latin word for strips of land not allocated by the cadaster and possibly without owners: subsicivum. A subsicivum is a useful term for such strips which are unexploited, without proper names, possibly nurturing all kinds of (small) wildlife, possibly covered in rubbish which people have dumped because the land had no value or defender. They are common ground, amongst other things. Sprackland has an imaginative relationship to such terrain. They are pristine in odd ways, for example that they were, some of them, never cultivated and so never touched by insecticides. Subsicivus was also used of time, so leisure time; when we ourselves are not being useful.

Strands is about walking the beaches near where she lives, in Lancashire, and picking up what the sea throws away. The objects are stranded and strands of a larger story. This is a really irresistible book. The idea is comparable with Blackburn's but on the opposite coast. A tea-cup from a transatlantic liner is one of the high points.

An anthology of alternative landscape poetry is *The Ground Aslant*, edited by Harriet Tarlo. This was extremely successful; presumably people feel a residual guilt about reading nature poetry about the countryside and this is resolved by the idea that they are reading something difficult and risky. My feeling about the book is that parts of it were indispensable to the modern history of poetry, while other parts weren't very good. I was surprised at the omissions from the introduction, so I didn't think it gave a history of the genre that was solid, but it did list some components.

Nancy Gaffield, *Continental Drift* (2014, 84pp)
Continental drift is one of the fundamental factors of geology but was a rejected thesis for roughly four decades after it was first developed and proposed by Alfred Wegener. It explains how the earth's crust is divided by faults into plates and that new crust is constantly, if slowly, appearing and disappearing along these faults. The name refers to the movement of continents, as phenomena created by tectonic plates. The term functions

in the book to bring to attention the impermanence of even very large-scale arrangements, and the reality of planetary-scale interactions, with the implication that you can't just throw waste into the ocean (or the sky) and expect it to disappear. The amount of new crust emerging (from under the mid-Atlantic fault, for example) is very small in a given year, and humans are also very small in relation to geology but also are a product of it, in the sense that we eat what the earth produces and that our dwelling is in places brought about by geology. A poem called 'zu Babel' runs:

> Bittern in the reed beds neck the sky and go boom. Babbling, inhabiting the borders. That place unreason lives. Coppiced chestnuts, conifer plantations woods older than Babylon. European oaks tell of eruption – yellow fog, dim sun, summer frost, famine. Learning to weapon, maraud. Bronze follows copper follows bluebell, anemone, dog's mercury, herb paris, columbine, bird's nest orchid. Mystery flowers, hordes of swords, spearheads, sickles, chisels.
>
> Released from dendrochronology pentatonic monody for four voices. Drones. Rare lady orchid fringes the escarpment outside time.

zu Babel comes out of the collocation *der Turmbau zu Babel*, the tower of Babel. That was a human project (of irrational scale and arrogance) in which an original language broke down and was split, so that people could no longer understand each other. We can say first that this is a theme about the borderline between language and not-language, which the poem slips across:

> Loosening the bands of syntax
> morpheme by morpheme
> mother plaiting pain
> the name she gave you
> all that remains.

– and secondly that the poems are constructed of interweaving themes and that the movement between local peaks, moving away from a high point and going on while allowing its unstated implications to go on revealing themselves, is a key to the design. But also, we can reveal that the texture of the poem is attractive and even tender; we actually want to be there, and empathy with the poet as a source of benign language is the landscape even if rather complex abstract ideas are being developed as the book goes on.

If we look for the connection between *mother* and *syntax* it is evident that syntax is not part of the first language which very young children speak and that language acquisition is associated with the mother-child bond and flourishes inside that bond. Disturbance of language might, quite often, be traced back to a disturbance in the mother-child relationship – perhaps the arrival of another child. It is not normal to experience the dissolution of syntax: acquisition is normally in one direction only. The poem is not just about the origin of language but about the origin of (European) society. *Babylon* is in some relationship to *babble*: not that the city was named for language (*Bab-el* means "gate of the gods") but that the meaningless but fluent babble of very young children mysteriously connects with the "severed" languages which other people suddenly could not understand. All children babble in the same way and fall away from that when they acquire a language, with its words and grammar.

Unreason is the home of the unreasoning. That might apply to every organism. It is possible that the origin of language is reversible because words arrive with humans and there was a landscape without language which preceded that, and surrounded it.

This poetry is intelligent because it is beautiful and we can even say that it has intellectual beauty. It is full of landscapes and organisms – identifying a fault line which divides abstract philosophy from thinking about full-colour parts of the three-dimensional world. The poems are full of natural symbols and are not producing formal symbolic statements, those adjacent to either law or quantifying for example. By implication that second discourse includes human beings as subjects and feelings as real percepts in the same way as things (or even commodities?). The organisms mentioned are good to think with, but they also resist reason: Europe is not being seen as something empty which is tolerant of uninhibited development or devastation, razing as clearance. That abstract thought which knows infinite power because it has done away with anything which could resist it, deprived reality of reality, is first being made visible as a thing, a part of the conceptual landscape; and then called out. We are being taken to "that place unreason lives". Dendrochronology is "exact measurement of time by reading growth bands of trees"; it tells us that a forest can be older than Babylon (which is only there from the second millennium BC, in fact). We hear that bronze follows a series of (wild) flowers but we have just been hearing about ancient woodland. Surely these flowers are those which flourish in sunlit gaps in woodland, and the copper and bronze is here in its primary use of supplying adzes for cutting trees down. The Bronze Age forest clearances, then, are a primary moment of industrialisation: the landscape rewritten by new technology. We hear also of "swords, spearheads, sickles, chisels". A widely held theory has the early Bronze Age as the point where Indo-European language spilt over into eastern Europe, so was our phase of language acquisition in the sense that that language was identifiably related to modern English. The second page of the poem mentions exile (the root meaning of *wretch*) and again the boreal forest. "linked from the start your life/ and mine.": I am not sure if the *you* is the mother (who was plaiting) or the boreal forest which shaped Northern European dwelling. The poem 'zu babel' is part of a cycle called 'Music of the Phenomenal World' and this explains how the record of tree cover could be a monody for four voices, presumably four original tree species.

Gaffield is American. I notice the ability of her poetry to float conceptual fields without making explicit statements, so that the field remains lit up, in play, for long periods, without explicit propositions. This seems to be the American thing, it lets poems flourish in ideas without cutting them off. A field actually is static and it helps if you imagine a visual pattern which does not move forward as a sentence does. The field remains intact. I don't want to summarise the entire volume, in view of its complexity. But we need to think about 'Po-wa-Ha', a long evocation of the history of the south-west USA, so New Mexico and adjacent areas. The title is glossed as "the creative life force of Pueblo mythologies". Pueblo is Spanish for *village* but applied to Indians who lived in villages (as opposed to wanderers), so people of several different languages and ethnic names, in the south-west. The poem, over 30 pages, describes the Anasazi (the name means "former people", as the Navajo found their adobe villages intact but unpeopled), the development of the atomic bomb by a theoretical group at Los Alamos, and the devastation of two cities in Japan by the bombs, as the climax of the project. The poem offers complexes that incite us to invent patterns rather than bringing the patterns to a head (and an end), but for me there is a link between the desert ('Jornada del muerto') where the bomb was tested and the desert that occupied the site of Nagasaki; and between the disappearance of the Anasazi and the possible demise of a society due to nuclear warfare.

Mark Goodwin wrote in *Else* (2008) a kind of pastoral poetry set in north-west Leicestershire, but not entirely. The cover refers to the author living on a narrowboat on the river Soar, and I should confess that I grew up very near the Soar, in what must be more or less the same corner of the county. I thought *Else* was wonderful. *House At Out* needs more explaining. Take this slice –

>   wind   thrives in sky's tigh   t lipped pert
>   progress the winding   of cloth pulls heaped
>   eyes & speech   less beetles sky's heart open
>
>   with golden   coats take the push of cloud's
>   fingers amongst earth   corn's mat-talk molten
>   dryness & itch pick   up bundles of air take
>
>   solid verbs with you in your   hems fed them
>   down our throats your skirts or the turn-up fur
>   rows while stung   breeze st   rings bottoms of
>
>   your trousers unravel against the rotating parcel
>   of buttered day blades   of laughing cloth engra
>   ved with a soft   slit the mill   er   is giggling
>
>   with Egyptian   surrender
>   (from 'Mind Will' i.e. 'wind mill')

Prima facie we have a hiatus inserted in some of the lines, sometimes two hiatuses, so that words like *strings, furrows* are split; and the poem titles are compounds or compactions, so Gowl Un is "owl gown". Hoght Luise is 'light house'. 'Ridlite Werness' is 'wilderness rite'. In the poem, there is a physical windmill. 'blade of laughing cloth' may be the gaps between the sails of the mill turning round. 'buttered sky' may be what is seen through the sails, yellow with sunlight. A house defines an inside in a very deep sense, so *house at out* may define something which lingers outside, away from dwellings. The prelims list seven books since *Else*, so this is part of what may be a vast body of work. Others seem to have been published by concerns in Rugby and Sheffield. Goodwin explained some processes at a reading at Hootenanny, a series in Leicester, for which my notes apparently say *"taking last words of lines of P Riley poems and making new poems out of them. Like acronyms. Translating Goodland and Bletsoe by word substitution word by word to form new poems."* So part of what seemed like a far-flung programme was denaturing captured chains of language and substituting words to evolve a new poem, so that you have some kind of sound shadow underlying the visible surface. The idea of a Cultural Past consisting of Giles Goodland and Elisabeth Bletsoe is quite intoxicating. Another set-up was a group of sound-based pieces (exhibited in a gallery in Leicester), so that the raw material of a recited poem would be the start for an acoustic environment where the words would be blurred, and could also suggest new words. A theme might be releasing the materiality of language, dissolving its bonds of resistance so that it can be generative like number series and flow out in new sequences. A possible motive is the mismatch of the static and allover quality of landscape with the perpetually forward-moving nature of language, so that Goodwin is applying devices to make language stand still. This washes out human intentionality from the verbal events, allowing contemplation. Dissolving out movement allows the immensity of the land to become central, silently engulfing the merely human observer. Language often lives in houses, and is domestic, but language too can go outside, and this teeming intricacy allows a text to mimic what is not of human scale. The typography of *House* reminds me of Susan Howe. I am going to quote a passage from 'a smell of bells' as if it were prose: "hot bronze punch to nose burnt metal twists/ slicey stink pong of mineral crystal manipulated by heat & men & god / the fragrance of noise hangs at a brainstem encasing memories with vibrating shiny lattices that rust around a desire/ a sniffing bell pulls all sweeter smells off sky earth into its cavity / hangs out existing's stinks in our instant stretched beyond snouts of dogs or sharks after blood in vast's blue nostril of ocean gong going". There is in fact a bell foundry in the Soar valley, the only one in the country. This is clearly a solid description of the birth of a bell, and is part of a long poem called "Bell feeding" which is all about bells. We talked about being static – the poem lingers on its subject to get further into it than verbal convention allows. The poem punches through set rhythms of perception to give us more about a real subject, about metal and sound, than would otherwise be possible. The analogy between sound and smell seems to be through memory – memories are peculiarly locked up in smells, but church bells were also designed to wake the memory and make us aware of time. Time as an abstraction takes us, humans, beyond the awesome sensory powers of the dog and the shark, chained to the eternal present as they are. At the moment of casting, the bell metal would have been detectable as a smell, some element of it volatile, anticipating the volatile sounds it would later release. The ocean was introduced higher up as 'rust of ringing thick on a waist harsh round a mouth/ a submersible container of air falls through ocean' – the sound is a gulp of air falling through the quiet air as an ocean. The lattices are the fabric of the metal. This is an intricate poem, reminiscent perhaps of the Anglo-Saxon riddles in capturing an object through layers of language. So what we probably have in *House* (120pp) is sixty or so complex poems, all or most of them exploring features of the landscape of a part of the Midlands, most of them exploring impersonal forces, mass, depth, linguistic depth. A statement on Goodwin's website reads:

> I am at home on edges or 'at the edges'. I love balancing along fence rails or tree branches – poised between drops to my left & my right. The rim of a city holds an equal fascination. The city-rim is the cultural tightrope of our very late, flailing capitalist civilisation. To walk & imagine in these liminal lands is to occupy a wound of transition; still raw, and ugly & beautiful in equal measure because of that rawness. Walking this corridor, one can imagine deep & recent histories co-happening: a city-density on one side of an urban membrane is where peoples of all kinds have mixed to escape 'the wilderness'; the rural other is where most people used to dwell (in the true sense of that word) before The Great Theft of The Enclosures. One side is of the Fathers, the other of the Mothers. One side is mostly dark at night whilst one remains lit. Walking in these zones of 'between' I'm reminded that no living cell lives without a membrane that is porous.

*

People are convinced that there is a new landscape poetry, and that it was not there before about 1966, but it is hard to explain just what changed. One current of 'spatial poetry' had begun in 1966 with the *English Intelligencer* project ("myth, geography, landscape") and this is probably the moment of breach with an older poetry about travel and places. Because this current is flowing like a river too wide to see across still in 2022, it may be interesting to think about how it differed from the poetry of travel which already existed.

I came across a prose book by Alan Ross called *The Gulf of Pleasure*. It is about the Bay of Naples – the islands of Capri and Ischia and the shore. I was in a library where it was surrounded by books about the Southern Problem – the mezzogiorno as one of the poorest parts of Europe with fabulous inequality, recalcitrant feudal families, organised crime, the constant frustration of development ideas, mass emigration. Such a contrast with Ross presenting landscapes essentially as objects of pleasure – where the centre of the landscape is the observer, and actually the part of the observer which feels pleasure. Capri is turned into a painting of Capri – the connoisseur knows the painting and visits the real place to compare it with the painting and to collect the experiences which have already been defined as assets by a series of painters and writers. So just maybe the gap between poetry about landscape as it was in 1968 and the manner which came after that and which we can all recognise as new is the removal of the ego from the landscape – the positioning of the earth itself as the central character. Biography was removed from the picture to open the way for forces on a much vaster scale, evolving over a much longer rhythm of time. Volumes like *Wood and Windfall* (by John Holloway) and *The Taj Express* (by Alan Ross) defined the old landscape poetry quite different from the new landscape poetry. The old version was quite close to writing about dream holidays in exotic locations; the new form was interested in nature without man and it was open to the theme of nature being damaged and needing amends, suggesting that human intervention in nature was reckless and disproportionate. I like this story – but I think the real situation may be more complicated. Holloway said:

> Now, in the main of summer's
> Dry drench from the sun,
> The rock bleaches, blanches, sparkles.
> Jewelled weather; and
> The hillside seeds; brown whorl and horn,
> Shuck, husk and rasp, spiral and radial in
> An orchestra of sharpness.
> The chaff is armoured; an insured ripening.

> Twenty-three kinds of thistle. Yet
> The goats find a living.
> (from 'A Letter from the Argolid', published 1968)

This illustrates what changed. It does sound out of date. Yet the complexity of the whole poem, at about 250 lines, suggests that the transition involves values too complex to resolve in a convincing way.

It is noticeable that both Ross and Holloway write about Classical Mediterranean landscapes and have a deep awareness of Latin poets wandering through the same scenery. English landscape painting is diverse but at this point I find it hard to connect modern nature poetry with it. Modern poetry isn't cashing in a cultural memory from topographical painting – I stand to be proven wrong on this, but there seems to be a reluctance to project the body image into a landscape, even though the body image has the biological function of relating the body to a landscape containing assets we want to collect. If you wish for the destruction of the ego, that involves the destruction of the wish as one step along the route. At that point the aesthetic dimension and its ordering procedures wither away.

It is difficult to explain how you can have a huge growth in tourism to places outside Britain and yet the near disappearance of poems which want to describe landscape as a source of pleasure. Has poetry given up pleasure? Or projection of the self? Does political virtue end up as one more way of repressing visual sensibility?

Afterword

I never covered most of those 1,140 books (mentioned in the introduction) and feel much happier doing a source critique which suggests that there might be 2,300 or 3,400 significant books in the same period. I apologise – I am not covering everything. This is offered more like a radio programme which broadcasts a certain number of records every Sunday morning but does not promise to broadcast every record. Instead, there will be more records on R6 Music next Sunday morning. That is the offer.

I am more interested by older poets because they have seen more and because the connections of their lives are more tangled and obstinate and deep-rooted. An old tree has a root system with a difficult geometry. All the same there is something fundamental about being exposed to patterns you have never seen before.

The idea of writing a book that knowingly doesn't deal with everything is like composing a landscape painting where an essential part of the feel is that we don't think the landscape runs out exactly at the frame edge, rather the promise of boundlessness is the illusion on which it floats. Art is not something where we wish to exhaust and degrade everything in the course of realising its value. The pattern of poetry since the take-off in the early Seventies is that there is a wilderness, something far more extensive than what we can take in; I suspect that this feeling of dissolution of boundaries is within the poems as well.

I did a brief compilation and in the five quarters since I began writing this book the Poetry Book Society has listed another 540 titles on its website, none of which I have read. Maybe the scene changed as soon as I turned the camera off.

Bibliography

Except where otherwise stated, copyright in every quote in this book lies with the author and the date of this copyright is the date of publication as listed in this bibliography. Not all bibliographic entries reflect quotations in the text.

INTRODUCTION
Andrew Duncan, *A Poetry Boom* (Bristol: Shearsman Books, 2015)

GENERALISATIONS ABOUT THE POETRY WORLD
two sociologists: Brian Jackson, and Dennis Marsden, *Education and the Working Class* (Harmondsworth : Penguin, 1966)
Richard Sennett, *The Decline of Public Man* (London: Penguin, 2002 [originally 1974]).

LANGUAGE IS MADE OF RULES
Kenneth Allott, ed., *Mid-century Poetry* (Harmondsworth: Penguin, 1962)
my website: angelexhaust.blogspot.com, see label "history of taste"
Robert Ford, and Matthew Goodwin, *Revolt on the Right. Explaining Support for the Radical Right in Britain* (Abingdon: Routledge, 2014).

FOUNDATION TEXTS
Fernando Medina Ruiz, ed. and transl., *Popol Vuh literario* (Mexico City: Editorial Jus, 1983)
Steve Ely, *Englaland* (Ripon: Smokestack Books, 2015); *Incendium Amoris* (Ripon: Smokestack Books, 2017)
Dewi Stephen Jones: from Bobi Jones website at http://www.rmjones-bobi-jones.net/llyfrau/FfynhonnauU.pdf
— and: in Tony Bianchi (ed.), *Blodeugerdd Barddas o Farddoniaeth Gyfoes* (Aberystwyth: Cyhoeddiadau Barddas, 2005)
Anthony Julius, *Trials of the Diaspora. A History of Anti-Semitism in England.* (Oxford: Oxford University Press, 2010)
Kevin Nolan, *Loving Little Orlick* (London: Barque Press, 2006)
A.J. Pollard, *Imagining Robin Hood* (London: Routledge, 2004)
Martin Thom, *Cloud* (Cambridge: Equipage, 2020)

IDENTIFICATION
Willis D. Ellis, ed. and trans., *Sourcebook of Gestalt Psychology* (London: Routledge and Kegan Paul, 1950)
Charles Rycroft, *Psychoanalysis and Beyond* (London: Chatto & Windus, 1985) at p.263

THEIR TRAJECTORY WAS JUST LARGE
Michael Ayres, *a.m.* (Cambridge: Salt Publishing, 2003)

Andrea Brady, *Vacation of a Lifetime* (Cambridge: Salt, 2001)
Melanie Challenger, *Galatea* (Cambridge: Salt, 2006)
Giles Goodland, *Capital* (Cambridge: Salt, 2006)
Emily Hasler, *Natural Histories* (Cambridge: Salt, 2011)
Siân Hughes, *The Missing* (Cambridge: Salt, 2010)
David Kennedy, *The President of Earth* (Cambridge: Salt, 2002)
Peter Larkin, *Terrain Seed Scarcity* (Cambridge: Salt, 2001)
Chris McCabe, *The Hutton Inquiry* (Cambridge: Salt, 2005)
Anna Mendelssohn (Grace Lake), *Implacable Art* (Cambridge: Folio-Equipage, 2000)
Rod Mengham, *Unsung* (Cambridge: Salt, 2001)
Eleanor Rees, *Andraste's Hair* (Cambridge: Salt, 2007)
Anthony Rowland, *Green Ginger* (Cambridge: Salt, 2008)
Victor Tapner, *Flatlands* (Cambridge: Salt, 2010)
Mark Waldron, *The Itchy Sea* (Cambridge: Salt, 2011)
Tony Williams, *Midlands* (Rugby: Nine Arches, 2014)
Anna Woodford, *Birdhouse* (Cambridge: Salt, 2010)

CULTURAL ASSET MANAGEMENT
Allott ut supra.
Andrew Lambirth, *A is a Critic. Writings from* The Spectator (London: Unicorn Press, 2013)

VERTICEGARDEN
Ford and Goodwin, *Revolt on the Right*. ut supra
Haley Jenkins, *nekorb* (London: Veer, 2017)
Nat Raha, *Octet* (London: Veer, 2010); *[of sirens. body & faultlines]* (London: Veer, 2015)

INSIGNIFICANCE, OR STRUCTURE ENGULFED BY SURFACE
Lowenthal, David, *The Heritage Crusade and the Spoils of History* (London: Viking, 1996)
'Laibach Lyrik' in: Denise Riley, *Mop Mop Georgette* (London: Reality Street, 1993)
Raphael Samuel, *Island Stories. Unravelling Britain* (London: Verso, 1998)

POEMS ON COMMUNAL WELLBEING
Jay Bernard, *surge* (London: Chatto and Windus, 2019)
Keith Jafrate, *Songs for Eurydice* (Exeter: Stride, 2004)
Simon Jenner, *Winstanley* (Hove: Waterloo Press, 2021)
Toby Martinez de las Rivas, *Black Sun* (London: Faber and Faber, 2018)
and:
interview with James Brookes in *Prac Crit* on line at www.praccrit.com.

kenotic: J K Mozley, *Some Tendencies in British Theology* (London: SPCK, 1951); ditto, *The Doctrine of the Atonement* (New York: Charles Scribner's Sons, 1916)

LOCAL KNOWLEDGE
Tim Allen, Norman Jope, Mark Goodwin: *Portland: A Triptych* (Newton-le-Willows: Knives Forks and Spoons, 2019)
Elisabeth Bletsoe, *Birds of The Sherborne Missal* (Exeter: Shearsman Books, 2021)
gestalt: Ehrenzweig, Anton, *The Hidden Order of Art* (London: Phoenix Press, 2000)
Neil Pattison, Reitha Pattison, Luke Roberts, eds. *Certain Prose of* The English Intelligencer (Cambridge: Mountain Press, 2012)
John Cowper Powys, *Wolf Solent* (Harmondsworth: Penguin, 1964)

DEVOLUTION/DISASSEMBLY: SCOTTISH POETS
Ascherson, Neal, *Stone Voices. The Search for Scotland* (London: Granta, 2002)
Janette Ayachi, *Hand Over Mouth Music* (Liverpool: Pavilion Poets, Liverpool University Press, 2019)
Lesley Duncan and Alan Riach, eds., *The Smeddum Test* (Kilkerran: Kennedy & Boyd, 2013).
William Gillies in *Litreachas & Eachdraidh: Rannsachadh na Gàidhlig 2* (Glasgow: Department of Celtic, 2006)
Iain MacWhirter, *Road to Referendum* (s.l., Cargo Publishing, 2014)
Rody Gorman, *Zonda? Khamsin? Sharaav? Camanchaca?* (Inverness: Leabhraichean Beaga, 2006)
An Guth, ed. Rody Gorman (Dublin: Coisceim/An Guth, 2006 and other years)
Gerard MacEoin in *Celtic Cosmology, Perspectives from Ireland and Scotland*, ed. Jacqueline Borsje et al. (Toronto: Pontifical Institute of Mediaeval Studies, 2014)
Peter Mackay, & Iain S. MacPherson, eds., *Leabhar Liath. 500 years of Gaelic Love and Transgressive Verse* (Edinburgh: Luath Press, 2016)
Donald Meek, 'Bàird na feicheadamh linn agus an creideamh Crìosdail', published in *Rannsachadh na Gàidhlig 2000* (Glasgow: Department of Celtic, 2002).
Ríona Ní Fhrighil, *Briathra, Béithe agus Banfhilí* (Dublin: An Clóchomhar Tta, 2008)
Pádraig Ó Fiannachta, *Léas Eile ar ár Litríocht* (Maigh Nuad: An Sagart, 1982)
Calum Rodger, ed., *makar / unmakar* (Tarland: Tapsalteerie, 2019)
Stewart Sanderson, *The Sleep Road* (Tarland: Tapsalteerie, 2021)
Maria Sledmere and Rhian Williams, eds., *the weird folds* (s.l., Dostoyevsky Wannabe, 2020)

Molly Vogel, *Florilegium. Poems with a glossary* (Bristol: Shearsman Books, 2020)

SERIAL

Wayne Burrows, *Exotica Suite and Other Fictions* (Nottingham: Shoestring Press, 2015); *Eastern Bloc Songs. Party, Pop and Politics* (Birmingham: Centrala, 2018)

'Interaction between text and reader' in Wolfgang Iser, *Prospecting. From reader response to literary anthropology* (Baltimore: The Johns Hopkins University Press, 1989)

Daniel zur Höhe/Anthony Mellors, *Winter Journey* (Llangattock: Aquifer, 2022)

Jon Stone, *The School of Forgery* (Cambridge: Salt, 2012)

BRITISH SOUTH ASIAN POETS

Kazim Ali, *The Voice of Sheila Chandra* (s.l., Platypus Press, 2021)

Mona Arshi, *Small Hands* (Liverpool: Pavilion Poets, Liverpool University Press, 2015)

Nuzhat Bukhari, *Brilliant Corners* (London: CB Editions, 2021)

—Bukhari: Arnold Hauser, *Der Manierismus. Ursprung der modernen Kunst und Literatur* (Munich: Deutscher Taschenbuch Verlag, 1979)

Khaled Hakim / Sister Ray, *The Routines: 1983–2000* (London: Contraband Books, 2021)

SPLENDOURS AND CHAGRINS

Will Harris, *Rendang* (London: Granta: 2020)

Fawzi Karim, *Plague Lands and other poems* (Manchester: Carcanet Press, 2011)

Yousif M. Qasmiyeh, *Writing the Camp* (Talgarreg: Broken Sleep Books, 2021)

Stephanie Sy-Quia, *Amnion* (London: Granta: 2021)

Jay G. Ying, *Katabasis* (Sheffield: Smith/Doorstop, 2020)

ANGLO-WELSH

John Goodby and Lyndon Davies, eds., *Edge of Necessary. Welsh Innovative Poetry 1966–2018* (Llangattock: Aquifer Books, 2018)

River Rheidol: see Rhys Jones' essay 'Pair Dadeni?', (in: *Cof Cenedl*, ed. Geraint H. Jenkins, vol. 22; Llandysul: Gwasg Gomer, 2007)

Robert Minhinnick, *King Driftwood* (Manchester: Carcanet Press, 2008)

Cris Paul, *stenia cultus handbook: maps and annotations* (London: Veer Books, 2010)

Rhys Trimble, *Keinc* (Blaenau Ffestiniog: Cinnamon Press, 2010)

SHORT STRINGS, POLYRECOMBINANT

Ira Lightman, *Duetcetera* (Exeter: Shearsman Books, 2008).

Ira Lightman interview in *The Argotist*, online

WEST-BLOC DISSIDENTS: ALTERNATIVE POETRY
Didier Eribon, *Michel Foucault* (Cambridge, MA: Harvard University Press, 1991)
Ian Heames, *Arrays* (collected edition; Cambridge: Face Press; 2015)
Heather Phillipson, *INSTANT-fLEX 718* (Tarset: Bloodaxe, 2013)
J.H. Prynne, 'Letter to Andrew Duncan' (Matlock: *Grosseteste Review*, #15, 1984)
Nicholas Spicer, *Lines on the Surface* (London: Contraband, 2013)

TRIUMPHS AND PANICS
Dorothy Lehane, *Ephemeris* (Rugby: Nine Arches Press, 2014)
Luke Roberts, *False Flags* (Cambridge: Mountain Press, 2011); *Glacial Decoys* (no publisher, no place, 2021)
John Robinson, *The Cook's Wedding* (Snitterfield: Ragged Raven Press, 2001)
Ian Seed, *Makers of Empty Dreams* (Bristol: Shearsman Books, 2014)
Hannah Silva, *Forms of Protest* (London: Penned in the Margins, 2013)
Maria Stadnicka, *Somnia* (Newton-le-Willows: Knives Forks and Spoons Press: 2020)
Samantha Walton, *Self Heal* (Norwich: Boiler House Press, 2018)

THE HUMAN VOICE
Emily Berry, ed., *The Best British Poetry 2015* (Cambridge: Salt, 2015)
Caroline Bird, *Rookie* (Manchester: Carcanet, 2022)
Mark Ford, *Soft Sift* (London: Faber and Faber, 2001)
Melissa Lee-Houghton, *Beautiful Girls* (London: Penned in the Margins, 2013)
Eleanor Perry, *Venusberg* (London: Veer, 2015)
Sam Riviere, *Kim Kardashian's Marriage* (London: Faber & Faber, 2015)
Sophie Robinson, *rabbit* (Norwich: Boiler House Press, 2018)

PISTACHIO EUPHORIA SORBET
Maria Sledmere, *Leave Bambi Alone* (Glasgow: Motel Mermaid, 2022)
Nathan Thompson, *the arboretum towards the beginning* (Exeter: Shearsman Books, 2008)

SOCIOLINGUISTICS & OPAQUE
Jasmina Bolfek-Radovani. *Knitting drum machines for exiled tongues* (Stourpaine: Tears in the Fence, 2022)
Christine De Luca, *Northern Alchemy* (Patrician Press, 2020)
———, 'Not on a Raised Beach' in *Lallans* magazine, 2001.
L Kiew, *Unquiet* (London: Offord Road Books, 2019)
Robert Owen Jones, *Hir oes i'r iaith* (Llandysul: Gwasg Gomer, 1997)
Meic Stephens, *Wilia* (s.l., Cyhoeddiadau Barddas, 2014)
Mary Wiliam, *Blas ar iaith Blaenau'r Cymoedd* (Llanrwst: Gwasg Carreg Gwalch 1990)

PRIVATISATION AND RELIGION
Geraldine Clarkson, *Monica's Overcoat of Flesh* (Rugby: Nine Arches Press, 2020)
Peter Davidson, *The Palace of Oblivion* (Manchester: Carcanet, 2008)
Sarah Law, *Ascension Notes* (Exeter: Shearsman Books, 2009)
Richard Skelton, *Stranger in the Mask of a Deer* (London: Penned in the Margins, 2021)

BY LAND AND SEA
Some Prose of The English Intelligencer, ut supra
Nancy Gaffield, *Continental Drift* (Bristol: Shearsman Books, 2014)
Mark Goodwin, *House At Out* (Bristol: Shearsman Books, 2015)
Lesley Harrison, *Disappearance* (Bristol: Shearsman Books, 2020)
John Holloway, *Wood and Windfall* (London: Routledge and Kegan Paul, 1965)
Jean Sprackland, *Green Noise* (London: Vintage Digital, 2018)

Permission Acknowledgements

Many of the quotations in this book have been made under the fair-use norms prevailing in the UK. For those cases where specific permission was required for longer quotes, we are grateful to the following authors and publishers:

Attempts to clarify copyrights in the cases of Bobi Jones (1929–2017) and Dewi Stephen Jones (1940–2019) have been unsuccessful. If anyone should have further information that would assist us in resolving this, the publishers would be pleased to hear from them.

Alice James Books for an excerpt from Kazim Ali's *The Voice of Sheila Chandra* (New Gloucester, ME: Alice James Books, 2020), copyright © Kazim Ali, 2020.

Michael Ayres, for excerpts from 'Marshal' published in *Grille*, edited by Simon Smith, Issue 3, 1994, and 'Deposition' published in *Angel Exhaust*, edited by Andrew Duncan, copyright © Michael Ayres, 1994; excerpt from 'Zeiss', published in Michael Ayres, *a.m.* (Cambridge: Salt Publishing, 2003); copyright © Michael Ayres, 2003.

Elisabeth Bletsoe and Shearsman Books for 'Tayle mose, long-tailed tit' published in *Birds of the Sherborne Missal* (Bristol: Shearsman Books, 2021); copyright © Elisabeth Bletsoe, 2021, and for an excerpt from 'The 'Oary Man' published in *Pharmacopoeia and other early poems* (Exeter: Shearsman Books, 2010); copyright © Elisabeth Bletsoe, 1993, 2010.

Jasmina Bolfek-Radovani and Tears in the Fence for excerpts from 'What is the colour of dépaysement?', 'Knitting drum machines for exiled tongues', 'All that Zagreb jazz' published in *Knitting drum machines for exiled tongues* (Stourpaine: Tears in the Fence, 2022); copyright © Jasmina Bolfek-Radovani 2022.

Tilla Brading for 'Movement from the Hills' published in *Possibility of an Inferno* (Nether Stowey: Odyssey Poets, 1997); copyright © Tilla Brading, 1997.

Andrea Brady, for 'Hard on Soft Fatal (*for Madeleine Albright*)' published in *Vacation of a Lifetime* (Cambridge: Salt Publishing, 2001); copyright © Andrea Brady, 2001.

Bloodaxe Books for Zoë Brigley, 'Day 8: Quarry', published in *The Secret* (Tarset: Bloodaxe Books, 2007); copyright © Zoë Brigley, 2007.

CB Editions for excerpts from Nuzhat Bukhari, 'Last Gardener of Aleppo', published in *Brilliant Corners* (London: CB Editions, 2021); copyright © Nuzhat Bukhari, 2021.

Shoestring Press for excerpts from 'A Simultaneous Translation' and 'Black Glass' published in Wayne Burrows, *Exotica Suite and Other Fictions* (Nottingham: Shoestring Press, 2015); copyright © Wayne Burrows, 2015.

Salt Publishing for excerpts from Melanie Challenger, 'The Service of the Heart', published in *Galatea* (Cambridge: Salt Publishing, 2006); copyright © Melanie Challenger, 2006.

Christine De Luca: for an excerpt from 'Not on a raised beach', published in *Lallans* magazine, special issue *A sklent at Shaetlan*, 2001; copyright © Christine De Luca 2001; Christine De Luca and Patrician Press for an excerpt from 'Conundrums', published in *Northern Alchemy* (Manningtree: Patrician Press, 2020); copyright © Christine De Luca, 2020.

Steve Ely for 'One of us', 'The Battle of Brunanburh', 'Yellowhammer' from *Englaland* (Ripon: Smokestack Books, 2015); copyright © Steve Ely, 2015; 'Seditiones, caedem et rapinam' from *Incendium Amoris* (Smokestack Books, 2017); copyright © Steve Ely, 2017.

Peter Finch for the poem 'RNLD TOMOS', published in *Selected Later Poems* (Bridgend: Seren Books, 2007); copyright © Peter Finch, 2007.

Giles Goodland for 'Dream Capital' and 'Zero Capital' from *Capital* (Cambridge: Salt Publishing, 2006); copyright © Giles Goodland, 2007.

Rody Gorman for 'Suathadh Eile' published in *Zonda? Khamsin? Sharaav? Camanchaca?* (Inverness: Leabhraichean Beaga, 2006). Original text copyright © Rody Gorman, 2006; English translation copyright © Rody Gorman, 2024.

Khaled Hakim and Contraband Books for excerpts from *The Routines 1983–2000* (London: Contraband Books, 2021). Copyright © Khaled Hakim, 2021.

Ian Heames for excerpts from *Arrays* (Cambridge: Face Press, 2015); copyright © Ian Heames, 2015.

Haley Jenkins for excerpts from *nekorb* (London: Veer, 2017); copyright © Haley Jenkins, 2017.

Simon Jenner and Waterloo Press for excerpts from *Winstanley* (Hove: Waterloo Press, 2021); copyright © Simon Jenner, 2021.

Norman Jope and Knives, Forks & Spoons Press for excerpts from 'Veästa' published in *Portland: A Triptych* (Newton-le-Willows: Knives Forks & Spoons Press, 2019); copyright © Norman Jope, 2019.

Carcanet Press for two excerpts from *Plague Lands and other poems*, translated by Anthony Howell & Abbas Karim (Manchester, Carcanet Press 2011); copyright © Fawzi Karim, Anthony Howell, Abbas Karim, 2011.

L. Kiew for an excerpt from 'Swallow', published in *The Unquiet* (London: Offord Road Books, 2019); copyright © L. Kiew, 2019.

Nine Arches Press for 'Solidarity' and 'Coronal Mass Ejection' published in Dorothy Lehane, *Ephemeris* (Rugby: Nine Arches Press, 2014); copyright © Dorothy Lehane, 2014.

Ira Lightman for 'REMEMBER the led better' published in *Duetcetera* (Exeter: Shearsman Books, 2008); copyright © Ira Lightman 2008.

Carcanet Press for excerpts from 'The Hourglass' and 'To Those on the Promontory' published in Robert Minhinnick, *King Driftwood* (Manchester: Carcanet Press, 2008); copyright © Robert Minhinnick, 2008.

Kevin Nolan for excerpts from 'WRZBRNO', 'Denmark: thinking of John Wieners', 'Eirleach', 'Life as a Bracket', 'Ear Missing, published in *Loving Little Orlick* (London: Barque Press, 2006); copyright © Kevin Nolan, 2006.

Cris Paul for 'Cas' and an excerpt from 'Dream of the Rood, a translation' published in *stenia cultus handbook* (London: Veer Books, 2010); copyright © Cris Paul, 2010.

Bloodaxe Books for excerpts from Heather Phillipson, '1960s Monochrome Hollywood Paraphernalia ($47, collection only)' and 'The One Coat That Could Have Made Winter Worth Living Through', published in *INSTANT-fLEX 718* (Tarset: Bloodaxe Books, 2011); copyright © Heather Phillipson, 2011.

Nat Raha for excerpts from *Octet* (London: Veer Books, 2010), copyright © Nat Raha, 2010.

Salt Publishing for an excerpt from Eleanor Rees, 'Night River', published in *Andraste's Hair.* (Cambridge: Salt Publishing, 2007); copyright © Eleanor Rees, 2007.

Luke Roberts for an excerpt from 'Terraform lecture notes', published in *False Flags* (Cambridge: Mountain Press, 2011); copyright © Luke Roberts, 2011.

Tapsalteerie for excerpts from 'The Lunnasting Stone', 'Inchkeith' and 'Sleepwalking' published in Stewart Sanderson, *The Sleep Road* (Tarland: Tapsalteerie, 2021); copyright © Stewart Sanderson, 2021.

Ian Seed and Shearsman Books for 'Chrysalis' and an excerpt from 'Chances', published in *Makers of Empty Dreams* (Bristol: Shearsman Books, 2014); copyright Ian Seed, 2014.

Maria Sledmere for excerpts from *Leave Bambi Alone* (Glasgow: Mermaid Motel, 2022); copyright © Maria Sledmere, 2022.

Maria Stadnicka and Knives, Forks and Spoons Press for 'Spring Cleaning' from *Somnia* (Newton-le-Willows: Knives Forks and Spoon Press, 2020); copyright © Maria Stadnicka, 2020.

Victor Tapner for 'Arrow Maker' from *Flatlands* (Cambridge: Salt Publishing, 2007); copyright © Victor Tapner, 2007.

Martin Thom for excerpts from *Cloud. A Coffee Cantata* (Cambridge: Equipage, 2020); copyright © Martin Thom, 2020.

The Estate of Chris Torrance for 'The Theatre of its Protagonist's Desires' by Chris Torrance, published in *Acrospirical Meanderings in a Tongue of the Time* (London: Albion Village Press, 1973); copyright © Chris Torrance, 1973.

Rhys Trimble for excerpts from *Keinc* (Blaenau Ffestiniog: Cinnamon Press, 2010); copyright © Rhys Trimble, 2010.

Molly Vogel for 'Antonyms' and excerpts from 'The Child Dreaming in a Poet's House' and 'Verse Riddles' published in Molly Vogel, *Florilegium* (Bristol: Shearsman Books, 2020); copyright © Molly Vogel, 2020.

Nine Arches Press for an excerpt from 'But Tell Me…' published in Tony Williams, *Midlands* (Rugby: Nine Arches Press, 2014); copyright © Tony Williams, 2014.

Smith|Doorstop for excerpts from 'Cursed Resources' and 'Visible Waves' published in Jay G Ying, *Katabasis* (Sheffield: Smith | Doorstop, 2020); copyright © Jay G. Ying, 2020.

Other texts listed below have been quoted under the fair-use rule:

Tim Allen, excerpt from 'Pontoon', published in *Portland: A Triptych* (Newton-le-Willows: Knives Forks & Spoons Press, 2019); copyright © Tim Allen, 2019.

Mona Arshi, excerpt from 'You Are Not', published in *Small Hands* (Liverpool: Pavilion Poets, Liverpool University Press, 2015); copyright © Mona Arshi, 2015.

Janette Ayachi, excerpt from 'I Laughed So Much I Lost My Voice', published in *Hand Over Mouth Music* (Liverpool: Pavilion Poets, Liverpool University Press, 2019); copyright © Janette Ayachi, 2019.

David Barnett, excerpt from 'West Kennet – Long Barrow', published in *All the Year Round* (Wales: Envoi Poets Publications, 1995); copyright © David Barnett, 1995.

Caroline Bird, excerpt from 'Flatmate' published in *Watering Can* (Manchester: Carcanet Press, 2009); copyright © Caroline Bird, 2009.

Geraldine Clarkson, excerpt from 'For Our Extinguished Guests' published in *Monica's Overcoat of Flesh* (Rugby: Nine Arches Press, 2020); copyright © Geraldine Clarkson, 2020.

Peter Davidson, excerpts from 'The Spy's Letters' and 'A Choice of Emblems', published in *The Palace of Oblivion* (Manchester: Carcanet Press, 2008); copyright © Peter Davidson, 2008.

Nancy Gaffield, excerpt from 'zu Babel' published in *Continental Drift* (Bristol: Shearsman Books, 2014), copyright © Nancy Gaffield, 2014.

Mark Goodwin, excerpt from 'Mind Will' published in *House At Out* (Bristol: Shearsman Books, 2015); copyright © Mark Goodwin, 2015. Statement from author's website (no longer available) copyright © Mark Goodwin.

John Holloway, excerpt from 'A Letter from the Argolid' published in *Wood and Windfall* (London: Routledge and Kegan Paul, 1965); copyright John Holloway, 1965.

Sarah Law, excerpt from 'Poetry etc – an unauthorised manifesto', published in *Ascension Notes* (Exeter: Shearsman Books, 2009); copyright © Sarah Law, 2009.

Toby Martinez de las Rivas, excerpt from 'Allegory of the Church / Hanged Owl', published in *Black Sun* (London: Faber & Faber, 2018), copyright © Toby Martinez de las Rivas, 2018.

Alistair McDonald, excerpt from 'Edenburg', published in *The Smeddum Test – 21st Century Poems in Scots* (Edinburgh: Kennedy & Boyd, 2012); copyright © Alistair McDonald 2012.

John Robinson, excerpts from 'A Speculative History of Theft', published in *The Cook's Wedding* (Snitterfield: Ragged Raven Press, 2001); copyright © John Robinson, 2001.

Sophie Robinson, excerpts from 'Cancer, Leo Rising' and 'Four ways to trap a rabbit' from *rabbit* (Norwich: Boiler House Press, 2018).

Nicholas Spicer, excerpt from 'Counter Turn / First Ode' published in *Lines on the Surface* (London: Contraband Books, 2013); copyright © Nicholas Spicer, 2013.

Meic Stephens, excerpt from 'Wteri' published in *Wilia – Cerddi 2003–2013* (Aberystwyth: Cyhoeddiadau Barddas, 2014); copyright © Meic Stephens, 2014.

Stephanie Sy-Quia, excerpt from *Amnion* (London: Granta, 2021), copyright © Stephanie Sy-Quia, 2021.

Alice Tarbuck, excerpt from 'Musée de la chasse et de la nature', published in *the weird folds: everyday poems from the anthopocene* (ed. Maria Sledmere & Rhian Williams; Manchester: Dostoyevsky Wannabe, 2020); copyright © Alice Tarbuck, 2020.

Nathan Thompson, excerpt from 'The Texan with the Instamatic', published in *the day maybe died* (Newton-le-Willows: Knives Forks & Spoons Press, 2011); copyright © Nathan Thompson, 2011.

Mark Waldron, excerpt from 'Of Course, We've All Seen this Kind of Thing Before', published in *The Itchy Sea* (Cambridge: Salt Publishing, 2011); copyright © Mark Waldron, 2011.

Samantha Wynne-Rhydderch, excerpt from 'Deacon Brodie's Predecessors: 2. The Surf Report' published in *Rockclimbing in Silk* (Bridgend; Seren Books, 2001); copyright © Samantha Wynne-Rhydderch, 2001.

Index

Ali, Kazim, 207-9
Allen, Tim, 162-3
anthologies: *The Best British Poetry 2015*, 283, 291; *Edge of Necessary*, 229-37; *An Guth* 170; *makar/unmakar* 180-1; *Poetry 1900–2000*, 229; *The Smeddum Test*, 168; *The Weird Folds*, 181-2
Arshi, Mona, 205-7
avant-garde, the, 9-10, 30-2, 118-128, 229-41, 249-51, 252-65
Ayachi, Janette, 173-5
Ayres, Michael, 89-91
BAME poetry, 118-122, 149-51, 173-5, 201-14, 215-28, 299-301, 303-6, 309-10
Barnett, David, 232-3
Bernard, Jay, 149-52
Bird, Caroline, 288-90
Bletsoe, Elisabeth, 153-7, 159, 230-1
Bolfek-Radovani, Jasmina, 303-6
Brading, Tilla, 233-4
Brady, Andrea, 98-99
breakdown of mainstream-innovative divide, 9-10
Brigley, Zoë, 231
Bukhari, Nuzhat, 202-5
Burrows, Wayne, 197-9
Challenger, Melanie, 101-4
Clarkson, Geraldine, 315-6
cultural conservatism, 39-45, 107-117
Davidson, Peter, 311-14
De Luca, Christine, 306-9
domestic anecdote, 129-38
drum and trumpet history, 39, 129
elites, 15, 16-17, 19, 40-1, 43
Ely, Steve, 64-71
exclusion/inclusion process, the, 13, 15, 16-17, 21-2, 46-7
Finch, Peter, 233

Ford, Mark, 290-1
Gaffield, Nancy, 320-4
Goodland, Giles, 93-6
Goodwin, Mark, 160, 324-26
Gorman, Rody, 170-1
Hakim, Khaled, 209-14
Harris, Will, 215-8
Harrison, Lesley, 318-9
Hasler, Emily, 97-8
Heames, Ian, 258-61
Holcombe, Robert, 199
Holloway, John, 327-8
Hughes, Siân, 104
Jafrate, Keith, 139-43
Jenkins, Haley, 124-8
Jenner, Simon, 148-9
Jones, Dewi Stephen, 59-64
Jones, Bobi, 59-63
Jope, Norman, 161-2
Karim, Fawzi, 218-221
Kennedy, David, 92
Kiew, L, 309-10
Lake, Grace, 87-8
landscape or ecological poetry, 10, 153-64, 318-328
language generation procedures, 244-251
Larkin, Peter, 86
Law, Sarah, 314-5
Lee-Houghton, Melissa, 286-7
Lehane, Dorothy, 266-70
Lightman, Ira, 244, 249-51
Martinez De Las Rivas, Toby, 143-7
Mccabe, Chris, 96-7
Mellors, Anthony, 192-7
Mengham, Rod, 88-9
Minhinnick, Robert, 263-7, 241-3
Nagra, Daljit, 299-301
Nolan, Kevin, 52-9
Paul, Cris, 238-9
Perry, Eleanor, 287-8
Phillipson, Heather, 263-5
privatisation, 24-29

Qasmiyeh, Yousif M., 226-8
Raha, Nat, 118-122
reader-text interaction, 183-200
Rees,Eleanor, 99-101
refugium, 114-117
Riviere, Sam, 291-3
Roberts, Luke, 270-4, 318
Robinson, John, 281-2
Robinson, Sophie, 284-6
Rowland, Anthony, 105
Sanderson, Stewart, 178-180
Scottish poetry, 166-82, 306-9, 311-14
Seed, Ian, 276-8
Silva, Hannah, 278-9
Skelton, Richard, 317
Sledmere, Maria, 181, 295-7
sociolinguistics, 168-70, 299-310
Spicer, Nicholas, 261-3
Sprackland, Jean, 319-20
Stadnicka, Maria, 274-6
Stephens, Meic, 231-2, 235, 301-3
Stone, Jon, 187-9
Sy-Quia, Stephanie, 221-3
Tapner, Victor, 84-5
Tarbuck, Alice, 182
Thom, Martin, 71-5
Thompson, Nathan, 294-5
Torrance, Chris, 234
Trimble, Rhys, 239-41
Vogel, Molly, 175-8
volume of output, 11, 12, 23
Waldron, Mark, 92-3
Walton, Samantha, 279-81
Warsaw Pact culture, 192-8
Welsh poetry, 59-64, 229-243, 301-3
Williams, Tony, 104-5
Woodford, Anna, 89
Wynne-Rhydderch, Samantha, 236
Ying, Jay G, 223-6

www.ingramcontent.com/pod-product-compliance
Ingram Content Group UK Ltd.
Pitfield, Milton Keynes, MK11 3LW, UK
UKHW042342250126
10300UKWH00031B/81